Palgrave Studies in Globalization, Culture and Society

Series Editors
Jeroen de Kloet
Centre for Globalisation Studies
University of Amsterdam
Amsterdam, The Netherlands

Esther Peeren
Centre for Globalisation Studies
University of Amsterdam
Amsterdam, The Netherlands

Palgrave Studies in Globalization, Culture and Society traverses the boundaries between the humanities and the social sciences to critically explore the cultural and social dimensions of contemporary globalization processes. This entails looking at the way globalization unfolds through and within cultural and social practices, and identifying and understanding how it effects cultural and social change across the world. The series asks what, in its different guises and unequal diffusion, globalization is taken to be and do in and across specific locations, and what social, political and cultural forms and imaginations this makes possible or renders obsolete. A particular focus is the vital contribution made by different forms of the imagination (social, cultural, popular) to the conception, experience and critique of contemporary globalization. Palgrave Studies in Globalization, Culture and Society is committed to addressing globalization across cultural contexts (western and non-western) through interdisciplinary, theoretically driven scholarship that is empirically grounded in detailed case studies and close analyses. Within the scope outlined above, we invite junior and senior scholars to submit proposals for monographs, edited volumes and the Palgrave Pivot format. Please contact the series editors for more information: b.j.dekloet@uva.nl / e.peeren@uva.nl

More information about this series at
http://www.palgrave.com/gp/series/15109

Chow Yiu Fai

Caring in Times of Precarity

A Study of Single Women
Doing Creative Work
in Shanghai

palgrave
macmillan

Chow Yiu Fai
Hong Kong Baptist University
Kowloon Tong, Hong Kong

Palgrave Studies in Globalization, Culture and Society
ISBN 978-3-319-76897-7   ISBN 978-3-319-76898-4   (eBook)
https://doi.org/10.1007/978-3-319-76898-4

Library of Congress Control Number: 2018954418

Cover illustration: Artwork by Justin Wong, photograph taken by Jeroen de Kloet.

This Palgrave Macmillan imprint is published by the registered company Springer Nature Switzerland AG
The registered company address is: Gewerbestrasse 11, 6330 Cham, Switzerland

ACKNOWLEDGEMENTS

It just occurred to me that I should write my acknowledgements—now that I am back in Shanghai to do fieldwork once again.

I am staying in the same neighbourhood, wandering through the same streets and alleys, and going to the same noodle shops and cafés. Inertia, insistence, intimacy. This is where I met all the women you will meet in this book, where I listened to their stories, felt their trust, and was enthralled by their struggles, pleasures, and above all, sheer accomplishment of living their lives in this place, at this time. These memories and impressions have morphed into a constant susurration as well as a resounding reminder for me to write this book well. I hope I have done a good job, at least good enough that I would dare to let them read it. I thank all of you, who were willing to talk to me. I know it was not always easy; let us continue trying to make it easier.

Without the Humanities in the European Research Area (HERA) project "Creating the 'new' Asian woman: entanglements of urban space, cultural encounters and gendered identities in Shanghai and Delhi (SINGLE)", this book would not exist at all. In 2013, the European Commission funded the research proposal to investigate single women in the two cities, and the principal investigators—Christiane Brosius, Melissa Butcher, and Jeroen de Kloet—invited me to join their research team. I thank these three PIs. And I also thank my fellow researchers, Laila Abu-Er-Rub, Lucie Bernroider, Maddalena Chiellini, Penn Ip, and Pi Chenying, for all the wonderful moments in Heidelberg, Delhi, Shanghai, and Leiden. Remember the karaoke night? I thank Lena Scheen, who was not in the team, but was one big reason why I was in the team. I will not explain this beyond calling it serendipity. Through the HERA project, I also had the pleasure to get to know the scholar Kinneret Lahad, whose work on single women remains inspiring and empowering for me; the curator and academic Wayne Modest, whose energy and engagement continually enlighten me; as well as artists Li Xiaofei and Guo Qingling, who became one of my anchor points when I was in Shanghai, and my friends. Talking about Shanghai, I would like to thank Afa, Ah Ching, Anna, Jude, Melody, Tingyun, and many others, who made me feel less like a stranger.

This book project was my very first monograph. Monograph. How daunting! Luckily, I was guided or cautioned—"What? You have not started writing yet?"—by people who were more experienced than I, to the extent that I knew, at the very least, I must reserve time to concentrate on, very simply put, writing. I thank Hong Kong Baptist University for granting me sabbatical leave. I am particularly grateful to my colleagues, Iris Chao, Gladys Chong, John Nguyet Erni, Leung Pui Man, Lucetta Kam, K.C. Lo, Eva Man, and Daisy Tam, as well as the supporting team of the Department of Humanities and Creative Writing—Chester Chan, Donald Chan, Bonnie Fung, Jacky Ho, and Fiona Lu—for indulging my writing spree. I thank the Amsterdam Centre for Globalisation Studies and the Amsterdam School of Cultural Analysis—personified as Esther Peeren, Patricia Pisters, and Jeroen de Kloet—for hosting me. That half a year felt so insouciant and quiet.

I have just written the word monograph, which is usually understood as a treatise on a single subject, authored by a single person. How I would love to believe that this was entirely my own effort. Of course, it was not.

I thank all the scholars who, in their own ways, have been telling me that I can do it. Ien Ang, Kees Brants, Rey Chow, Stephen Chu, Anthony Fung, Joke Hermes, Koichi Iwabuchi, Giselinde Kuipers, Helen Hok-Sze Leung, Song Hwee Lim, Tak-Wing Ngo, Tejaswini Niranjana, Leonie Schmidt, Shu-mei Shih, and my dear PhD supervisor Liesbet van Zoonen, who believed in my potential as an academic much earlier than I did myself. I thank Zoénie Deng, Lin Jian, Tan Jia and Sonia Wong for supporting me with literature alerts and other research help. I thank Wang Rui and Yvette Wong, my two primary research assistants for offering me concrete support throughout the entire book project. Both Virgos, even born on the same day, they lived up to the expectations of being meticulous and attentive to detail—I owe them for all the reminders of all the details of my research. I meant to list out precisely what they did for me, but then, I realized no long list of tasks would be better than a simple cheer: my dear Rui and Yvette, long live our friendship!

I thank Vincent So for helping me with formatting and tidying up all stylistically loose ends (it must have been nightmarish for you); Chen Min, Roman Chen Ziqing, and Cai Qingyang for your great assistance during fieldwork in Shanghai; and Zhang Qian, and all the transcribers. I thank Patrick Jered for copyediting the entire book. It was not only a matter of ensuring the linguistic quality, but much more importantly, of reassuring me that someone like you would always be there. I thank the anonymous reviewer(s), and the (former) editors at Palgrave: Lucy Batrouney, Heloise Harding, and Martina O'Sullivan. I thank David Hesmondhalgh and Fran Martin for gracing the back cover with your endorsements. For the front cover, I thank Justin Wong for allowing me to use your artwork, and Jeroen de Kloet for the photograph of this.

Right, finally, Jeroen. These days, you have been somewhat disturbed. Just the other day, you sent a message to me: "I lost Ernie!" I could already imagine the distress and anguish you were feeling. Indeed, you were disturbed, quite seriously. The loss of an "object," a "toy" that you had been using as the centre point of your photographic project hit you like the loss of a dear one. That kind of immediacy, sincerity, and I think, humanity—it reminds me of a notion in Chinese 赤子之心: the heart of a child (haha, I know you will call me Sinocentric for this). This heart keeps on inspiring me. More than a decade ago, it inspired me to embark on an academic life; during the research and writing of this book, it inspired me through your conversations, your accommodations, and your distractions, ultimately to let me continue believing in what I was doing, if only for the pleasure. Thank you.

Chow Yiu Fai

This work was supported by the Humanities in the European Research Area (HERA) under the funded-project "Creating the 'New' Asian Woman: Entanglements of Urban Space, Cultural Encounters and Gendered Identities in Shanghai and Delhi" (SINGLE Project Nr: 586, 2013–2016).

A NOTE ON LANGUAGE

All English translations are mine, unless otherwise stated. For citation of Chinese personal names using English spelling, I have followed the Chinese convention, that is, family name first. However, when the persons involved preferred using an English first name, I have followed the English convention, putting the family name last. For citation of other Chinese proper names or titles, I have generally put their English equivalents in the text, followed by pinyin (the standard Romanization of Chinese characters adopted in mainland China) and Chinese characters in brackets. Chinese characters printed in this book belong to the simplified version used in mainland China, unless otherwise warranted, for instance, when the names and titles concerned are from areas where the classical version of Chinese characters remains preferred.

Contents

CHAPTER 1

Living on My Own, Creatively, Precariously

This book project originated from my personal observations and curiosity. In addition to my academic pursuits, I have been working for many years as a creative writer. My base has been Hong Kong. In the past decade, my base has spread to mainland China. When I started visiting mainland China more frequently, I started to notice this: many of the media people I met were women, and many of them single. I started to wonder about the relationship between single women and creative work. Does their singlehood help them deal more effectively with creative work demands? Or, conversely, do their work demands actually strengthen their choice or necessity to remain single? Or, are they just fine with being single and doing their work? ... I simply did not know, but I suspected that there must be something about their working lives, their private single lives, that was embodied in the women I came across.

When I consolidated these initial observations and curiosity into a research project, I realized something about its historicity. These single women doing creative work are actually straddling a historical, precarious conjuncture, configured by two peculiar trajectories in our globalizing times.

First, increasing numbers of people do not subscribe to traditional forms of shared living; they lead a single life. Whether as a matter of choice or an act of necessity, singlehood has become possible by processes of urbanization and modernization, and all the conveniences they afford. For the first time in human history, as argued by Ulrich Beck and Elisabeth

© The Author(s) 2019

Chow Y. F., *Caring in Times of Precarity*, Palgrave Studies in Globalization, Culture and Society, https://doi.org/10.1007/978-3-319-76898-4_1

Beck-Gernsheim, as well as Eric Klinkenberg, people do not necessarily need a family.[1] Citing Klinenberg's work, a 2017 commentary on China announced in its headline: "The single society has come!"[2] According to the latest available official figures published in 2014 and 2015, among the total national population of 1.368 billion, 21.5 per cent of those aged 20 and above are single. Among those aged 20 to 59, 170 million are single, 40.4 per cent of whom are female.[3]

At the same time, single people continue to be stigmatized. Single women, particularly—as Kinneret Lahad repeatedly shows in her series of studies—have had to wrestle with the accusation, and sometimes internalized self-accusation of being unnatural, unattractive, pathological, eccentric, desperate, and egocentric; in short, single women are often led to believe they are lesser women while the ideology of marriage, family, and above all, motherhood continues to be privileged.[4] In the Chinese context, the widely circulated term "3S ladies"—single, seventies (born in the 1970s)—has stuck, testifying to the negative stereotype single women in China have to wrestle with.[5] Another term, *shengnü* (剩女)—literally, leftover women—referring to single urban professional women in their late twenties, was introduced by the official Women's Federation in 2007, to remind women not to be too demanding and to get married before it is too late.

Second, increasingly more people are attracted to the promises of creative work, and so, join the creative workforce. The discourse of the creative industries—and its underpinning ideologies of self-fulfilment, flexibility, and freedom—has globalized profoundly, especially with the influential and upbeat thinking on creative class and creative city by Richard Florida.[6] Creative labour in China, as yet understudied, offers a unique prism to view how such a globalized discourse is articulated in the context of China. Creative work is supposed to give you more autonomy, flexibility, and job satisfaction, and is generally considered more human. Paradoxically, in return for such presumably desirable work, creative workers often sacrifice more regular working hours and good job security. They bear the risks and responsibilities individually, struggle with their work–life balance, and tolerate multiple demands, demoralization, and exploitation.[7] In her latest book on creative work, Angela McRobbie critically reframes the call to be creative as "a potent and highly appealing mode of new governmentality," adding, "this mode of neoliberal governmentality is also a general and widespread mode of precarization."[8] While scholarship is building on "Creative China," existing studies show a preference

for issues concerning the political economy, for instance, or creative policies and industry practices,[9] as well as concerning the nation itself, such as,
for instance, the promotion of freedom and the exercise of "soft power."[10]

Straddling this historical, precarious conjuncture, this book zooms in
on one particular group of "precariat": single women in Shanghai who
earn their living by various forms of creative (self-)employment. While
negotiating their share of the uncanny creative work ethos, they also find
themselves interpellated as latent or actual *shengnü* in a society configured
by a mix of Confucian values, heterosexual ideals, and global images of
womanhood. Put differently, despite all the purported undesirability of
single womanhood and creative work, they are still living as single women
doing creative work. Following these women's professional, social, and
intimate lives in the urban space, this book is, first and foremost, an
attempt to understand a woman's life in both its work and after-work time
and practices, defying the artificial demarcations of singlehood as personal,
and creative work as professional. At the same time, this book fills a
research gap by bringing into dialogue two fields of studies: while studies
on the creative class have neglected gender and affective dimensions, studies on single women, on the contrary, often privilege the personal and
leave behind issues of work. Thus premised, it aims to study the Chinese
case not only for its specificities, but ultimately, for its mobilization as a
method, following Chen Kuan-hsing's "Asia as method."[11] My intention
is to explore the world of these single women in China, to see if there are
new paths to follow outside of—or crisscrossing with—the well-trodden
paths of thinking on single womanhood and creative work.

As I shall explicate in the following chapters, what these women have to
say urges me to write a book that converses with, but departs from, dominant thinking on precarity, which foregrounds and critiques the contemporary need to be flexible, mobile, and spontaneous to the extent of
self-exploitation and acceptance of insecurity. My approach refuses to see
these women's singlehood and creative labour necessarily as problems,
and them as victims. I do not want to; I cannot. Although the women I
have got to know may have their share of difficulties, hardships, and quandaries, they show a strong sense of caring for their lives despite *and* because
of these difficulties, hardships, and quandaries. This book seeks to understand, empirically and specifically, their everyday struggles and pleasures in
a city such as Shanghai. Ultimately, it aims to address an urgent issue in
our contemporary mode of existence: how (far) can one take care of oneself in times of precarity?[12] Teasing out the local experiences of such a

global question, I continue by asking: while these Chinese women are dealing with the multiple demands of singlehood and creative jobs, how do they maintain a sense of well-being, obtain pleasure, and exercise agency? In other words: how can one take care of oneself in the midst of everyday precarity? And how, and how far, do they experience such precarity? And how do global scripts related to womanhood, love, and creative work inform their aspirations? In other words, this inquiry is about local modes of precarity implicated in global ideologies and imaginaries pertaining to (ideal) womanhood and its intersection with creative labour. Ultimately, my aim is to hold up the Shanghai case as an opening to re-enter scholarship on precarity: perhaps, for these Chinese women, precarity is a human condition known to them, suitable for them, and available to them? Perhaps "precarity" is a male-centric and Western-centric notion? Driven by its local, empirical insights, this book aims to rethink the global condition of precarity; it pushes current debates on precarity beyond the domain of labour towards the domain of care.[13]

In the rest of this introductory chapter, I will start by contextualizing the research by offering a historical account of (single) womanhood and (creative) work in contemporary globalized urban China. The chapter continues with discussions, particularly in their intersections with the concerns of precarity and what the single women in this inquiry have to say about their lives. The specificities of the Chinese women, both in terms of being "Chinese" and "women," lead me to argue for the limits of the politics of precarity, and to propose an ethics of care. I will then present the women, and the methods I have used to converse with them. Chapter 1 ends by presenting the organizational logic of the book and the gist of the subsequent chapters.

THE CHINESE CONTEXT

Any account that dares to cover the colossal changes of the last decades in the colossal country of China is bound to be sketchy, jumpy, and unfinished. Even if I confine it to the realms of (single) womanhood and (creative) work, I will exclude much more than I include. For our purposes, allow me, therefore, to focus on two historical moments: the Communist Revolution of 1949, and the opening up of the Chinese economy to the global capitalist system, starting in 1978.[14]

Mao's famous call for women to "hold up half of the sky" is often quoted as an epitome of the post-1949 exercise to achieve a radical form of gender equality. Organized by the State and the Party, the exercise was part and parcel of the Marxist doctrine of casting female subordination in the larger project to erase all kinds of class and socioeconomic inequalities. While the modernization of women had already begun in the Republican, pre-1949 period, Mao's era is considered to have brought in drastic changes to ideals and practices of Chinese femininity. Women, for instance, were no longer required to look feminine; they were attired in ostensibly sexless uniforms, the so-called Mao suit, also worn by fellow male comrades. Women were also deemed suitable and capable of taking up work traditionally regarded as masculine. Gender equality, in this period, was coterminous with gender sameness. With the retreat of revolutionary and emancipatory enthusiasm in the wake of the Cultural Revolution, as well as the opening up of the country, femininity returned with capitalistic intensity and velocity. While Chinese women sought to demand back their deprived womanhood and individuality, the market supplied them with consumer products that promised beauty and personal style, and choice became the mantra for women to chart their futures and careers. Just when neo-liberal post-feminism—in its depoliticizing and apoliticizing tendency of proclaiming the completion of the feminist project, with equality being understood as a personal matter of choice and agency, as argued by Judith Lakämper[15]—seems to circulate globally to characterize contemporary China, state feminism, it must be noted, remains, often functioning in tandem with values and norms loosely called traditional, but in effect, patriarchal and heteronormative.

As critics point out, the post-1949 drive to emancipate women was sturdily grounded in the economically dominant thinking of Marxism. The concern and the official measures were never genuinely about gender, or the cultural. As women were urged to take up public labour, men were never required to hold up the half sky of domestic work. Patriarchy, and the androcentric values mutually imbricated, were left firmly in place. In 2007, as noted earlier, the official Women's Federation introduced the term *shengnü* to stigmatize single womanhood and pressurize women into matrimony.[16] The term became hugely popularized into yet another disciplinary device for single urban professional women in their late twenties to take heteronormative arrangements as the order of the day, a supplement to the persistent Confucian and familial values in Chinese society. Illustrative of the kind of state feminism in contemporary China, President Xi Jinping has repeatedly articulated the importance of such values and women's contribution to their maintenance.[17] One spectacular display of parental concern and pressure on their daughters to get married is the parents' occupation of public parks in big cities to place placards to attract prospective sons-in-law, forming what is sometimes called the "marriage markets."[18] Other widely circulated terms such as the aforementioned "3S ladies" and "3 high ladies"—high educational level, high salary, high expectations—testify to the negative stereotyping that single women in China have to endure.[19] The other manifestation of how single women are portrayed as always seeking partners is the hugely popular television dating show, *If You Are the One* (*Feicheng Wurao*, 非诚勿扰), and various television drama series in China.[20] To underline the hegemony of matrimony, about 30 to 40 per cent of Chinese have been reported to prefer a bad marriage to singlehood.[21] Hardly surprising, but nonetheless disheartening, is the report that the divorce rate doubled in the decade through 2016—from 1.46 to 3 for every 1000 people in China.[22]

Such is the paradoxical situation Chinese women find themselves in. While the country has started to open itself up to market reforms, enabling increasing exposure to and encounters with global flows of symbolic and material goods, they have more opportunities, space, and choices. At the same time, they are constantly reminded to find a man, and to get married. They are asked to perform the double stunt of being modern and traditional, simultaneously. We will discuss this in greater detail in the following chapter. Suffice it to say, this seems to be something that Chinese women have been struggling with since the modernization of the nation. Reverting to the opportunities, space, and choices they have, I will continue with another aspect of their lives that has undergone drastic change through the two historical moments I pinpointed; this is their life not only as a woman, but also as a worker. If the state, in the early revolutionary decades, was regulating everything pertaining to economy, from the macro policies of five-year plans to the micro arrangement of personal jobs, market reforms since the late 1970s have opened up the Chinese economy to the global capitalist system with the more recent attempt—for our purpose here—to move from the paradigm "made in China" to "created in China."[23]

In 1978, the words *gaige kaifang* (改革开放) became national policy that would herald dramatic transformations in the decades to come. Orchestrated by leader Deng Xiaoping, it announced an opening up (*kaifang*) of the hitherto secluded nation as well as an introduction of market reforms (*gaige*) to the hitherto planned economy. While foreign companies and capital started to find their way into China, the accelerating privatization of state companies crushed the job allocation system—security and the "iron rice bowls" included—that had been installed and ensured by the communist authorities. Employment became individualized. In this reforming context, China followed closely what was happening in the rest of the world. In 2001, China joined the World Trade Organization (WTO). While *gaige*, the actual reforms put into practice, attract most Western attention, it was *kaifang*, as noted by Lily Chumley, that marked a fundamental shift in the way the party and the state started to govern China. Simply translated to "opening up," *kaifang* can mean several things in the Chinese language: to bloom; to lift restrictions; to be opened up to the public; to start up; to be privatized. The connotation, as it applies to human minds, is perhaps the one most pertinent to the transformations in the cultural and creative industries in China[24]: open-minded.[25] The decade following China's joining of the WTO witnessed a process of integrating the global rhetoric and promises offered by the creative industries into official polices at various levels of administration. In 2007, the then President Hu Jintao delivered his annual address to the National Congress of the Communist Party of China. Amidst the expected tributes and assertions of commitment to socialist ideals, he introduced something less expected: "cultural creativity."[26]

> We must … stimulate the cultural creativity of the whole nation, and enhance culture as part of the soft power of our country in order to better guarantee the people's basic cultural rights and interests, to enrich the cultural life in Chinese society and to inspire the spiritual outlook of the people to be more elevated and more progressive.[27]

The national motto changed from *gaige kaifang* (改革开放) to *gaige chuangxin* (改革创新),[28] as *chuangxin* (innovate, invent, create 创新) replaced *kaifang* (open, open-door 开放) as the key exponent of policy directives generalized by the term *gaige* (reform 改革). It could also be seen as a logical step to concretize what was already contained in the notion of *kaifang* into *chuangxin*: the mind is opened; now, it is time to utilize it, to put it into practice. Hu's vision of creativity and the creative industries agenda thus developed, as I argue elsewhere, were linked to "soft power, to the cultural and the spiritual, to the scenario when the country grooms and shows its symbolic strength."[29] Initiatives subsequently flowed from various institutions under national, regional, and municipal governments, aiming—not unlike their counterparts in the West—to secure strength of a more materialistic kind, namely economic, and in correspondence with Hu's vision, soft national power. In 2011, Li Wuwei, an academic, policymaker, and opinion leader in creative practices, published an article calling for the advancement of creative industries into the international arena. Taking the Korean wave as an example, Li was hoping for the China Wind to blow across the world.[30] In his address to the National Congress, 10 years after Hu, President Xi Jinping described the development of cultural industries not in terms of the China Wind, but the China Dream. Listing a series of tasks in rather loose terms—from perfecting the modern cultural industries and market system, and fostering a new cultural ecology, to organizing the Beijing Winter Olympics—the new leader articulated the goal of "enhancing national cultural soft power."[31]

The state-led cultural creativity directive has led to remarkable transformations in the cultural creative landscape of the nation. By 2012, as noted by Justin O'Connor and Xin Gu, "many Chinese cities, towns or even villages had built or had plans for CICs [creative industry clusters] in some shape or form."[32] Concomitantly, we see a long string of policy papers, consultation reports, and economic analyses.[33] The series of the official *Blue Book of China's Culture: Annual Report on Development of China's Cultural Industries* (文化蓝皮书:中国文化产业发展报告), published by the influential Chinese Academy of Social Sciences, as well as the *Blue Book of Cultural Brands: Annual Report on Development of Cultural Brands in China* (文化品牌蓝皮书:中国文化品牌产业发展报告), published by a research institute attached to Zhongnan University, have been offering analyses of the nation's creative economy and compiling reports on creative industries during recent years.[34] Numerous similar reports have been published, predominantly in the Chinese language, for various more specific purposes, for instance, concerning a specific district, a specific region, or a specific industry or cluster of industries.[35] Correspondingly, the training of young people in related sectors has been intensified. In 1997, the government commenced an expansion plan for higher education to cater to the requirements of knowledge for the creative economy; by 2009, the number of university students majoring in art and design already exceeded those of other disciplines.[36] The single women in this inquiry were among them. Like their contemporaries in other parts of the world, they became part of the creative workforce.[37]

SINGLE WOMANHOOD: BIG STRESS, BIG BUSINESS

This account of what has happened to womanhood and work in China since the Communist Revolution in 1949, as I cautioned earlier, is inevitably lacking. If I do not and cannot aspire to a comprehensive contextualization, I do wish to leave something that functions as a kind of palimpsest. That is, if you happen to come across a single woman in urban China, who may wear similar clothes as her counterparts in New York City or London, do similar creative jobs, frequent similar cafés, watch similar series on Netflix—yes, she may share many similarities with their Western counterparts at this particular conjuncture, but she has grown up in the context specified earlier. There are traces from the past that the present overwrites, but never completely; these are traces that we need to reckon with. We will come back to the Chinese specificities in a while. First, we will take a tour through the theorizations and see how far they can help us understand what is happening in this part of the world.

In tandem with the historical conjuncture mapped out at the start of this chapter, numerous publications have presented knowledge on single womanhood and creative work. In her 2017 book, based on the experience of single women in Israel, Kinneret Lahad offers a long, but by no means complete list of works published on the increasingly palpable phenomenon of women going solo.[38] What lynchpins this collection of works is the widespread and persistent framing of single women as unnatural, unattractive, pathological, and egocentric—a lesser woman, with whom there must be something wrong. While single women are constructed as somehow lacking, single womanhood is a state of being best avoided. In Bella DePaulo's poignant formulation, "unsingling" themselves is the only viable and desirable option for single women.[39] In the footsteps of these works, this book is, in the first place, a supplement to the field of scholarship on single womanhood, providing the supplement of the experience in the Chinese context. At the same time, it also serves as a supplement to the emerging series of works on Chinese single women. So far, studies on single women in China have largely focused on urban-dwelling and middle-class categories; they mainly confirm the expected—that single women in China are experiencing similar marginalization and stigmatization as found in the Western contexts.[40] Singlism, "the discrimination and mistreatment of single persons,"[41] is haunting contemporary China. Wrestling with a constellation of power—Confucian values, state propaganda, and parental pressure—these women find themselves summoned to unsingle themselves and realize their lives as women through matrimony and maternity. At the same time, there is a resurgence of male privilege from the time prior to the top-down drive for gender equality and sameness in the early decades after the Communist Revolution.[42] The emergence and popularity of derogatory and disciplinary terms, such as "3S ladies" and *shengnü*, as well as popular cultural phenomena, such as dating shows and marriage markets, speak volumes about the dire scenario that Chinese single women are living in.

It is not only a war of symbolic positions, but also a contestation for a larger share of real profits. While single women have become increasingly visible and have become subjects for media productions, as we shall see in Chap. 2, that visibility has not readily or necessarily been translated into understanding and compassion. The high media profile of "leftover women," as observed by Liu Liqun and Zhang Jingjie, does not mean that these women and their single culture are receiving sincere attention. In their sharp formulation, the media are selling "leftover women" for their "eyeball return," that is, for the economic benefits readily harvested from their popular visibility and appeal.[43] Taking the dating show *If You Are the One* as an example, media scholars cite its advertising revenues for the year 2012 at RMB1.819 billion[44], a record for a provincial-level satellite television company.[45] Similarly, dating sites such as Jiayuan (世纪佳缘), Baihe (百合网), and Zhenai (珍爱网) also managed to cash in on the emergence of the marriage market. According to internet consultancy firm iResearch, the total revenues of dating sites in China climbed from US$74 million in 2010 to US$290 million in 2015.[46] To fine-tune their business models, Jiayuan has succeeded in getting listed on Nasdaq, while Baihe has branched out into the film industry—its *shengnü* and marriage-related film *I Do* (我愿意, 2012) earned the company RMB5 million in profits.[47] Indeed, as observed by Arianne Gaetano, an entire industry has emerged out of the "unmarried crisis," an industry "consisting of expert advice columns and self-help books, television talk shows, professional marriage counsellors, divorce lawyers, and a plethora of creative match-making services."[48]

To this list of businesses, I could easily add items ingeniously introduced to cash in on the presumed desperation to find Mr Right. During my field trips in Shanghai, I visited a Love Club, or *lian'ai xunlianying* (恋爱训练营), literally "love training camp," which demanded a fee of RMB4500, as of end 2014, for a three-month course to train participants, mostly single women in their mid-20s and mid-30s, to become more skilled in securing intimate relationships.[49] On November 11, 2016, I attended a party to "celebrate" Singles Day (光棍节), itself a creation of Chinese online shopping portals, which has become a kind of annual festivity, and a consumption peak, in the same league as the Valentine's Day.[50] In 2017, online shopping figures for the major online shopping platform Tianmao (or Tmall) reached RMB168.2 billion on this particular day.[51] While the goal of Singles Day is not so much to honour singlehood as to reiterate the urgency to leave it (*tuoguang* 脱光)[52], the party I went to was held in Shanghai's hip live house venue, Mao Live. Not exactly based on the Western convention of partying, it was more like a series of games for the RMB200 entrance-fee-paying participants—again, more females than males—to get in touch, sometimes literally. And I could also readily add to Gaetano's list of businesses what I have observed, as will have any other casual traveller to Shanghai or other Chinese cities: the omnipresence of advertisements for beauty products and services. *Meinü jingji* (beauty economy 美女经济), as termed by the locals, plays into young Chinese women's beliefs in the advantages that good looks bring to their love and work lives.[53]

MORE THAN SINGLE WOMEN: CREATIVE WORK, PRECARITY

The single women I spoke with do report their anxiety and stress, and the perception of negativity surrounding their single status. Parents urge them, and friends encourage them, to get married. At least one of them joined the Love Club, while others have told me that their friends have. They take care of their appearance, and never looked out of place at the trendy cafés and shopping malls where we met. They consume to give shape to their individuality and femininity. In short, they indeed experience the constant interpellation to "unsingle," and they do keep themselves in the "market" by consuming. However, they are more than that. To begin with, if we are to use the term "market," then we must not confine ourselves to the marriage market, but also the job market. They are more than victims hard-pressed by the two walls of patriarchal heteronormativity and neo-liberal consumerism. They are also, very importantly, workers. Throughout this book, I want to argue that singlism is not only about the marginalization and stigmatization of single women, but also about the reductionist way of seeing them as marginalized and stigmatized. In this sense, to see single women as more than single women, and also as (creative) workers, is not only an empirically-driven starting point for the inquiry; it is an attempt at intervention. It seeks to move beyond the paradigm of seeing them as single, of understanding their lives in terms of singlehood, of lacking something, and of negativity—it seeks to view them as more than this. This book fills two research lacunae in existing scholarship on single women in China. On the one hand, it is the first to situate the investigation of single women in intersection with their creative work. On the other, it inserts a gender dimension into studies on "Creative China," which are dominated by issues of political economy and national well-being.[54]

Once the move is made to connect these two hitherto strangely disparate fields of studies—single womanhood and creative work—we cannot but engage with one theme that has been informing studies on the latter. If single women are living personal lives devoid of the securities afforded by heteronormativity, they, as creative workers, are confronted with increasing uncertainty as far as their work lives are concerned. And if the possibility of single womanhood and the appeal of creative work, as noted at the beginning of this chapter, represent two peculiar trajectories in our globalizing times, then our globalizing times are arguably best characterized by the keyword "precarity." It spares no one, to cite Nancy Ettlinger's alarming formulation.[55] As observed by Donna McCormack and Suvi Salmenniemi in their leading article for a special issue on "biopolitics of precarity and the self," reflections and discussions on precarity can be organized into two major lines of inquiry.[56] For the first, emblematized by Judith Butler's post-911 treatise, *Precarious Life*, precarity is evoked to attempt a "non-violent ethics, one that is based upon an understanding of how easily human life is annulled."[57] When we realize the vulnerability of what counts as human, Butler posits that we may feel related, responsible, and interdependent as human beings living with precarity. While this take on precarity borders on the existential, Butler foregrounds its political dimension, in the sense that the burden of vulnerability, despite its humanity, is not evenly distributed across humanity—certain populations are, quite simply, more vulnerable and more susceptible to violence than others. Finally, to Butler, the ethics of vulnerability, of understanding the fundamental relationality not only of human beings but of all things in the world, opens up the possibility of a collective politics. Such is the politics of precarity.

The other line of inquiry follows precarity as the latest mutation of capitalism, taking it, in McCormack and Salmenniemi's formulation, as "a paradigmatic feature of our post-Fordist, post-welfare and neoliberal times."[58] Concerned with precarity's impact on work and workers, thinkers have put forward a variety of notions, united in their observation and critique of the increasing informalization, flexibilization, and precarization of employment in our midst. Lauren Berlant puts forward "cruel optimism" as the way that optimistic fantasies of upward mobility become precisely, and cruelly, what lure people to endure conditions of precarity, and at the same time, thwart them from ever realizing the very fantasies that drive them.[59] Precarious living and working conditions, according to Isabell Lorey, are no longer the predicament of the poor, but are becoming increasingly normal for other strata of society, such that precarity has become "a fundamental governmental instrument of governing."[60] Predicating similarly on the prevalence of precarity, Guy Standing integrates "precarity" and "proletariat" and neologizes the term "precariat" to foreground the experience of exploitation and the possibility of a new subjectivity.[61] For all its intertwining with high mobility, unstable labour conditions, and affective investment—creative workers are said to move readily to vibrant cities, and are prepared to tolerate unfair or inhuman conditions for doing what they like—creative work has become a prime site to investigate the contemporary mechanisms and ramifications of precarity and precarization.[62]

This book converses with this impressive body of scholarship on precarity and (creative) work with two particular assertions—that of the gendered, personal experiences (of singlehood), and that of the local, specific realities (in contemporary China).[63] To examine precarity as complex, lived realities is to be, at the same time, informed by the critique on works on precarity, precariat, and precarization, that the knowledge so far produced and circulated is predominantly conceived of and necessitated by scenarios unfolded and conceptualized in Western contexts, say, the Global North.[64] The precariat, as Standing admits, is not a homogeneous group. My inquiry into the single, female creative workers in Shanghai, in this sense, is an attempt to resist dehistoricizing and flattening precarious experiences, and to offer a more specific, empirical understanding of what is taking place elsewhere. I stand by scholars who work on Chinese labour issues, who insist on locality and complexity in seeing and thinking about the Chinese case. While similar practices of exploitation and processes of precarization are evident, Chinese characteristics are not to be erased, such as class distinctions, the legal system and practices, and the importance of the state.[65] To this, I add the experiences of single women living in contemporary Shanghai.

From Precarity to Love of *Zheteng*

If, as stated by Ronaldo Munck, "precariousness has always been a seemingly natural condition" for the workers in the Global South,[66] I argue in this book that it is probably also a female thing. From what I am about to explicate in the following chapters, the single women may not choose for their precarious lives, but they stand by their lives and find ways to negotiate the multiple demands of singlehood and creative work. If freedom is, at least partly, what they claim to enjoy, despite and perhaps because of such negotiation, they know that this freedom does not come for free, either literally or figuratively. For the creative work they do, these women report similar experiences of exploitation as their colleagues elsewhere, such as long working hours and job insecurity, as well as gender-specific ones, such as gender discrimination and sexual harassment. By and large, they do like the work they do and find ways to do, using David Hesmondhalgh and Sarah Baker's emphasis, their "good work,"[67] particularly through the practice of *chuangye* (创业): starting up a business of their own.

While the flexibility and unpredictability of creative work affects their private lives, it also enables them to lead the private lives they prefer. Creative work and single life seem to be mutually constituted, sometimes with sadness, sometimes with delight. Concerning their love lives, the single women shared anecdotes with me of being pressurized to marry, and of the cultural practice of *xiangqin* (相亲), gatherings arranged, usually by parents, for singles to meet potential marital partners, which are as numerous as the tactics they use to deal with them. However painful it is for me to witness, and for them to live in a society still so stubbornly hostile to single women, they live on. They continue the search for their version of a good relationship, doing what they enjoy as singles, co-habiting with people other than marital partners, pursuing their cultural interest as a community of their own making, navigating from place to place between the longing for stability and the sweet charm of mobility and novelty, of things unknown and unpredictable. To be able to keep on changing would be how they would like to imagine their life. Amidst all the perlocutionary acts and dark consequences that compel women to get a life that is more secure, predictable, and respectable, the single women working in the creative industries, as we will get to know later throughout the book, do differently. If "party-ism, familism, and pedagogy," according to Jeroen de Kloet and Anthony Fung, constitute the major forces that try to mould contemporary Chinese youth to docility and conformity,[68] these single women demonstrate the potential of living differently.

One of them tells me how and why women live their lives differently, since they are more readily "led" by love, by family, by getting pregnant and raising children, and by many other personal factors that are contingent, defying planning and calculation. To her, she says, women are simply more wont to insecurity and unpredictability. Another, talking about her previous employment as a journalist for a well-known financial newspaper, says she could have settled for security, away from troubles and difficulties. But she chose, instead, to start her own business. "The state of being single, the state of doing creative things, it's insecure, but we love *zheteng* (折腾). This circle of people loves *zheteng*." This Chinese term 折腾— literally meaning tossing from side to side, and figuratively referring to suffering physical and mental agitation—is often used by the single women in this inquiry. As much as their experiences corroborate Lorey's poignant observation that "[p]recarization is not an exception, it is rather the rule,"[69] they are not ruled by this. They experience precarity, they know it, and they are fond of it.

My empirical scrutiny in the context of contemporary China compels me to rethink single womanhood, creative work, and the negative framing of marginalization and precarization, and ultimately, albeit tentatively and probably provocatively, the politics of the historical conjuncture of our time. I want to make three remarks.

First, guided by what the single women in this inquiry have to say about themselves, I want to reiterate the complexity of their lived realities not only in terms of empirical difference, but also as a theoretical exigency. In tandem with Western-based feminist scholarship which, cogently and correctly, concerns itself with globalizing neo-liberalism and the individualizing, depoliticizing discourse of post-feminism, this book positions itself as an exercise in understanding women's lives, never homogenously or universally, never a priori, but always on their own terms, in their own contexts. I align with feminist scholars working in non-Western contexts who, in the words of Luo Wei and Sun Zhen, flag up the danger of "(1) a theoretical blending of third world women as a coherent, identical group without class, ethnic, or racial distinctions; (2) an uncritical offering of third world women's oppression as universality; and (3) a problematic dichotomy between the supposedly powerless, victimized 'average third world women' and their educated, modern Western counterparts."[70]

Second, the single women and creative workers in this inquiry have, time and again, told me about their single and work lives evoking a scenario not entirely alienated, but affectively different, from the one posited by critical thinkers such as Lakämper, Lorey, McRobbie, and Standing. When creative workers are said to be suffering from processes of precarization, and women are cautioned about the false consciousness of choice and freedom, what will unfold in this book is that they do not subscribe to such insights; they feel rather differently about their lives. I am not asking which is right or wrong; I am asking the question of connection, and possible mobilization. Elsewhere, I have argued that hope, in the sense of caring and daring to imagine a certain, better future, is not the privilege of the progressive Left. The state-capital nexus is very skilled in managing and distributing their version of hope, by way of popular culture.[71] If the last decade of populist triumph can serve as evidence, they are more skilled than we are. Indeed, more than a decade ago, Chantal Mouffe, in her reflection on hope, already articulated her discontent with the moral and rationalist approach of what she calls "the Left." To realize the radical project of a better society for everyone, Mouffe reminds the leftist practitioners that it is not merely a matter of who is right or wrong, but a matter of passion. "[W]e are clearly facing a difficulty in terms of the way passion can be mobilized."[72] I suspect part of that difficulty is that we sometimes fail to deal with, reckon with, and connect with how people feel. In our urgency to remind them of what they should do, we forget what they are doing, forget to connect, forget that such a connection is vital in mobilizing passion.

Third, following on from the deliberations on mobilization and politics, I want to resonate the second remark with another act of forgetting, of the political realities in other contexts. To continue with the call for politics on the basis of our aversion to post-feminism and our concern for precarization is probably intellectually correct, but is empirically—or should we say, realistically—inadequate. It goes against the caution reiterated by researchers in experiences not situated in the Global North, simply and complicatedly, that we cannot always be informed by the politics argued elsewhere in Western democracies. As far as China is concerned, Wang Hui presents the contemporary conjuncture as one devoid of space for political debate, one where state control is severe, and the party, a mechanism of power *sans* political ideals, leading the author to declare "the end of the revolution," the title of his book.[73] In a related vein, Lee Ching Kwan warns against a certain curious preference, or probably wishful thinking, to look at what is claimed to be a mounting wave of labour strikes, class consciousness, and worker empowerment. Such an empowerment thesis, the author argues, is hardly substantiated with empirical evidence. The labour activism that did emerge "remains a politics of necessity rather than a politics of freedom."[74] Meng Bingchun and Huang Yanning, reflecting on the misogynist discourse surrounding Singles Day, observe similarly a waning class consciousness in tandem with what they call "patriarchal capitalism." Poignantly, they refer to contemporary China as "a low point in the history of Chinese feminism."[75] Not to forget that on the eve of International Women's Day in 2015, five Chinese feminists, who were planning demonstrations against sexual harassment in different cities, were arrested for "disorderly conduct" and detained for more than a month. This does not mean that feminist activism has been stifled—Li Maizi, one of the arrested, published an essay in the UK newspaper *The Guardian* two years later, to articulate her persistent hope for the Chinese feminist movement.[76] This also does not mean I do not stand by such forms of activism for a better world. What I want to highlight here is that when we think about the politics surrounding workers and women in the Chinese context, we need to think specifically.[77]

RECOGNITION, REFUSAL, CARING

This is, thus, not only a case of Western theory, Asian reality; it is also an instance of what I alluded to earlier in this introductory chapter: how we can use the Asian reality as method to rethink Western theory. Before I move on, I must reiterate this: all of these cautions, grounded in empirical investigation of the Chinese case, do not mean that things are fine, that these women and workers are fine, and that we should cease to be interested and invested in striving for a world that is less precarious, less stigmatizing, more equal, and more free. I am arguing for an alternative, another possibility of thinking and doing politics, there and perhaps elsewhere. To reach this final goal of the introductory chapter, I need three stepping stones, offered by recognition, refusal, and caring.

I borrow the term "recognition" from Nancy Fraser's seminal piece, where she builds on Charles Taylor's and Axel Honneth's works and argues forcefully and schematically about the pitfalls of doing "politics of redistribution" alone, if we are to pursue justice in the post-socialist era. For Fraser, it is essential to adopt a "bivalent" approach in which the "politics of recognition" must be integrated with that of redistribution. The dilemma, and thus the solution, is how to address injustice simultaneously on the cultural and socioeconomic fronts—in the case of the feminist project, how to integrate gender identity and class interests.[78] I underwrite the importance to recognize, but not or not only in the sense of a group, as a collectivity of women, whose experiences and specificities run the risk of being flattened and homogenized, by an over-coded language of marginalization and stigmatization, into one *single* narrative. We need to recognize them as individuals. The single women we are going to meet in this book—with their specific socioeconomic and personal backgrounds, educated, middle-class, living in a big city, creatively-oriented— will, I hope, urge us to see them not only as marginalized and stigmatized, but as individuals who refuse to be pressurized into a life that is expected of them, with the seductions of security and predictability, and trepidations of contingency and precarity if lived otherwise. Yes, to refuse, as posited by Marcel Mauss—as if to refuse a gift, an offer of goodwill presumed by the one offering, for instance, the advice by the state and by the parents to get married before it is too late, or the prospect of earning more money with jobs that are more lucrative than the creative ones.[79] The single women in this book are not necessarily resisting, at least not in an active and conscious sense, but they are refusing, sometimes successfully, sometimes not or not entirely. Nevertheless, as Carole McGranahan notes, "[r]efusal is optimistic. Refusal involves attachments, connections to a goal, relations to ambitions. It is a no committed to generating a yes."[80]

And the attachments, goals, and ambitions are to be found in the lives they have to build, of their own accord, and on their own.[81] The "yes" is a yes to themselves, to their capacity in not only refusing, but also in caring for themselves precisely in these precarizing times. If we speak the word "precarity," we pronounce "care"; if we write "precarity," we almost spell the word "care." Word plays aside, the step I want to attempt is to take the politics of precarity to the ethics of care; ethics, in the Foucauldian sense of "the relation to oneself."[82] When we look at how the single women in this book relate to themselves, we see not only what some would call a post-feminist and neo-liberal fantasy, but also how they refuse, how they live their lives—we see "care of the self." This is not to trivialize the struggles, the anxieties, the subordination they experience, or to override the experiences of those with other specificities, such as migrant workers or rural women—it is to acknowledge and connect to the complexity of women's engagement with the regulatory world they are living in, above all, the efforts, the passion, the triumphs, however occasional they may be. As Foucault reminds us, "[i]t would not be possible for power relations to exist without points of insubordination that, by definition, are means of escape."[83]

This book, while not written in Foucauldian language, resonates with his "insistence on the transformative power of the common, the everyday and the mundane."[84] Here is also the departing point of my take on precarity. When Lorey questions "why protests against government through insecurity are so difficult and rare," she means to take it as "problematizing the obvious dominance of the servile side of precarious self-government," and the concomitant, hegemonic mode of labour that implicates the whole person.[85] My reply, or the reply I can formulate from what I have learned from this inquiry, is that they do not protest because they do not experience the myriad of ways to meander through precarity as being servile, at least not only as servile. Negativity is not what integrates the insecurity of single womanhood and creative work into a new subjectivity, as proposed by Standing in his "precariat." They actually love *zheteng*. Nor do I think a sense of vulnerability, the realization of interdependency, offers a good basis to drive the politics of precarity as far as the women in this book are concerned. Butler invokes Levina's notion of "face," a face for us to recognize one another's vulnerability in, and the ethical responsibility towards one another, generating the possibility of a politics against the precarity of life.[86] Relatedly, Lorey finds us in a "care crisis," and pleads for more time and effort to care for others, to practice what she sees as a feminist political resistance movement *Precarias a la deriva*: a "care community."[87]

Given the contemporary Chinese context, where politics of such a collective kind is quite improbable and dangerous, where the memory of collectivism is a return to gender sameness and a planned economy, where the new generation of single women-cum-creative workers may feel vulnerable and precarious but nonetheless are surviving and thriving in their vulnerability and precarity—given this context, I want to call forth not so much an ethics of vulnerability, but an ethics of care; not on the inter-relationality of us, but the relationality towards oneself. I want to insert a provocative call into our search for alternative ways for imagining and achieving a better society: perhaps the call is not so much for the precariat or the precarized to recognize others' faces, others' vulnerability, to care for others, to realize a care community; the call is also for the precariat and the precarized to recognize themselves, to recognize their capability to refuse and to care for themselves, to survive and thrive through precarity, fearless of precarity—a call to be more individual. Du Yaquan, when making a plea for the reform of the individual at the beginning of the twentieth century, the beginning of modern China, argues that until the individual realizes "his own frail and unhealthy body, his impotent and weak spirit, his shallow and incapable mind, and his disordered and purposeless life, social reform will be no more than a remote dream."[88] Disrupted by the Communist Revolution in 1949 and the reform transformations since the 1970s, the contemporary configuration of China may require another reform of the individual, to realize quite the opposite of Du's formulation—to realize her body, spirit, mind, and life, like the single women in this inquiry, to build a life of their own, on their own.

Maybe we need more individuals caring for themselves in times of precarity, more individuals refusing to live a stable life, refusing security, and stability, and any imagination that any institutions may offer them this—after all, the Chinese population remembers and understands such processes as institutionalization, formalization, and securitization, rather differently.[89] Maybe we need more people to recognize their own potential to refuse, to care. Maybe we need more precarity, to such an extent that someday, things may toss about, and eventually, topple. This is the politics of precarity, and the recognition of the caring capacity, that this book wants to provoke with, about China, and elsewhere.[90]

In 2016, I was curating an exhibition on single women in Shanghai in connection with this research project, entitled "Precariously Yours." I discussed with Li Xiaofei, an artist-curator and my partner on the Shanghai side, about the Chinese translation of the title. Apparently, there was no readily accepted equivalent, and it was not easy to translate. Xiaofei checked online and found this expression: *yaoyao yuzhui* (摇摇欲坠), tossing, swaying, trembling, about to, wanting to fall, to topple.

HERE THEY ARE

The empirical core of this book is made up of the experiences of 25 single women: seven born in the 1990s, 10 in the 1980s, seven in the 1970s, and one in the 1960s.[91] While 10 of them were born and grew up in Shanghai, the rest moved to the city either as a university student or as a working adult. They operate in a variety of creative sectors, from mass media to new media, from advertising to art and culture. They are journalists, musicians, designers, artists, producers, vloggers, account executives, and have many more diverse occupations. Some are employed; some do freelance work; and some consider themselves as entrepreneurs. The inclusive and open nature of inquiry is deliberate, for two reasons. First, I do not want to presuppose anything. If my goal is to find out how these single women do their creative work, I should refrain from presupposing certain creative work (for instance, that of an artist) and certain ways of doing creative work (for instance, that of a freelancer) are categorically different (for instance, more precarious). Second, I do not want to define and confine what creative work or the creative worker is. There are attempts: from Florida's "creative core" and "creative professionals" (which include, among others, "health care workers") to the IPR (intellectual property regime)-driven definition introduced by the UK Department for Culture, Media and Sports.[92] Given the persistent discussion over what Lily Kong calls the "ambiguities and opacities" of creative industries, I opted for a bottom-up approach: as long as the single women considered themselves to be doing creative work, they were welcome to participate in this research project.[93] Such inclusiveness and openness, I hope, will oppose any tendency to universalize and flatten the experience of creative work.

With the same urge to canvass complexity, I also opted for a loose mobilization of the term "single." The single women whose experiences are collected in this book are mostly single in the typical sense, that is, never-married, but they also include divorced women and single mothers, those living with others, and those with—but not living with—a partner or partners. In other words, in terms of marital background or habitation status, they vary. In deciding what to include as "single" for my investigation, I have considered the various ways my fellow researchers have guided their projects. Gavin Jones' research team, in their study on the single population in Singapore and East Asia in general, used two pointers to recruit their subjects: aged between 30 and 44, and never-married.[94] They included singles living with their family and having a relationship during the time of research. On the other hand, Lahad chose to exclude the latter category. In her book on the Israeli case, Lahad refers to what she calls "long-term singles" or "late singlehood," terms that have emerged in the local public discourse. They cover women who are "not in a committed long-term relationship, and do not have children … whose status is no longer regarded socially acceptable."[95] Her study includes divorced women who are not inclined to find a new partner, but not single mothers, widows, or women with permanent partners. Similarly mobilizing a vernacular neologism, but keeping its parameters vague, the book published by Luo et al. focuses on "leftover women" (*shengnü*) in China. It analyses the phenomenon without defining "single women," whether in terms of age or other biographical details.[96] Wu Shuping's popular, biographically accented book on Chinese single women contains lengthy interviews with 20 women aged between 21 and 36.[97]

Soon after I started my fieldwork, I realized the possible pitfalls of confining the women in this inquiry to any fixed set of yardsticks. Must they live on their own? Quite a few of them actually live with their families or with flatmates. Must they be never-married? I do not see why their experiences as single women should be less single due to this marital background. Must they be older than a certain age? I have come across younger women telling me of the pressure to get married, as well as older women actively seeking a partner. The best approach, I presume, is not to impose anything, save for the very acknowledgement, by themselves, that they are single—best in the sense of serving the purpose of this inquiry, which is primarily an investigation of how single women experience and live their lives. As long as they perceive themselves as being single, they experience and live in the regime surrounding singlehood, particularly single womanhood, discursively and otherwise. In their discussion of Chinese women younger than 25 years of age, Luo et al. note a more intense anxiety about being left over, the anxiety of "*shengnü*-to-be."[98] During the process of recruiting subjects, I said, consistently and simply, that I was looking for single women, without any taglines. The diversity of age, marital background, and habitation status, and the existence of current relationships subsequently found among the single women, nods again to the inclusiveness and openness of this inquiry. After all, lynchpinning this book is its refusal to reduce the complexity of single women's lives.

Basic information on these 25 single women is listed in Appendix I for easy reference. They were recruited by myself, my research assistants, our circles of friends, and the networks of creative professionals and feminist activists I have built up throughout the years of my own creative and academic work in mainland China. Generally based in Hong Kong, I went to Shanghai twice to conduct two rounds of fieldwork: February to March 2015, and October to November 2016. During these four months, I conducted in-depth, semi-structured, face-to-face interviews with all of the subjects. The interviews, usually not longer than an hour, took place at a time and place of their convenience. I would start by asking them some basic information, and followed up with questions as prompted by the information they supplied; I would make sure that our conversations covered their work and love lives. This is inevitably a challenge to the interviewing and analytical skills of the investigator, who must negotiate between sincerity to take the interviewees' subjective experiences seriously, and awareness of the forces configuring such experiences that the interviewees may not be aware of themselves, the tension between structure and subjectivity, of speaking with them or for them. At the same time, I also conducted site visits, either prompted by the interviews, for instance, to the Love Club in Shanghai, or occasioned by chance encounters, for instance, to the party on November 11. I went with interviewees to dinners, to visit their studios, to check out their music, and generally, to sensitize myself to their lived worlds. The interviews were recorded and transcribed verbatim, and the site visits were documented with notes and photographs. Qualitative research techniques were employed for the strengths of their generally intensive research design.[99] Such a design does not aspire to offer grand narratives or common patterns of large populations; it aims to investigate subjective experiences and the interpretation of a small number of cases, ultimately advancing knowledge and understanding of the global phenomena under study.

For the specific inquiry on Kunqu (昆曲), seven additional single women were recruited for their shared interest in this operatic art and its possibility for community building. Given the nature of this inquiry, focus groups were organized in addition to the data collected during the interviews. I managed to host one during my last week in Shanghai. The third and last round of fieldwork took place in the early half of 2017. I needed to entrust this to three research assistants, as my teaching commitments at my university did not allow me to visit Shanghai for another extended period of time. I personally recruited these assistants in Shanghai, and explained the projects to them. One of them, a Kunqu lover herself, helped me with the Kunqu inquiry; the other two supported my investigations using mapping and visual methods. They worked under my instruction and supervision, and were in constant communication with me. While the responsibility is mine, I remain grateful to them.[100] More methodological details of this round of fieldwork can be found in Chaps. 6, 7, and 8. Details of all the interviews and focus group meetings are to be found in Appendix II. I explained the research project and possible privacy concerns to the women, all of whom gave explicit consent to use materials collected during the different rounds of fieldwork, including the images reproduced in Chap. 8 (some of which show their faces recognizably). The names used in this book were suggested by the interviewees themselves.

THE REST OF THE BOOK

I will end this introductory chapter with an introduction of the organization logic of the book and the gist of the subsequent chapters. The single women who have kindly agreed to tell us about their lives may be unmarried, unpartnered, but it will be doing them an injustice to attach the epithet "single" to their lives. What I want to do in the following empirical chapters is precisely to problematize the understanding of "single" in relation to these single women; they are never really single in many senses. The rest of the book is thus structured on this paradoxical premise—namely, that these single women are always with someone or something: their representations, their "generation," their work, their (imaginary) romantic lovers, their friends, their fellow strangers in the city, themselves.

There is indeed something paradoxical about single women; while they are socially marginalized, they seem to command mass appeal and feature strongly in Chinese cultural productions. Chapter 2 takes popular media as a lens to trace the discursive formulations surrounding Chinese single women in an urban setting. Following an overview of the representation of ideal womanhood in magazines, films, advertising, television dating shows, and drama, I will focus on *Ode to Joy*, a hit series surrounding five single women who happen to live on the same floor in a residential complex in Shanghai. The success of the series, scripted by a woman, owes itself to the sharp and sympathetic portrayal of the difficulties, complexities, and above all, joy—as the series title points at—of single womanhood in a city such as Shanghai; it also leads to criticism of its erasure of class inequalities. I will end with an analysis of the five actresses' participation in the 2017 Spring Festival Gala, when their subversive potentials were being performed, and at the same time, cleansed.

Chapter 3 continues with another sort of discursive formation that single women in China live with—that of the generation. Similar in its underpinning logic of era and time, yet different from the Generation X, Y, and Z in the Western or global context, the single women in this inquiry prefer to refer themselves to *qilinghou*, *balinghou*, and *jiulinghou*, the post-1970s, -1980s, and -1990s, the vernacular terms grounded in temporality and epochality that emerged into wide circulation among Chinese media and populations.[101] I will zoom in on the lives of three single women to explicate historically the different eras and perhaps different Chinas that they were born into: one-child policy, economic reforms and growth, start-up culture, and the increasing participation in processes of globalization. They testify to generational distinctions as vividly as generational ambiguities, posing implicit questions about the usefulness and limitation of the generational paradigm.[102] In any case, they, like many fellow Chinese people, continue to talk of themselves in such collectivity, together with the empowerment and disempowerment afforded by such a generational discourse.

Thus contextualized, the inquiry continues in Chap. 4 to discuss work—or more specifically, creative work—and the single women doing it. I will situate my study amidst a body of critical scholarship that tries to make sense of what is taking place in creative work with fast-changing technologies, economies, and politics. This chapter is supplemented with the subjective experiences of the creative workers themselves in two ways I regard as significant. First, it chooses to suspend the concern of exploitation and alienation to make space for what these single women have to say about work—and particularly, good work.[103] Despite all the demands, struggles, and failures, the single women evoke a general sense of doing good with what they do. I will use *chuangye*, the setting up of a business, a term often mobilized to illustrate what they see as good work. Second, it inserts a gendered dimension, female singlehood, into discussions on creative work, to look at work not in isolation, but in intersection with their lives as single women.[104] Three overlapping scenarios concerning creative work and singlehood are narrated: mutual constitution; how creative work makes it easier to lead a single life; and how career success makes it more difficult to leave a single life.

Chapter 5 should be read as a continuation of Chap. 4, to explore the single women's lives in domains of intimacy. It situates the exploration in China, where vectors of coercion such as Confucian values, state propaganda, and parental pressure, usher urban-dwelling and middle-class women into realms of marginalization and anxiety.[105] Focusing on the lived experiences of single women, the chapter documents their negative accounts as well as coping tactics towards the pressure to get married, especially surrounding the much-cited and hated experience of *xiangqin*, or arranged meetings with candidates for marriage. Aversion to pressure is one thing; wish and will to romance is another. Chapter 5 continues to trace their longings and the tactics they use to find a partner. In any case, the single women, when they are single, invariably articulate and celebrate their freedom and autonomy, gesturing to global narratives of singlehood, of femininity, and ultimately, of what they consider a "good life." The chapter ends with the case of three self-proclaimed lesbian women in order to supplement the largely heteronormative narrative of their fellow single women with their specific experiences of loving and living.

For these single women with creative proclivity, one component of their understanding of a good life is, clearly, the enjoyment of art and culture in the city in which they live. Incidentally, many of the single women I came across share a common interest in Kunqu—generally considered one of the oldest forms of operatic arts in China—as fans, as apprentices, as teachers, as organizers, or as promoters. And they know one another. Chapter 6 offers a case study of a community built on "informal sociality."[106] After a historical overview of Kunqu in the context of Shanghai, the inquiry presents what they do with Kunqu in their after-work lives; how and why this community of informal sociality came into being; and what this passion, friendship, and shared contacts with regard to a creative practice means to these single women. This case study engages with three lines of scholarship: first, deliberations on (imagined) community and citizenship[107]; second, creative labour studies that often frame "sociality" among creative workers in professional terms[108]; and third, fandom studies as well as audience research that attempt to redefine what fans and audiences are in our time.[109]

While many studies on single women centre on time, the single women in this inquiry live their lives in one common space: Shanghai.[110] Cued by their remarks about the ease and freedom offered by the trendy cafés where we usually met, as well as by the "spatial turn" in humanities—the increasing interest in the interaction between place and people—Chap. 7 uses the method of the "mattering map" to recuperate mobile narratives of such interactions with an additional axis of work.[111] From their mapping of the sites that matter to them, the chapter tracks their movement to Shanghai, followed by their relocation trajectories as well as everyday mobility, and immobility. In doing so, it engages with certain claims that cool places attract creative talents,[112] and their right not so much to the city,[113] but *in* the city. Questions concerning a sense of belonging, security, convenience, choice, and freedom, are discussed, culminating in the complexity of their mobility being part and parcel of their mooring.

While this book opens with a discussion of how single women in contemporary China are being represented, it ends with their self-representations. Fundamentally, Chap. 8 is an attempt, the most explicit one among the chapters, to let the subjects mobilize their creative skills and speak for themselves. Inspired by visual methodology in general, and image-elicitation techniques in particular, this chapter has two goals.[114] It documents visual materials created by the single women that best represent their lives as single woman in Shanghai: we see cats, a horse, a panda, a playing card, and pastiches of various sorts, sometimes with their faces included, sometimes not. At the same time, it presents the narratives elicited from these materials as singularity, as personal narratives vis-à-vis the grander narratives thrust upon them, as outlined in Chap. 2. This final main chapter, while opening up areas for examination otherwise unexamined, overlooked, and finally erased from any understanding of their lives, ends with a note of intense longing evoked by their self-presentation: to change and to keep on changing. Chapter 9 concludes the book with an epilogue.

I will end this introductory chapter with a literary quotation. In 1933, Lu Xun published a somewhat cynical piece of prose, titled "Shanghai Girls," in which he described the subjects of his piece in the following way:

> Those females accustomed to life in Shanghai soon become well aware of the glory they have, knowing at the same time the danger inherent in it.[115]

I choose not to read this, however, with cynicism. I read the complexity, the awareness of one's own life, the exigency to take care of oneself, and the following chapters contain what these single women are going to tell us, more than 80 years later.

NOTES

1. See Ulrich Beck and Elisabeth Beck-Gernsheim, *Individualization: Institutionalized Individualism and Its Social and Political Consequences* (London: Sage, 2002); Eric Klinenberg, *Going Solo: The Extraordinary Rise and Surprising Appeal of Living Alone*, 1 edition (London: Duckworth Overlook, 2012).
2. Tao Shun (陶舜), "单身社会来了 [The Single Society Has Come]," 腾讯网 *[Tengxun Wang]* (blog), August 24, 2017, http://view.news.qq.com/original/intouchtoday/n3993.html.
3. Mu Guangzong (穆光宗), "'单身社会'来临未必是好事 [The Advent of 'Single Society' May Not Be a Good Thing]," 中國網 *[China.Org.Cn]* (blog), August 27, 2017, http://big5.china.com.cn/gate/big5/opinion.china.com.cn/opinion_20_170420.html.
4. See Kinneret Lahad, *A Table for One: A Critical Reading of Singlehood, Gender and Time* (Manchester: Manchester University Press, 2017);

Kinneret Lahad, "'Am I Asking for Too Much?' The Selective Single Woman as a New Social Problem," *Women's Studies International Forum* 40, no. Supplement C (2013): 23–32; Kinneret Lahad and Avi Shoshana, "Singlehood in Treatment: Interrogating the Discursive Alliance between Postfeminism and Therapeutic Culture," *European Journal of Women's Studies* 22, no. 3 (2015): 334–49. See also Bella M. DePaulo and Wendy L. Morris, "Singles in Society and in Science," *Psychological Inquiry* 16, no. 2–3 (2005): 57–83; Jill Reynolds, *The Single Woman: A Discursive Investigation* (London: Routledge, 2008); Elizabeth A. Sharp and Lawrence Ganong, ""I'm a Loser, I'm Not Married, Let's Just All Look at Me": Ever-Single Women's Perceptions of Their Social Environment," *Journal of Family Issues* 32, no. 7 (2011): 956–80.

5. See Luo Wei and Sun Zhen, "Are You the One? China's TV Dating Shows and the Sheng Nü's Predicament," *Feminist Media Studies* 15, no. 2 (2015): 239–56 ("Are You the One" is the authors' translation of the dating show "If You Are the One"); Su Xing (苏醒) and Tian Renbo (田仁波), "'城市剩女'群体生存焦虑问题研究 [Research on Living Anxiety of Shengnü in Cities]," *Journal of Qujing Normal University* 31, no. 2 (2012): 116–20.

6. In his 2017 book, Florida admits he was overly optimistic about the power of the creative class and creative city to revitalize a better version of urban life, as he posited in the bestseller published 15 years earlier. His earlier work has been and remains influential. See Richard Florida, *The Rise of the Creative Class* (New York: Basic Books, 2002); Richard Florida, *The New Urban Crisis: How Our Cities Are Increasing Inequality, Deepening Segregation, and Failing the Middle Class and What We Can Do About It* (New York: Basic Books, 2017).

7. See Nicholas Garnham, "From Cultural to Creative Industries," *International Journal of Cultural Policy* 11, no. 1 (2006): 15–29; Rosalind Gill and Andy Pratt, "In the Social Factory?: Immaterial Labour, Precariousness and Cultural Work," *Theory, Culture & Society* 25, no. 7–8 (2008): 1–30; Richard Lloyd, *Neo-Bohemia: Art and Commerce in the Postindustrial City* (New York: Routledge, 2006); Toby Miller, "From Creative to Cultural Industries," *Cultural Studies* 23, no. 1 (2009): 88–99; Andrew Ross, *Nice Work If You Can Get It: Life and Labor in Precarious Times* (New York: NYU Press, 2009).

8. Angela McRobbie, *Be Creative: Making a Living in the New Culture Industries*, 1 edition (Cambridge, UK; Malden, MA: Polity, 2016), 14.

9. See Anthony Y. H. Fung and John Nguyet Erni, "Cultural Clusters and Cultural Industries in China," *Inter-Asia Cultural Studies* 14, no. 4 (2013): 644–56; Michael Keane, *Creative Industries in China: Art, Design and Media* (Malden: Polity, 2013); Winnie Wong, *Van Gogh on*

Demand: China and the Readymade (Chicago; London: University Of Chicago Press, 2014); Pang Laikwan, *Creativity and Its Discontents: China's Creative Industries and Intellectual Property Rights Offenses* (Durham: Duke University Press, 2012); Niu Weilin (牛维麟) and Peng Yi (彭翊), 北京文化创意产业集聚区发展研究报告 *[Beijing Cultural Creative Industry Clusters Development Study Report]* (Beijing: 中国人民大学出版社 [People's University Press], 2009); Zhang Xiaoming (张晓明), Hu Huilin (胡惠林), and Zhang Jiangang (章建刚), eds., 文化蓝皮书.中国文化产业发展报告 *[Blue Book of China's Culture: Annual Report on the Development of China's Cultural Industries]* (Beijing: 社会科学文献出版社 [Social Sciences Academic Press], 2002).

10. See Matthew Chew, "Contemporary Re-Emergence of the Qipao: Political Nationalism, Cultural Production and Popular Consumption of a Traditional Chinese Dress," *The China Quarterly* 189 (2007): 144–61; Jeroen de Kloet, *China with a Cut: Globalisation, Urban Youth and Popular Music* (Amsterdam: Amsterdam University Press, 2010); Keane, *Creative Industries in China*; Justin O'Connor and Gu Xin, "Shanghai: Images of Modernity," in *Cultures and Globalization: Cities, Cultural Policy and Governance*, ed. Helmut K. Anheier and Yudhishthir Raj Isar (London: Sage, 2012), 288–99; Wang Jing, "The Global Reach of a New Discourse: How Far Can 'Creative Industries' Travel?," *International Journal of Cultural Studies* 7, no. 1 (2004): 9–19.

11. Chen Kuan-Hsing, *Asia as Method: Toward Deimperialization* (Durham, NC: Duke University Press, 2010).

12. Guy Standing, *The Precariat: The New Dangerous Class* (London; New York: Bloomsbury Academic, 2011).

13. See Anne Allison, *Precarious Japan* (Durham: Duke University Press, 2013); Maribel Casas-Cortés, "A Genealogy of Precarity: A Toolbox for Rearticulating Fragmented Social Realities in and out of the Workplace," *Rethinking Marxism* 26, no. 2 (2014): 206–26; Donna McCormack and Suvi Salmenniemi, "The Biopolitics of Precarity and the Self," *European Journal of Cultural Studies* 19, no. 1 (2016): 3–15; Standing, *The Precariat*.

14. The post-1949 account of gender and womanhood in China is a simplifying and synthesizing one, based on the much more detailed and complex works by writers on the topic, including Gail Hershatter, *Women in China's Long Twentieth Century* (Berkeley: University of California Press, 2007); Jeanne Hong Zhang, "Gender in Post-Mao China," *European Review* 11, no. 2 (2003): 209–24; Yang Jianli (杨剑利), 女性与近代中国社会 *[The Female and Modern China Society]* (Beijing: 中国社会出版社 [China Society Press], 2007); Luo, Wang, and Jiang, 中国剩女调查; Meng Bingchun and Huang Yanning, "Patriarchal Capitalism with

Chinese Characteristics: Gendered Discourse of 'Double Eleven' Shopping Festival," *Cultural Studies* 31, no. 5 (2017): 659–84.; Harriet Evans, *The Subject of Gender: Daughters and Mothers in Urban China* (Maryland: Rowman & Littlefield, 2008).

15. Judith Lakämper, "Affective Dissonance, Neoliberal Postfeminism and the Foreclosure of Solidarity," *Feminist Theory* 18, no. 2 (2017): 119–35.

16. See Leta Hong Fincher, *Leftover Women: The Resurgence of Gender Inequality in China* (London, New York: Zed Books, 2014); Sandy To, *China's Leftover Women: Late Marriage Among Professional Women and Its Consequences* (London, New York: Routledge, 2015).

17. See, for instance, Ye Pan (叶攀), "'平语'近人—习近平谈妇女如何全面发展 ['Ping Yu' Intimacy—Xi Jinping Talks about Personal Development of Women]," 中国新闻网 *[Chinanews.Com]*, October 12, 2015, http://www.chinanews.com/gn/2015/10-12/7565191.shtml; Yan Yan (闫妍) and Qin Hua (秦华), "充分发挥妇女在家庭文明建设中的独特作用 [Full Potential of the Unique Role of Women in the Construction of Family Civilization]," 中国妇联新闻 *[Zhongguo Fulian Xinwen]*, May 18, 2015, http://acwf.people.com.cn/n/2015/0518/c99058-27015970.html.

18. Making use of this problematic, cosmetic brand SKII launched a video in 2016 showing daughters speaking "back" to their parents by placing similar placards in the People's Park of Shanghai. The introductory text reads: "Today, Chinese women face immense pressure to get married before they turn 27. In many Chinese cities, so-called marriage markets are a common sight, where parents go to post and match personal ads. A number of brave Chinese women have finally stood up to speak their mind against society's labels and their parents' pressures. A marriage market in Shanghai's People's park was taken over by personal messages from hundreds of independent women, stating that they want to control their own destiny." The video became viral and caused intense discussion on the *shengnü* phenomenon. See: "SK-II: Marriage Market Takeover," video, 4:16, April 6, 2016, https://www.youtube.com/watch?v=irfd74z52Cw.

19. Luo and Sun, "Are You the One?"; Su and Tian, "'城市剩女'群体生存焦虑问题研究"; To, *China's Leftover Women*.

20. See Li Luzhou, "If You Are the One: Dating Shows and Feminist Politics in Contemporary China," *International Journal of Cultural Studies* 18, no. 5 (2015): 519–35; Luo and Sun, "Are You the One?" See Chap. 2 for detailed discussion on representations of single women in Chinese popular cultural productions.

21. That single women are framed as *the* problematic category does not only foreground the entrenched sexism in Chinese society; it also elides the social plight confronting a large number of single men. Calculating the

sex ratio of cohorts already born, Das Gupta et al. argue that Chinese men, particularly "poor men in low-income provinces," will be the ones failing to get married, not women; "one in five Chinese men will fail to marry in 2020." They urge us to pay attention to the "bride shortage" and the subsequent social challenges of elderly men for the state in the nearby future of China. See Monica Das Gupta, Ethan Jennings Sharygin, and Avraham Ebenstein, "China's Marriage Market and Upcoming Challenges for Elderly Men" (The World Bank, 2010). See also Wei-Jun Jean Yeung and Hu Shu, "Coming of Age in Times of Change: The Transition to Adulthood in China," *The ANNALS of the American Academy of Political and Social Science* 646, no. 1 (2013): 149–71.

22. Viola Zhou, "China's Marriage Rate Slumps as More Singles Say 'I Don't'," *South China Morning Post*, September 6, 2017, http://www.scmp.com/news/china/society/article/2109868/marriage-rate-down-divorce-rate-more-chinese-couples-say-i-dont.

23. See Michael Keane, *Created in China: The Great New Leap Forward* (London; New York: Routledge, 2007). In this connection, I would like to explicate my general reference to China in this book. While many writers prefer the term "post-socialist China," I would continue with the more banal way of calling the historical period this book covers and the women in this book grew up in: "contemporary." Ideologically, "post-socialist" denotes a disappearance of class politics; and mundanely, it refers to the dismantling of socialist institutions. These two features do apply to China. However, as this book aims to understand contemporary China in terms of both gender and work, I do not want to foreground class politics a priori by pre-fixing China as "post-socialist." In any case, as observed by Lily Chumley, "many scholars argued that Chinese post-socialism was really neoliberalism." (See Lily Chumley, *Creativity Class: Art School and Culture Work in Postsocialist China* (Princeton: Princeton University Press, 2016): 16). At the same time, it will be misleading to understand the "post-" here to envisage a China moving forward and leaving socialism totally behind. Following this, to call the China under study "contemporary" is my way to include its "residual" socialism, post-socialism, and neo-liberalism. For its messiness, "contemporary" conjures the coevalness between China and the rest of the world—especially pertinent to single womanhood and creative work—whereas the term "post-socialist" immediately distinguishes China as a case apart. As this book strives to show, China is both a case apart and not.

24. It should be noted that "cultural industries," (*wenhua chanye* 文化产业) given its Marxist inclinations, have been the official term. However, with the increasing adoption of the global creative industries agenda, contemporary China has started to use "creative industries" (*chuangyi chanye* 创意产业) sometimes as replacement for, and sometimes in combination with the older term ("cultural creative industries").

25. Chumley, *Creativity Class*, 22–23.

26. Keane, *Creative Industries in China*, 31.

27. Ibid.

28. Pang, *Creativity and Its Discontents*.

29. Chow Yiu Fai, "Hong Kong Creative Workers in Mainland China: The Aspirational, the Precarious, and the Ethical," *China Information* 31, no. 1 (2017): 46.

30. Li Wuwei (厉无畏), "发展创意产业 让世界刮起中国风 [Developing a Creative Industry That Blows China Wind across the World]," 人民网 *[People.Cn]*, March 11, 2011, http://finance.people.com.cn/GB/71364/14119345.html.

31. The address was delivered on 18, October 2017 in Beijing. For the full text of President Xi's address, see "十九大開幕 習近平發表工作報告 [Opening of 19th National Congress—Working Report by Xi Jinping]," 香港經濟日報 *[Hong Kong Economic Times]*, October 18, 2017, http://china.hket.com/article/1927215.

32. Justin O'Connor and Xin Gu, "Creative Industry Clusters in Shanghai: A Success Story?" *International Journal of Cultural Policy* 20, no. 1 (2014): 1–20.

33. For a detailed account of the emergence and development of cultural industries in China, see Keane, *Created in China*. For a plea to return to cultural industries grounded in a theoretical and policy critique of creative industries, see Lily Kong, "From Cultural Industries to Creative Industries and Back? Towards Clarifying Theory and Rethinking Policy," *Inter-Asia Cultural Studies* 15, no. 4 (2014): 593–607. See also Miller, "From Creative to Cultural Industries."

34. The persistent usage of the term "cultural industries" underlines the officially sanctioned and ideologically-oriented emphasis on Chinese culture and civilization, at the expense of the presumably Western concoctions of creativity and creative industries. See, for instance, Zhang, Hu, and Zhang, 文化蓝皮书·中国文化产业发展报告; Zhang Xiaoming (张晓明), Wang Jiaxin (王家新), and Zhang Jiangang (章建刚), eds. 文化蓝皮书·中国文化产业发展报告 *[Blue Book of China's Culture: Annual Report on the Development of China's Cultural Industries]*. Beijing: 社会科学文献出版社 [Social Sciences Academic Press], 2012–2016; Ouyang, Youquan (欧阳友权), ed. 文化品牌蓝皮书·中国文化品牌发展报告 *[Blue Book of Cultural Brands: Annual Report on the Development of Cultural Brands in China]*. Changsha: 中南大学中国文化产业品牌研究中心 [Zhongnan University China's Cultural Industries Brands Research Centre], 2006.

35. See, for instance, Desmond Hui, "From Cultural to Creative Industries: Strategies for Chaoyang District, Beijing," *International Journal of Cultural Studies* 9, no. 3 (2006): 317–31; Niu Weilin (牛维麟) and Peng

Yi (彭翊), 北京文化创意产业集聚区发展研究报告 *[Beijing Cultural Creative Industry Clusters Development Study Report]* (Beijing: 中国人民大学出版社 [People's University Press], 2009); Ye Xin (叶辛) and Kuai Dashen (蒯大申), 上海文化发展报告 *(2011) [Shanghai Cultural Development Report (2011)]* (Beijing: 社会科学文献出版社 [Social Sciences Academic Press], 2011); Fung and Erni, "Cultural Clusters and Cultural Industries in China."

36. For a book-length study of art education in contemporary China, see Chumley, *Creativity Class*.

37. Like the account of gender and womanhood in China after 1949, this outline of the introduction of reform and opening up policies in China remains, indeed, an outline. In-depth analyses are to be found in the following works, on which I have drawn, in rough strokes, for the current purposes. For anthologies over the economic reforms and their aftermath, see Stephan Feuchtwang and Athar Hussain, eds., *The Chinese Economic Reforms* (London: Croom Helm, 1983); Shenggen Fan, Xibao Zhang, and Arjan de Haan, *Narratives of Chinese Economic Reforms: How Does China Cross the River?* (Singapore; Hackensack, NJ: World Scientific, 2010). For an excellent study of neo-liberal development in China and the production of desires and subjectivities, see Lisa Rofel, *Desiring China: Experiments in Neoliberalism, Sexuality, and Public Culture* (Durham: Duke University Press, 2007). For a list of Chinese-language publications that appear in connection with the 20th anniversary of reforms in 2008, see Zhou Yiping (周一平) and Zhou Lei (周雷), "2008 年改革开放史研究述评 [Overview of Researches on the History of Chinese Economic Reform 2008]," 当代中国史研究 *[Dangdai Zhongguo Shi Yanjiu]*, no. 1 (2008): 102–9.

38. For the list of references, see Lahad, *A Table for One*, 25. Here, I cite some of the latest studies: Laura Dales, "Single Women and Their Households in Contemporary Japan," in *The Global Political Economy of the Household in Asia*, ed. Juanita Elias and Samanthi J. Gunawardana (Basingstoke: Palgrave Macmillan, 2013), 110–126; Laura Dales, "Ohitorisama, Singlehood and Agency in Japan," *Asian Studies Review* 38, no. 2 (2014): 224–42; Lynn Jamieson and Roona Simpson, *Living Alone: Globalization, Identity and Belonging* (London: Palgrave Macmillan, 2013); Lynne Nakano, "Single Women in Marriage and Employment Markets in Japan," in *Capturing Contemporary Japan: Differentiation and Uncertainty*, ed. Satsuki Kawano, Glenda Susan Roberts, and Susan Orpett Long (Honolulu: University of Hawaii Press, 2014), 163–182; Jesook Song, *Living on Your Own: Single Women, Rental Housing, and Post-Revolutionary Affect in Contemporary South Korea* (Albany: SUNY Press, 2014); Eleanor Wilkinson, "Single People's

Geographies of Home: Intimacy and Friendship beyond 'the Family,'" *Environment and Planning A* 46, no. 10 (2014): 2452–68.

39. Bella DePaulo, "Holiday Spirit, 21st Century Style: Kay Trimberger and I Share Our Vision," *Living Single* (blog), November 23, 2008, http://www.psychologytoday.com/blog/living-single/200811/holiday-spirit-21st-century-style-kay-trimberger-and-i-share-our-vision.

40. An exception is Penn Tsz Ting Ip's inquiry of single female migrant workers in Shanghai's beauty parlours. While the demands of affective labour impact negatively on these women's possibility in forming other affective relationships, Ip argues it can also be enabling. See Penn Tsz Ting Ip, "Desiring Singlehood? Rural Migrant Women and Affective Labour in the Shanghai Beauty Parlour Industry," *Inter-Asia Cultural Studies* 18, no. 4 (2017): 558–80.

41. Lahad, *A Table for One*, 3.

42. See Hong Fincher, *Leftover Women*; Luo and Sun, "Are You the One?"; To, *China's Leftover Women*; Wang Changfeng (王昌逢), "社会性别视角下的[剩女]现象分析 [An Analysis of the 'Leftover Women' Phenomenon from the Perspective of Gender]," 中共山西省直机关党校学报 [*ZhongGong Shanxisheng Zhi Jiguan Dangxiao Xuebao*], no. 6 (2010): 46–47; Wang Haiping and Douglas A. Abbott, "Waiting for Mr. Right: The Meaning of Being a Single Educated Chinese Female Over 30 in Beijing and Guangzhou," *Women's Studies International Forum* 40, no. Supplement C (2013): 222–29; Zhang Jun and Sun Peidong, "'When Are You Going to Get Married?' Parental Matchmaking and Middle-Class Women in Contemporary Urban China," in *Wives, Husbands and Lovers: Marriage and Sexuality in Hong Kong, Taiwan, and Urban China*, ed. Deborah S. Davis and Sara L. Friedman (Stanford: Stanford University Press, 2014), 118–44; Luo Aiping (罗爱萍), Wang Feng (王蜂), and Jiang Yu (江宇), 中国剩女调查 [*China's Shengnü Survey*] (Guangzhou: 广东人民出版社 [Guangdong renmin chuban she], 2014).

43. Liu Liqun (刘利群) and Zhang Jingjie (张敬婕), "'剩女'与盛宴—性别视角下的'剩女'传播现象与媒介传播策略研究 ['Leftover Women' and Grand Banquet: Study of the Media Portrait of 'Leftover Women' and Strategies behind Media Coverage from a Gender Perspective]," 妇女研究论丛 [*Collection of Women's Studies*], no. 5 (2013): 80.

44. RMB stands for *renminbi*, the currency in mainland China. As at the day of checking (June 18, 2018), 1 RMB equals US$ 0.16.

45. Liu and Zhang, "'剩女'与盛宴," 80.

46. Ibid.

47. Ibid.

48. Arianne Gaetano, "Single Women in Urban China and the 'Unmarried Crisis': Gender Resilience and Gender Transformation," in *Working*

Papers in Contemporary Asian Studies; No. 31 (Lund: Centre for East and South East Asian Studies, Lund University, 2010).

49. See the following blog post for a report of the field visit. Pi Chenying, "Fieldwork Report: Love Club," *HERA SINGLE* (blog), December 2, 2014, http://www.hera-single.de/love-club/.

50. Also known as the Double Eleven, the four "1"s that denote the date of November 11 lend themselves to symbolize single people. Initially, an event aimed at university students, it became a consumption festival in 2009, when major online retailers decided to offer big discounts on November 11. For a brief history of Singles Day, see Meng and Huang, "Patriarchal Capitalism with Chinese Characteristics."

51. See 阿里足跡團隊 (Ali news team), "2017 天貓雙11全日成交額 1682 億元人民幣 再刷新紀錄 [2017 Tmall November 11th Full-Day Turnover of RMB 168.2 Billion Breaks New Record]," 阿里足跡 *[Alibabanews. Com]*, November 12, 2017, http://alibabanews.com/article/2017tianmaoshuang11quanrichengjiaoe1682yiyuanrenminbi-zaishuaxinjilu.

52. *Tuoguang* 脱光, which used to mean "undress" or "go naked," has become a vernacular term referring to the act or wish to leave singlehood.

53. Gary Xu and Susan Feiner, "Meinü Jingji/China's Beauty Economy: Buying Looks, Shifting Value, and Changing Place," *Feminist Economics* 13, no. 3–4 (2007): 307–23. See also Meng Zhang, "A Chinese Beauty Story: How College Women in China Negotiate Beauty, Body Image, and Mass Media," *Chinese Journal of Communication* 5, no. 4 (2012): 437–54; Liu and Zhang, "'剩女'与盛宴." For a book-length treatise on Chinese bodies and modernities, see Fran Martin and Larissa Heinrich, *Embodied Modernities: Corporeality, Representation, And Chinese Cultures* (Honolulu: University of Hawaii Press, 2006).

54. See, for instance, de Kloet, *China with a Cut*; Jullien, *The Silent Transformations*; Keane, *Creative Industries in China*; O'Connor and Gu, "Shanghai: Images of Modernity"; Wong, *Van Gogh on Demand*.

55. Nancy Ettlinger, "Precarity Unbound," *Alternatives* 32, no. 3 (2007): 322.

56. McCormack and Salmenniemi, "The Biopolitics of Precarity and the Self."

57. Judith Butler, *Precarious Life: The Powers of Mourning and Violence* (London: Verso, 2004): xvii.

58. McCormack and Salmenniemi, "The Biopolitics of Precarity and the Self," 7.

59. Lauren Berlant, *Cruel Optimism* (Durham: Duke University Press, 2011).

60. Isabell Lorey, *State of Insecurity: Government of the Precarious* (London: Verso, 2015): 63.

61. Standing, *The Precariat.*

62. See Mark Banks and Justin O'Connor, "After the Creative Industries," *International Journal of Cultural Policy* 15, no. 4 (2009): 365–73; Michael Curtin and Kevin Sanson, *Precarious Creativity: Global Media, Local Labor* (Oakland, CA: University of California Press, 2016); David Hesmondhalgh and Sarah Baker, *Creative Labour: Media Work in Three Cultural Industries* (London: Routledge, 2011); Damian Hodgson and Louise Briand, "Controlling the Uncontrollable: 'Agile' Teams and Illusions of Autonomy in Creative Work," *Work, Employment and Society* 27, no. 2 (2013): 308–25; McRobbie, *Be Creative*; Gerald Raunig, *Factories of Knowledge, Industries of Creativity* (Los Angeles, CA: Semiotext(e), 2013); Chow, "Hong Kong Creative Workers in Mainland China."

63. I would also like to draw attention to a body of empirical studies examining contemporary working conditions which, however, do not necessarily mobilize the notion of precarity explicitly, for instance: Arlie Russell Hochschild, *The Outsourced Self: Intimate Life in Market Times*, 1 edition (New York: Metropolitan Books, 2012); Lloyd, *Neo-Bohemia*; Barbara Ehrenreich, *Nickel and Dimed: On (Not) Getting By in America* (New York: Holt Paperbacks, 2010); Vicki Smith and Esther B. Neuwirth, *The Good Temp* (New York: Cornell University Press, 2010).

64. See Jan Breman, "A Bogus Concept?," *New Left Review*, no. 84 (2013): 130–38; Ronaldo Munck, "The Precariat: A View from the South," *Third World Quarterly* 34, no. 5 (2013): 747–62.

65. Lee Ching Kwan, "Precarization or Empowerment? Reflections on Recent Labor Unrest in China," *The Journal of Asian Studies* 75, no. 2 (2016): 317–33; Lee Ching Kwan and Zhang Yonghong, "The Power of Instability: Unraveling the Microfoundations of Bargained Authoritarianism in China," *American Journal of Sociology* 118, no. 6 (2013): 1475–1508. See also Olga Gurova and Daria Morozova's study of young fashion designers in contemporary Russia, which also argues for the need to heed the specific, local political context when examining labour issues. In Olga Gurova and Daria Morozova, "Creative Precarity? Young Fashion Designers as Entrepreneurs in Russia," *Cultural Studies* 32, no. 5 (2018): 704–26.

66. Munck, "The Precariat," 747.

67. Hesmondhalgh and Baker, *Creative Labour.*

68. Jeroen de Kloet and Anthony Y. H. Fung, *Youth Cultures in China* (Cambridge: Polity, 2017).

69. Lorey, *State of Insecurity*, 1.

70. Luo and Sun, "Are You the One?," 241. See also Chandra Talpade Mohanty, "Under Western Eyes: Feminist Scholarship and Colonial Discourses," *Feminist Review*, no. 30 (1988): 61–88.

71. Chow Yiu Fai, "Hope Against Hopes: Diana Zhu and the Transnational Politics of Chinese Popular Music," *Cultural Studies* 25, no. 6 (2011): 783–808.

72. Mary Zournazi, *Hope: New Philosophies for Change* (New York: Routledge, 2002): 129.

73. Wang Hui, *The End of the Revolution: China and the Limits of Modernity* (London; New York: Verso Books, 2011).

74. Lee, "Precarization or Empowerment?," 329–330.

75. Meng and Huang, "Patriarchal Capitalism with Chinese Characteristics," 682.

76. For more, see Tania Branigan, "Five Chinese Feminists Held over International Women's Day Plans," *The Guardian*, March 12, 2015, sec. World news, http://www.theguardian.com/world/2015/mar/12/five-chinese-feminists-held-international-womens-day; Li Maizi, "I Went to Jail for Handing out Feminist Stickers in China," *The Guardian*, March 8, 2017, sec. Opinion, http://www.theguardian.com/commentis-free/2017/mar/08/feminist-stickers-china-backash-women-activists. For a study of feminist media practices before and after the 2015 detention, see Tan Jia, "Digital Masquerading: Feminist Media Activism in China," *Crime, Media, Culture* 13, no. 2 (2017): 171–86. For a book-length study on feminist resistance in China, see Leta Hong Fincher, *Betraying Big Brother: China's Feminist Resistance* (London: Verso, Forthcoming 2018).

77. To be clear on this point, I am not making a plea for Asian or Chinese exceptionalism. Nor do I declare that local realities must be explained by local theories. Rather, it is part and parcel of the general reminder of the persistent inequality in knowledge production between, say, the West and the Rest. Elsewhere, I organized with two colleagues a special issue to discuss the issue in the context of the "Asian Century." See Chow Yiu Fai, Sonja van Wichelen, and Jeroen de Kloet, "Introduction: At Home in Asia? Place-Making, Belonging and Citizenship in the Asian Century," *International Journal of Cultural Studies* 19, no. 3 (2016): 243–56. See also the special issue published on "East Asian Theory" by Margaret Hillenbrand, "Communitarianism, or, How to Build East Asian Theory," *Postcolonial Studies* 13, no. 4 (2010): 317–34.

78. For Fraser's article, comments by Iris Marion Young and Judith Butler, and Fraser's rejoinders to their comments, see Nancy Fraser, "From Redistribution to Recognition? Dilemmas of Justice in a 'Post-Socialist' Age," *New Left Review*, no. 212 (1995): 68–93; Iris Marion Young, "Unruly Categories: A Critique of Nancy Fraser's Dual Systems Theory," *New Left Review*, no. 222 (1997): 147–160; Nancy Fraser, "A Rejoinder to Iris Young," *New Left Review*, I, no. 223 (1997): 126–29; Judith Butler, "Merely Cultural," *New Left Review*, no. 227 (1998): 33–44.

79. Marcel Mauss, *The Gift: Forms and Functions of Exchange in Archaic Societies*, trans. Ian Cunnison (New York: W. W. Norton, 1967).

80. Carole Mcgranahan, "Refusal and the Gift of Citizenship," *Cultural Anthropology* 31, no. 3 (2016): 335.

81. I borrow this formulation from Melvyn Bragg's beautiful novel *Grace and Mary*. Speaking of or on behalf of Grace, a woman betrayed by the man who left her nothing but illusion and a daughter in late-nineteenth-century Cumbria, Bragg writes: "She would have to build a life of her own and on her own." In Melvyn Bragg, *Grace and Mary* (London: Sceptre, 2014), 242.

82. Michel Foucault, "On the Genealogy of Ethics: An Overview of Work in Progress," in *The Foucault Reader*, ed. Paul Rabinow (New York: Pantheon, 1984), 340–72.

83. Michel Foucault, "The Subject and Power," *Critical Inquiry* 8, no. 4 (1982): 794.

84. Jeffrey Nealon, *Foucault Beyond Foucault: Power and Its Intensifications since 1984* (Stanford: Stanford University Press, 2007): 78.

85. Lorey, *State of Insecurity*, 5.

86. Butler, *Precarious Life*.

87. Lorey, *State of Insecurity*.

88. Du Yaquan (杜亚泉), "个人之改革 [Reforming the Individual]," 1914. Reprint in 杜亚泉卷(中国近代思想家文库) *[Du Yaquan Volume (Chinese Modern Thinkers Collection)]* (Beijing: 中国人民大学出版社 [People's University Press], 2014).

89. Just as I was drafting this introductory chapter, an essay was published online, on October 13, 2017, in which author Li Xiaotong articulates the danger not of precarization, but precisely the opposite: the danger of security, of a steady job with promised salary. Titled "Your damned salary is dragging you down," the essay, apparently touching a nerve in society, instantly went viral. On the WeChat platform it was originally posted, it soon reached 100,000 views, the maximum shown, and the reposting on other platforms received a similar response. For the original post, see: http://mp.weixin.qq.com/s/m3LIy33IKoZBMs6dqaobZg.

90. This, the provocative call for a different kind of politics surrounding precarity, should never silence political concerns articulated from experiences other than the single women creative workers in this book, for instance, migrant workers. For excellent studies on migrant workers in contemporary China, see the works by Pun Ngai and Jack Qiu: Pun Ngai, *Made in China: Women Factory Workers in a Global Workplace* (Durham: Duke University Press, 2005); Pun Ngai, "Gender and Class: Women's Working Lives in a Dormitory Labor Regime in China," *International Labor and Working-Class History* 81 (2012): 178–81; Pun Ngai, *Migrant Labor in*

China (Cambridge: Polity Press, 2016); Jack Linchuan Qiu, *Working-Class Network Society: Communication Technology and the Information Have-Less in Urban China* (Cambridge, Massachusetts: MIT Press, 2009); Jack Linchuan Qiu, "'Power To the People!': Mobiles, Migrants, and Social Movements in Asia," *International Journal of Communication* 8 (2014): 376–91; Jack Linchuan Qiu, "Locating Worker-Generated Content (WGC) in the World's Factory," in *The Routledge Companion to Labor and Media,* ed. Richard Maxwell (New York: Routledge, 2015), 303–14; Jack Linchuan Qiu, *Goodbye iSlave: A Manifesto for Digital Abolition* (Champaign: University of Illinois Press, 2017). For a sophisticated study on Chinese migrant workers and their cultural mediations and politics, see Sun Wanning, *Subaltern China: Rural Migrants, Media, and Cultural Practices* (Rowman & Littlefield, 2014).

91. In fact, I have interviewed 26 women. Subsequently, one of them, born in the 1980s, withdrew from the research, saying she did not want to be "labelled as single woman."

92. See Florida, *The Rise of the Creative Class*; Department of Culture, Media, and Sport, "Creative Industries Mapping Documents" (London: DCMS, 2001).

93. Kong, "From Cultural Industries to Creative Industries and Back?"

94. Gavin W. Jones, Zhang Yanxia, and Pamela Chia Pei Zhi, "Understanding High Levels of Singlehood in Singapore," *Journal of Comparative Family Studies* 43, no. 5 (2012): 731–50.

95. Lahad, *A Table for One*, 2–3.

96. Luo, Wang, and Jiang, 中国剩女调查.

97. Wu Shuping, *Single in the City: A Survey of China's Single Women* (Beijing: Long River Press, 2012).

98. Luo, Wang, and Jiang, 中国剩女调查, 18.

99. Rom Harré, *Social Being: A Theory for Social Psychology* (Basil Blackwell, 1979); Hesmondhalgh and Baker, *Creative Labour*.

100. I would like to acknowledge my research assistants again: thank you, Chen Min, Roman Chen Ziqing, and Cai Qingyang.

101. See de Kloet and Fung, *Youth Cultures in China*; Li Chunling (李春玲), "静悄悄的革命是否临近?—从80后和90后的价值观转变看年轻一代的先行性 [Is the Quiet Revolution Imminent?—The Advances of the Younger Generation from the Transformative Values of the Post-80s and Post-90s]," 河北学刊 *[Hebei Xue Kan]*, no. 3 (2015): 100–104; Li Hui (李慧), "对'70后'命名的思考 [Reflection on the Term of 'Post-70s']," 安徽文学:下半月 *[Anhui Wenxue: Xia Banyue]*, no. 8 (2009): 319–20; Yuan Yue (袁岳) and Zhang Jun (张军), 我们90后 *[We the Post-90s]* (浙江大学出版社 [Zhejiang daxue chubanshe], 2011).

102. See Alan France and Steven Roberts, "The Problem of Social Generations: A Critique of the New Emerging Orthodoxy in Youth Studies," *Journal of Youth Studies* 18, no. 2 (2015): 215–30; Andy Furlong, Dan Woodman, and Johanna Wyn, "Changing Times, Changing Perspectives: Reconciling 'Transition' and 'Cultural' Perspectives on Youth and Young Adulthood," *Journal of Sociology* 47, no. 4 (2011): 355–70.

103. Hesmondhalgh and Baker, *Creative Labour*.

104. See Brooke Erin Duffy, "The Romance of Work: Gender and Aspirational Labour in the Digital Culture Industries," *International Journal of Cultural Studies* 19, no. 4 (2016): 441–57; Melissa Gregg, *Work's Intimacy* (London: Polity Press, 2011).

105. See Hong Fincher, *Leftover Women*; Luo and Sun, "Are You the One?"; To, *China's Leftover Women*; Wang, "社会性别视角下的 [剩女] 现象分析 [An Analysis of the 'Leftover Women' Phenomenon from the Perspective of Gender]"; Wang and Abbott, "Waiting for Mr. Right"; Zhang and Sun, "'When Are You Going to Get Married?' Parental Matchmaking and Middle-Class Women in Contemporary Urban China."

106. Richard Sennett, *Together: The Rituals, Pleasures and Politics of Cooperation* (New Haven: Yale University Press, 2012).

107. See Max Weber, "The Distribution of Power Within the Gemeinschaft: Classes, Stände, Parties," in *Weber's Rationalism and Modern Society: New Translations on Politics, Bureaucracy, and Social Stratification*, ed. Tony Waters and Dagmar Waters (New York: Palgrave Macmillan, 2015), 37–58; Benedict Anderson, *Imagined Communities: Reflections on the Origin and Spread of Nationalism* (London: Verso, 1991).

108. Lily Kong, "The Sociality of Cultural Industries," *International Journal of Cultural Policy* 11, no. 1 (2005): 61–76.

109. See Matt Hills, *Fan Cultures* (Hove: Psychology Press, 2002); Henry Jenkins, *Convergence Culture: Where Old and New Media Collide* (New York: NYU Press, 2006).

110. See for instance Lahad, *A Table for One*.

111. See David J. Bodenhamer, Trevor M. Harris, and John Corrigan, "Deep Mapping and the Spatial Humanities," *International Journal of Humanities and Arts Computing* 7, no. 1–2 (2013): 170–75; Lawrence Grossberg, "Is There a Fan in the House? The Affective Sensibility of Fandom," in *The Adoring Audience: Fan Culture and Popular Media*, ed. Lisa A. Lewis (London: Routledge, 1992), 50–65.

112. Florida, *The Rise of the Creative Class*.

113. David Harvey, *Rebel Cities: From the Right to the City to the Urban Revolution* (London; New York: Verso Books, 2012).

114. See Marcus Banks, *Visual Methods in Social Research* (London: Sage, 2001); Sarah Pink, *Doing Visual Ethnography*, 3rd Edition (London:

SAGE, 2013); Gillian Rose, *Visual Methodologies: An Introduction to Researching with Visual Materials* (London: Sage, 2012).

115. This is my adaptation of the translation collected in Lu Xun, "Shanghai Girls," in *Lu Xun: Selected Works*, trans. Yang Xianyi and Gladys Yang, vol. 3 (Beijing: Foreign Languages Press, 1980), 332–33.

REFERENCES

Allison, Anne. *Precarious Japan*. Durham: Duke University Press, 2013.

Anderson, Benedict. *Imagined Communities: Reflections on the Origin and Spread of Nationalism*. London: Verso, 1991.

Banks, Marcus. *Visual Methods in Social Research*. London: Sage, 2001.

Banks, Mark, and Justin O'Connor. "After the Creative Industries." *International Journal of Cultural Policy* 15, no. 4 (2009): 365–73.

Beck, Ulrich, and Elisabeth Beck-Gernsheim. *Individualization: Institutionalized Individualism and Its Social and Political Consequences*. London: Sage, 2002.

Berlant, Lauren. *Cruel Optimism*. Durham: Duke University Press, 2011.

Bodenhamer, David J., Trevor M. Harris, and John Corrigan. "Deep Mapping and the Spatial Humanities." *International Journal of Humanities and Arts Computing* 7, no. 1–2 (2013): 170–75.

Bragg, Melvyn. *Grace and Mary*. London: Sceptre, 2014.

Breman, Jan. "A Bogus Concept?" *New Left Review*, no. 84 (2013): 130–38.

Butler, Judith. "Merely Cultural." *New Left Review*, no. 227 (1998): 33–44.

Butler, Judith. *Precarious Life: The Powers of Mourning and Violence*. London: Verso, 2004.

Casas-Cortés, Maribel. "A Genealogy of Precarity: A Toolbox for Rearticulating Fragmented Social Realities in and out of the Workplace." *Rethinking Marxism* 26, no. 2 (2014): 206–26.

Chen, Kuan-Hsing. *Asia as Method: Toward Deimperialization*. Durham, NC: Duke University Press, 2010.

Chew, Matthew. "Contemporary Re-Emergence of the Qipao: Political Nationalism, Cultural Production and Popular Consumption of a Traditional Chinese Dress." *The China Quarterly* 189 (2007): 144–61.

Chow, Yiu Fai. "Hong Kong Creative Workers in Mainland China: The Aspirational, the Precarious, and the Ethical." *China Information* 31, no. 1 (2017): 43–62.

Chow, Yiu Fai. "Hope Against Hopes: Diana Zhu and the Transnational Politics of Chinese Popular Music." *Cultural Studies* 25, no. 6 (2011): 783–808.

Chow, Yiu Fai, Sonja van Wichelen, and Jeroen de Kloet. "Introduction: At Home in Asia? Place-Making, Belonging and Citizenship in the Asian Century." *International Journal of Cultural Studies* 19, no. 3 (2016): 243–56.

Chumley, Lily. *Creativity Class: Art School and Culture Work in Postsocialist China.* Princeton: Princeton University Press, 2016.

Curtin, Michael, and Kevin Sanson. *Precarious Creativity: Global Media, Local Labor.* Oakland, CA: University of California Press, 2016.

Dales, Laura. "Ohitorisama, Singlehood and Agency in Japan." *Asian Studies Review* 38, no. 2 (2014): 224–42.

Dales, Laura. "Single Women and Their Households in Contemporary Japan." In *The Global Political Economy of the Household in Asia*, edited by Juanita Elias and Samanthi J. Gunawardana, 110–126. Basingstoke: Palgrave Macmillan, 2013.

Das Gupta, Monica, Ethan Jennings Sharygin, and Avraham Ebenstein. "China's Marriage Market and Upcoming Challenges for Elderly Men." The World Bank, 2010. http://documents.worldbank.org/curated/en/9487714682 12988136/Chinas-marriage-market-and-upcoming-challenges-for-elderly-men.

Department of Culture, Media, and Sport. "Creative Industries Mapping Documents." London: DCMS, 2001.

DePaulo, Bella. "Holiday Spirit, 21st Century Style: Kay Trimberger and I Share Our Vision." *Living Single* (blog), November 23, 2008. http://www.psychologytoday.com/blog/living-single/200811/holiday-spirit-21st-century-style-kay-trimberger-and-i-share-our-vision.

DePaulo, Bella M., and Wendy L. Morris. "Singles in Society and in Science." *Psychological Inquiry* 16, no. 2–3 (2005): 57–83.

Du, Yaquan (杜亚泉). "个人之改革 [Reforming the Individual]." In 杜亚泉卷 (中国近代思想家文库) *[Du Yaquan Volume (Chinese Modern Thinkers Collection)]*. Beijing: 中国人民大学出版社 [People's University Press], 1914.

Duffy, Brooke Erin. "The Romance of Work: Gender and Aspirational Labour in the Digital Culture Industries." *International Journal of Cultural Studies* 19, no. 4 (2016): 441–57.

Ehrenreich, Barbara. *Nickel and Dimed: On (Not) Getting By in America.* New York: Holt Paperbacks, 2010.

Ettlinger, Nancy. "Precarity Unbound." *Alternatives* 32, no. 3 (2007): 319–40.

Evans, Harriet. *The Subject of Gender: Daughters and Mothers in Urban China.* Maryland: Rowman & Littlefield, 2008.

Fan, Shenggen, Xibao Zhang, and Arjan de Haan. *Narratives of Chinese Economic Reforms: How Does China Cross the River?* Singapore; Hackensack, NJ: World Scientific, 2010.

Feuchtwang, Stephan, and Athar Hussain, eds. *The Chinese Economic Reforms.* London: Croom Helm, 1983.

Florida, Richard. *The New Urban Crisis: How Our Cities Are Increasing Inequality, Deepening Segregation, and Failing the Middle Class and What We Can Do About It.* New York: Basic Books, 2017.

Florida, Richard. *The Rise of the Creative Class.* New York: Basic Books, 2002.

Foucault, Michel. "On the Genealogy of Ethics: An Overview of Work in Progress." In *The Foucault Reader*, edited by Paul Rabinow, 340–72. New York: Pantheon, 1984.

Foucault, Michel. "The Subject and Power." *Critical Inquiry* 8, no. 4 (1982): 777–95.

France, Alan, and Steven Roberts. "The Problem of Social Generations: A Critique of the New Emerging Orthodoxy in Youth Studies." *Journal of Youth Studies* 18, no. 2 (2015): 215–30.

Fraser, Nancy. "A Rejoinder to Iris Young." *New Left Review*, I, no. 223 (1997): 126–29.

Fraser, Nancy. "From Redistribution to Recognition? Dilemmas of Justice in a 'Post-Socialist' Age." *New Left Review*, no. 212 (1995): 68–93.

Fung, Anthony Y. H., and John Nguyet Erni. "Cultural Clusters and Cultural Industries in China." *Inter-Asia Cultural Studies* 14, no. 4 (2013): 644–56.

Furlong, Andy, Dan Woodman, and Johanna Wyn. "Changing Times, Changing Perspectives: Reconciling 'Transition' and 'Cultural' Perspectives on Youth and Young Adulthood." *Journal of Sociology* 47, no. 4 (2011): 355–70.

Gaetano, Arianne. "Single Women in Urban China and the 'Unmarried Crisis': Gender Resilience and Gender Transformation." In *Working Papers in Contemporary Asian Studies; No. 31*. Lund: Centre for East and South East Asian Studies, Lund University, 2010.

Garnaut, Ross, and Ligang Song, eds. *China: Twenty Years of Economic Reform*. Canberra: Asia Pacific Press, 1999.

Garnham, Nicholas. "From Cultural to Creative Industries." *International Journal of Cultural Policy* 11, no. 1 (2006): 15–29.

Gill, Rosalind, and Andy Pratt. "In the Social Factory?: Immaterial Labour, Precariousness and Cultural Work." *Theory, Culture & Society* 25, no. 7–8 (2008): 1–30.

Gregg, Melissa. *Work's Intimacy*. London: Polity Press, 2011.

Grossberg, Lawrence. "Is There a Fan in the House? The Affective Sensibility of Fandom." In *The Adoring Audience: Fan Culture and Popular Media*, edited by Lisa A. Lewis, 50–65. London: Routledge, 1992.

Gurova, Olga, and Daria Morozova. "Creative Precarity? Young Fashion Designers as Entrepreneurs in Russia." *Cultural Studies* 32, no. 5 (2018): 704–26.

Harré, Rom. *Social Being: A Theory for Social Psychology*. Basil Blackwell, 1979.

Harvey, David. *Rebel Cities: From the Right to the City to the Urban Revolution*. London; New York: Verso Books, 2012.

Hershatter, Gail. *Women in China's Long Twentieth Century*. Berkeley: University of California Press, 2007.

Hesmondhalgh, David, and Sarah Baker. *Creative Labour: Media Work in Three Cultural Industries*. London: Routledge, 2011.

Hillenbrand, Margaret. "Communitarianism, or, How to Build East Asian Theory." *Postcolonial Studies* 13, no. 4 (2010): 317–34.

Hills, Matt. *Fan Cultures.* Hove: Psychology Press, 2002.

Hochschild, Arlie Russell. *The Outsourced Self: Intimate Life in Market Times.* 1 edition. New York: Metropolitan Books, 2012.

Hodgson, Damian, and Louise Briand. "Controlling the Uncontrollable: 'Agile' Teams and Illusions of Autonomy in Creative Work." *Work, Employment and Society* 27, no. 2 (2013): 308–25.

Hong Fincher, Leta. *Betraying Big Brother: China's Feminist Resistance.* London: Verso, 2018.

Hong Fincher, Leta. *Leftover Women: The Resurgence of Gender Inequality in China.* London, New York: Zed Books, 2014.

Hui, Desmond. "From Cultural to Creative Industries: Strategies for Chaoyang District, Beijing." *International Journal of Cultural Studies* 9, no. 3 (2006): 317–31.

Ip, Penn Tsz Ting. "Desiring Singlehood? Rural Migrant Women and Affective Labour in the Shanghai Beauty Parlour Industry." *Inter-Asia Cultural Studies* 18, no. 4 (2017): 558–80.

Jamieson, Lynn, and Roona Simpson. *Living Alone: Globalization, Identity and Belonging.* London: Palgrave Macmillan, 2013.

Jenkins, Henry. *Convergence Culture: Where Old and New Media Collide.* New York: NYU Press, 2006.

Jones, Gavin W., Zhang Yanxia, and Pamela Chia Pei Zhi. "Understanding High Levels of Singlehood in Singapore." *Journal of Comparative Family Studies* 43, no. 5 (2012): 731–50.

Jullien, Francois. *The Silent Transformations.* London; New York: Seagull Books, 2011.

Keane, Michael. *Created in China: The Great New Leap Forward.* London; New York: Routledge, 2007.

Keane, Michael. *Creative Industries in China: Art, Design and Media.* Malden: Polity, 2013.

Klinenberg, Eric. *Going Solo: The Extraordinary Rise and Surprising Appeal of Living Alone.* 1 edition. London: Duckworth Overlook, 2012.

de Kloet, Jeroen. *China with a Cut: Globalisation, Urban Youth and Popular Music.* Amsterdam: Amsterdam University Press, 2010.

de Kloet, Jeroen, and Anthony Y. H. Fung. *Youth Cultures in China.* Cambridge: Polity, 2017.

Kong, Lily. "From Cultural Industries to Creative Industries and Back? Towards Clarifying Theory and Rethinking Policy." *Inter-Asia Cultural Studies* 15, no. 4 (2014): 593–607.

Kong, Lily. "The Sociality of Cultural Industries." *International Journal of Cultural Policy* 11, no. 1 (2005): 61–76.

Lahad, Kinneret. *A Table for One: A Critical Reading of Singlehood, Gender and Time.* Manchester: Manchester University Press, 2017.

Lahad, Kinneret. "'Am I Asking for Too Much?' The Selective Single Woman as a New Social Problem." *Women's Studies International Forum* 40, no. Supplement C (2013): 23–32.

Lahad, Kinneret, and Avi Shoshana. "Singlehood in Treatment: Interrogating the Discursive Alliance between Postfeminism and Therapeutic Culture." *European Journal of Women's Studies* 22, no. 3 (2015): 334–49.

Lakämper, Judith. "Affective Dissonance, Neoliberal Postfeminism and the Foreclosure of Solidarity." *Feminist Theory* 18, no. 2 (2017): 119–35.

Lee, Ching Kwan. "Precarization or Empowerment? Reflections on Recent Labor Unrest in China." *The Journal of Asian Studies* 75, no. 2 (2016): 317–33.

Lee, Ching Kwan, and Yonghong Zhang. "The Power of Instability: Unraveling the Microfoundations of Bargained Authoritarianism in China." *American Journal of Sociology* 118, no. 6 (2013): 1475–1508.

Li, Chunling (李春玲). "静悄悄的革命是否临近?—从80后和90后的价值观转变看年轻一代的先行性 [Is the Quiet Revolution Imminent?—The Advances of the Younger Generation from the Transformative Values of the Post-80s and Post-90s]." 河北学刊 *[Hebei Xue Kan]*, no. 3 (2015): 100–104.

Li, Hui (李慧). "对'70后'命名的思考 [Reflection on the Term of 'Post-70s']." 安徽文学:下半月 *[Anhui Wenxue: Xia Banyue]*, no. 8 (2009): 319–20.

Li, Luzhou. "If You Are the One: Dating Shows and Feminist Politics in Contemporary China." *International Journal of Cultural Studies* 18, no. 5 (2015): 519–35.

Li, Maizi. "I Went to Jail for Handing out Feminist Stickers in China." *The Guardian*, March 8, 2017, sec. Opinion. http://www.theguardian.com/commentisfree/2017/mar/08/feminist-stickers-china-backash-women-activists.

Li, Wuwei (厉无畏). "发展创意产业 让世界刮起中国风 [Developing a Creative Industry That Blows China Wind across the World]." 人民网 *[People.Cn]*, March 11, 2011. http://finance.people.com.cn/GB/71364/14119345.html.

Liu, Liqun (刘利群), and Zhang Jingjie (张敬婕). "'剩女'与盛宴—性别视角下的'剩女'传播现象与媒介传播策略研究 ['Leftover Women' and Grand Banquet: Study of the Media Portrait of 'Leftover Women' and Strategies behind Media Coverage from a Gender Perspective]." 妇女研究论丛 *[Collection of Women's Studies]*, no. 5 (2013): 76–82.

Lloyd, Richard. *Neo-Bohemia: Art and Commerce in the Postindustrial City.* New York: Routledge, 2006.

Lorey, Isabell. *State of Insecurity: Government of the Precarious.* London: Verso, 2015.

Lu, Xun. "Shanghai Girls." In *Lu Xun: Selected Works*, translated by Xianyi Yang and Gladys Yang, 3:332–33. Beijing: Foreign Languages Press, 1980.

Luo, Aiping (罗爱萍), Wang Feng (王蜂), and Jiang Yu (江宇). *中国剩女调查 [China's Shengnü Survey].* Guangzhou: 广东人民出版社 [Guangdong renmin chuban she], 2014.

Luo, Wei, and Zhen Sun. "Are You the One? China's TV Dating Shows and the Sheng Nü's Predicament." *Feminist Media Studies* 15, no. 2 (2015): 239–56.

Martin, Fran, and Larissa Heinrich. *Embodied Modernities: Corporeality, Representation, And Chinese Cultures.* Honolulu: University of Hawaii Press, 2006.

Mauss, Marcel. *The Gift: Forms and Functions of Exchange in Archaic Societies.* Translated by Ian Cunnison. New York: W. W. Norton, 1967.

McCormack, Donna, and Suvi Salmenniemi. "The Biopolitics of Precarity and the Self." *European Journal of Cultural Studies* 19, no. 1 (2016): 3–15.

Mcgranahan, Carole. "Refusal and the Gift of Citizenship." *Cultural Anthropology* 31, no. 3 (2016): 334–41.

McRobbie, Angela. *Be Creative: Making a Living in the New Culture Industries.* 1 edition. Cambridge, UK; Malden, MA: Polity, 2016.

Meng, Bingchun, and Yanning Huang. "Patriarchal Capitalism with Chinese Characteristics: Gendered Discourse of 'Double Eleven' Shopping Festival." *Cultural Studies* 31, no. 5 (2017): 659–84.

Miller, Toby. "From Creative to Cultural Industries." *Cultural Studies* 23, no. 1 (2009): 88–99.

Mohanty, Chandra Talpade. "Under Western Eyes: Feminist Scholarship and Colonial Discourses." *Feminist Review*, no. 30 (1988): 61–88.

Mu, Guangzong (穆光宗). "'单身社会'来临未必是好事 [The Advent of 'Single Society' May Not Be a Good Thing]." 中国网 *[China.Org.Cn]* (blog), August 27, 2017. http://big5.china.com.cn/gate/big5/opinion.china.com.cn/opinion_20_170420.html.

Munck, Ronaldo. "The Precariat: A View from the South." *Third World Quarterly* 34, no. 5 (2013): 747–62.

Nakano, Lynne. "Single Women in Marriage and Employment Markets in Japan." In *Capturing Contemporary Japan: Differentiation and Uncertainty*, edited by Satsuki Kawano, Glenda Susan Roberts, and Susan Orpett Long, 163–182. Honolulu: University of Hawaii Press, 2014.

Nealon, Jeffrey. *Foucault Beyond Foucault: Power and Its Intensifications since 1984.* Stanford: Stanford University Press, 2007.

Ngai, Pun. "Gender and Class: Women's Working Lives in a Dormitory Labor Regime in China." *International Labor and Working-Class History* 81 (2012): 178–81.

Ngai, Pun. *Made in China: Women Factory Workers in a Global Workplace.* Durham: Duke University Press, 2005.

Ngai, Pun. *Migrant Labor in China.* Cambridge: Polity Press, 2016.

Niu, Weilin (牛维麟), and Peng Yi (彭翊). 北京文化创意产业集聚区发展研究报告 *[Beijing Cultural Creative Industry Clusters Development Study Report]*. Beijing: 中国人民大学出版社 [People's University Press], 2009.

O'Connor, Justin, and Xin Gu. "Creative Industry Clusters in Shanghai: A Success Story?" *International Journal of Cultural Policy* 20, no. 1 (2014): 1–20.

O'Connor, Justin, and Xin Gu. "Shanghai: Images of Modernity." In *Cultures and Globalization: Cities, Cultural Policy and Governance*, edited by Helmut K. Anheier and Yudhishthir Raj Isar, 288–99. London: Sage, 2012.

Ouyang, Youquan (欧阳友权), ed. 文化品牌蓝皮书:中国文化品牌发展报告 *[Blue Book of Cultural Brands: Annual Report on the Development of Cultural Brands in China]*. Changsha: 中南大学中国文化产业品牌研究中心 [Zhongnan University China's Cultural Industries Brands Research Centre], 2006.

Pang, Laikwan. *Creativity and Its Discontents: China's Creative Industries and Intellectual Property Rights Offenses*. Durham: Duke University Press, 2012.

Pi, Chenying. "Fieldwork Report: Love Club." *HERA SINGLE* (blog), December 2, 2014. http://www.hera-single.de/love-club/.

Pink, Sarah. *Doing Visual Ethnography*. 3rd Edition. London: SAGE, 2013.

Qiu, Jack Linchuan. *Goodbye iSlave: A Manifesto for Digital Abolition*. Champaign: University of Illinois Press, 2017.

Qiu, Jack Linchuan. "Locating Worker-Generated Content (WGC) in the World's Factory." In *The Routledge Companion to Labor and Media*, edited by Richard Maxwell, 303–14. New York: Routledge, 2015.

Qiu, Jack Linchuan. "'Power to the People!': Mobiles, Migrants, and Social Movements in Asia." *International Journal of Communication* 8 (2014): 376–91.

Qiu, Jack Linchuan. *Working-Class Network Society: Communication Technology and the Information Have-Less in Urban China*. Cambridge, Massachusetts: MIT Press, 2009.

Raunig, Gerald. *Factories of Knowledge, Industries of Creativity*. Los Angeles, CA: Semiotext(e), 2013.

Reynolds, Jill. *The Single Woman: A Discursive Investigation*. London: Routledge, 2008.

Rofel, Lisa. *Desiring China: Experiments in Neoliberalism, Sexuality, and Public Culture*. Durham: Duke University Press, 2007.

Rose, Gillian. *Visual Methodologies: An Introduction to Researching with Visual Materials*. London: Sage, 2012.

Ross, Andrew. *Nice Work If You Can Get It: Life and Labor in Precarious Times*. New York: NYU Press, 2009.

Sennett, Richard. *Together: The Rituals, Pleasures and Politics of Cooperation*. New Haven: Yale University Press, 2012.

Sharp, Elizabeth A., and Lawrence Ganong. "'I'm a Loser, I'm Not Married, Let's Just All Look at Me': Ever-Single Women's Perceptions of Their Social Environment." *Journal of Family Issues* 32, no. 7 (2011): 956–80.

Siebert, Sabina, and Fiona Wilson. "All Work and No Pay: Consequences of Unpaid Work in the Creative Industries." *Work, Employment and Society* 27, no. 4 (2013): 711–21.

SK-II. *SK-II: Marriage Market Takeover*, 2016. https://www.youtube.com/watch?v=irfd74z52Cw.

Song, Jesook. *Living on Your Own: Single Women, Rental Housing, and Post-Revolutionary Affect in Contemporary South Korea*. Albany: SUNY Press, 2014.

Standing, Guy. *The Precariat: The New Dangerous Class*. London; New York: Bloomsbury Academic, 2011.

Su, Xing (苏醒), and Renbo (田仁波) Tian. "'城市剩女'群体生存焦虑问题研究 [Research on Living Anxiety of Shengnü in Cities]." *Journal of Qujing Normal University* 31, no. 2 (2012): 116–20.

Sun, Wanning. *Subaltern China: Rural Migrants, Media, and Cultural Practices*. Rowman & Littlefield, 2014.

Tan, Jia. "Digital Masquerading: Feminist Media Activism in China." *Crime, Media, Culture* 13, no. 2 (2017): 171–86.

Tao, Shun (陶舜). "单身社会来了 [The Single Society Has Come]." *腾讯网 [Tengxun Wang]* (blog), August 24, 2017. http://view.news.qq.com/original/intouchtoday/n3993.html.

To, Sandy. *China's Leftover Women: Late Marriage Among Professional Women and Its Consequences*. London, New York: Routledge, 2015.

Wang, Changfeng (王昌逢). "社会性别视角下的 [剩女] 现象分析 [An Analysis of the 'Leftover Women' Phenomenon from the Perspective of Gender]." *中共山西省直机关党校学报 [ZhongGong Shanxisheng Zhi Jiguan Dangxiao Xuebao]*, no. 6 (2010): 46–47.

Wang, Haiping, and Douglas A. Abbott. "Waiting for Mr. Right: The Meaning of Being a Single Educated Chinese Female Over 30 in Beijing and Guangzhou." *Women's Studies International Forum* 40, no. Supplement C (2013): 222–29.

Wang, Hui. *The End of the Revolution: China and the Limits of Modernity*. London; New York: Verso Books, 2011.

Wang, Jing. "The Global Reach of a New Discourse: How Far Can 'Creative Industries' Travel?" *International Journal of Cultural Studies* 7, no. 1 (2004): 9–19.

Weber, Max. "The Distribution of Power Within the Gemeinschaft: Classes, Stände, Parties." In *Weber's Rationalism and Modern Society: New Translations on Politics, Bureaucracy, and Social Stratification*, edited by Tony Waters and Dagmar Waters, 37–58. New York: Palgrave Macmillan, 2015.

Wilkinson, Eleanor. "Single People's Geographies of Home: Intimacy and Friendship beyond 'the Family.'" *Environment and Planning A* 46, no. 10 (2014): 2452–68.

Wong, Winnie. *Van Gogh on Demand: China and the Readymade*. Chicago; London: University Of Chicago Press, 2014.

Wu, Shuping. *Single in the City: A Survey of China's Single Women*. Beijing: Long River Press, 2012.

Xu, Gary, and Susan Feiner. "Meinü Jingji/China's Beauty Economy: Buying Looks, Shifting Value, and Changing Place." *Feminist Economics* 13, no. 3–4 (2007): 307–23.

Yan, Yan (闫妍), and Qin Hua (秦华). "充分发挥妇女在家庭文明建设中的独特作用 [Full Potential of the Unique Role of Women in the Construction of Family Civilization]." *中国妇联新闻 [Zhongguo Fulian Xinwen]*, May 18, 2015. http://acwf.people.com.cn/n/2015/0518/c99058-27015970.html.

Yang Jianli (杨剑利). *女性与近代中国社会 [The Female and Modern China Society]*. Beijing: 中国社会出版社 [China Society Press], 2007.

Ye, Pan (叶攀). "'平语'近人—习近平谈妇女如何全面发展 ['Ping Yu' Intimacy—Xi Jinping Talks about Personal Development of Women]." *中国新闻网 [Chinanews.Com]*, October 12, 2015. http://www.chinanews.com/gn/2015/10-12/7565191.shtml.

Ye, Xin (叶辛), and Kuai Dashen (蒯大申). *上海文化发展报告 (2011) [Shanghai Cultural Development Report (2011)]*. Beijing: 社会科学文献出版社 [Social Sciences Academic Press], 2011.

Yeung, Wei-Jun Jean, and Shu Hu. "Coming of Age in Times of Change: The Transition to Adulthood in China." *The ANNALS of the American Academy of Political and Social Science* 646, no. 1 (2013): 149–71.

Young, Iris Marion. "Unruly Categories: A Critique of Nancy Fraser's Dual Systems Theory." *New Left Review*, no. 222 (1997): 147–160.

Yuan, Yue (袁岳), and Zhang Jun (张军). *我们90后 [We the Post-90s]*. Hangzhou: 浙江大学出版社 [Zhejiang daxue chubanshe], 2011.

Zhang, Jeanne Hong. "Gender in Post-Mao China." *European Review* 11, no. 2 (2003): 209–24.

Zhang, Jun, and Peidong Sun. "'When Are You Going to Get Married?' Parental Matchmaking and Middle-Class Women in Contemporary Urban China." In *Wives, Husbands and Lovers: Marriage and Sexuality in Hong Kong, Taiwan, and Urban China*, edited by Deborah S. Davis and Sara L. Friedman, 118–44. Stanford: Stanford University Press, 2014.

Zhang, Meng. "A Chinese Beauty Story: How College Women in China Negotiate Beauty, Body Image, and Mass Media." *Chinese Journal of Communication* 5, no. 4 (2012): 437–54.

Zhang, Xiaoming (张晓明), Hu Huilin (胡惠林), and Zhang Jiangang (章建刚), eds. *文化蓝皮书:中国文化产业发展报告 [Blue Book of China's Culture: Annual Report on the Development of China's Cultural Industries]*. Beijing: 社会科学文献出版社 [Social Sciences Academic Press], 2002.

Zhang, Xiaoming (张晓明), Wang Jiaxin (王家新), and Zhang Jiangang (章建刚), eds. *文化蓝皮书:中国文化产业发展报告 [Blue Book of China's Culture: Annual Report on the Development of China's Cultural Industries]*. Beijing: 社会科学文献出版社 [Social Sciences Academic Press], 2012.

Zhou, Viola. "China's Marriage Rate Slumps as More Singles Say 'I Don't.'" *South China Morning Post*, September 6, 2017. http://www.scmp.com/news/china/society/article/2109868/marriage-rate-down-divorce-rate-more-chinese-couples-say-i-dont.

Zhou, Yiping (周一平), and Zhou Lei (周雷). "年改革开放史研究述评 [Overview of Researches on the History of Chinese Economic Reform 2008]." 当代中国史研究 *[Dangdai Zhongguo Shi Yanjiu]*, no. 1 (2008): 102–9.

Zournazi, Mary. *Hope: New Philosophies for Change*. New York: Routledge, 2002.

"十九大開幕　習近平發表工作報告 [Opening of 19th National Congress—Working Report by Xi Jinping]." 香港經濟日報 *[Hong Kong Economic Times]*, October 18, 2017. http://china.hket.com/article/1927215.

阿里足跡團隊 (Ali news team). "2017 天貓雙11全日成交額1682億元人民幣 再刷新紀錄 [2017 Tmall November 11th Full-Day Turnover of RMB 168.2 Billion Breaks New Record]." 阿里足跡 *[Alibabanews.Com]*, November 12, 2017. http://alibabanews.com/article/2017tianmaoshuang11quanrichengjiaoe1682yiyuanrenminbi-zaishuaxinjilu.

CHAPTER 2

Living with Their Own Images

"Happiness is always waiting for you / Only fools do not go for it / Brave yourself, survive it / Dreams and love belong to you"—these are some of the chorus lines from "Happiness Is Always Waiting for You," arguably the most popular theme song from *Ode to Joy* (*Huanle Song* 欢乐颂), which was definitely the most popular television drama series in mainland China in 2016.[1] Roughly comparable to the New York-based *Sex and the City*, this series is set in Shanghai, and follows the love lives and work lives of five single women from different socioeconomic backgrounds, who happen to live on the same floor in the same building. Premiered on April 18, the series achieved a daily record of 600 million views while attracting an abundance of postings and discussions on China's microblogging sites; on the most searched list of Weibo, the series attracted more than 4 billion hits.[2]

While *Ode to Joy*'s success may be phenomenal, the mobilization of single women for cultural productions is hardly exceptional in contemporary China. Take films, for instance: 2015 saw the release of *The Last Woman Standing* (*Shengzheweiwang* 剩者为王), a romantic comedy centring around the search for true love by a leftover woman with a successful career. Take dating shows: *If You Are the One* (*Feicheng Wurao* 非诚勿扰) was launched in 2010 and remains a ratings success after more than a decade on nationwide television and computer screens. Take advertising: remember the viral video launched by SKII I, cited in Chap. 1?

© The Author(s) 2019
Chow Y. F., *Caring in Times of Precarity*, Palgrave Studies in
Globalization, Culture and Society,
https://doi.org/10.1007/978-3-319-76898-4_2

Reverting to the lyrics cited at the head of this chapter, are we not lis-tening to the voice of a wilful, strong, and independent woman? A call for agency, freed from the patriarchal structure? Or another rendition of the post-feminist, neo-liberal female subjectivity? Or should we actually listen further? For instance, to other parts of the theme song, when they sing "Happiness… comes in the most unexpected moments"—perhaps reiter-ating passivity in the face of destiny. This is merely one song from one television drama series.

Informed by the centrality and popularity of single womanhood in pop-ular cultural productions in China during the past years, what I aim to do in this chapter is as follows. I will first offer an overview of the representa-tions of single women across a plethora of genres and platforms. I will then zoom in on a number of television drama series and tease out more from this genre, known to be particularly popular among female audiences in the Chinese context.[3] Finally, I will focus on the success of *Ode to Joy*, where I will conduct a textual analysis of the first season as well as of media commentaries and audience responses.[4] In short, this chapter seeks to take popular media as a lens to examine the development to the latest discursive formations surrounding Chinese single women in an urban setting. Considering the sheer amount of media productions in China—in 2016 alone, there were 10,084 magazine titles, 144 state-approved television channels, 517 films released, and RMB 597.3 billion in advertising sales—the following accounts do not aspire to include everything, but sufficient to be indicative of what is going on.[5]

Magazines

A glance at the magazine section of any pavement newsstand would suffice to confirm the large number of publications, glossy and tabloid, dedicated to a female readership. Corresponding with its counterpart in the West, the Chinese magazine market is tilted heavily towards magazines offering a mix of lifestyle tips, career advice, beauty secrets, and celebrity features, loosely grouped under the term "women's magazines."[6]

Updating earlier studies on the same magazines in China,[7] Zhang Yuliang investigates major portraits of women in four women's magazines with very different styles and readerships. He identifies three dominant figures of womanhood: "iron lady," "good wife," and "trendy woman."[8] First, the state-sponsored magazine *Zhongguo Funü* ("China Women") continues to construct the figure of the "iron lady" as sexless, patriotic, and dedicated to work, presumably upholding the Maoist mantra of gender equality—"women hold up half the sky." Second, in contradistinction to communist ideology that urges women to come out to the public arena as an "iron lady," *Zhongguo Funü*, somewhat ironically, but conforming to persistent practices of state feminism, also constructs the other figure of the "good wife" who, aspiring to domestic bliss, would rather stay in the private sphere and be a good support for her man, whether as wife or mother, or preferably both. Two other state-sponsored magazines, *Jiating* ("Family")—reporting heavily on family values and celebrity lives—and *Nüyou* ("Girlfriend")—dominated by marriage and love features as well as beauty tips—do the same. Third, the figure of the "trendy woman," mostly found in *Cosmopolitan*, embodies a sense of autonomy and a passion for consumption, culminating in the typical successful career women who emerged in mid-1990s China.

Ling Qi conducts textual analysis on nearly 150 articles drawn from five leading women's magazine websites, all dealing with the theme of *shengnü* (leftover women).[9] They show a remarkable consistency across the websites, focusing on why women are left single and how they can leave the single life—or unsingle. They continue to frame singlehood as an undesirable state for women's lives, displaying to the reader possibilities for looking better and sexier, and eventually, to succeed in the marriage market. In tandem with this emphasis on beautification and sexualization, the websites of these women's magazines pay scant attention to their achievements as working persons. In short, Ling confirms earlier findings that show the tendency of commercial women's magazines to reiterate a consumerist lifestyle, and to foreground women as consumers, rather than producers.[10]

Assuming a different entry point, Sun Shengwei and Chen Feinian choose magazines targeted at a more general readership to understand the media's framing of women and their issues. Based on 202 articles drawn from three Chinese mainstream magazines between 1995 and 2012—the period chosen by the researchers for its salience in demonstrating changes following the intensified market reforms in the mid-1990s—their findings show a "stagnation, if not decline, in women's status in China."[11] While the two most frequently discussed topics are "delaying marriage and relationship issues" and "dissolution of marriage," the researchers observe diminishing coverage of gender inequality amidst a resurgence of traditional gender roles and family values calling for "women to return home."[12]

FILMS

Inspired by French New Wave icon François Truffaut's assertion that film is a woman's art form, Huang Ying offers a handy, albeit inevitably sketchy, overview and analysis of female characters in China, paying particular attention to post-millennium releases.[13] Stereotype is the thread that, according to Huang, connects female characters in disparate eras in earlier Chinese (film) history: from "the insulted and the injured," when China first produced films shortly after the turn of the nineteenth century (1905) to "the melancholic" in post-war films; to "the androgynous and the sexless" during the post-Revolution years; to "the model and the conceptual" during the Cultural Revolution; to "the reformulated" (notably, by Zhang Yimou and other male directors of the so-called Fifth Generation of Chinese Cinema) in the 1970s and 80s; and finally, to "the searcher for individuality and emancipation" in the consumerist society of the 1990s.[14] The post-millennium films are, however, far more complex. On the one hand, we see female characters who depart radically from the stereotypically humble, submissive, and suffering oriental woman, a departure famously encapsulated in a one-liner in a film directed by its own main actress: "I love you, but it doesn't concern you."[15] Often intertwined in the scripts of such films are men who are disappointing, selfish, or conspicuously absent. On the other hand, the women in post-millennial Chinese films continue to be objectified by the male gaze,[16] while many characters who are not particularly lovable are praised in the films for being "practical" and "tolerant" of their male spouses' mischievous behaviour.[17] Zhang Yuanyuan observes a similar paradox in a study of Chinese films post-2000: the female characters are both objects under the male gaze as well as independent and rebellious women.[18] Zhang attributes this paradox to the emergence of consumerism in China—in particular, the beauty economy, or the eyeball economy, as mentioned in the previous chapter.[19]

Following a similar, historical approach, Dai Jinhua retrieves from Chinese film history not only the stereotypical women, but also the "invisible."[20] For Dai, female characters in Chinese films after 1949 can be "Qin Xianglian (kind, miserable, powerless, needing help), Hua Mulan (woman soldier with obscured gender), sacrificing mother (living for saving male heroes), and oriental sexual objects (gazed by male and the whole western world)"—but not themselves.[21] The mother figure is particularly intriguing, as female characters in Chinese films, especially by Fifth-Generation directors, often mobilize their bodies to rebel against marriage and the patriarchal order in which marriage and motherhood are ensconced.[22] In their study of blockbusters, Carol Liebler's research team supplements this history of changes and increasing complexity with a harsh reminder. From their content analysis of 332 characters in 50 hit films from 2002 to 2011, the investigators conclude that women are more likely than men "to be young, sexualized, and conform to an ideal image," and that the content creators for these films are seldom women.[23] While their study generally corroborates earlier inquiries that find the portrayal of female characters in Chinese films to be consistently conventional,[24] it argues that such character constructions "serve as further impetus for women to engage with the beauty economy."[25]

Advertising

Then, we come to the obvious partner in the consumerist crime: advertising. Despite its intimate relationship with consumerist society and the beauty economy, advertising is far less linked to academic inquiry on gender. This is all the more remarkable when any casual traveller in virtually any city will observe the dominance of female images, usually beautiful and sexy, luring gazers to notice a wide range of products, not necessarily targeted at women, but quite often associated with bodily embellishment, such as cosmetics and fashion. China is no exception in this[26]—although for a few decades after the Communist Revolution in 1949, commercial forms of advertising familiar in capitalist societies were entirely unknown. Such forms of advertising were considered "a wasteful capitalist business practice and [were] banned."[27] It was in the late 1970s and early 1980s, when market reforms were launched, that commercial advertising became recognized as an important way to revitalize the economy, heralding the arrival of China in the global advertising and consumer culture.

The short history of advertising in contemporary China may also provide an explanation for the scarcity of research. Among existing studies that are anchored to gender discussions, researchers generally agree that neither the Confucian, pre-Mao, docile, and respectful woman from Chinese traditions, and the post-Mao, androgynous, and strong woman from the Revolution, engender sufficient advertising appeal.[28] Analysing 427 advertisements selected from 30 top magazines, both local and foreign, Kineta Hung and Stella Li verify their hypothesis that magazine advertisements, particularly the images they mobilize, reiterate cultural characteristics believed to be embodied in traditional and modern Chinese women.[29] The researchers identified four female types: nurturer, strong woman, flower vase, and urban sophisticate. Their analysis shows that more than 80 per cent of advertisements carry one or more images from these four types of contemporary Chinese women, who constitute the "multiple feminine ideals" Chinese women are exposed to.[30] Among these, the urban sophisticate proves to be the most popular image, followed by flower vase, strong woman, and nurturer. Hung and Li contend that the emphasis on a woman's appearance and taste underscores the consumerist drive scripted in the advertisements, especially regarding fashion, cosmetics, and lifestyle products. Later studies confirm the dominance of decorative roles performed by women in magazine and subway advertising.[31]

Vis-à-vis such decorative representations of women, another image that seems to lead a strenuous life in China's advertising world is the "New Woman" (*xin nüxing*), who emerged in the 1930s, when Republican China was striving to modernize the nation. According to Megan Ferry's study, the "New Woman" represents all the progressiveness of the time, embodying, at the same time, the excesses of a modern woman, such as licentiousness and unruliness, particularly in the form of sexual autonomy.[32] While this image was mobilized to sell products deemed modern in the 1930s, it resurfaced in the 1990s in variations of nostalgia, nonetheless commercial. In the words of Dai Jinhua, nostalgia is packaged as something fashionable in order to sell.[33] Advertising with such images of "New Woman" may indeed, as Ferry critiques, erase the presence of poor, rural, and older women; such an "icon of progressive modernity" aids "in the construction of young (urban) female identities in China today."[34] Doreen Wu and Agatha Chung offer a more sanguine reading.[35] The researchers analyse the images of "modern Chinese woman" in 164 award-winning TV commercials selected from both Hong Kong and mainland China. While their analysis shows a much stronger presence of modern rather than traditional women, it also finds in mainland advertisements a stronger tendency to represent women "in more modern than traditional dimensions such as in the aspects of role portrayals, appearance/projection, voice-over, and functions of speech."[36] They consider this more modern representation to be a legacy of the communist doctrine and promotion of gender equality since 1949, which has "significantly stimulated women's emancipation from the traditional roles."[37]

TELEVISION: DATING SHOWS

Whether *If You Are the One* (*IYAO*, literally "do not disturb if not sincere") is the most popular and high-profile production in Chinese television history remains a moot point; however, the dating show is quite likely the most researched and written-about phenomenon among researchers on Chinese media and culture. Before zooming in on this spectacular TV success, I will attempt a brief history of dating shows.

The first dating show was screened in China in the late 1980s, a decade after the economic reforms were introduced. Entitled *Television Matchmaker* (*Dianshi Hongniang* 电视红娘), the forerunner of *IYAO* did not actually offer dating services, but aired a series of marriage advertisements sent from the audience. Quite a lacklustre forerunner for its successful successor, the "rigid and reserved" show attracted very few viewers when it was first aired.[38] After the show managed to persuade a male marriage seeker in front of the camera, more men followed suit. Indeed, according to Li Zhonglian, producer and host of the show, those who sent in their requests were predominantly male. When a girl finally appeared on the show, she was accused of losing face for her family in public,[39] highlighting strong social stigma against female agency. In any case, the show "pioneered heterosexual marriage matchmaking on television and shifted the topic of individual intimacy from the private to the public."[40] With accelerated marketization of the Chinese economy and increasing importance of local television stations, a second generation of dating shows emerged, with good-looking and well-presented marriage-seekers enjoying real on-screen speed-dating and matching-making games.[41] In 2010 came another wave of dating shows in China, which managed to turn this genre into a "new" tradition in the twenty-first century.[42] As the flagship show of this tradition, *IYAO* has continued to achieve top ratings.[43] Its audience figures are second only to the national evening news and the subsequent weather forecast on CCTV-1.[44]

Modelled on the global format *Take Me Out*, every episode of *IYAO* presents an exercise in matchmaking between 24 young women and one man. Dressed-up and made-up as glamorous television personalities, these women "wield their 'power' of questioning, challenging and switching stage lights on and off to determine the success and failure of each individual male player."[45] Grounding the show to the "increasingly conservative Chinese media, which is ardently performing its capitalist turn amidst market reform," Li Luzhou analyses almost all the episodes from January

2010 to March 2012, concluding that "women are essentialized, represented as subordinates and dependents who need material support from men, and [are] encouraged to become sexual subjects by internalizing the male gaze."[46] The show, according to this inquiry, is lynchpinned by the leftover women ideology. While taking a different route of analysis—stage arrangements and hidden rules of *IYAO*—Luo Wei and Sun Zhen's inquiry comes to a similar conclusion.[47] They find the shows playing, or perhaps preying, on the predicament of Chinese single women, particularly the *shengnü*. The fact that the women are often seen as lashing out with harsh interrogations of the bachelors, Li argues, is not exactly a reassertion of the "New Woman" figure; rather, it is more a commercial trick than a sincere way to empower women.[48] "Chinese feminism is pseudo-feminism; its nature is to reap without sowing," as one audience member summarized it.[49] It represents a Chinese version of Western post-feminist popular culture and sensibilities, emphasizing choice and agency, cleansing feminist politics.[50] Wu Jing, on the other hand, offers a more sympathetic reading, explaining the show's representation of female individualization as traversing between the freedom and constraints configured by a rapidly changing society.[51]

In addition to the importance, and thus, influence of commercial interests in the television sector, researchers also draw attention to state involvement, particularly with increasing social critique and moral anxiety towards the presumably blatant materialistic values articulated by the female participants of *IYAO*.[52] Ma Nuo, a woman expressing her expectations of potential husbands, infamously said she would rather cry in a BMW than laugh on the back seat of a bicycle.[53] Ensuing controversies surrounding similar materialistic aspirations led to intervention by the State Administration of Radio, Film and Television (SARFT) in 2010. Chen Siyu notes a radical change after the state intervention, with the single women in the show subsequently aspiring to a caring, respectful, and romantic man instead of a rich guy.[54] Similarly, Guo Shaohua's analysis of the episodes from 2010 and 2013 observes major modifications after state intervention, which, ironically, enhance *IYAO's* criticality in presenting more diversified gender representations, nurturing public debate culture, and including social commentaries on dating issues.[55] For all its complications with the market and state interests, and for all its traditional and modern representations of women, *IYAO*, in Wang Pan's summary, "draws public discussion and debate on multiple social and moral issues," including gender inequality, filial piety, love, and marriage.[56]

TELEVISION: DRAMA

During the period of the Cultural Revolution, television dramas, like other media products, towed the official ideological line, according to which romance, love, and gender relationships were considered inappropriate in a time of mass mobilization. When the television industry started rehabilitating itself, after 1976, increasing numbers of drama series appeared on Chinese screens, with an increasing presence of female characters entangled in stories of love and romance. It took almost a decade before a nationwide hit series was produced, in 1985, entitled *Finding the World Back* (*Xunzhao Huilai de Shijie* 寻找回来的世界). The series narrates the story of a young female teacher, who insists on teaching in a reformatory school against the wishes of her fiancé. This popular drama series introduced to the Chinese audience an independent woman who defied her familial and romantic relationships for the sake of her own dream, which is as personal as it is steeped in the communist ideal "to serve the people."

As in other media platforms and genres, increasing marketization of Chinese society started to have an impact on the television industry.[57] Two influential productions span the modern–traditional paradigm found in other media products mentioned earlier. Mobilizing a new professional breed engendered by the market reforms, Guangdong Television's *Public Relations Girls* (*Gongguan Xiaojie* 公关小姐) launched in 1989, heralded the start of the genre of "urban business dramas." The series follows the life of a single woman who moved from Hong Kong to Guangzhou, her personal trajectory and professional life in public relations resonating with the larger context of economic changes in China. In 1990, even more popular—and causing unprecedented waves of discussion in society—was Beijing Television Art Centre's *Yearning* (*Kewang* 渴望). Generally considered China's first women-centred long-running serial, and a successful predecessor to other similar series to come,[58] *Yearning* narrates the relationships between friends and family members, zooming in on the lives of so-called ordinary people. Most significantly, it reworks the traditional female ideals of "virtuous wives and good mothers" in the modern Chinese context. The self-sacrificing protagonist Liu Huifang represents the epitome of traditional women in China, which in turn, also corresponds to the representation of Oshin in a Japanese drama, which was the first to enter the Chinese television market, in 1980, with great success.[59]

Riding on the popularity of *Yearning*, many women-centred drama series emerged, with increasing diversity and mingling of genres and representations of women. Academic as well as popular discourses have proposed a variety of genre names, but as Manfred Kops and Stefan Ollig argue, such differentiation is "necessarily a messy job."[60] I will confine this brief account to the five genres most relevant to our purposes: family ethics drama,[61] women empowering drama,[62] costume drama,[63] romantic drama,[64] and pink drama.[65]

For a family ethics drama, *Yearning*'s heroine remains prototypical. Similar self-sacrificing and virtuous women are found in *Big Sister* (*Dajie* 大姐, 2004), *New Era of Marriage* (*Xinjiehun Shidai* 新结婚时代, 2006), and *Double Sided* (*Shuangmianjiao* 双面胶, 2007). Gradually, more "independent" female protagonists appeared. In *Dwelling Narrowness* (*Woju* 蜗居, 2009), another milestone in Chinese television history, Haizao leaves her boyfriend to become the mistress of a rich man, ushering in a controversial kind of woman, no longer sacrificing her own interests for family and traditional values, ready to do what she can under the new Chinese capitalism for upward mobility. Probably less polemically, other family ethics dramas of this period feature women managing difficulties involving their families and careers, not necessarily finding this easy, but no longer suffering in silence. *Hot Mom* (*Lama Zhengzhuan* 辣妈正传, 2013) depicts different types of educated, middle-class career women, all of whom are considerably detached from their families, including a workaholic who ignores her husband.

After the Chinese popularity of a Korean drama *Dae Janggeum* in 2005, series portraying strong women started to appear more frequently on Chinese TV screens.[66] Within this genre, noted for its connection with Maoist feminism, the "women empowerment trilogy," created by the same production team, is particularly popular: *Silent Tears* (*Nüren Buku* 女人不哭, 2006), *Living with a Smile* (*Xiaozhe Huoxiaqu* 笑着活下去, 2007), and *Woman Is Not Easy* (*Nüren Burongyi* 女人不容易, 2016). Courage, in these series, is what the female protagonists show in their struggles, and success is what they ultimately gain.

Another popular genre is costume drama featuring women, particularly empresses and court ladies, mostly from Chinese historical legends, wielding power, sometimes seen as independent, more often as aggressive and manipulative. Take, for instance, *Wu Zetian* (武则天, 1995), *Empresses in the Palace* (*Hougong Zhenqiongzhuan* 后宫甄嬛传, 2011), and *Legend of Miyue* (*Miyuezhuan* 芈月传, 2015). These dramas hook audiences in with the ladies' intrigues, tricking and victimizing their male counterparts, which, in their own ways, are subversive to the feudal and patriarchal system.[67]

At the same time, Chinese television continues to release drama series that mobilize urban romance as the main organizing principle of their stories.[68] Such series feature women who are gentle, tender, and longing for true love, for instance, *The Young Man Meets the Woman (Xiaonanren Yushang Danüren 小男人遇上大女人*, 2012), *Honey Bee Man (Woai Nanguimi 我爱男闺蜜*, 2014), and *Pretty Li Huizhen (Piaoliang de Li Huizhen 漂亮的李慧珍*, 2017). Under the influence of the "Korean wave," adaptations appear in China that follow Korean originals in fabricating romantic fantasies and female characters who are chasing them. Despite the conventionally romanticized framing of women, these drama series also contain less conventional elements: for instance, older female characters falling in love.

Integrating other genres, particularly those involving romance and empowerment, pink drama, the latest invention in recent Chinese television history, foregrounds women who are single, childless, and urban. They are successful at work, but confused in personal relationships.[69] Loosely modelled on similar single women characters in Western television dramas, notably *Sex and the City* (1998–2004), the Chinese variants include *Pink Ladies (Fanhong Nülang 粉红女郎*, 2003), *The Daughter Has to Get Married (Dainü Dangjia 大女当嫁*, 2010), *3S Lady (Danshen Nüwang 单身女王*, 2011), *The Golden Age of the Leftover Ladies (Shengnü de Huangjin Shidai 剩女的黄金时代*, 2011), *We Get Married (Zanmen Jiehunba 咱们结婚吧*, 2014), and arguably the most recent hit series, *Ode to Joy (Huanle Song 欢乐颂*, 2016). Before I attempt a more detailed analysis of *Ode to Joy*, suffice it to say that (single) women, who are no longer bound to the traditional, familial context, are represented as modern by shopping. And pink-collar women, who have benefited from better education and employment opportunities, are able to enter into fashionable professions, outnumbering the "middle-class housewives" and "flower vases" as new role models.[70]

Amidst the shifting representational environment in China, a central figure has emerged in pink drama from 2008: *shengnü*. These single women are labelled as leftover, and the pressure for them to get married sustains many story lines. In the following section, I will focus on the latest representation of single women in a drama series that is interesting for my analysis not only due to its immense popularity, but also for its refreshingly realistic portrayal of single women in contemporary Chinese society.[71]

ODE TO JOY!

> To promote the prosperous development of arts and culture, the most fundamental element is to create excellent works that can face up to this great nation and this great epoch.[72]

These words, cited from an important address by President Xi Jinping in 2014, articulate a change of course in cultural productions, a change towards closer links with the nation, the epoch, the "reality," writ small, as argued by Fan Yali, in the everyday lives of its populations[73]—one of which is the urban middle class. More than three decades of economic reforms have transformed China into the second largest economic entity in the world, with an increasing population that can loosely be grouped under the term "middle class." This middle class, as noted by Wu Changchang, has become the key target audience of television dramas and variety shows by media institutions, state-run or otherwise, in post-millennium China.[74] In 2011, for instance, Shanghai-based Dragon TV (*Shanghai Dongfang Weishi*, 上海东方卫视) realigned the market position of its prime-time drama to "tie in with the new driving force in the cities." Five years later, Dragon TV reiterated the gist of Xi's address at an annual conference: the urgency to script its drama productions with "the DNA of urban realities … reflecting truly the thinking and living of China's new generation of young people."[75] It was at this conjuncture that *Ode to Joy (OtJ)* was created; Dragon TV was a co-producer.

In a rare interview with the press, scriptwriter Yuan Zidan stresses the basis of her scenarios in the series: her own life.[76] She was working for an advertising agency in Shanghai, often working overtime until 10 pm, and feeling lost. Yuan says the scriptwriting assignment saved her life. However, knowing the precarity of creative work, she did not dare to resign, and continued to write for the series while doing her agency job—for three years. The experiences of work and love lives in the series, Yuan reiterates, were informed by her own. Commended by the official *People's Daily* (Overseas edition) as "daring and insightful," *OtJ* is exemplary, according to the commentary, for its realistic sensitivity to women's status and discursive power in contemporary China, breaking new ground in television dramas about urban life.[77] Another essay points to its title, and praises the series as an ode to women's joy, laying bare, at the same time, "the traditional patriarchy and the straightjacket that Confucian ideology has been imposing on Chinese women for centuries."[78] On the other hand, *OtJ* is also criticized for its "pseudo-feminism" and its representation of women as "stereotypical," created from masculinist perspectives.[79] Similarly, another author calls it "a bowl of poisonous chicken soup," taking issues with the materialistic fantasies propagated in the series which, as fantasies go, are alluring but doomed.[80]

Between these polemic responses, one can find gradations of positive and negative feedback on the television series, whether on academic or popular platforms, most of which agree on one point: in the show's five characters, "you seem to see traces of yourself or those close to you."[81] Let me now introduce these five single women who enthralled millions of viewers during those months in 2016, with their lives, living together as neighbours on the 22nd floor of a building called Ode to Joy.[82]

Andi

The five characters in the series are cleverly modelled on different types of women, clearly discernible and discursively circulated, in contemporary Chinese society. Andi, a successful career woman who graduated from a top American university, remained in the United States, and made her way up the corporate ladder, would readily be identified in the Chinese vernacular terminology as *haigui* (returning from overseas 海归) and *gaofu-mei* (tall, rich, and beautiful 高富美). While such women seem to have the world at their fingertips, Andi fulfils another stereotypical image of successful career women: high in I.Q., low in E.Q, extremely capable in the office, but totally helpless in love. Returning to Shanghai to work for her old male friend's investment company, Andi's hidden agenda is to search for her lost brother.

The search, a journey back to a darker past, guides her away from the usual trajectory of her time—namely, a race towards an ever brighter future. After all, she breaks her enviable career for an unsure, personal mission. Her brother, it transpires, has been abandoned time and again due to his mental problems, and so, Andi fears for the same. As much as this fear confines her, it also frees her. While she, particularly in the earlier part of the series, seems to be clumsy, inexperienced, and rather closed in terms of human relationships, Andi's awareness of her vulnerability, of her possible inadequacy as a partner in a loving relationship, guides her to make choices that are unexpected, according to dominant societal values. Despite the obvious compatibility and desirability of Wei Wei, a man who belongs to the elite of contemporary China, Andi decides to stay single by the end of the season. Her choice to refuse Wei and go on a vacation is perhaps also a choice to refuse the temptation of coupledom, and a confirmation of a possible, good single life.

Fan Shengmei

Characterized as the typical *baijinnü*—women worshipping gold 拜金女—Fanjie (elder sister Fan, as she is called intimately by others in the series) works as a senior HR personnel in a company with foreign investments. In the series, she is often seen as donning facial masks, making herself up, choosing (fake) brand clothes and handbags, generally devoting her time to self-beautification, with one primary goal: to find some *gaofushuai* (tall, rich, handsome 高富帅) guy to marry. In her bedroom in an apartment shared with Guanguan and Qiuyin, Fanjie stands on many occasions in front of the mirror, lamenting her poor accommodation and dreaming of having her own place, purchased by a husband who can afford it. Almost cynical about love, she lectures Qiuyin on the uselessness of a man who is only good at being handsome. "Handsome?… What's the use of that? Can we eat it?… If you get to marry such a guy, you are actually committing suicide."

At the same time, being the oldest of the gang at 30, Fanjie often functions as an older sister, a post-1980s girl, always ready with street-smart advice and practical support.[83] As the series unfolds, Fanjie is revealed as having always been a victim of her patriarchal family. Growing up in a rural area, Fanjie learned to live with a culture that values boys more than girls. Becoming the financial mainstay of her family, she works hard to earn money, only to be abused by her family and her elder brother, both financially and emotionally, leading to her famous one-liner: "One's family is one's destiny." While most Chinese women would long to become the successful and beautiful Andi, they are more likely to end up like Fanjie. Commenting on her eagerness to package and market herself, one commentator asks rhetorically: "What other resources can Fan Shengmei rely on?"[84] For women like her, "work is the only source of security, we should never risk our lives on those men losers." Using the pun of her name—"sheng" can mean leftover, as in *shengnü* as well as victory—another commentator argues that she should be seen as a winning, not leftover, woman.[85]

In a lengthy monologue towards the end of the series, Fanjie emotionally expresses to her four neighbour-friends her predicament as a single woman working and living in Shanghai. Owing to its distinctive treatment, in a script otherwise peppered with witty and speedy dialogue, allow me to cite Fanjie extensively here:

> I am also a woman, why am I like this? It's not easy at all being on my own in Shanghai... Every day, I pretend to be stronger, to be tougher, but in reality, you have all seen through me. My family has been like this for years. There is nothing I can do, however hard I try... I am also a woman, I also want to have a beautiful and glamorous appearance... That's why I want to find a good person to marry, a person who can give me everything I want. But now, I am at this age, who would still want to do that for me?

Qu Xiaoxiao

An embodiment of *fuerdai*, the second generation of wealthy parents 富二代, Xiaoqu, as she is called in the series, is spoiled, feral, and egoistic. Born and wont to an insouciant life, she has spent her years abroad having fun, rather than gaining knowledge as she is supposed to do as a university student. Xiaoqu reluctantly returns to Shanghai following an urgent plea from her mother. Apparently, Xiaoqu's half-brother, from his father's former marriage, is threatening to take hold of her father's business. With the help of her earlier friends, particularly a young man—and later, of her female neighbours—Xiaoqu learns to run a start-up with her habitual mix of laziness, shrewdness, and playfulness. In matters of love, Xiaoqu seems more experienced than the others, sometimes to the point of being cynical. Sceptical of Qiuyin's office romance, she single-handedly runs a test: she flirts with Qiuyin's boyfriend, steals his attention, and successfully exposes his abusive way of conducting relationships.

On the edge of becoming a caricature of *fuerdai*, who are not, or cannot be, sympathetic, Xiaoqu morphs into a more complex character. The audience discovers how she takes care of the stray cats of the neighbourhood, and how she feels intensely insecure when she falls in love with a medical doctor. Xiaoqu becomes painfully aware of the disadvantage of being spoiled, of being given the luxury of material abundance, but not the incentive to enrich herself, to the extent that she feels inferior to the knowledgeable person she craves to be. What makes Xiaoqu eventually someone with the potential to pull the audience—particularly young women not as fortunate as her—over to her side, is the unfairness her family inflicts on her. Despite the fact that her half-brother is equally spoiled, he is the heir, and is favoured by their father, unlike Xiaoqu. This blatant manifestation of patriarchy, this unfairness, is a shared experience of women across different classes, notwithstanding the disparities in many other dimensions of their lives. When Xiaoqu increasingly manages to win the trust of her father and runs her own start-up, she says, contentedly if not conceitedly: "I'm earning my own money now. I don't have to take money from [my father], I can even support [my family]."

Guan Ju'er

Probably the plainest of the five, Guanguan can easily be summarized as the-girl-next-door type: harmless, simple, and easily pleased. Coming from a middle-class family, she has moved to Shanghai to study, and then, stays as intern in an international company, which, to many Chinese graduates her age, is a dream trajectory. Guanguan works hard, often at the expense of her personal life; we see her conduct online conferences with overseas colleagues and hug a cushion lamenting her chronic lack of sleep. In a sense, a tough woman determined to move upward, Guanguan, however, often relies on her parents for arranging her life, from buying her clothes to getting her the internship job. Guanguan is the typical mediating pacifier of the group, thanks to her openness to all views, and thus, the deficiency of her own. However, the always smiling woman turns out to have a clear mind, or heart, in matters of love. Despite her lack of love stories and experiences, Guanguan declines the pursuit of her old university classmate, choosing to follow where her heart goes, probably a hopeless affair. She is in love with the same man Xiaoqu loves.

Indeed, in spite of the general dependency on her parents, something perceived to be typical of the post-1990s generation in contemporary China where their parents are generally better off, Guanguan is also independent, almost rebellious. Not only is she determined not to marry for marriage's sake and settle for someone ready and easy, Guanguan chooses for a more tortuous path and tries, in her own way, to stay hopeful for what she truly believes in. This takes place, in the context of the series, when her mother keeps nagging her and pushing her to find a partner and leave singlehood, a common experience among women in China who have to deal with the stigma of being leftover women and their parental concern and pressure to get married. Compared with Andi, who has all the resources to stay single and respectable, Guanguan's refusal of a convenient access to the heteronormative comfort zone is potentially empowering to many others who would otherwise perceive themselves as ordinary and filially pious. However ordinary and filially pious these women are, they may still choose, with the kind of sharpness reminiscent of the kitchen knife Guanguan is carrying when the neighbour-friends join in a threatening debt negotiation for Fanjie and her family.

Qiu Yingying[86]

Qiuyin, literally "earthworm" but sounding like her real name, is another small-town woman who is trying her luck in a big city such as Shanghai. She is simple, perhaps naïve; straightforward, perhaps unthoughtful. At the same time, she is optimistic, and capable of forgetting and surviving bad experiences, one of the tactics cherished in both her love and work life, despite or because of her incapability precisely in her love and work life. Unlike Andi, Fanjie, or Xiaoqu, Qiuyin is neither intelligent, nor well-trained in human relationships, nor blessed with family affluence. In the series, we witness how Qiuyin falls not only in love with a senior colleague, but also into a trap set by the "bad guy". In the end, she loses both her romantic dream and her job at a small local company, whose reaction towards Qiuyin portrays the kind of office practices and politics that are biased against women.

Throughout the series, Qiuyin remains, by and large, such a simple, naïve, straightforward, and unthoughtful person. While this personality is often detrimental, Qiuyin also benefits from it. After she loses her job, Qiuyin goes to a job market along with hundreds of other young jobseekers. In a realistic rendition of such occasions in big Chinese cities, she comes across her former lover. Against all decorum, particularly the kind of professional coolness supposed to be demonstrated in a competitive environment such as a job market, Qiuyin launches into a tirade of complaints against him, in public. This unlikely outburst is not only good for the melodrama; it is good for Qiuyin too—it earns her the attention and respect by a man in charge of a job booth. He recruits her, and the job leads, further in the series, to Qiuyin's own start-up in the coffee business. That Qiuyin is arguably the least popular character of the series may well be indexing the Chinese reluctance to speak up, and the persistent expectation of a young woman being demure.

Poisonous Chicken Soup?

"The young women who live on the 22nd floor of Ode to Joy have their own small problems, and their own small expectations." This and its variations form a recurring narrative device throughout the series: non-diegetic commentaries by a male voice-over. Whether this device—borrowed from the original online novel—works dramatically is disputable; the commentary points to the multiplicity of womanhood as articulated and constructed by the five protagonists in *OtJ*. This multiplicity is probably possible due to the genre: television drama. A total of 42 episodes, each lasting almost an hour, offers an immense time span for character development and elaboration. The paradox of *OtJ* is that the five characters are reiterating and cementing stereotypes, while reinventing and confusing them. Similarly paradoxical is its take on "reality": the series, as noted earlier, has been commended for its exceptionally realistic content, especially in comparison with other television drama productions, but it has also been critiqued for its construction of fantasy around such reality.

One oft-heard feedback is the incredible elision of, or triumph over, class interests and incompatibilities. As much as the five single women are distinguished on the socioeconomic axis—throughout the series, we know how Andi and Xiaoqu are protected by their careers and families, and their three neighbours are struggling with precarity and their attempts to move upward—they seem to co-habit in their everyday lives beyond the distinctions, together in a building euphemistically called "Ode to Joy." One commentator notes a land transaction in Shanghai one week after the final episode: RMB 70–80,000 per square metre. Citing experts, Wu Daozi concludes pointedly that the value of Andi and Qu's fixed assets will soon double, as will the rent of their three neighbours. "By then, will poor people and rich people live so joyfully and harmoniously together?" he asks.[87] After the first season, another commentator concludes as follows: "All the attempts to change one's class backgrounds fail totally."[88] The drama series has brewed some chicken soup with a dose of poison—the title of the commentary—that viewers have to divulge, digest, and absorb into their system: one's class background determines everything. For most of the viewers of *OtJ*, the harsh fact of life in China remains: "I'd like to live like Andi, play like Xiaoqu, but I live like Qiuyin, work like Guanguan, and I end up as Fanjie."[89]

I underwrite this line of critique. At the same time, I want to flag up some additional dimensions, some ways of looking at their everyday lives that intersect with their socioeconomic backgrounds and gender experiences. Deliberating on their lives, or more precisely, how they deal with all the vicissitudes, the problems, the precarity, of their lives, it remains pertinent to check their class privileges, or lack thereof. But sometimes, there are other tactics and logics that help them survive. The first is technology. When I am viewing the series, one of the things that jumps out and catches my attention is the prevalence of technology, often mobilized to deal with everyday problems of all sorts, not necessarily to offer ontological security, but helping with mundane insecurity all the same.

The second dimension is togetherness. The first time the five women appear in one scene, the moment that kick-starts their relationship, is an incident. They are trapped when an under-maintained elevator gets stuck—an analogy of the malfunctioning society? We witness their fear, only to notice their different ways of expressing it. Andi, notwithstanding the strong career woman she is, struggles visibly to stay composed, until the usually spoiled Xiaoqu takes hold of her hand, saying: "We are all afraid, no need to pretend." Holding hands, a specifically feminine gesture and tactic, they survive the scare. There are many other incidents that demonstrate how the women gather together intimately and intelligently to support each other. Sometimes, the collective and connective action informs a major story line, such as Fanjie's debts and family troubles. It takes all of them to pool their resources together to help Fanjie, from taking care of her visiting family, to backing her up in negotiations with the gangsters who are blackmailing the family.

As illustrated by the elevator incident, space is the third dimension that *OtJ* lays bare in portraying the everyday lives these single women. I will confine myself to sketch just a few observations. To begin with, they are shown in their homes as much as in their offices. While it may go without saying that women are associated not only with domesticity, but also with work, professionalism and engagement with society at large is not always a given. The reader may recall the media representations listed earlier in this chapter. In this connection, the drama series also makes use of another technique of association to present the women. Put crudely, they are often placed in trendy cafés, top-notch restaurants, and high-end spas, to underline their modernity, while Guanguan, for instance, is lured by her parents to a matching occasion that takes place in a restaurant decorated in a style loosely called traditionally Chinese. To launch a critique, however justifiably, that these modern, commercial places have become part and parcel of the women in *OtJ* is not only beside the point, but missing the centrality of consumption in constructing a self of being modern. In addition to such spatial associations, *OtJ* is shot with many a scene that one can think of as these women's spatial appropriation. The malfunctioning elevator is one. More frequently seen in the series are two other mise-en-scènes: a pedestrian walkway and the waterfront of the Bund.

While I do not disagree with other possible explanations for the arrange-ments—logistically handier, visually attractive, offering a sense of urbanity, and so forth—I want to insert one reading, namely, that the single women in the series show that they can claim the public spaces in Shanghai, how-ever temporarily. Fanjie's long monologue, cited earlier, is delivered on the waterfront to the other four women, with the cityscape as their back-drop. It is as if Fanjie is voicing, venting her struggles not only to her friends, but also to the city at large. A necessary extension of both spatial association and appropriation concerns these women's mobility: they need to be able to move before they can be somewhere else. Throughout the series, one constantly sees how Fanjie travels, vies for her space, and uses her mobile phone in the crowded subway trains of Shanghai, while Andi and Xiaoqu, with their privileged backgrounds, traverse the city in the comfortable and secluded space of a luxury car. It is in the mobility afforded by Andi's BMW that she starts building up her closeness with Qu and Guan, who accept Andi's offer of a ride to their offices.

Spring Festival Gala

The analyses in the chapters to come will be sensitized by these complex portrayals of single women in between tradition and modernity, emancipa-tion and consumption, empowerment and victimhood, the reproductive and the productive, between stereotypes and more. There will be more when the empirical core of this book ushers in the single women doing creative work in Shanghai, when they start elaborating on their precarious lives and how they take care of themselves. Mobilization of technology, the togetherness, and spatial use will re-emerge when we come to it. For the time being, let us follow the five characters of *OtJ* to some huge video walls, perfectly choreographed dancers, colourful costumes, upbeat music, and stunning stunts… As in past years, CCTV's 2017 Spring Festival Gala, arguably the "most watched television programme in the world,"[90] was opened with a spectacle of enchanting technological prowess and incredi-ble human skills. Presented by China Central Television on the eve of every lunar new year since 1983, the five-hour extravaganza continues to "showcase government achievements, eulogizes socialist virtues, and sets the ideological tone for political events that have occurred in the previous year."[91] In 2017, however, the opening act was conspicuous not only in what was displayed, but also in what was not: men. Taking front stage were three teenage boys, often criticized as being feminine, and five women known to the nation as single women.[92] The teenage boys were the immensely popular pop formation TF Boys, and the five young women were the actresses starring in *OtJ*.[93]

While this lineup could readily and easily be explained by the performers' popularity, their prominence in such an ideologically significant show feeds into questions reminiscent of the crisis of Chinese masculinity.[94] That the new year should be heralded by a group of artists representing (feminized) youth and (single) womanhood must be another alarming piece of evidence for the Chinese intellectuals, predominantly male, who announced a "search for real men" in the 1990s. Responding to a globalizing and modernizing China, they were wrestling with the loss of the typical masculine advantage of physical stamina to feminine skills, as well as with the Western versions of ideal manhood, which remain, by and large, the global hegemonic norm.[95] Of course, this crisis, like many other cases of moral panic, is occasioned by a sense of threat as much as an occasion for those who feel threatened to reorganize and reassert themselves.[96]

Indeed, during the opening act of Spring Festival Gala 2017, while the boys and the women sang, most of the performance, entitled "Beautiful Chinese Year," was accomplished by impressive choreography on a grand scale, acrobatic acts, and special effects in the style of what director Zhang Yimou terms "square aesthetics," something only authoritarian regimes such as Beijing and Pyongyang are purportedly capable of.[97] As in the opening ceremony of the Beijing Olympics 2008, such aesthetics and such a performance was intended to flex the muscles of a strong nation, a show or showing-off of what discipline, hard work, and big money can do.[98] The men might have been absent on the front stage, but the masculinist longing was everywhere.

That the five women from *OtJ* were always pushed back to where they were supposed to be—namely, a stereotypical framing of womanhood—was clear in the other segments surrounding the Gala show. In one, they were assigned by two male presenters the task of making dumplings, presumably a family tradition at Chinese New Year. In the other, they were asked to make a group selfie, led by a feminizing statement that the five women must be fighting to avoid having the least flattering position in the picture.[99] The five women, continuing their television roles as single working women in a big city such as Shanghai, were then asked by two male presenters five questions, said to be often raised when single working women return to their hometown for Chinese New Year. The five questions were: (1) Hey, did you get fatter again? (2) How's your work? How much is your salary? Got a big year-end bonus? (3) Got a boyfriend? What is your type, let auntie introduce one to you? (4) Heard that you are doing good, about to buy a flat? (5) Why no baby yet? What are you waiting for?

Scripted and packaged as a comical game, these questions are, at the same time, reiterating the social norms and pressures single working women are subjected to, particularly during the holiday period of family reunions. In recent years, rent-a-boyfriend services have developed from a media sensation to a more commonplace practice, precisely to help single women deal with stressful days such as the spring festival period.[100] Ironically, thanks to the comical aspiration of the game, which specified a facial expression as reply, the five single working women, unlike their counterparts in real life, did not need to say anything. Instead, they made grimaces, all open to slightly different interpretations, but invariably dismissive. In particular, Wang Ziwen responded to her own as well as the other four questions with a constant smirk on her face, remarkably in line with the fearless Qu Xiaoxiao she played in the drama series. Whether it was a lingering confusion or conflation between on- and off-screen realities on my part as a member of the audience, the same confusion or conflation might well also play out to my fellow audience members. In any case, the five women, using their acting skills, managed to brush off the essentially nasty questions as dandruff on their shoulders; they were annoying, but ultimately, insignificant. In fact, during the dumpling-making segment, the five women refused similarly to be framed in a domesticated manner. When asked to choose their favourite ingredient, Qiao Xin (Guan Ju'er) replied "lotus seed," which, according to Chinese word play, has always been a symbol of reproductivity. The male presenter was quick in voicing this symbolic association and insinuating Qiao's desire to become a mother. Qiao, undistractedly, continued explaining her choice as something else.

By the end of their performance at the Spring Festival Gala, the five women from *OtJ* were asked to take a selfie again. They took turns to look into the camera, and shook their heads as animation effects were automatically added to their selfies. This was to premiere and promote a new App soon to be launched by CCTV to the nation, with the intention of expanding their ideological and market share in the media world of contemporary China. In that sense, these five women, like many of their colleagues, found themselves in a situation where their subversive potentials as alternative versions of femininity would always be "cleansed," to use a verb I used somewhere else, by an "exercise of collaboration between the market and state ideology".[101] They were confronted with the state and the market's attempt to represent them as nation-loving, dumpling-making, and selfie-taking women. This, in turn, is succinctly what their fellow single women in Chinese society have to encounter in their everyday lives; they are constantly being foregrounded, discussed, and represented. Whether disciplinary or emancipatory, stereotyping or interrogating, provocative or prescriptive—or probably all of these—such representations are the symbolic realities single women in China have to live with. Later in this book, some of the women I have enlisted for this research project will keep such symbolic realities on hold, enjoy a moment of choosing, and show us the images of themselves they believed to be themselves: their self-representations. For now, we will move on to the empirical and analytical core of the book, and hear what single women have to say about their work, their love, and their lives in contemporary China.

NOTES

1. According to one major Chinese music site, this song enjoys the number of highest hits—3.38 million among the 10 songs released as original sound track. See http://www.xiami.com/album/2100316560?spm=0.0.0.0.0.dwTO8C&from=search_popup_album.

2. These figures are cited in Wang Tianyue (王天玥), "电视剧《欢乐颂》的意识形态色彩研究 [A Study on the Ideological Colours of TV Drama 'Ode to Joy']," 西部广播电视 [Xibu Guangbo Dianshi], no. 9 (2016): 100; and Jing Ji (荆棘), "《欢乐颂》:碗现实主义的毒鸡汤 ['Ode to Joy': A Bowl of Realist Poisonous Chicken Soup]," 齐鲁周刊 [Wilu Zhoukan], no. 19 (2016): 64–65.

3. As noted by Cai Shenshen, "[a]s females compose the bulk of Chinese TV drama spectators, the ambiguities and hardships facing women are more likely to lift audience ratings." In Cai Shenshen, Television Drama in Contemporary China: Political, Social and Cultural Phenomena (London; New York: Routledge, 2016): 8. See also Michael Keane, "Television Drama in China: Remaking the Market," Media International Australia 115, no. 1 (2005): 82–93; Zhang Kai (张开), "女性观众喜爱电视剧成因分析[A Study on the Reasons Why Television Drama Series Are Popular among Female Audiences]," 现代传播:中国传媒大学学报 [Xiandai Chuanbo: Zhongguo Chuanmeidaxue Xuebao], no. 6 (2009): 65–68.

4. The second season opened in May 2017, arguably less valued, and inciting hostility for its heavy product placement. For an analysis of its dwindling popularity, see Ye Zi (叶子), "《欢乐颂2》难复第一季辉煌?主创聊

季播探索之路 ['Ode to Joy 2' Unable to Attain the Height of Season One? Show Creator Discusses the Initial Exploration of the Show]," *新浪娱乐 [Sina Entertainment]* (blog), June 7, 2017, http://ent.sina.com.cn/v/m/2017-06-07/doc-ifyfuzmy2393679.shtml.

5. Upon inquiry by my research assistant, an official governmental response from The State Administration of Press, Publication, Radio, Film and Television to her has provided these figures. Additional information is cited from: "中国广告媒体新世代(一): 新媒体刺激市场需求 [New Generation of Advertising Media in China (I): New Media Stimulate Market Demand]," *商贸全接触 [Hong Kong Means Business]* (blog), April 21, 2016, http://hkmb.hktdc.com/tc/1X0A5VYH; "2016年全国新闻出版业基本情况 [Overview of the National Press and Publication Industry in 2016]" (国家新闻出版广电总局 [State Administration of Press, Publication, Radio, Film and Television], 2017), http://www.sapprft.gov.cn/sapprft/govpublic/6677/1633.shtml.

6. See Marjorie Ferguson, *Forever Feminine: Women's Magazines and the Cult of Femininity* (Exeter, NH: Heinemann, 1983); Angela McRobbie, "Jackie: An Ideology of Adolescent Femininity," in *Popular Culture: Past and Present*, ed. Bernard Waites, Tony Bennett, and Graham Martin (London: Croom Helm, 1982), 263–83; Janice Winship, *Inside Women's Magazines* (London: Pandora Press, 1987).

7. See Chen Guiqin (陈桂琴), "试论女性时尚杂志中的女性角色问题 [Discussions on the Issues of Female Characters in Women Fashion Magazines]" (暨南大学 [Chi Nan University], 2003); Luo Yunjuan (罗韵娟) and Hao Xiaoming (郝晓鸣), "媒体女性形象塑造与社会变革—《中国妇女》杂志封面人物形象的实证研究 [Shaping Women's Image in Media and The Social Revolution—An Empirical Study of the Cover Figure's Image from Women of China]," *中国传媒报告 [China Media Report]* 1 (2015): 87–99; Sun Lu [孙璐], "论当代传媒中女性刻板印象的嬗变 [On Changing Female Stereotypes in Contemporary Media]" (苏州大学 [Soochow University], 2004).

8. Zhang Yuliang (张裕亮), "铁姑娘、贤内助、时尚女— 中国女性杂志建构的女性形象 [Iron Lady, Better Half and Fashion Girl: Women's Image in Women's Magazines in China]," *China Media Report Overseas* 6, no. 1 (2010): 92.

9. The five women's magazines are *Marie Claire, Cosmopolitan, Rayli, Elle,* and *Nüyou.* For more see Qi Ling, "A New Dynamic of Gender Discourses? A Textual Analysis of the Representation of Shengnü in Television Dramas and Women's Magazines' Websites" (The Chinse University of Hong Kong, 2013), 49.

10. See Zhou Chen, "The Embodiment of Transforming Gender and Class: Shengnü and Their Media Representation in Contemporary China"

(University of Kansas, 2011); Wei Qiong (危琼), "报纸对'剩女'的媒介形象塑造 [The Media Representation of 'Shengnü' Image by News]," 新闻世界 [News World], no. 9 (2010): 112–14.

11. Sun Shengwei and Chen Feinian, "Reprivatized Womanhood: Changes in Mainstream Media's Framing of Urban Women's Issues in China, 1995–2012," *Journal of Marriage and Family* 77, no. 5 (2015): 1091.

12. In Sun and Chen, "Reprivatized Womanhood," 1105. The three mainstream magazines, understood as "nationally distributed, market-driven," are *Sanlian Shenghuo Zhoukan* (*Life Weekly*), *Nandu Zhoukan* (*Southern Metropolis Weekly*), and *Xin Zhoukan* (*New Weekly*). For more see Sun and Chen, "Reprivatized Womanhood," 1097.

13. Huang Ying (黄颖), "镜像内外的困囿与突围—论新世纪以来中国电影中的女性形象 [The Restraint and Breakout Inside/Outside of the Mirror: On Female Representation of Contemporary Chinese Cinema]," 当代电影 [Contemporary Cinema], no. 12 (2016): 142–45.

14. See Dai Jinhua (戴锦华), "性别与叙事:当代中国电影中的女性 [Gender and Narration: Women in Contemporary Chinese Films]," 天涯 [Tianya] 11, no. 5 (2003); Hu Xin (胡辛) and He Jing (何静), "难以超越的性别视角-1949年后中国男导演的女性电影叙事管窥 [Unsurpassable Gender Perspective: Female Narration by Chinese Male Directors since 1949]," 江西社會科學 [Jianxi Social Science], no. 8 (2008); Qin Xiaohong (秦晓红), "女性生存状态的中国镜像—论中国电影中的女性形象建构 [Chinese Mirror of Female Existence—On the Construction of Female Images in Chinese Films]," 湖南社会科学 [Hunan Shehui Kexue] 3, no. 44 (2006): 138–41; Wang Zhenzhen (王臻真), "消费文化中的性别图景——近年中国电影中的女性形象 [Gender Images in Consumer Culture—Female Representation in Recent Chinese Films]," 当代文坛 [Dangdai Wentan], no. 1 (2015): 103–9.

15. Huang, "镜像内外的困囿与突围," 143.

16. Mulvey, Laura. *Visual and Other Pleasures*. 1975. Reprint, London: Macmillan, 1989.

17. Huang, "镜像内外的困囿与突围," 143.

18. Zhang Yuanyuan (张媛媛), "浅析几部国产电影中的女性角色 [On the Female Roles in Several Chinese Domestic Films]," 云南农业大学学报 [Yunnan Nongye Daxue Xuebao] 4, no. 6 (2010): 88–90.

19. See also Chris Berry, "Representing Chinese Women: Researching Women in the Chinese Cinema," in *Dress, Sex and Text in Chinese Culture*, ed. Antonia Finnane (Clayton: Monash Asia Institute, 1999), 198–211; Qin, "女性生存状态的中国镜像."; Wang Pan, "Inventing Traditions: Television Dating Shows in the People's Republic of China," *Media, Culture & Society* 39, no. 4 (2017): 504–19.

20. Dai, "不可见的女性."

21. Carol M. Liebler, Jiang Wei, and Chen Li, "Beauty, Binaries, and the Big Screen in China: Character Gender in Feature Films," *Asian Journal of Communication* 25, no. 6 (2015): 588.

22. See Chris Berry and Mary Ann Farquhar, *China on Screen: Cinema and Nation* (New York, NY: Columbia University Press, 2006); Tan See-Kam, Peter X. Feng, and Gina Marchetti, "Introduction," in *Chinese Connections: Critical Perspectives on Film, Identity, and Diaspora*, ed. Tan See-Kam, Peter X. Feng, and Gina Marchetti (Philadelphia, PA: Temple University Press, 2009), 1–5.

23. Liebler, Jiang, and Chen, "Beauty, Binaries, and the Big Screen in China," 584.

24. See Rey Chow, "Fetish Power Unbound: A Small History of 'Woman' in Chinese Cinema," in *The Oxford Handbook of Chinese Cinemas*, ed. Carlos Rojas and Eileen Chow, Oxford Handbooks (Oxford, New York: Oxford University Press, 2013); Zhou Xuelin, "'From behind the Wall' The Representation of Gender and Sexuality in Modern Chinese Film," *Asian Journal of Communication* 11, no. 2 (2009): 1–17.

25. Liebler, Jiang, and Chen, "Beauty, Binaries, and the Big Screen in China," 596.

26. See Beverley Hooper, "Flower Vase and Housewife: Women and Consumerism in Post-Mao China," in *Gender and Power in Affluent Asia*, ed. Krishna Sen and Maila Stivens (London: Routledge, 1998), 167–93; Perry Johansson, "Chinese Women and Consumer Culture: Discourses on Beauty and Identity in Advertising and Women's Magazines 1985–1995" (Stockholms Universitet, 1998).

27. Hung and Li, "Images of the Contemporary Woman in Advertising in China," 11.

28. See Hooper, "Flower Vase and Housewife"; Johansson, "Chinese Women and Consumer Culture"; Hung and Li, "Images of the Contemporary Woman in Advertising in China."

29. Kineta Hung and Stella Yiyan Li, "Images of the Contemporary Woman in Advertising in China," *Journal of International Consumer Marketing* 19, no. 2 (2006): 7–28.

30. Ibid., 21.

31. See also Cheng Hong and Wan Guofang, "Holding up Half of the 'Ground': Women Portrayed in Subway Advertisements in China," in *Commercializing Women: Images of Asian Women in the Media*, ed. Katherine Toland Frith and Kavita Karan (USA: Hampton Press, 2008); Zhang Lin, Pataradech "Tony" Srisupandit, and Debra Cartwright, "A Comparison of Gender Role Portrayals in Magazine Advertising: The United States, China and Thailand," *Management Research News* 32, no. 7 (June 19, 2009): 683–700.

32. Megan M. Ferry, "Advertising, Consumerism and Nostalgia for the New Woman in Contemporary China," *Continuum* 17, no. 3 (2003): 277–90.
33. Dai Jinhua, "Imagined Nostalgia," trans. Judy T. H. Chen, *Boundary 2* 24, no. 3 (1997): 143–61.
34. Ferry, "Advertising, Consumerism and Nostalgia," 277.
35. Doreen D. Wu and Agatha Man-kwan Chung, "Hybridized Images: Representations of the 'Modern Woman' across Mainland China and Hong Kong TV Commercials," *Journal of Asian Pacific Communication* 21, no. 2 (2011): 177–95.
36. Ibid., 192.
37. Ibid.
38. Wang, "Inventing Traditions."
39. Wen Lifang (温丽芳), "电视相亲节目的前世今生 [The Past and Present of Television Dating Shows]," 山西晚报 *[Shanxi Wanbao]*, February 27, 2010.
40. Wang, "Inventing Traditions," 506.
41. Jiang Xiaobin (蒋肖斌), "从《电视红娘》到《非诚勿扰》—电视相亲节目的历史考察 [From 'Television Matchmaker' to 'If You Are the One': A Historical Investigation of Television Dating Shows]," 现代视听 *[Xiandai Shiting]*, no. 9 (2011): 43–46.
42. See Wang, "Inventing Traditions."
43. See Xiong Yan (熊艳), "《非诚勿扰》何以领跑收视冠军 [How Does 'If You Are the One' Remain a Rating Champion]," 视听 *[Shiting]*, no. 6 (2013): 26–27.
44. See Fan Lu (范璐), "江苏卫视下战书:《非诚勿扰》不怕模仿 [Jiangsu Television Welcomes Competition: 'If You Are the One' Is Not Afraid to Be Imitated]," *Shanxi Wanbao [山西晚报]*, May 27, 2010.
45. Luo Wei, "Packaged Glamour: Constructing the Modern Bride in China's Bridal Media," *Asian Women* 28, no. 4 (2012): 89.
46. Li Luzhou, "If You Are the One: Dating Shows and Feminist Politics in Contemporary China," *International Journal of Cultural Studies* 18, no. 5 (2015): 531.
47. Luo Wei and Sun Zhen, "Are You the One? China's TV Dating Shows and the Sheng Nü's Predicament," *Feminist Media Studies* 15, no. 2 (2015): 239–56. "Are You the One" is these authors' translation of "If You Are the One."
48. Li, "If You Are the One," 532.
49. Ibid., 531.
50. See Li, "If You Are the One"; Luo and Sun, "Are You the One?".
51. Wu Jing, "Post-Socialist Articulation of Gender Positions: Contested Public Sphere of Reality Dating Shows," in *Women and the Media in Asia* (London: Palgrave Macmillan, 2012), 220–36.

52. See Guo Shaohua, "When Dating Shows Encounter State Censors: A Case Study of If You Are the One," *Media, Culture & Society* 39, no. 4 (2017): 487–50; Chen, "Disciplining Desiring Subjects through the Remodeling of Masculinity"; Li, "If You Are the One."

53. Chen, "Disciplining Desiring Subjects through the Remodeling of Masculinity." 101.

54. Ibid., 112.

55. Guo, "When Dating Shows Encounter State Censors."

56. Wang, "Inventing Traditions," 514. See also Tania Lewis, Fran Martin, and Sun Wanning, *Telemodernities: Television and Transforming Lives in Asia* (Durham: Duke University Press, 2016) for an excellent comparative study on "lifestyle" television shows in India, mainland China and Taiwan, which demonstrates similar complexity of identity and modernity constructions.

57. Zhu Ying, Michael Keane, and Bai Ruoyun, eds., *TV Drama in China* (Hong Kong: Hong Kong University Press, 2008).

58. Huang Ya Chien, "Pink Dramas: Reconciling Consumer Modernity and Confucian Womanhood," in *TV Drama in China*, ed. Zhu Ying, Michael Keane, and Bai Ruoyun (Hong Kong: Hong Kong University Press, 2008), 103–14.

59. See James Lull, *China Turned On: Television, Reform and Resistance* (London: Routledge, 2013): 176; Yasushi Watanabe and David L. McConnell, eds., *Soft Power Superpowers* (Armonk, NY: M.E. Sharpe, 2008): 119.

60. Manfred Kops and Stefan Ollig, *Internationalization of the Chinese TV Sector* (Berlin: LIT Verlag Münster, 2007): 92.

61. See James F. Scotton and William A. Hachten, *New Media for a New China* (Chichester: Wiley-Blackwell, 2010); Han Yujuan (韩玉娟), "新世纪家庭伦理剧女性形象变迁 [Changes of Female Representation in Family Drama of the New Century]," 艺术科技 *[Yishu Keji]*, no. 3 (2015): 52–53.

62. Ma Yan (马艳), "女性励志剧中的人物功能分析 [Analysis of the Characters in Female Inspirational Drama]," 中国电视 *[China Television]*, no. 2 (2009): 36–40.

63. See Zhu Ying and Chris Berry, *TV China* (Bloomington, IN: Indiana University Press, 2009); Zhou Ting (周婷), "宫廷剧中女性形象对都市白领女性形象的解构—基于34位都市白领女性对《后宫甄嬛传》看法研究 [The Deconstruction of Metropolitan White Collar Female Image in Historical Court Drama—A Study Based on the Analysis of 34 White Collar Female on 'Empresses in the Palace']," 声屏世界 *[Voice and Screen World]*, no. 7 (2014): 35–37; Ling, "A New Dynamic of Gender Discourses? A Textual Analysis of the Representation of Shengnü in

Television Dramas and Women's Magazines' Websites"; Zhu, Keane, and Bai, *TV Drama in China*.

64. Peter J. Kitson, *Forging Romantic China: Sino-British Cultural Exchange 1760–1840* (Cambridge: Cambridge University Press, 2013).

65. See Zhu, Keane, and Bai, *TV Drama in China*; Scotton and Hachten, *New Media for a New China*.

66. Ma, "女性励志剧中的人物功能分析."

67. See Yang Yan (羊艳), "解读女性宫廷剧的大众文化意义 [Deconstructing the Popular Culture Significance of Female Historical Court Drama]," 电影文学 *[Movie Literature]*, no. 21 (2011): 112; Zhou, "宫廷剧中女性形象对都市白领女性形象的解构," 35; Cai, *Television Drama in Contemporary China*.

68. See Cai, *Television Drama in Contemporary China*; Zhu, Keane, and Bai, *TV Drama in China*, 77.

69. See Zhu Ying, *Television in Post-Reform China: Serial Dramas, Confucian Leadership and the Global Television Market* (London; New York: Routledge, 2008); Huang, "Pink Dramas."

70. See Marc Blecher, *China Against the Tides: Restructuring Through Revolution, Radicalism and Reform* (New York: Continuum, 2003); Huang, "Pink Dramas."

71. For more comprehensive inquiries on media in contemporary China, see, for instance, Stephanie Hemelryk Donald, Michael Keane, and Hong Yin, eds., *Media in China: Consumption, Content and Crisis* (London; New York: Routledge, 2014); Sun Wanning and Jenny Chio, eds., *Mapping Media in China: Region, Province, Locality* (London; New York: Routledge, 2012).

72. Specifically on art and culture work, the address, delivered on October 15, 2014, was reminiscent of the famous address by Mao in Yan'an on the same topic in 1942. See Xi's full address on: http://news.xinhuanet.com/politics/2015-10/14/c_1116825558.htm.

73. See Fan Yali (樊亚丽), "电视剧《欢乐颂》的人物形象塑造与时代美学精神 [The Construction of Character Image and the Spirit of Contemporary Aesthetics in TV Series 'Ode to Joy']," 当代电影 *[Contemporary Cinema]*, no. 7 (2016): 13.

74. Wu Changchang (吴畅畅), "欢乐颂:阅现实主义的'颂'歌? [Ode to Joy: Ode to Realism?]," 上海艺术家 *[Shanghai Yishujia]* 0, no. 4 (2016): 94–96.

75. Wu, "欢乐颂," 94.

76. *Ode to Joy* is an adaptation of an online novel with the same name, which was serialized from 2010 to 2012. The original writer, Anai, has refused interviews and her identity remains unknown. Rumour has it that she held a senior position in a major corporation, an allusion to the character

Andi created in her novel. All she ever disclosed was "I have been retired for a long time" (as cited in Dai Wei [戴维], "《欢乐颂》大结局了 我们和神秘的作者阿耐聊了聊 ["Ode to Joy" Finale: Chatting with the Mysterious Author A-Nai]," 都市快报 [Dushi Kuaibao], May 15, 2016). While largely following the original, the television adaptation also shows certain changes, some of which are to avoid political sensitive issues (see Wu, "《欢乐颂》热映背后的中国都市残酷物语."). For instance, in the novel, Andi's father is a government official with Cultural Revolution background; in the television drama, he is an economist. Fan's family problem is solved not by a local police officer as in the novel, but by a lawyer in the series. See also Yang Yang (楊洋), "《歡樂頌》編劇袁子彈: 人生沒有彎道超車 ["Ode to Joy" Scriptwriter Yuan Zidan: No Chicane Overtaking in Life]," 壹讀 [READ01.COM] (blog), May 19, 2016, https://read01.com/gNzjn5.html.

77. Yan Wei (闫伟), "《欢乐颂》为都市剧的创新探路 ["Ode to Joy" Discovering Innovative Pathways for Urban Drama]," 人民日报海外版 [People's Daily (Overseas Edition)], May 9, 2016, Overseas edition edition, http://paper.people.com.cn/rmrbhwb/html/2016-05/09/content_1677453.htm.

78. Li Yang (李阳), "一曲女性的欢歌—电视剧《欢乐颂》评析 [An Ode to Women—An Analysis of TV Series 'Ode to Joy']," 美与时代 [Beauty & Times] 0, no. 7 (2016): 121.

79. Lu Yuying (吕玉莹) and Zhao Qiang (赵强), "'伪女性主义'宣言书—浅析《欢乐颂》 ['Pseudo-Feminism' Manifesto—An Analysis of 'Ode to Joy']," 戏剧之家 [Home Drama], no. 19 (2016): 139.

80. Jing, "《欢乐颂》."

81. Li Huan (李欢), "浅析电视剧《欢乐颂》中女性形象的文化认知 [An Analysis of the Cultural Recognition of Female Images in TV Series 'Ode to Joy']," 大众文艺 [Dazhong Wenyi], no. 21 (2016): 205.

82. See also Pamela Robertson Wojcik's analysis of what she calls the "apartment plot" in American films and TV shows. In her book, Wojcik argues the mobilization of such apartment plot transforms the conception of home from privacy, stability, and family to visibility, mobility, and community. In Pamela Robertson Wojcik, The Apartment Plot: Urban Living in American Film and Popular Culture, 1945 to 1975 (Durham, NC: Duke University Press, 2010).

83. See Chap. 3 for a discussion on this popular generational paradigm in contemporary China: as post-80s, post-90s and so forth.

84. Jing, "《欢乐颂》," 65.

85. Liu Yuan (刘沅), "是'胜女',不是'剩女'—电视剧《欢乐颂》中樊胜美形象解读 [Is 'Winning Woman,' Not 'Leftover Woman'—Representational Analysis of Fan Shengmei in TV Series 'Ode to Joy']," 湖南大众传媒职

业技术学院学报 *[Journal of Hunan Mass Media Vocational Technical College]* 16, no. 5 (2016): 36–39.

86. The five protagonists—Andi, Fanjie, Xiaoqu, Guanguan, and Qiuyin—are performed by Tao Liu, Xin Jiang, Wang Ziwen, Zi Yang, and Xin Qiao.

87. Wu Daozi (吴稻子), "《欢乐颂》热映背后的中国都市残酷物语 [The Cruel Story of Chinese Cities behind the Popularity of 'Ode to Joy']," 端传媒 *[Initium Media]*, May 23, 2016, https://theinitium.com/article/20160523-mainland-huanlesong/. In addition, according to Fang et al., the decade from 2003 to 2013 saw a hike of 13.1 per cent in property prices in top-tier cities in China. For their examination of the housing market in urban China, see Hanming Fang et al., "Demystifying the Chinese Housing Boom," *NBER Macroeconomics Annual* 30, no. 1 (2016): 105–66.

88. Jing, "《欢乐颂》," 64.

89. Wu, "《欢乐颂》热映背后的中国都市残酷物语."

90. Clarence Tsui, "Celine Dion to Perform on China Central Television's New Year's Gala Show," *The Hollywood Reporter*, February 6, 2013, http://www.hollywoodreporter.com/news/celine-dion-perform-cctvs-new-419121.

91. See Zhang Lin and Anthony Fung, "The Myth of 'Shanzhai' Culture and the Paradox of Digital Democracy in China," *Inter-Asia Cultural Studies* 14, no. 3 (September 1, 2013): 401–16.

92. There are heated discussions on the alleged femininity of TF Boys in the Chinese cyberspace, for instance, here on Baidu, a major search engine in China, with the heading: *Why do we say TF Boys are feminine?* See: https://zhidao.baidu.com/question/624579474937514484.html.

93. For the opening act featuring the five actresses of *Ode to Joy*, see: https://www.youtube.com/watch?v=AHyIDjjPtow; for the dumpling fragment, see: https://www.youtube.com/watch?v=CQ0NgrWyr2A; for the chatting fragment, see: https://www.youtube.com/watch?v=4FEvGkWnaF8.

94. For a recent commentary related to this crisis, see Zheng Yuli, "'Save Our Boys': China's Made-up Masculinity Crisis," *Sixth Tone* (blog), July 31, 2017. Pointing to one central concern surrounding the annual college entrance examination *gaokao*: "Are the girls scoring higher or the boys," the author connects it to two components: the fear that "the boys are not performing as well as the girls in a variety of fields," and "the boys are increasingly losing their so-called masculine temperament." See an English version of Zeng's commentary on: http://www.sixthtone.com/news/1000562/save-our-boys-chinas-made-up-masculinity-crisis. For a recent investigation on the consequence of such masculinity crisis, see Tian Xiaoli and Deng Yunxue, "Organizational Hierarchy, Deprived

Masculinity, and Confrontational Practices: Men Doing Women's Jobs in a Global Factory," *Journal of Contemporary Ethnography* 46, no. 4 (2017): 464–89. Studying "men doing women's jobs" in a factory in China, Tian and Deng note a sense of deprived masculinity among the male workers who resort to offensive language, flirting, and sexual harassment as their defence tactics. For a related commentary, which understands the crisis of masculinity as a discursive device to divert attention from persistent gender issues under patriarchy, see Li Yinhe (李银河), "中国已经阴盛阳衰了吗? [Has China Already Become High in Femininity and Low in Masculinity?]," *李银河的博客 [Li Yinhe's Blog]* (blog), June 4, 2018, http://liyinhe.blog.caixin.com/archives/181848.

95. Chow Yiu Fai, "Subcultures: Role of Media," in *The International Encyclopedia of Media Effects* (New Jersey: John Wiley & Sons, Inc., 2017).
96. Erich Goode and Nachman Ben-Yehuda, "Moral Panics: Culture, Politics, and Social Construction," *Annual Review of Sociology* 20 (1994): 149–71.
97. See "延展思考的时空尺度 文化起飞 [Extending Thinking on Time and Space: A Cultural Takeoff]," *工商时报 [Gongshang Shibao]*, March 17, 2014, http://www.chinatimes.com/cn/newspapers/20140317000072-260202.
98. See Gladys Pak Lei Chong, *Chinese Subjectivities and the Beijing Olympics* (London: Rowman & Littlefield International, 2017).
99. The upfront, thus a visually larger, fatter and supposedly less attractive face.
100. Celia Hatton, "Boyfriends for Hire to Beat China's Wedding Pressure," *BBC News*, February 7, 2013, sec. China, http://www.bbc.com/news/world-asia-china-21192131.
101. Chow Yiu Fai, "Hope Against Hopes: Diana Zhu and the Transnational Politics of Chinese Popular Music," *Cultural Studies* 25, no. 6 (2011): 803.

REFERENCES

"2016年全国新闻出版业基本情况 [Overview of the National Press and Publication Industry in 2016]." 国家新闻出版广电总局 [State Administration of Press, Publication, Radio, Film and Television], 2017. http://www.sapprft.gov.cn/sapprft/govpublic/6677/1633.shtml.

Berry, Chris. "Representing Chinese Women: Researching Women in the Chinese Cinema." In *Dress, Sex and Text in Chinese Culture*, edited by Antonia Finnane, 198–211. Clayton: Monash Asia Institute, 1999.

Berry, Chris, and Mary Ann Farquhar. *China on Screen: Cinema and Nation.* New York, NY: Columbia University Press, 2006.

Blecher, Marc. *China Against the Tides: Restructuring Through Revolution, Radicalism and Reform.* New York: Continuum, 2003.

Cai, Shenshen. *Television Drama in Contemporary China: Political, Social and Cultural Phenomena.* London; New York: Routledge, 2016.

Chen, Guiqin (陈桂琴). "试论女性时尚杂志中的女性角色问题 [Discussions on the Issues of Female Characters in Women Fashion Magazines]." 新闻学硕士论文 [MA thesis of Journalism], 暨南大学 [Chi Nan University], 2003.

Chen, Siyu. "Disciplining Desiring Subjects through the Remodeling of Masculinity: A Case Study of a Chinese Reality Dating Show." *Modern China* 43, no. 1 (2017): 95–120.

Chen, Zhou. "The Embodiment of Transforming Gender and Class: Shengnü and Their Media Representation in Contemporary China." Thesis, University of Kansas, 2011.

Cheng, Hong, and Guofang Wan. "Holding up Half of the 'Ground': Women Portrayed in Subway Advertisements in China." In *Commercializing Women: Images of Asian Women in the Media,* edited by Katherine Toland Frith and Kavita Karan. USA: Hampton Press, 2008.

Chong, Gladys Pak Lei. *Chinese Subjectivities and the Beijing Olympics.* London: Rowman & Littlefield International, 2017.

Chow, Rey. "Fetish Power Unbound: A Small History of 'Woman' in Chinese Cinema." In *The Oxford Handbook of Chinese Cinemas,* edited by Carlos Rojas and Eileen Chow. Oxford Handbooks. Oxford, New York: Oxford University Press, 2013.

Chow, Yiu Fai. "Hope Against Hopes: Diana Zhu and the Transnational Politics of Chinese Popular Music." *Cultural Studies* 25, no. 6 (2011): 783–808.

Chow, Yiu Fai. "Subcultures: Role of Media." In *The International Encyclopedia of Media Effects.* New Jersey: John Wiley & Sons, Inc., 2017.

Dai, Jinhua. "Imagined Nostalgia." Translated by Judy T. H. Chen. *Boundary 2* 24, no. 3 (1997): 143–61.

Dai, Jinhua (戴锦华). "不可见的女性:当代中国电影中的女性与女性的电影 [Invisible Women: Women and Female Films in Contemporary Chinese Cinema]." *当代电影 [Contemporary Cinema]*, no. 6 (1994): 37–45.

Dai, Jinhua (戴锦华). "性别与叙事:当代中国电影中的女性 [Gender and Narration: Women in Contemporary Chinese Films]." *天涯 [Tianya]* 11, no. 5 (2003).

Dai, Wei (戴维). "《欢乐颂》大结局了 我们和神秘的作者阿耐聊了聊 ["Ode to Joy" Finale: Chatting with the Mysterious Author A-Nai]." *都市快报 [Dushi Kuaibao]*. May 15, 2016. http://hzdaily.hangzhou.com.cn/dskb/html/2016-05/15/content_2263672.htm.

Donald, Stephanie Hemelryk, Yin Hong, and Michael Keane, eds. *Media in China: Consumption, Content and Crisis*. London; New York: Routledge, 2014.

Fan, Lu (范璐). "江苏卫视下战书:《非诚勿扰》不怕模仿 [Jiangsu Television Welcomes Competition: 'If You Are the One' Is Not Afraid to Be Imitated]." *Shanxi Wanbao [山西晚报]*, May 27, 2010. http://media.people.com.cn/GB/40724/11715400.html.

Fan, Yali (樊亚丽). "电视剧《欢乐颂》的人物形象塑造与时代美学精神 [The Construction of Character Image and the Spirit of Contemporary Aesthetics in TV Series 'Ode to Joy']." 当代电影 *[Contemporary Cinema]*, no. 7 (2016): 13–19.

Fang, Hanming, Quanlin Gu, Wei Xiong, and Li-An Zhou. "Demystifying the Chinese Housing Boom." *NBER Macroeconomics Annual* 30, no. 1 (2016): 105–66.

Ferguson, Marjorie. *Forever Feminine: Women's Magazines and the Cult of Femininity*. Exeter, NH: Heinemann, 1983.

Ferry, Megan M. "Advertising, Consumerism and Nostalgia for the New Woman in Contemporary China." *Continuum* 17, no. 3 (2003): 277–90.

Goode, Erich, and Nachman Ben-Yehuda. "Moral Panics: Culture, Politics, and Social Construction." *Annual Review of Sociology* 20 (1994): 149–71.

Guo, Shaohua. "When Dating Shows Encounter State Censors: A Case Study of If You Are the One." *Media, Culture & Society* 39, no. 4 (2017): 487–503.

Han, Yujuan (韩玉娟). "新世纪家庭伦理剧女性形象变迁 [Changes of Female Representation in Family Drama of the New Century]." 艺术科技 *[Yishu Keji]*, no. 3 (2015): 52–53.

Hatton, Celia. "Boyfriends for Hire to Beat China's Wedding Pressure." *BBC News*, February 7, 2013, sec. China. http://www.bbc.com/news/world-asia-china-21192131.

Hooper, Beverley. "Flower Vase and Housewife: Women and Consumerism in Post-Mao China." In *Gender and Power in Affluent Asia*, edited by Krishna Sen and Maila Stivens, 167–93. London: Routledge, 1998.

Hu, Xin (胡辛), and He Jing (何静). "难以超越的性别视角-1949年后中国男导演的女性电影叙事管窥 [Unsurpassable Gender Perspective: Female Narration by Chinese Male Directors since 1949]." 江西社會科學 *[Jianxi Social Science]*, no. 8 (2008).

Huang, Ya Chien. "Pink Dramas: Reconciling Consumer Modernity and Confucian Womanhood." In *TV Drama in China*, edited by Ying Zhu, Michael Keane, and Ruoyun Bai, 103–14. Hong Kong: Hong Kong University Press, 2008.

Huang, Ying (黄颖). "镜像内外的困囿与突围—论新世纪以来中国电影中的女性形象 [The Restraint and Breakout Inside/Outside of the Mirror: On Female Representation of Contemporary Chinese Cinema]." 当代电影 *[Contemporary Cinema]*, no. 12 (2016): 142–45.

Hung, Kineta, and Stella Yiyan Li. "Images of the Contemporary Woman in Advertising in China." *Journal of International Consumer Marketing* 19, no. 2 (2006): 7–28.

Jiang, Xiaobin (蒋肖斌). "从《电视红娘》到《非诚勿扰》—电视相亲节目的历史考察 [From 'Television Matchmaker' to 'If You Are the One': A Historical Investigation of Television Dating Shows]." *现代视听 [Xiandai Shiting]*, no. 9 (2011): 43–46.

Jing, Ji (荆棘). "《欢乐颂》:一碗现实主义的毒鸡汤 ['Ode to Joy': A Bowl of Realist Poison Chicken Soup]." *齐鲁周刊 [Wilu Zhoukan]*, no. 19 (2016): 64–65.

Johansson, Perry. "Chinese Women and Consumer Culture: Discourses on Beauty and Identity in Advertising and Women's Magazines 1985–1995." Doctoral thesis, Stockholms universitet, 1998.

Keane, Michael. "Television Drama in China: Remaking the Market." *Media International Australia* 115, no. 1 (2005): 82–93.

Kitson, Peter J. *Forging Romantic China: Sino-British Cultural Exchange 1760–1840*. Cambridge: Cambridge University Press, 2013.

Kops, Manfred, and Stefan Ollig. *Internationalization of the Chinese TV Sector*. Berlin: LIT Verlag Münster, 2007.

Lewis, Tania, Fran Martin, and Wanning Sun. *Telemodernities: Television and Transforming Lives in Asia*. Durham: Duke University Press, 2016.

Li, Huan (李欢). "浅析电视剧《欢乐颂》中女性形象的文化认知 [An Analysis of the Cultural Recognition of Female Images in TV Series 'Ode to Joy']." *大众文艺 [Dazhong Wenyi]*, no. 21 (2016): 205.

Li, Luzhou. "If You Are the One: Dating Shows and Feminist Politics in Contemporary China." *International Journal of Cultural Studies* 18, no. 5 (2015): 519–35.

Li, Yang (李阳). "一曲女性的欢歌—电视剧《欢乐颂》评析 [AAn Ode to Women—An Analysis of TV Series 'Ode to Joy']." *美与时代 [Beauty & Times]*, no. 7 (2016): 120–21.

Li, Yinhe (李银河). "中国已经阴盛阳衰了吗?[Has China Already Become High in Femininity and Low in Masculinity?]." *李银河的博客 [Li Yinhe's Blog]* (blog), June 4, 2018. http://liyinhe.blog.caixin.com/archives/181848.

Liebler, Carol M., Wei Jiang, and Li Chen. "Beauty, Binaries, and the Big Screen in China: Character Gender in Feature Films." *Asian Journal of Communication* 25, no. 6 (2015): 584–99.

Ling, Qi. "A New Dynamic of Gender Discourses? A Textual Analysis of the Representation of Shengnü in Television Dramas and Women's Magazines' Websites." MPhil diss., The Chinse University of Hong Kong, 2013.

Liu, Yuan (刘沅). "是'胜女',不是'剩女'—电视剧《欢乐颂》中樊胜美形象解读 [Is 'Winning Woman,' Not 'Leftover Woman'—Representational Analysis of Fan Shengmei in TV Series 'Ode to Joy']." *湖南大众传媒职业技术学院学报 [Journal of Hunan Mass Media Vocational Technical College]* 16, no. 5 (2016): 36–39.

Lu, Yuying (吕玉莹), and Zhao Qiang (赵强). "'伪女性主义'宣言书——浅析《欢乐颂》['Pseudo-Feminism' Manifesto—An Analysis of 'Ode to Joy']." 戏剧之家 *[Home Drama]*, no. 19 (2016): 139–41.

Lull, James. *China Turned On: Television, Reform and Resistance.* London: Routledge, 2013.

Luo, Wei. "Packaged Glamour: Constructing the Modern Bride in China's Bridal Media." *Asian Women* 28, no. 4 (2012): 83–115.

Luo, Wei, and Zhen Sun. "Are You the One? China's TV Dating Shows and the Sheng Nü's Predicament." *Feminist Media Studies* 15, no. 2 (2015): 239–56.

Luo, Yunjuan (罗韵娟), and Hao Xiaoming (郝晓鸣). "媒体女性形象塑造与社会变革—《中国妇女》杂志封面人物形象的实证研究 [Shaping Women's Image in Media and The Social Revolution—An Empirical Study of the Cover Figure's Image from Women of China]." 中国传媒报告 *[China Media Report]* 1 (2015): 87–99.

Ma, Yan (马艳). "女性励志剧中的人物功能分析 [Analysis of the Characters in Female Empowering Drama]." 中国电视 *[China Television]*, no. 2 (2009): 36–40.

McRobbie, Angela. "Jackie: An Ideology of Adolescent Femininity." In *Popular Culture: Past and Present*, edited by Bernard Waites, Tony Bennett, and Graham Martin, 263–83. London: Croom Helm, 1982.

Mulvey, Laura. *Visual and Other Pleasures.* London: Macmillan, 1975.

Qin, Xiaohong (秦晓红). "女性生存状态的中国镜像—论中国电影中的女性形象建构 [Chinese Mirror of Female Existence—On the Construction of Female Images in Chinese Films]." 湖南社会科学 *[Hunan Shehui Kexue]* 3, no. 44 (2006): 138–41.

Scotton, James F., and William A. Hachten. *New Media for a New China.* Chichester: Wiley-Blackwell, 2010.

Sun, Lu (孙璐). "论当代传媒中女性刻板印象的嬗变 [On Changing Female Stereotypes in Contemporary Media]." 传播学硕士论文 [MA thesis of Communication Studies], 苏州大学 [Soochow University], 2004.

Sun, Shengwei, and Feinian Chen. "Reprivatized Womanhood: Changes in Mainstream Media's Framing of Urban Women's Issues in China, 1995–2012." *Journal of Marriage and Family* 77, no. 5 (2015): 1091–1107.

Sun, Wanning, and Jenny Chio. *Mapping Media in China: Region, Province, Locality.* London; New York: Routledge, 2012.

Tan, See Kam, Peter X. Feng, and Gina Marchetti. "Introduction." In *Chinese Connections: Critical Perspectives on Film, Identity, and Diaspora*, edited by See Kam Tan, Peter X. Feng, and Gina Marchetti, 1–5. Philadelphia, PA: Temple University Press, 2009.

Tian, Xiaoli, and Yunxue Deng. "Organizational Hierarchy, Deprived Masculinity, and Confrontational Practices: Men Doing Women's Jobs in a Global Factory." *Journal of Contemporary Ethnography* 46, no. 4 (2017): 464–89.

Tsui, Clarence. "Celine Dion to Perform on China Central Television's New Year's Gala Show." *The Hollywood Reporter*, February 6, 2013. http://www.hollywoodreporter.com/news/celine-dion-perform-cctvs-new-419121.

Wang, Pan. "Inventing Traditions: Television Dating Shows in the People's Republic of China." *Media, Culture & Society* 39, no. 4 (2017): 504–19.

Wang, Tianyue (王天玥). "电视剧《欢乐颂》的意识形态色彩研究 [A Study on the Ideological Colors of TV Drama 'Ode to Joy']." *西部广播电视 [Xibu Guangbo Dianshi]*, no. 9 (2016): 100.

Wang, Zhenzhen (王臻真). "消费文化中的性别图景——近年中国电影中的女性形象 [Gender Images in Consumer Culture—Female Representation in Recent Chinese Films]." *当代文坛 [Dangdai Wentan]*, no. 1 (2015): 103–9.

Watanabe, Yasushi, and David L. McConnell, eds. *Soft Power Superpowers*. Armonk, NY: M.E. Sharpe, 2008.

Wei, Qiong (危琼). "报纸对'剩女'的媒介形象塑造 [The Media Representation of 'Shengnü' Image by News]." *新闻世界 [News World]*, no. 9 (2010): 112–14.

Wen, Lifang (温丽芳). "电视相亲节目的前世今生 [The Past and Present of Television Dating Shows]." *山西晚报 [Shanxi Wanbao]*, February 27, 2010.

Winship, Janice. *Inside Women's Magazines*. London: Pandora Press, 1987.

Wojcik, Pamela Robertson. *The Apartment Plot: Urban Living in American Film and Popular Culture, 1945 to 1975*. Durham, NC: Duke University Press, 2010.

Wu, Changchang (吴畅畅). "欢乐颂:一阕现实主义的'颂'歌? [Ode to Joy: Ode to Realism?]." *上海艺术家 [Shanghai Yishujia]* 0, no. 4 (2016): 94–96.

Wu, Daozi (吴稻子). "《欢乐颂》热映背后的中国都市残酷物语 [The Cruel Story of Chinese Cities behind the Popularity of 'Ode to Joy']." *端传媒 [Initium Media]*, May 23, 2016. https://theinitium.com/article/20160523-mainland-huanlesong/.

Wu, Doreen D., and Agatha Man-kwan Chung. "Hybridized Images: Representations of the 'Modern Woman' across Mainland China and Hong Kong TV Commercials." *Journal of Asian Pacific Communication* 21, no. 2 (2011): 177–95.

Wu, Jing. "Post-Socialist Articulation of Gender Positions: Contested Public Sphere of Reality Dating Shows." In *Women and the Media in Asia*, 220–36. London: Palgrave Macmillan, 2012.

Xiong, Yan (熊艳). "《非诚勿扰》何以领跑收视冠军 [How Does 'If You Are the One' Remain a Rating Champion]." *视听 [Shiting]* 0, no. 6 (2013): 26–27.

Yan, Wei (闫伟). "《Q: 欢乐颂》为都市剧的创新探路 ["Ode to Joy" Discovering Innovative Pathways for Urban Drama]." *人民日报海外版 [People's Daily (Overseas Edition)]*. May 9, 2016, Overseas edition edition, sec. 12. http://paper.people.com.cn/rmrbhwb/html/2016-05/09/content_1677453.htm.

Yang, Yan (羊艳). "解读女性宫廷剧的大众文化意义 [Deconstructing the Popular Culture Significance of Female Historical Court Drama]." *电影文学 [Movie Literature]*, no. 21 (2011): 111–12.

Yang, Yang (楊洋). "《欢乐颂》编剧袁子弹:人生没有弯道超车 ['Ode to Joy' Scriptwriter Yuan Zidan: No Chicane Overtaking in Life]." 壹讀 [READ01. COM] (blog), May 19, 2016. https://read01.com/gNzjn5.html.

Ye, Zi (叶子). "《欢乐颂2》难复第一季辉煌?主创聊季播探索之路 ['Ode to Joy 2' Unable to Attain the Height of Season One? Show Creator Discusses the Initial Exploration of the Show]." 新浪娱乐 [Sina Entertainment] (blog), June 7, 2017. http://ent.sina.com.cn/v/m/2017-06-07/doc-ifyfuzmy2393679. shtml.

Zeng, Yuli. "'Save Our Boys': China's Made-up Masculinity Crisis." Sixth Tone (blog), July 31, 2017. http://www.sixthtone.com/news/1000562/save-our-boys-chinas-made-up-masculinity-crisis.

Zhang, Kai (张开). "女性观众喜爱电视剧成因分析 [A Study on the Reasons Why Television Drama Series Are Popular among Female Audiences]." 现代传播:中国传媒大学学报 [Xiandai Chuanbo: Zhongguo Chuanmeidaxue Xuebao], no. 6 (2009): 65–68.

Zhang, Lin, and Anthony Fung. "The Myth of 'Shanzhai' Culture and the Paradox of Digital Democracy in China." Inter-Asia Cultural Studies 14, no. 3 (2013): 401–16.

Zhang, Lin, Pataradech "Tony" Srisupandit, and Debra Cartwright. "A Comparison of Gender Role Portrayals in Magazine Advertising: The United States, China and Thailand." Management Research News 32, no. 7 (2009): 683–700.

Zhang, Yuanyuan (张媛媛). "浅析几部国产电影中的女性角色 [On the Female Roles in Several Chinese Domestic Films]." 云南农业大学学报 [Yunnan Nongye Daxue Xuebao] 4, no. 6 (2010): 88–90.

Zhang, Yuliang (张裕亮). "铁姑娘、贤内助、时尚女—中国女性杂志建构的女性形象 [Iron Lady, Better Half and Fashion Girl: Women's Image in Women's Magazines in China]." China Media Report Overseas 6, no. 1 (2010): 79–94.

Zhou, Ting (周婷). "宫廷剧中女性形象对都市白领女性形象的解构—基于34位都市白领女性对《后宫甄嬛传》看法研究 [The Deconstruction of Metropolitan White Collar Female Image in Historical Court Drama—A Study Based on the Analysis of 34 White Collar Female on 'Empresses in the Palace']." 声屏世界 [Voice and Screen World], no. 7 (2014): 35–37.

Zhou, Xuelin. "'From behind the Wall' The Representation of Gender and Sexuality in Modern Chinese Film." Asian Journal of Communication 11, no. 2 (2009): 1–17.

Zhu, Ying. Television in Post-Reform China: Serial Dramas, Confucian Leadership and the Global Television Market. London; New York: Routledge, 2008.

Zhu, Ying, and Chris Berry. TV China. Bloomington, IN: Indiana University Press, 2009.

Zhu, Ying, Michael Keane, and Ruoyun Bai, eds. TV Drama in China. Hong Kong: Hong Kong University Press, 2008.

"中国广告媒体新世代(一): 新媒体刺激市场需求 [New Generation of Advertising Media in China (I): New Media Stimulate Market Demand]." *商贸全接触 [Hong Kong Means Business]* (blog), April 21, 2016. http://hkmb.hktdc.com/tc/1X0A5VYH.

"延展思考的时空尺度 文化起飞 [Extending Thinking on Time and Space: A Cultural Takeoffc]." *工商时报 [Gongshang Shibao]*, March 17, 2014. http://www.chinatimes.com/cn/newspapers/20140317000072-260202.

CHAPTER 3

Living with a Generation—*Qilinghou, Balinghou, Jiulinghou*

"I think it makes good sense to talk about a generation. Our generation. I know people are quite different, but there are things that our generation must accept."
Jennifer *(born in 1975).*

"We post-1980s know a lot, but sometimes it's hard to put it into practice. We are not like the post-1970s."
Michelle *(born in 1983).*

"Yes, I always want to start up my own business. Perhaps I wasn't this sure, but once I started, I knew I liked this. I like being responsible for my own staff, for everyone. I want to make the company big, and get it listed."
Skipper *(born in 1991).*

I opened this chapter with three quotations from three of the single women I spoke with. We will get to know them later; here, I have introduced them to launch the start of the empirical and analytical core of this book: an investigation of the experiences of single women in creative work along the generational paradigm. This is a data-driven choice. During the initial fieldwork, something struck me: many of my subjects spoke generationally. Their generational discourses are not only a matter of age in the personal, individual sense, but also bound up with a very historical weft that is specific to China; for instance, the post-1990s (*jiulinghou* 九零后)

© The Author(s) 2019
Chow Y. F., *Caring in Times of Precarity*, Palgrave Studies in Globalization, Culture and Society,
https://doi.org/10.1007/978-3-319-76898-4_3

with their confidence and earnestness to do start-up projects; the post-1980s (*balinghou* 八零后) with the introduction of the one-child policy; the post-1970s (*qilinghou* 七零后) with the intertwining of the lives of their contemporaries towards the end of the Cultural Revolution. While this underscores the need to explore the lives of these Chinese women in those temporal and epochal lights, it may also testify to the discursive power of "generation"—and particularly, "Chinese generations."

This chapter continues with a critical account of studies that seek to employ social generations as an important, if not dominant, way to analyse (young) people's relationship with their life courses. The chapter moves on to insert the Chinese case where, as if in correspondence with the increasing popularity of such generational theories, terms grounded in temporality and epochality emerged and circulated widely in contemporary China: terms such as *jiulinghou, balinghou, qilinghou*. Academic studies and popular books were published to demarcate, define, and problematize these generations of Chinese youth.[1] This chapter outlines the genealogies of such terms and reviews this collection of publications. Meanwhile, as cued by my subjects, historical features, such as the one-child policy, economic reforms and growth, start-up culture, and the increasing participation in processes of globalization will be documented to configure a wider context to understand their subjective accounts as single women doing creative work. In this wider, historical context, Chap. 3 will present these women's narration of their generational experiences. Based on insights thus gained, the chapter will examine the usefulness of such generational theories as well as their limitations.

GENERATION XYZ

Baby Boomers, Generation X, Generation Y, Generation Z. Just this morning, as I indulged my habit of reading the weekend edition of a Dutch newspaper, I read a four-page feature on the "millennials," presumably referring to those born between 1980 and 2000.[2] "Also known as Generation Y," so opens the feature, "millennials," however, are more about a subgroup of twenty-somethings, who are "young, smart, and full of doubts," living between "choices, uncertainty and stress."[3] In another article on career stress, an "experience expert" pinpoints the abundance of choices, and thus, the challenges of having to choose, as the major source of stress for his generation of twenty- and thirty-somethings.[4] The evocation of generation in such catchy phrases, and as an explanatory framework, has become quite an indispensable feature in Western media, and through the globalization of media, also in media elsewhere. It is not only in news or other popular media that these collective terms are used; academically, the so-called generational paradigm or theory is applied to "a wide range of diverse disciplines and areas of study,"[5] often literally in the "applied" sense, such as analysing consumption behaviours of different generations.[6]

In itself, "generation" is an old term. According to David Kertzer, the concept of generation enjoys a "privileged place" in Western societies with its "codification in the Bible," and in "the most disparate societies of Africa, Asia and Australia," the concept is incorporated into their "notions of social order."[7] However, its more recent revival in academic and popular discourse is usually attributed to the seminal work by German sociologist Karl Mannheim, published originally in German in 1928, and its English translation published in 1952.[8] While the term generation has become, in our time, something like a ready answer to many phenomena, its emergence as a concept started off as a series of questions. What makes a generation? What makes people born in the same period of time a generation? Towards such a series of questions, which were raised by the end of nineteenth century, Mannheim's work proffers the key definition for future scholars. Among the numerous contemporary studies that cite Mannheim as their theoretical grounding, I will confine myself to two.

Outlining the theoretical underpinning for an investigation into the post-1980s generation in China, Lian Hongping observes four key points in Mannheim's conception of generation.[9] First, generational consciousness is fostered in a major disruption of social continuity. Second, such consciousness evolves during the formative years of one's life, when one is young. Third, these young people take such consciousness with them throughout their lives. And fourth, generations are not homogenous, and there are intra-generational differences, which Mannheim calls "stratification of experience."[10] In their lead article for a special issue on intergenerational inequality, Camille Peugny and Cècile van de Velde focus on the genealogy of Mannheim's conception of generation throughout the twentieth century: from consciousness, through values, to inequality.[11] Mannheim, according to the authors, distinguishes two levels of the generation-making process. Those who are born at the same period of time share the same "generation status"—the first level. Their potential to form a generation is actualized when they partake in a "common destiny," shaped by historical and social developments, and their experiences to become the "generation as actuality"—the second level.[12] If "conscious-ness" was the keyword for the earliest generational understanding, Peugny and van de Velde foreground "values" as the new keyword when the con-cept resurfaced in the 1950s and 1960s due to its intricate connections with the many youth social movements of those decades. Samuel Eisenstadt's influential book *From Generation to Generation*, published in 1956, uses the term "generational" "to offer what is in effect a compara-tive analysis of social youth movements depending on the type of societies and forms of social integration they propose."[13] The shift of the accent onto values also led to what Margaret Mead calls the "generation gap,"[14] morphing into generational conflict, ultimately—with the emergence of a generation of young people, by the end of 1960s through the 1970s, blessed with the democratization of education, and yet, frustrated with employment opportunities—towards the focus on socioeconomic inequal-ity between generations.

For all its popularity in academic and popular discourse, the notion of "generation" remains an ongoing contention, a powerful but slippery concept.[15] One common line of questioning is its lack of precision and easy conflation with a cluster of similar terms. Kertzer, for instance, notes the multiple meanings of "generation" found in sociological literature and seeks to clarify the term into four categories: "generation as a principle of kinship descent; generation of cohort; generation as life stage; and genera-tion as historical period."[16] However, despite his and others' attempts towards conceptual clarification, he predicts somewhat pessimistically that "the term continues to be employed in a polysemous manner guaranteed to sow confusion."[17]Another critique pinpoints the contribution of gen-erational thinking to youth studies, and paradoxically, its possible disser-vice at the same time. Johanna Wyn and Dan Woodman, whose important work has been instrumental in establishing the centrality of generational theory in the field of youth studies, rightly highlights its importance in breaking up the old model of conceptualizing youth as a linear, transi-tional period to adulthood, relocating young people "within specific sets of economic, social, cultural and political conditions."[18] At the same time, by shifting the analytical attention from biography to history, Alan France and Steven Roberts raise the tendency of generational theory or paradigm to overlook the impact of biographical dimensions on young people, such as class and gender.[19] They plead for an exploration of "the interrelation-ship between macro- and micro-processes that underpin the everyday social practice of young people."[20]

GENERATION POST-XXXX

The Chinese case is different—but not entirely—from the Western or "global" case. To resist the tempting pull of Chinese exceptionalism, I want to begin with the observation that terms such as Generation X, Y, and Z are also in circulation in China, applied to their Chinese contemporaries. Among academic studies, Dou Wenyu, Wang Guangping, and Zhou Nan, for instance, investigate the media consumption patterns of China's Generation X consumers.[21] There are other studies that note the different historical trajectory China took, and propose different categorical frameworks. Sometimes, they are entirely distinct from the mainstream Western usage, for instance, the generations of "the era with limited choice, the great Gatsby and the dreamers" corresponding, respectively, to the China of pre-consumerism, that is, 1949–1976; the Golden Age of Chinese consumerism, that is, 1976–2011; and the post-consumerist China, that is, 2012–present.[22] Sometimes, the Chinese generations are delineated distinctly until they fold into the global configuration mirroring the integration of China itself into global cultural flows, such as: the Cultural Revolution generation (born during 1949–1966), the Transitional generation (1967–1978), and the Millennials (1979–1990),[23] and a variant of these—the Cultural Revolution generation (1961–1966), the Social Reform generation (1971–1976), and the Millennials (1981–1986).[24] While the latter two generational frameworks use the same global term "millennials," they have slightly different demarcations of the birth period, which are also different from the one proposed in the Dutch news report I came across. Another chronological way to name the Chinese generations is to draw a baseline at the Communist Revolution and the establishment of the People's Republic of China, and to call those growing up after 1949, symbolically, the First Generation, leading, sequentially, to those growing up after 1989 being the Fifth Generation.[25]

This variety of generational terms and frameworks is largely due to attempts by scholars to facilitate understanding of the Chinese case; they may be useful, but are inevitably top-down and artificial. As Yi Xiang's research team notes, "[i]n Chinese society, generations are usually labeled by birth decade, i.e. 'Born in the 1960s', 'Born in the 1970s' and 'Born in the 1980s'."[26] According to Stanley Rosen, these terms are now used in "virtually all areas of Chinese life to refer to individuals ... and phenomena."[27] Indeed, these are the terms emerging from society, that are catching on and eventually become part of the everyday lexicon that contemporary Chinese people use to describe their generations. I will continue using these vernacular terms to refer to the generations in the Chinese case. For the purposes of this book, I will discuss the three of them, to which my subjects are supposed to belong: *qilinghou*, *balinghou*, and *jiulinghou*. As is the case for many vernacular terms, it is difficult, if not impossible, to trace their origins with exactitude.

According to the sources I located, both *qilinghou* and *balinghou* emerged as collective labels for writers. Novelist Chen Wei, born in 1973, is alluded to as the one who started using the term *qilinghou* as the organizing principle for a literary magazine he launched in 1996.[28] In 2003, a young writer, Gong Xiaobing, built on Chen's term and referred to his own generation of writers as *balinghou*.[29] With the nationwide popularity of contemporary writers such as Han Han and Guo Jingming, the term "*balinghou* writer" caught on and became prominent on various media platforms. On February 2, 2004, 20-year-old Chun Shu became the first Chinese writer to appear on the cover of *Time Magazine*. In the feature entitled "Breaking Out: China's Youth Finally Dare to Be Different," Chun Shu and her contemporary, Han Han, were presented as being typical of a new generation of Chinese youth called *balinghou*.[30] Riding on the international validation of *Time Magazine* and the national nomenclatural popularity of *balinghou*, the other post-19XX terms became increasingly dominant in the media and in popular conceptions of the Chinese generations.[31] I will sieve the abundance of media report to outline dominant understandings of the three generations before we move on to the stories of the three generations of Chinese single women.

Qilinghou *(Post-1970s, Born Between 1970 and 1979)*

In many ways, this is an in-between generation, or in Zhu Qi's words, a "vacuum" generation. "On the one hand, traditional values from earlier generations are disappearing from the *qilinghou* generation; on the other hand, *qilinghou* have not yet developed their own characteristics."[32] Growing up in a China where people enjoyed better economic prospects and a more open society, this generation is, at the same time, confronted with the kind of moral struggles, social competition, and self-actualization that was unknown to their predecessors.[33]

Qilinghou were "born in an era of instability," as summarized in an article discussing the emergence of the Chinese generations, which configures their characteristics as "being resigned, conservative and persevering."[34]

Similarly pinpointing the burgeoning reform and opening up of China when *qilinghou* were born, the article explains their formative years as the time when China underwent radical transformations, and hence, their general values lean towards stability and conservatism.[35] Not always enjoying opportunities the later generations would take for granted (for instance, education), *qilinghou* tend to follow the aspirations of their fathers—namely, to work hard, to try hard, and to achieve upward mobility.[36]

Balinghou *(Post-1980s, Born Between 1980 and 1989)*

Compared with their predecessors, the post-1980s are considered more fortunate, in the sense that their childhood years were spent in a relatively stable China, where the economy took flight and communication technology landed.[37] At the same time, all this novelty also led them into uncharted territory, to a sense of being lost, and of not knowing what to do.[38] They are usually considered to be a problematic generation: "egotistic, irresponsible, myopic."[39] Confronted with a rapidly changing China, *balinghou* find the values they learned from their predecessors to be outmoded and unreliable, and yet, they are struggling to find their own. Thanks to the democratization of education, they were well trained but not necessarily well suited, they fear, to a good future.[40] In Lian Hongping's analysis, the dramatic social changes confronted by the post-1980s generation include an affluent economic life, a diversified cultural structure, the one-child policy, the mass production of education, globalization, and an open society.[41] While these changes largely correspond to the other analyses mentioned earlier, the one-child policy is particularly revealing.

According to Lian, *balinghou*'s experiences of growing up as the first generation of single children shape them in two significant ways. On the one hand, in the absence of big families, they relate to society at large, making them more susceptible to social trends and the media (strengthened by the arrival of communication technology such as television). On the other hand, "excessive care from parents reduces their experience of equal communication," contributing to their inability to empathize with others, and thus, to their egoism and individualistic tendencies.[42] Another report calls them "Little Emperors sitting atop a family pyramid of two doting parents and four eager-to-please grandparents," or the "Me Generation."[43] In this regard, a major theme that underwrites many surveys on the youth attitudes and behaviours of the post-1980s generation is "the inroads that Western culture has made into the belief systems of Chinese youth,"[44] which is, at the same time, a source of anxiety about the influence of Western political ideas such as liberalism and democracy, as well as a reason to celebrate the impact of global consumption on Chinese youth as an antidote to political restlessness. China joined the World Trade Organization in 2001. Indeed, the *balinghou* is also the generation that grew up in the aftermath of the Tiananmen Square Protests in 1989. To deal with their legitimacy crisis, as noted by Rosen, the Chinese regime took on cultural and economic forms from the West, and succeeded in incorporating many *balinghou* into the stratum of the "middle class"—the target audience of television drama and variety shows, as noted in Chap. 2—and during the process, into a generation of people individually struggling for their own well-being.[45]

Jiulinghou *(Post-1990s, Born Between 1990 and 1999)*

The Chinese youth born in the 1990s grew up in an economic and cultural environment not unlike that of their preceding generation. What distinguishes them is probably their clear pursuit of happiness.[46] In many ways, their living conditions are better, and the online world, enabled by a fast-developing internet system, affords them access to flows and quantities of information previously unheard of. Relatively unburdened by economic worries and political upheavals, they have learned to become more independent, more confident, and more free: free from the traditions that the post-1980s generation might still be confronted with, free to do what they aspire to. Very often, their aspirations are for "a successful career and high-quality life."[47] The potential tension between career and life, for the *jiulinghou*, should be resolved by three keywords: personal interest, freedom, and career development. Compared with the post-1970s and the post-1980s generations, for whom security and money are considered of primary importance amidst an urge to change, the post-1990s care and dare to pursue what they want: a better life, something more intrinsic than, for instance, a good income. As analysed by one report, the confidence of the *jiulinghou* is largely grounded in their being the only child of their parents, who are mostly post-1960s, at the peak of their earning capacity, and thus, providing robust financial support for their *jiulinghou* children.

Post-post

If the above outline of the Chinese generations prompts the reader to ask how distinct they actually are, this is as inevitable as it is understandable. While there are myriads of reports and studies, each seeking to define these three generations in a lucid manner, taken together, they often show inconsistencies and disparities, discombobulating, and inviting questions concerning intra- and intergenerational variations.

As such, I will conclude this account of the Chinese generations with a reminder. In a feature discussing *qilinghou, balinghou,* and *jiulinghou,* one of the contributing authors brings in what was then taking place in China, to question the usefulness or correctness of these labels. In 2008, when the feature was published, a serious earthquake hit Sichuan, causing severe casualties and damage. Recalling the participation of many young men and women of the post-1980s generation in front-line work helping earth-quake survivors, and the appeals of children, the post-1990s generation, at the disaster scene who urged, "help my classmate first," the author wonders how they would fulfil the egoist and apathetic images usually associated with these two Chinese generations,[48] gesturing to the limits of such popular labels to describe people of different ages. Nonetheless, they remain powerful discursive formations and explanatory frameworks, which were especially useful when I started meeting and listening to the women in Shanghai. I have selected three of these women, partly as their accounts index to similar narrations of their generational peers, partly as I intend to give more space for the readers to get acquainted with their experiences, to immerse themselves in their lives, and to know them. After all, this is the first time that the women in this book start talking to us, properly and substantially.

The Single Women Generations

Jennifer *(Born in 1975)*

I think it makes good sense to talk about a generation. Our generation. I know people are quite different, but there are things that our generation must accept. Our personalities, our thinking are connected to our past and what we experienced during our period of growing up. Let me call it social subconsciousness, a sort of collective subconsciousness. I didn't understand it at first, but later, I realized it's very important. In the Chinese subconsciousness of my parents' generation, as long as a woman stays single, she is a failure. However successful she is at work, as long as she is single, that means no man wants her. When a woman is not wanted by any man, what does that mean? It means she is ugly; it means she has many issues; it means she is picky...

I am 41. I was 23 when I got married. I was a fresh graduate, far too young, and totally inexperienced ... He was my neighbour. My parents introduced us. They were very traditional, they believed a girl should, well, in the 1990s in China, there was this wave of unemployment, what we call *xiagangchao*, don't know if you have heard of it?[49] My parents lost their jobs, and our family was in a very anxious state. We relied on our savings. My mother wanted to have me, her daughter, to earn money as soon as possible. But it wasn't a good time to find a job for anyone, not to mention for a fresh graduate. And then, my mother thought, OK then, get married. So, she introduced me to this man. I was very obedient, so I got married. He was born in 1970, five years older than me. It was ridiculous, but we indeed got married. It was a product of the time. My mother thought that his family conditions were quite alright, and our family was really in difficulties. In any case, a girl must get married and have her own family. My parents had a daughter and a son. They really believed that they lived for their children. This is exactly what I keep on telling myself: I live for myself ... After my mother passed away, my daughter told me: mom, you really should enter another phase of your life now. You used to be doing everything for the family, for granny, and for me. Now you should live for yourself. Even a child said that to me, I felt I was indeed too ... (sobbing.)

When my parents lost their jobs during *xiagangchao*, it was difficult for them. It's not like they didn't have any skills, but since they spent their lives working for the same state-run enterprise, in the same jobs, they trained up only one set of skills ...

Our move to Shanghai was rather coincidental. The parents of my husband were from Shanghai; same generation as my parents. They were both *zhiqing*.[50] My husband's father was from Shanghai, and his mother from Wuhan. So, they moved to Wuhan. And now with a different government policy, they wanted to go back to Shanghai. I was rather submissive and obedient, and I didn't have a job in Wuhan, so I thought it might be fun to move to Shanghai, and we did. In Wuhan, I only once got a short-term job, and since then, I failed to find any job again. Then, I got married and got pregnant ...

After we moved to Shanghai in 2000, my husband's family told me: "you've got to find a job, you can't always stay home." Well, they thought that I needed to find a job, to support myself. I also felt that I should. Actually, staying home all the time was not easy. I didn't know what to do. They helped me, as it's not easy for someone without any working experience to find a job. They helped me, and so, I started ...

Sometimes, I do imagine what it would be like if I hadn't left Wuhan. But then if I never left Wuhan and my parents, I would never have earned the money to take care of their illnesses ...

My husband became jobless in 2009. He had hated his job for a long time. Since he became jobless, we spent four very unhappy years together. In 2011, we divorced ... My parents were conservative; they thought I have a daughter and she should have a family, so no matter how my husband was, he's still the father of my child ... In the end, it was my husband who filed the divorce application, not me. He had been without a job for a long, long time, and he cared for nothing. It's me who supported our family, and our daughter. He was home every day, and he got depressed ... But when he filed the application, I refused to sign the papers. And according to Chinese law, it required the consent of both parties to get a divorce. There was pro-crastination ... At some point, your heart just shuts down, dead ... Finally, we were divorced. For two years, I didn't sleep well. I was blaming myself, but above all, I felt the unfairness. I did so well, why should I be treated this way? It was so unfair. I didn't really hate my daughter's father. I just asked myself why was I not good enough? I earned money, I supported the family, I took care of all the domestic chores, I didn't demand anything. Why did he treat me so unfairly? Why did God treat me so unfairly? ... Luckily, I got support from my friends. And after my husband filed the divorce applica-tion, my parents also changed their mind and offered me more support. I moved out, and lived on my own. I felt that I should not continue my old life, I should have a better life. It was the start ...

My father passed away last year. His death dealt me a big blow. He jumped to his death ... I guess he was suffering from depression. But for his genera-tion, it's not something you can talk about. He kept on suppressing his feelings, until he couldn't take it anymore. He had a very good relationship with my mother ... It was the time when my mother was diagnosed with cancer. My father was the one taking care of her, and my brother was still living with them ... It was just too much, too much pressure for him ... This January, my mother passed away. I know it's probably a very unfilial thing to say, but you know, I finally feel relieved.

Michelle *(Born in 1983)*

My undergraduate major was commercial English, mainly about trading and commerce, international trading kind of thing. My first job was foreign trading and merchandizing. It's very tough, very stressful. It's a foreign enterprise. After two years, I thought, "I am young, I don't have to stay in the same business ..." I wasn't worried at all. So I crossed over to the cultural circle. It's probably my rebellious genes. I felt that I didn't have to follow in the footsteps of my parents' generation. They stayed in the same job, at the same institution till they retired. I didn't want that kind of life. I wanted to try something new ...

Many people find me strange. Usually, when you change jobs, you get a better salary, a higher position. Why would I change to a job with worse terms? But then, I thought I liked the new job; first, because it had a more comfortable environment, and second, because they had good people. I did think about the salary. But then, maybe after a year or two, I may change again. My current state of mind is: I want to do something that is within my capability, something I can handle ...

For issues like getting married, I am very particular. Say, you want to marry me and have a child. Ok, I may agree with this demand, which is rather normal. But may I also raise my own demand that I don't want to have a child, or I don't want to have a child this early? Many men cannot accept this. Frankly, a lot of people get married because of reproduction. I always wonder why people should get married. Why can't they simply live together? ... I must emphasize that their attitude isn't wrong. Their mothers want to have grandchildren. They want to get married with you because they want a family, they want a child. But at this time, I don't want a child, I wouldn't like to have a child. Some friends of mine agreed to become a DINK [double income no kids] family before they got married. They shared the same attitude, and they found the right person. I think that's the perfect situation. I haven't had that kind of luck yet, I haven't found that kind of man ...

Pressure? If you talk about social pressure, basically, I have become sort of numb after so many setbacks. Some of my colleagues are post-1995, and they are married! Regarding family pressure, well, I think I am lucky. My parents have been good to me. They got to know each other through match-making. In three months' time, they got married. For their generation, it was considered late; they were 33. So, were they suited to each other? Not at all. One is a Taurus; the other, Gemini. They have very different values, very different temperaments. But they have survived. They often have quarrels, but they are old enough not to talk about divorce. Their sense of responsibility, sense of family is stronger than our generation's. My dad often tells me, "it's good to be on one's own." He also says if he didn't get married, he would be having a good life too … His only demand of me is: "be happy." He tells me not to care about having a family or not, because family may not add value to your sense of happiness; perhaps the opposite. "Don't make it difficult for yourself," he tells me … And my mom also, basically, she is not a good mother in the eyes of many people, she loves fun …

I was born in the 1980s. It was a time when China launched its reform policy, opening itself up. It's also an embarrassing time, somewhere between old and new. In my body, there is this clash between a more progressive way of thinking and a more traditional way of thinking. In the bodies of us *bailinghou*, there is this contradiction. We started having contact with foreign cultures, we started to know about the outside world. At the same time, we inherited traditional attitudes from our parents. That's the contradiction. On the one hand, we are doing something rather progressive. On the other hand, I am deeply traditional. And I can easily understand why other people are having such traditional thoughts. Just like I can easily understand why they think that getting married is to have descendants. It's only me, an individual, who fails to do it, who doesn't want it. That's it … We post-1980s know a lot, but sometimes, it's hard to put it into practice. We are not like the post-1970s. Their generation lived in the time when China still allowed families to have more than one child. We post-1980s are the generation of the one-child policy. It's sad, and our generation has become an experiment of the time. We are compelled by state policy to be the only child of the family. You know, I could have had a younger sister or younger brother. But due to official regulations, my mom had an abortion. Let's not talk about the human rights side; for me, my epoch has decided that from the day I was born, I would be alone …

Last year was a strange year for me. Within one week, I lost two family members: my aunt, my father's younger sister, and my grandpa. Within one week, in the same weekend, and I attended two funerals in a matter of three days. Both of them passed away right in front of me … Actually, during the past two years, I started to feel that people could leave you for ever. And I don't even dare to think of my parents leaving me. I often joke to my parents, I tell them: our goal is to go to an old people's home together; when I am 60, the three of us go there together and you both have to take care of me at least till I retire. I always tell my parents to take good care of themselves. I have to admit that I am not quite capable of taking care of them. I just hope we enjoy good health. It's just far too expensive to fall ill in

Shanghai … I always tell them, "your daughter doesn't earn much money, doesn't have many capabilities." I just hope that we three stay healthy …

These years, I haven't left Shanghai for any extended period of time. I haven't tried living and working outside Shanghai. I believe it's partly because of my parents. Sometimes, I do think, if one day they are no longer here, well, I don't have any siblings and I don't have any other family members that I must support, I may then pick up a backpack and go to any city, go somewhere I have never been to. And then, if I come across a place I like, I may simply settle down there. For now, my parents are still alive, they have a big impact on my life. It's not like I rely on them, but I feel, like what I said, some sort of tradition in my heart. I have strong feelings towards my parents. The three of us keep very close contact. Wherever we are, we stay in contact. On a daily basis. Like my dad, he just learned how to use WeChat and he is using it a lot to communicate with me. When I finish seeing some performance, for instance, he will send me a message, asking me where I am, when I go home, and so forth.

Skipper *(Born in 1991)*

I applied for a lot of art schools in the United States. I got scholarships from all of them … And I got an offer from quite a famous institution of art and design. Famous artists studied there. So, I went to New York City. My boyfriend was in NYC too, that's also why I wanted to study there. But later, he moved to Chicago, so I moved too … My major was game design; my minor was online programme design. My school was the biggest college of commercial art in the country … I found the disciplines I chose challenging. I started designing my own website when I was 18. I was in the third year of my senior secondary school. I drafted the template of this website. I also registered my own company at the same time. I needed to register the website template, and for this, we needed a registered company. My mom helped me. She said if I was serious, I should take this step …

When I was in my third year at university, I used that website for my graduation project. And I attracted an investor. He signed a contract with me when he visited the United States. So, I went back to China, as a kind of gap year. But after my return, I found out that the investor was unreliable, and the so-called contract was not legal. In the end, I broke up with him. But at that point, I had already formed my own team. I spent another two months to find new capital. And then, I started again … It took me six months to settle the contract problem with the first investor, though. My family is quite well-off. They offered me 1 million RMB to cover the expenses. Well, if my family couldn't have afforded it, then I might have had to leave it like that ... Yes, I always wanted to start up my own business. Perhaps I wasn't this sure, but once I started, I knew I liked this. I like being responsible for my own staff, for everyone. I want to make the company big, and get it listed... Our company's goal is to become the largest of its kind in China, to be the largest distribution platform and copyright dealer among the youth sectors. Our App is both a distribution platform and a copyright dealer. We carry a lot of original music. Our goal for this year is to occupy 20 per cent of the market share, and next year, another 20 per cent. I am only talking about the post-1990s and post-2000s in first-tier cities. Their populations are about 100 million. So, our goal is 20 million ...

I personally am very interested in opinion management in culture and media. Ten years ago, it was the old media. Now, it's the new media. But how it takes shape is yet to be seen. So, there are opportunities ... In cultural industries, if you want to have your own voice, you have to grab the opinion leaders. For us, our opinion leaders are the post-1990s and post-2000s living in first-tier cities. They set the trends, they make what's fashionable. We pass something to them, and they will pass it on ... This is the online business model. If you are able to really start up, you will earn the first batch of money. If you earn the most and become the first, you must kill the second, the third, and the fourth. Otherwise, you won't survive ...

We are free on Saturdays and Sundays. Only the marketing team has to be on duty all the time. Can't be otherwise, as we are doing online business. I need time off. I keep a rabbit. We all need to live. And I also need to do some skincare chores, to date people ... Our office is housed in a villa. Quite good, quite quaint. Many start-ups in Shanghai are housed in such villas. Perhaps it's related to the history of this city. But then, there are not so many success start-up stories in Shanghai. Perhaps we are not hardworking enough. Many of us care a lot about quality of life ... We were actually thinking of another office location, in a kind of start-up park. But we found out we didn't like that place enough. We would like to have an *ayi* to cook for us.[51] But there, we wouldn't have a kitchen. Here, we have a kitchen, we have space for sleeping; we have a bathroom. It's an entire villa ...

We often have to work overtime during the weekends. Basically, half a day. As for me, I am more free. But I still spend a lot of time on work. I also work during my free days. I work seven days a week, but I will balance it with my life. This is something that I can control ... I am also renting a whole villa as my residence, with someone from my company. A designer partner. It's in the best part of the French concession area. Expensive shops around ...

I broke up with my boyfriend the moment I returned to China. Actually, we broke up before my return. Now, I have two boyfriends—one in Shanghai, and one in Beijing, both stable. Probably they know of each other's existence. But I have never asked. Like, you are dating someone, and you tell him you are his girlfriend. He wouldn't ask you if you have another boyfriend, right? That would be a strange question. Usually, people don't ask that kind of question. Therefore, I don't need to tell them … Well, I am Pisces, can't really choose. It's difficult for me to say goodbye to either one of them. So, we stay together. We just continue to stay together, that's all. It's been more than a year, with both of them. I met the guy in Shanghai shortly after my return. Half a year later, I got to know the other guy in Beijing. I knew my Shanghai boyfriend from the IT circle. He's also busy with his start-up. My Beijing boyfriend also, he has his own business. Both are CEOs. But both of their companies are not running well, almost closing. Well, actually one already stopped, the other is about to. I am thinking of recruiting the Beijing guy to Shanghai. If he's in Shanghai, I may need to choose. It's complicated. I want to discuss with my Shanghai boyfriend about an open relationship. My Beijing boyfriend is OK, he has a girlfriend in Beijing too …

A fortune teller told me I would get married when I was 26. That is two years from now. I believe him. It's better to believe him than anyone else. I grew up in Guangdong, my dad was from there. We believe in fortune telling. He also told me I would be doing fine, I would be rich. Seems he's right. My parents do not put pressure on me. Probably they also believe in the fortune teller. Then, just wait for two more years. Actually, my parents think that I spend too much time on my boyfriends. I like my life now. Being single is good. I like it. This is the kind of life I choose.

MORE THAN GENERATIONAL

The "work hard, try hard, move upward" spirit of the *qilinghou*, the in-betweenness of tradition and modernity of the *balinghou*, the confident, free, and above all, carefree *jiulinghou*—in many ways, these values do form some threads running through the self-narrations of Jennifer, Michelle, and Skipper. In many ways, they do offer evidence to validate the relevance of the generational paradigm in the Chinese case of post-1970s, -1980s, and -1990s. It is also clear in their self-narrations that generational thinking occupies an important role, and the specific terms of *qilinghou*, *balinghou*, and *jiulinghou* find their place here and there. But then, I must hasten to add the following. When I think of all the stories I have listened to during my fieldwork, I may also choose not to tease out the running threads of generations, but to be bewildered by the warp and woof of a far more complicated fabric called life.

Let me use Skipper's account to illustrate the limitations of the generational paradigm. I will take two particular articulations of her love and work life as starting points. To begin with, Skipper mentions her current relationship with two men who are based in two cities. She is managing this love life of hers without any clear longing for a heteronormative future, supported, one may argue, by the typical surety of *jiulinghou*, who pursue what they like and consider to be a better life. Skipper's contemporary, Siqi, a journalist born in 1991, had a relationship for some years. Disagreeing on the prospect of marriage—she did not want to get married—they split up. In this sense, Siqi is as sure as Skipper. Siqi also presents her parents as "understanding" people who do not interfere with her current single life. However, when she once joked with her mother that she would not consider marriage at all, her mother rejected the idea as "irrational." While not exerting direct pressure on her, her mother did try to arrange possible marriage partners for Siqi to meet. She declined. Her mother did not persist. Siqi's friend, Jiayin, has more problems and less confidence in dealing with her relationship and her family. Born in 1990, one year older than Siqi and Skipper, Jiayin is a designer whose dream is to go and live in New York City before she turns 30. However, she did not share the dream with her family or with her boyfriend. Her boyfriend, born in 1992, is a "traditional Chinese man." Even though they started their relationship only a few months before our interview took place, he was already proposing to spend Chinese New Year with Jiayin's family at her hometown, an act signifying a stable relationship and matrimonial intentions, if not an actual arrangement. However, Jiayin still dreams of going to New York and she would like to keep "a loving relationship," meaning not wanting to rush into marital life, which, to her, usually seems to kill the spark of love. Her mother, on the other hand, has been putting pressure on her. She keeps on asking Jiayin if she has a boyfriend. Jiayin only gives her a simple "yes," without providing further information, "not even a photo." Jiayin knows all too well that if her mother knew more, she would demand more. For the time being, instead of standing up and striving for her own version of a good life, in the post-1990s way, like Skipper, Jiayin describes her manner of coping as "escapist."

Such is the intra-generational diversity that perhaps not so much disrupts the generational paradigm, but at least poses questions about its mobilization. In the words of France and Roberts, we should be cautious if "the deployment of the social generations framework has been done in a way that stretches the utility of some of the concepts introduced by Mannheim beyond their capacity."[52] It may not be wrong to say that post-1990s do form a generation who know what they want and do not hesitate in pursuing it; at least from what Skipper, Siqi, and Jiayin have to say, they do offer evidence for the formation of such a generation. However, while Skipper seems to be very sure and rather ruthless in conducting her love life, Siqi and Jiayin are more hesitant and reticent about what they want when facing their parents and potential partners.

I would like to make use of Skipper's other presumably *jiulinghou* hallmark: the confidence, and the insouciance afforded by her well-off parents, having her own career particularly in the form of a start-up company in the creative field, to illustrate another possibility of diversity: intergenerational. Skipper quit, or suspended, her university education in the United States and returned to Shanghai to start her own online business. While this resolve about one's career path may be part and parcel of Skipper's generation—allegedly unlike the hardworking and essentially conservative career choices of earlier generations—some of the single women I spoke with necessitate nuances. Lei was born in 1975, in Xi'an. She grew up and completed her education in the same town. Lei introduced Xi'an fondly as an "ancient city," referring to its historical importance in Chinese history, particularly its penchant for the archaic and the idealistic. Majoring in Chinese, Lei became interested in media work, a mutation of her dream to become a writer. For the generation born in the 1970s, according to Lei, everybody wanted to become a writer. In the China of that era, "the most intelligent, excellent and charming people" all had "writer" as their dream career. But when she was offered an internship opportunity at a local radio station, she accepted it, which turned into a regular job as host. Moving from Xi'an to Beijing and from radio to television, Lei finally resigned in 2016 and started her own new media platform, just as Skipper, who is more than 20 years her junior. Different from Skipper, who voluntarily left her studies, Lei became frustrated with her television job when all her programmes, for one reason or another, were scrapped. She could not accept having nothing to do, so she handed in her resignation. Similar to Skipper is her framing of this career choice, that it is something she knows she should do, she is capable of doing, and she will enjoy doing so. Recounting her various experiences in media work, Lei considers herself to be well trained in offering content, whether in text creation, radio broadcasting, or television production. "I will do it well … and I am doing something I like to do," she said. Lei believes that when you are committed and put in the ultimate effort, "you will earn money, you will earn happiness, you will earn respect. What else is more exciting?"

Born in 1984, in Hubei, Yang studied porcelain creation in Jingdezhen, the Chinese city historically known for this art and craft. "I love the surprise in the process. There can be huge discrepancies between what you set out to create and the final product." By the time Yang graduated, she decided she would like to become a journalist, and continued her postgraduate studies in Xiamen, majoring in advertising and journalism. For her first job, Yang was affiliated to an important financial daily, and took Shanghai as her base. Despite her frequent framing of herself as a *balinghou*, Yang shares with Skipper and Lei a sense of certainty and conviction about her career path. Despite an attractive and stable source of income— "I was already earning 300,000 RMB the first year after graduation, quite high among fresh graduates in China"—she decided to return to her first love: porcelain. She also decided to run her own business. "I don't like to be tied down, and I don't think I can work within an institution," Yang analyses herself this way. She tried the first time in 2010, at the age of 26, when she set up a company mainly trading in porcelain-related products. In less than six months, Yang had to give up this new venture and move elsewhere as her husband was assigned to a job outside Shanghai. Here, Yang embodied the contradictory demands often ascribed to her *balinghou* generation. She said she was simply following the normative way for a woman of her time, in the sense that they simply give in to family pressure and demands. She became a mother. In September 2013, she divorced; in October, she made a second attempt at her porcelain business. "I don't want to have a job that is only for survival," says Yang. Echoing Skipper and Lei, members of two other generations, she states, "I really want to do something I like to do, whether in terms of personality or interests." This became her version of a porcelain studio, partly offering a space for tea, coffee, and conversation, partly for displaying her porcelain works and running workshops. Yang has already opened two venues in the city, and is planning a third. "Doing porcelain work remains very very attractive to me, that's why I have started this business."

FROM META-NARRATIVES TO PERSONAL DETAILS

When I was drafting this chapter, I was in Beijing. With some inkling that it might be relevant, probably cued by the synopsis I read and the trailer I saw online, I went to see a Chinese film, *The Summer Is Gone*.[53] Inspired by his own biography, director and scriptwriter Zhang Dalei uses 110 minutes to describe one summer month in an Inner Mongolian city sometime in the early 1990s. This summer, usually bright and sunny but interrupted with thunderstorms and heavy showers, is largely narrated from the viewpoint of a child, who is under family and peer pressure to go to an elite secondary school. At the same time, he is absorbing the shock and sadness when his father needs to leave home for a job when his former employer, a state-run film studio, is privatized, a consequence of economic reforms. The film, shot entirely in black and white, is mesmerizing, poetic, and uncannily, adamantly set against any conventional narrative plot, underscoring the constant amazement seen in and by the eyes of the child, of all the changes taking place in the Chinese society during his childhood. It is difficult, if at all desirable, to predict what would become of this particular *balinghou*. We only get to view one month of his life. The Chinese title of the film, *Ba-yue* ("August" 八月), seems to me an oblique reflection on, if not critique against, the idea of *balinghou*, as if the title and the film are invoking the sheer complexity of one month's experience of a Chinese youth to question the simplifications writ large as the experience of a whole decade.

Qilinghou, balinghou, jiulinghou. And now, with the babies born after the new millennium, the term *linglinghou*, or post-2000s, has also started to circulate on Chinese media platforms. The popularity of these terms suggests the usefulness of a generational paradigm to China—but then, with Chinese characteristics. I have introduced the first three single women in this chapter to illustrate how they live as part and parcel of their generation. At the same time, the intra- and intergenerational diversity, as told by their contemporaries, urges us to acknowledge the complexity as lived by the child in the film cited in the last paragraph. In their study on women and their survival of precarity, Ionela Vlase and Rebekka Sieber realize how the meta-narrative of a happy nation—Switzerland, in their case— interpellates women living there to narrate their well-being.[54] Similarly, Julie Ann Wilson and Emily Chivers Yochim demonstrate how a meta-narrative of family autonomy and self-appreciation subjects women to what they call "mamapreneurialism" and a voluntary endurance of the heavy burden of making a home and working at home.[55] Perhaps, the generational paradigm may best be understood as one sort of meta-narratives—the meta-narratives of *qilinghou*, of *balinghou*, and of *jiulinghou*, that the single women in my study are ready to mobilize to draw the contours of their lives. As meta-narratives go, they remain operational and effective at a meta-level, waiting to be disrupted by myriads of personal details in the biographical vicissitudes. While the debates on the concept of generation remain at the abstract level, the crux of the matter is empirical. As noted by France and Roberts, "at an empirical level at least, there is a relative scarcity of case studies of generations to provide evidence of claims around a collective generational identity."[56] Again, Dan Woodman also cautions, "[t]he significant point for generational theorists is to not assume that divisions and inequalities are automatically and always the same from one generation to the next; this is and must be an empirical question."[57]

It is with this empirical reminder that I continue in the following chapters to look at how the single women I spoke with live their lives, perhaps as a generational member, but primarily as themselves. We will start with work.

NOTES

1. See, for instance, Jeroen de Kloet and Anthony Y. H. Fung, *Youth Cultures in China* (Cambridge: Polity, 2017); Li Chunling (李春玲), "静悄悄的革命是否临近?—从80后和90后的价值观转变看年轻一代的先行性 [Is the Quiet Revolution Imminent?—The Advances of the Younger Generation from the Transformative Values of the Post-1980s and Post-1990s]," 河北学刊 *[Hebei Xue Kan]*, no. 3 (2015): 100–104; Li Hui (李慧), "对'70后'命名的思考 [Reflection on the Term of 'Post-1970s']," 安徽文学: 下半月 *[Anhui Wenxue: Xia Banyue]*, no. 8 (2009): 319–20; Yuan Yue (袁岳) and Zhang Jun (张军), 我们90后 *[We the Post-1990s]* (浙江大学出版社 [Zhejiang daxue chubanshe], 2011).

2. Joke Mat, "Jong, Slim En Boordevol Twijfel," *NRC Handelsblad*, April 8, 2017. 30–33.

3. Ibid., 30–31.

4. Anne Corré, "Ik Wil Er 't Allerbeste van Maken," *NRC Handelsblad*, April 8, 2017, sec. E14–E15.

5. Alan France and Steven Roberts, "The Problem of Social Generations: A Critique of the New Emerging Orthodoxy in Youth Studies," *Journal of Youth Studies* 18, no. 2 (February 7, 2015): 215.

6. See, for instance, D. Jasun Carr et al., "Examining Overconsumption, Competitive Consumption, and Conscious Consumption from 1994 to 2004: Disentangling Cohort and Period Effects," *The ANNALS of the American Academy of Political and Social Science* 644, no. 1 (2012): 220–33; Michaela Pyšňáková and Steven Miles, "The Post-Revolutionary Consumer Generation: 'Mainstream' Youth and the Paradox of Choice in the Czech Republic," *Journal of Youth Studies* 13, no. 5 (2010): 533–47. And in the Chinese context, see Dou Wenyu, Wang Guangping, and Zhou Nan, "Generational and Regional Differences in Media Consumption Patterns of Chinese Generation X Consumers," *Journal of Advertising* 35, no. 2 (2006): 101–10; Jhony Choon Yeong Ng, Christina Maria Helminger, and Wu Qianyun, "A Generational Cohort Model for Consumers in China: The Rise and Fall of the Great Gatsby?" *A Generational Cohort Model for Consumers in China: The Rise and Fall of the Great Gatsby?* 7, no. 1 (2016): 53–66; Jin-Seok Yoo, "Young Consumers Drive China's New Economic Model," *SERI Quarterly* 6, no. 4 (2013): 113–18.
7. D. I. Kertzer, "Generation as a Sociological Problem," *Annual Review of Sociology* 9, no. 1 (1983): 125.
8. Kertzer argues that Spanish philosopher Josè Ortega y Gasset also formulated and published a similar concept of generation as Mannheim's in 1933, highlighting its conceptual importance in history and each generation's "special mission." See José Ortega Y. Gasset, *The Modern Theme* (New York: W. W. Norton Company, 1933), 15–19. However, at least for the last two decades of academic works using the generational paradigm I have located, most of them cite Mannheim, not Gasset.
9. Lian Hongping, "The Post-1980s Generation in China: Exploring Its Theoretical Underpinning," *Journal of Youth Studies* 17, no. 7 (2014): 965–81.
10. Karl Mannheim, "The Problem of Generations," in *Essays on the Sociology of Knowledge* (London: Routledge, 1928/1952), 276–322. 297.
11. Camille Peugny and Cécile Van de Velde, "Rethinking Inter-Generational Inequality," trans. Peter Hamilton, *Revue Française de Sociologie* 54, no. 4 (2013): 641–62.
12. Mannheim, "The Problem of Generations," 308.
13. Peugny and Van de Velde, "Rethinking Inter-Generational Inequality," 644.
14. Margaret Mead, *Culture and Commitment: A Study of the Generation Gap* (New York: Doubleday, 1970).
15. Jennie Bristow, *The Sociology of Generations: New Directions and Challenges* (London: Palgrave Macmillan, 2016).
16. Kertzer, "Generation as a Sociological Problem," 126.
17. Ibid., 142.

18. Johanna Wyn and Dan Woodman, "Generation, Youth and Social Change in Australia," *Journal of Youth Studies* 9, no. 5 (2006): 495–514.

19. France and Roberts, "The Problem of Social Generations."

20. Ibid., 227.

21. Dou, Wang, and Zhou, "Generational and Regional Differences in Media Consumption Patterns of Chinese Generation X Consumers."

22. Ng, Helminger, and Wu, "A Generational Cohort Model for Consumers in China."

23. See Jian Chen and Rong Lian, "Generational Differences in Work Values in China," *Social Behavior and Personality: An International Journal* 43, no. 4 (2015): 567–78.

24. Yi Xiang, Barbara Ribbens, and Caryn N. Morgan, "Generational Differences in China: Career Implications," *Career Development International* 15, no. 6 (2010): 601–20.

25. Stanley Rosen, "Contemporary Chinese Youth and the State," *The Journal of Asian Studies* 68, no. 2 (2009): 359–69.

26. Yi Xiang et al., "Variation in Career and Workplace Attitudes by Generation, Gender, and Culture Differences in Career Perceptions in the United States and China," *Employee Relations* 37, no. 1 (2015): 68.

27. See Rosen, "Contemporary Chinese Youth and the State," 362. In addition, for an account of the evolution of popular usage from "generations" to the epiphet "post," see Zhao Feng, "The Evolution from Generation to Post-XX," trans. Ted Wang, *Chinese Education & Society* 44, no. 2–3 (2011): 76–79.

28. Ma Er (马耳), "陈卫与'70后' [Chen Wei and the 'Post-1970s']," *豆瓣小组 [Douban Xiaozu]* (blog), September 21, 2011, https://www.douban.com/group/topic/22459586/.

29. Gong Xiaobing (恭小兵), "总结:关于80后 [Summarizing: About the Post-1980s]," *天涯论坛 [Tianya Luntan]*, July 11, 2003, http://bbs.tianya.cn/post-210-2-1.shtml.

30. See "Breaking Out: China's Youth Finally Dare to Be Different," *Time*, February 2, 2004.

31. Jiang Bing (江冰), "论'80后'文字文学 [On 'Post-1980s' Writing Literature]," *中国作家网 [Zhongguo Zuojiawang]*, April 23, 2008, http://www.chinawriter.com.cn/2008/2008-04-23/34533.html.

32. Zhu Qi (朱其), "'70后':这个名称意味着什么? [The Post-1970s: What Does This Name Mean?]," *美苑 [Meiyuan]*, no. 5 (2005): 5.

33. Ibid., 5.

34. Xin Hua (新华), "'70后、80后、90后',时代催生的'话题三重门' ['The Post-70s, Post-80s, Post-90s', the 'Topic Triple Door' Spawned by Eras]," in "'70后、80后、90后',被标签了吗? ["The Post-1970s, Post-1980s, Post-1990s": Are They Being Labeled?]," ed. Yanmin (李彦敏) Li, *乡音 [Xiangyin]*, no. 8 (2008): 42.

35. Yin Ming (尹铭), "'60后'眼中的'70后、80后、90后'['The Post-70s, Post-80s, Post-90s' in the Eyes of 'the Post-60s'],'" in "'70后、80后、90后',被标签了吗? ["The Post-1970s, Post-1980s, Post-1990s": Are They Being Labeled?]," ed. Yanmin (李彦敏) Li, 乡音 [Xiangyin], no. 8 (2008): 42–43.

36. Lao Bei (老北), "70后、80后与90后 [The Post-1970s, the Post-1980s and the Post-1990s]," 文化中国 [Wenhua Zhongguo] (blog), September 19, 2010, http://culture.china.com.cn/book/zxyd/2010-09/07/content_20882161.htm.

37. Yin, "'60后'眼中的'70后、80后、90后'," 43.

38. Ibid., 43.

39. Xin, "'70后、80后、90后',时代催生的'话题三重门'," 42.

40. Lao, "70后、80后与90后."

41. Lian, "The Post-1980s Generation in China." Also, for the details of the one-child policy, read He Wei He and Hui Zheng, "Under the One Child Policy Regime in China: Did Having Younger Sibling(s) Increase the Risk of Overweight and Underweight Status?," *Asian Population Studies* 13, no. 3 (2017): 267–91.

42. Lian, "The Post-1980s Generation in China," 970.

43. Li Li, "The 'Me Generation,'" *Beijing Review*, February 3, 2008, http://www.bjreview.com.cn/special/2008-02/03/content_101174.htm.

44. Rosen, "Contemporary Chinese Youth and the State," 365.

45. Ibid.

46. Lao, "70后、80后与90后."

47. Ibid.

48. Yin, "'60后'眼中的'70后、80后、90后'," 43.

49. Due to increasing marketization of the Chinese economy, state-run enterprises started a process of privatization in the 1990s, whereby workers retained their affiliation, but became de facto redundant and received no salary any more. This arrangement is officially called *xiagang*, literally stepping down from one's function, and the wave of unemployment *xiagangchao* 下岗潮. The film *The Summer Is Gone*, which I will mention later, is situated in this context.

50. *Zhiqing*, a short form of *zhishi qingnian* 知识青年, literally "intellectual youth," was coined by the Chinese Communist Party, originally referring to young people with a tertiary education. However, from the 1950s through the 1970s, *zhiqing* usually meant those young people who left cities for the countryside to labour with the farmers, voluntarily or not. They also included people with only junior or senior secondary education, not necessarily university. It was estimated that 12 to 18 million *zhiqing* were involved in this massive migration exercise. For a book-length investigation, read Helena K. Rene, *China's Sent-Down Generation: Public*

Administration and the Legacies of Mao's Rustication Program (Washington, DC: Georgetown University Press, 2013).

51. *Ayi*, literally auntie, is the vernacular Chinese term used to refer to female helpers with domestic chores.
52. France and Roberts, "The Problem of Social Generations," 223.
53. The arthouse film won the Best Feature Film award at the 53rd Golden Horse Awards in Taiwan. Kong Weiyi, who played the child, won the Best New Actor Award. The film was released in mainland China in March 2017.
54. Ionela Vlase and Rebekka Sieber, "Narrating Well-Being in the Context of Precarious Prosperity: An Account of Agency Framed by Culturally Embedded Happiness and Gender Beliefs," *European Journal of Women's Studies* 23, no. 2 (2016): 185–99.
55. Julie Ann Wilson and Emily Chivers Yochim, "Mothering Through Precarity," *Cultural Studies* 29, no. 5–6 (2015): 669–86.
56. France and Roberts, "The Problem of Social Generations," 221.
57. Dan Woodman, "Researching 'Ordinary' Young People in a Changing World: The Sociology of Generations and the 'Missing Middle' in Youth Research," *Sociological Research Online* 18, no. 1 (2013), Section 1.3.

REFERENCES

"Breaking Out: China's Youth Finally Dare to Be Different." *Time*, February 2, 2004.

Bristow, Jennie. *The Sociology of Generations: New Directions and Challenges.* London: Palgrave Macmillan, 2016.

Carr, D. Jasun, Melissa R. Gotlieb, Nam-Jin Lee, and Dhavan V. Shah. "Examining Overconsumption, Competitive Consumption, and Conscious Consumption from 1994 to 2004: Disentangling Cohort and Period Effects." *The ANNALS of the American Academy of Political and Social Science* 644, no. 1 (2012): 220–33.

Chen, Jian, and Rong Lian. "Generational Differences in Work Values in China." *Social Behavior and Personality: An International Journal* 43, no. 4 (2015): 567–78.

Corré, Anne. "Ik Wil Er 't Allerbeste van Maken." *NRC Handelsblad*, April 8, 2017, sec. E14-E15.

Dou, Wenyu, Guangping Wang, and Nan Zhou. "Generational and Regional Differences in Media Consumption Patterns of Chinese Generation X Consumers." *Journal of Advertising* 35, no. 2 (2006): 101–10.

France, Alan, and Steven Roberts. "The Problem of Social Generations: A Critique of the New Emerging Orthodoxy in Youth Studies." *Journal of Youth Studies* 18, no. 2 (2015): 215–30.

Gong, Xiaobing (恭小兵). "总结:关于80后 [Summarizing: About the Post-80s]." 天涯论坛 *[Tianya Luntan]*, July 11, 2003. http://bbs.tianya.cn/post-210-2-1.shtml.

He, Wei, and Hui Zheng. "Under the One Child Policy Regime in China: Did Having Younger Sibling(s) Increase the Risk of Overweight and Underweight Status?" *Asian Population Studies* 13, no. 3 (2017): 267–91.

Jiang, Bing (江冰). "论'80后'文字文学 [On 'Post-80s' Writing Literature]." 中国作家网 *[Zhongguo Zuojiawang]*, April 23, 2008. http://www.chinawriter.com.cn/2008/2008-04-23/34533.html.

Kertzer, D. I. "Generation as a Sociological Problem." *Annual Review of Sociology* 9, no. 1 (1983): 125–49.

de Kloet, Jeroen, and Anthony Y. H. Fung. *Youth Cultures in China*. Cambridge: Polity, 2017.

Lao, Bei (老北). "70后、80后与90后 [The Post-70s, the Post-80s and the Post-90s]." 文化中国 *[Wenhua Zhongguo]* (blog), September 19, 2010. http://culture.china.com.cn/book/zxyd/2010-09/07/content_20882161.htm.

Li, Chunling (李春玲). "静悄悄的革命是否临近?—从80后和90后的价值观转变看年轻一代的先行性 [Is the Quiet Revolution Imminent?—The Advances of the Younger Generation from the Transformative Values of the Post-80s and Post-90s]." 河北学刊 *[Hebei Xue Kan]*, no. 3 (2015): 100–104.

Li, Hui (李慧). "对'70后'命名的思考 [Reflection on the Term of 'Post-70s']." 安徽文学:下半月 *[Anhui Wenxue: Xia Banyue]*, no. 8 (2009): 319–20.

Li, Li. "The 'Me Generation.'" *Beijing Review*, February 3, 2008. http://www.bjreview.com.cn/special/2008-02/03/content_101174.htm.

Lian, Hongping. "The Post-1980s Generation in China: Exploring Its Theoretical Underpinning." *Journal of Youth Studies* 17, no. 7 (2014): 965–81.

Ma, Er (马耳). "陈卫与'70后' [Chen Wei and the 'Post-70s']." 豆瓣小组 *[Douban Xiaozu]* (blog), September 21, 2011. https://www.douban.com/group/topic/22459586/.

Mannheim, Karl. "The Problem of Generations." In *Essays on the Sociology of Knowledge*, 276–322. London: Routledge, 1928.

Mat, Joke. "Jong, Slim En Boordevol Twijfel." *NRC Handelsblad*, April 8, 2017.

Mead, Margaret. *Culture and Commitment: A Study of the Generation Gap*. New York: Doubleday, 1970.

Ng, Jhony Choon Yeong, Christina Maria Helminger, and Qianyun Wu. "A Generational Cohort Model for Consumers in China: The Rise and Fall of the Great Gatsby?" *A Generational Cohort Model for Consumers in China: The Rise and Fall of the Great Gatsby?* 7, no. 1 (2016): 53–66.

Ortega Y. Gasset, José. *The Modern Theme*. New York: W. W. Norton Company, 1933.

Peugny, Camille, and Cécile Van de Velde. "Rethinking Inter-Generational Inequality." Translated by Peter Hamilton. *Revue Française de Sociologie* 54, no. 4 (2013): 641–62.

Pyšňáková, Michaela, and Steven Miles. "The Post-Revolutionary Consumer Generation: 'Mainstream' Youth and the Paradox of Choice in the Czech Republic." *Journal of Youth Studies* 13, no. 5 (2010): 533–47.

Rene, Helena K. *China's Sent-Down Generation: Public Administration and the Legacies of Mao's Rustication Program*. Washington, D.C.: Georgetown University Press, 2013.

Rosen, Stanley. "Contemporary Chinese Youth and the State." *The Journal of Asian Studies* 68, no. 2 (2009): 359–69.

Vlase, Ionela, and Rebekka Sieber. "Narrating Well-Being in the Context of Precarious Prosperity: An Account of Agency Framed by Culturally Embedded Happiness and Gender Beliefs." *European Journal of Women's Studies* 23, no. 2 (2016): 185–99.

Wilson, Julie Ann, and Emily Chivers Yochim. "Mothering Through Precarity." *Cultural Studies* 29, no. 5–6 (2015): 669–86.

Woodman, Dan. "Researching 'Ordinary' Young People in a Changing World: The Sociology of Generations and the 'Missing Middle' in Youth Research." *Sociological Research Online* 18, no. 1 (2013).

Wyn, Johanna, and Dan Woodman. "Generation, Youth and Social Change in Australia." *Journal of Youth Studies* 9, no. 5 (2006): 495–514.

Xin, Hua (新华). "'70后、80后、90后',时代催生的'话题三重门' ['The Post-70s, Post-80s, Post-90s', the 'Topic Triple Door' Spawned by Eras]." Edited by Li Yanmin (李彦敏). 乡音 *[Xiangyin]*, no. 8 (2008): 42.

Yi, Xiang, Barbara Ribbens, Linna Fu, and Weibo Cheng. "Variation in Career and Workplace Attitudes by Generation, Gender, and Culture Differences in Career Perceptions in the United States and China." *Employee Relations* 37, no. 1 (2015): 66–82.

Yi, Xiang, Barbara Ribbens, and Caryn N. Morgan. "Generational Differences in China: Career Implications." *Career Development International* 15, no. 6 (2010): 601–20.

Yin, Ming (尹铭). "'60后'眼中的'70后、80后、90后' ['The Post-70s, Post-80s, Post-90s' in the Eyes of 'the Post-60s']." Edited by Li Yanmin (李彦敏). 乡音 *[Xiangyin]*, no. 8 (2008): 42–43.

Yoo, Jin-Seok. "Young Consumers Drive China's New Economic Model." *SERI Quarterly* 6, no. 4 (2013): 113–18.

Yuan, Yue (袁岳), and Zhang Jun (张军). 我们90后 *[We the Post-90s]*. Hangzhou: 浙江大学出版社 [Zhejiang daxue chubanshe], 2011.

Zhao, Feng. "The Evolution from Generation to Post-XX." Translated by Ted Wang. *Chinese Education & Society* 44, no. 2–3 (2011): 76–79.

Zhu, Qi (朱其). "'70后':这个名称意味着什么? [The Post-70s: What Does This Name Mean?]." 美苑 *[Meiyuan]*, no. 5 (2005): 5–6.

CHAPTER 4

Balancing Work/Life?

March 10, 2015, Tuesday morning. I walk into a rather posh shopping mall close to where I stay in Shanghai. It is a regular working day. The mall is quiet, and I follow a familiar route to the café where I often conduct my interviews. My research assistant, a native Shanghai woman, helped me find this venue, which is convenient for me as well as for the single women who have agreed to participate in my research project. The shopping mall stands right on top of a subway station. Indeed, most of the women I have invited confirm the place and time without much negotiation—weekday mornings or afternoons are not a problem for them. As this morning, I sit in the café, waiting, preparing, and looking around me. The spacious café exudes the kind of cosmopolitanism that makes it hard to remember that I am in Shanghai instead of some other global city, save for the Chinese patrons who happen to share the same café with me. There are only a few of them, mostly female. While I am checking my recorder and notes, they are chatting in pairs, or working singly on their laptops. That women tend to be willing to pay a higher price—yesterday evening, I spent 10 RMB on a noodle soup and 20 RMB on a beef dish, while the tall latté in front of me right now cost 31 RMB—to sit in such a café and claim privacy in a semi-public space is verified by my casual observations whenever I sit down or pass by cafés in this city.

Lulu, born in 1990, in Qingdao, arrives around noon. Working as a designer for an online cultural magazine, she grumbles about the transport time it takes her to travel from her home to work: two hours per day,

© The Author(s) 2019

Chow Y. F., *Caring in Times of Precarity*, Palgrave Studies in
Globalization, Culture and Society,
https://doi.org/10.1007/978-3-319-76898-4_4

an annoying encroachment on her free time. After our interview, Lulu decides to walk back to her office. It is a fine day, and it is nicer to take a little stroll than hurrying back, she says. As I have prepared for an hour as interval before the next interview, I walk with her. Lulu tells me that the flexibility of her working hours is something she cherishes. For instance, she can be at work around 10 am, which makes it possible for her to avoid the peak hours of Shanghai public transport. Some friends of hers, however, have to start sharply at 9 am, and their offices operate a registration system so that their bosses know exactly when they arrive. If they are late, their salaries will be docked. "I like my kind of freedom," Lulu says, repeating what she articulated earlier in the interview.

This is the kind of freedom mentioned to me by quite a few women, and often demonstrated by the very flexibility they can utilize to spend their time less like a "regular" office-bound employee. At the same time, there are also a couple of interviewees who must squeeze our meeting into their lunch breaks. Or like Valerie, born in 1979, in Hong Kong, who must leave promptly for her advertising agency to attend a conference call at 9 pm. Or like Skipper, whom we met in the previous chapter, who is busy with her start-up. She asks to have the interview close to her office in a creative district, and specifies the timing most convenient for her. I wait in the designated café. After half an hour, there is no sign of her. I call, and Skipper tells me she has forgotten the appointment. She will rush by as soon as she finishes her meeting. Another half an hour, and still no sign of her. She has forgotten, again. Too much to deal with, she sighs when she finally arrives. Such is the other side of their working lives that I have witnessed merely from the way our interviews take place.

Such is the complexity of creative work that I am interested in and want to tease out in Chap. 4. In the following sections, I will begin with discussions surrounding creative work, from the largely celebratory undertaking typified by Richard Florida's work, to the Marxist-inflected critique of exploitation and abuse camouflaged as flexibility and freedom. Acknowledging and aligning with the critical scholarship that seeks to theorize creative work, or labour—the more favoured term for its ready critical underpinning—I will depart from it and supplement it with the subjective experiences of creative work as explicated by the single women in Shanghai. I will do so along two axes. First, this chapter chooses to suspend the concerns about exploitation and alienation in lieu of empirical curiosity and the documentation of what they themselves have to say. More specifically, this empirical investigation builds on the important work on creative labour by David Hesmondhalgh and Sarah Baker, in which they defend the intrinsic value of work.[1] Second, it seeks not only to look at their work, but also to examine the intricate connections between their creative work and single lives, which is, at once, driven by the empirical work conducted as well as by the theoretical urge to insert a gendered dimension into discussing creative labour—these women's singlehood.[2]

DOUBLE LIFE OF CREATIVE WORK

With the publication of Florida's *The Rise of the Creative Class*,[3] urban planners and policymakers around the world, from North America and Europe, to the Asia-Pacific, have subscribed to his beliefs that the resources offered by creativity can provide a better economy and better future.[4] Despite convincing critiques challenging Florida's beliefs, whether for its statistical grounding, its argumentation, or its neo-liberal underpinning,[5] both popular and academic discourses have undergone a "creative" turn, in the sense that creativity and its related notions (creative city, creative industries, creative class) have become important issues for public discussions and academic studies. Corresponding to the different critical stances towards Florida's beliefs in creativity and the creative class, studies demonstrate a variety of responses to the premises that increasingly more people are attracted to the promises of creative work—autonomy, flexibility, satisfaction—and join the creative workforce. On the one hand, creative workers are seen as the driving force of economies and innovation, and are conceived, with varying degrees of celebration, as model entrepreneurs, pioneers in new form of working, and generally embodying a turn towards life.[6] Particularly in its convergence with technological possibilities such as digital platforms, the creative class is heralded with a high dose of optimism, encapsulated in the maxim of "DWYL"—Do What You Love.[7] On the other hand, for all its alleged desirability, creative work summons a surrender of security: no more regular working hours, short-term contracts, freelancing and a variety of arrangements that assign individual creative workers as the bearer of risks and responsibilities. They struggle to perform a balancing act between work and life,[8] surviving—without collective bargaining power and trade unions—the multiple demands and abuses, it is argued, for the interests of the state and the industries, not their own.[9] In the words of Angela McRobbie, one of the most lucid and staunch critics of the celebratory framing of creative work by Florida and like-minded thinkers, "[t]he call to be creative is a potent and highly appealing mode of new governmentality directed to the young in the educational environment, whose main effect is to do away with the idea of welfare rights by means of eclipsing normal employment altogether."[10]

Many new terms have emerged in order to grapple with what is happening in the field of creative labour, particularly amidst fast-changing technologies, economies, and politics. In her proposition of the term "aspirational labour," Brooke Erin Duffy[11] lists out, among others, "digital labour,"[12] "co-creative labour,"[13] "passionate labour,"[14] "hope labour,"[15] "venture labour,"[16] and "playbour."[17] These studies often posit creative workers as a typical category of precariat, using Andrew Ross' term, the "creative precariat."[18] The notion of precariat—a neologism integrating precarity and proletariat—was put forward by Guy Standing to foreground the experience of exploitation and the possibility of new subjectivity.[19] The call to be creative, according to McRobbie, and its "mode of neoliberal governmentality is also a general and widespread process of precarization."[20] Two intertwined lines of inquiry weave into this chapter. One engages with the "free labour debate," where unpaid labour, especially in the context of digital cultures, is understood from a wide range of perspectives: from a form of creative expression that would not have been possible otherwise, a tactic in career management in the hope of going professional and getting paid, to new modes of exploitation by the creative industries.[21] The other, emerging in recent years in response to a research lacuna, is predicated by the DWYL ideals or ideology to explore the affective dimensions of creative work and workers, their pressure, pain, and pleasure.[22] A special issue on the subject has included five contributions in addition to an introduction on labour and passion.[23]

These lines of inquiry on creative work, with their focus on labour conditions and affect, do not have the problematic of precarity as their central concern. However, taken as a whole, these studies shed light on, for instance, the need to respond to contingent work opportunities, the anxiety associated with hoping for eventual reward for one's free labour, the whimsical nature of pleasure and pain in work, and in short, the myriad of situations the precariat experiences during the process of doing their creative work. This appeal to examine precarity as complex, lived realities can also be seen as a response to one critique against the notion of the "precariat"—namely, the danger to dehistoricize and flatten problematic working conditions to those of the contemporary Global North.[24] As pointed out in Chap. 1, scholars working on Chinese labour issues, while noting similar process of precarization, highlight local, specific characteristics—for instance, class distinctions, the legal system and practices, and the importance of the state.[25] What I aim to do in the following sections aspires to do precisely that: to examine precarity in a local, specific context. While generally supporting the view that creative work can be demanding, exploitative, and precarious—as evidenced by Valerie and Skipper at the beginning of this chapter, and many of the other single women I spoke with, I am also impressed by the sense of flexibility and freedom that warms Lulu to her design job. I will spell out the darker sides of creative work later, only to afford myself room to suspend the critical concern for a subsequent investigation into other possible dimensions of creative work, especially in the Chinese context. This investigation is, above all, inspired by Hesmondhalgh and Baker's seminal work on creative labour.[26]

In the first place, I take their appeal to understand what is going on in creative work through creative workers' own accounts of their experiences.[27] This emphasis on "subjective experience" is pivotal in probing the specificities of creative work and workers. At the same time, I am persuaded by the ways the two scholars defend the intrinsic value of work, as well as its social contribution, against the post-structuralist critique that good work is impossible, and subjective experience thereof serves only to lubricate abuses in the capitalist system. Hesmondhalgh and Baker argue, instead, to take creative workers' experience seriously and propose to conceptualize creative labour in terms of "good and bad work," especially as experienced and articulated by the creative workers themselves. I am particularly attracted not only to what constitutes their good work, but also to how to get good work done, as articulated in the accounts offered by the women in this inquiry. In doing so, I want to delve into the cultural translations and slippages taking place when we use such a framework—that is built on experiences in the United Kingdom—in the context of China. To paraphrase Hesmondhalgh and Baker, this chapter aims to offer "a study of jobs that are considered particularly desirable in the times in which we live" in the Chinese context.[28]

"They Must Be Monsters"

During my search for participants in this research project, I came across quite readily *balinghou* and *jiulinghou*, the post-1980s and -1990s women, but I had difficulty in locating those born in the 1970s. So, I asked a female friend, who worked in the media, to help. Married herself, but sympathetic to my research, she came back a few days later with a couple of screenshots of her WeChat conversation with a designer friend. She was asking him to help, assuming that he, a homosexual man active in a variety of creative fields, might know some single women he could refer me to. After all, male homosexuals and single women, particularly of a certain age, usually mingle, she thought. "Single woman, *qilinghou*, and still doing creative work? They must be monsters," the designer wrote to my friend.

> "Monsters?" my friend asked. "In my circle of friends, no one has survived."
> "Why?" "Creative work is too tough. Those who stay must have special reasons."[29]

What this designer observes from the creative fields in which he navigates summarizes the list of exploitations and abuses pinpointed by critical thinkers on creative labour; those who survive, especially if they are single women, must be monsters. The Chinese term he used is *yaonie* (妖孽). Although a typical dictionary translation of this will yield the word "evildoer," I understand it in the context of the conversation to mean something like a monster, a freak, an unnatural creature, a creature of ill-fortune; somebody to whom evil is done, rather than somebody doing evil; someone who should not exist. Perhaps a monster, not so much in the sense of being non-human, but superhuman, albeit not to be envied. I will discuss the gender dimension of the designer's observation in the second half of this chapter. For now, he is quite correct when I recall the stories the single women told me about their creative work.

Xiaoqian, born in 1982, in Shanghai, was working for a major music platform based in Hangzhou at the time of our interview. Her creative career offers a typical curriculum vitae of the precariat: unpaid labour, part-time work, insecurity, work dominating life. During the last year of her undergraduate education in publishing and the Chinese language, Xiaoqian offered her free labour to a magazine house as part of their internship programme. During the subsequent two years, when she furthered her studies in media and journalism to prepare herself for the jobs she really wanted, she took on part-time jobs as a copywriter for an advertising agency. She needed to earn money to support her life. Many of Xiaoqian's fellow students did the same. After the copywriting job, she moved to an online radio station concentrating on music programmes.

Xiaoqian loved the music, but the studio was at the other end of Shanghai. She needed to spend almost three hours a day commuting to and from work, and as she put it, "the salaries are not that high." After three years, she longed for some rest, and so, she quit. In 2008, someone Xiaoqian had met while doing the radio job invited her to work for his newly established online music platform. She had to convince her parents of her plan to live in Hangzhou during the week and spend weekends with them in Shanghai. Since she joined the company, Xiaoqian has had to deal with a number of new bosses, "which means I am not sure if my performance is being recognized, which worries me." Xiaoqian is preparing for the worst, which is that they will fire her. But for the time being, she remains very dedicated to her work. In Hangzhou, Xiaoqian does not have many friends. "I often don't know the distinction between life and work. I've sort of lost myself. A couple of years ago, I wondered if I was married to [the online platform]." In less metaphoric terms, Xiaoqian works constantly, putting in regular overtime, until very late at night, or early morning. Xiaoqian tells me that she agreed to participate in this interview partly because she wanted to force herself to reflect on her life.

CHUANGYE AS ONE WAY OF DOING GOOD WORK

Xiaoqian is by no means exceptional in her precarious existence as a creative worker. Among the other women in the inquiry, one endures sleepless nights; one needs to put on "work clothes" while working at home in order to demarcate the boundaries between work and life; one was recruited to a job for a website, and worked there for three months until the boss disappeared—she did not receive a single cent of pay; one says, quite the opposite to Xiaoqian, "I don't want to think too much." There are many similar instances that make it difficult not to align with critical thinkers such as McRobbie, and interrogate the contemporary condition of creative labour, whether in the West or in China. And these are the experiences of women who have persisted, and are daring and caring enough to tell. Recalling the designer's allusion to the "monsterly" attributes one must have to survive in creative work, I have cause to think of the members of the creative precariat who were crushed, suffered exhaustion, or left, and were so suffocated by their sense of failure that they might not want to be reminded of this at all; or, at the other extreme, those who are simply too busy, or so preoccupied, that they cannot even afford spending time and energy talking with their dear ones, let alone an unknown researcher. One single woman tells me that the daily commute back home on the Shanghai subway with her boyfriend has become the only occasion that they are together.

This much is clear about creative work in a Chinese city such as Shanghai. However, despite all the negative aspects, creative work, as reminded by Hesmondhalgh and Baker, remains desirable to such an extent that people—the single women in this book included—continue to do it. I seek to understand this paradox through the notion of "good work," as proposed by these two authors, as an alternative way to investigate creative labour.

In their book-length treatise, Hesmondhalgh and Baker elucidate their understanding of the critical approaches influenced by neo-Foucauldian governmentality theory, Althusserian Marxism, post-structuralism, and deconstruction, and their central concern with the (self-)exploitation of creative labour. While sharing this concern, the two authors also foreground their "lack of political clarity about what forms better creative work would take."[30] They formulate the political principle underlying their search for a model of good work as follows: "work needs to be made better, for more people." Instead of questioning all the positive elements usually associated with creative work, and relegating them to a problematic process of internalization, self-exploitation, and essentially illusionary, they choose to see them as a "useful resource for understanding of good and bad work in the cultural industries."[31] With this understanding, their project is to talk back to the "seeming impossibility of any hope of good work in capitalist modernity" that is embedded in the critique of creative labour.[32] Instead of yielding to an over-deterministic badness, they have outlined a conception of good work as involving "autonomy, interest and involvement, sociality, self-esteem, self-realization, work-life balance and security."[33] Aligned with this line of thinking, I have listened to the accounts of the single women doing creative work in Shanghai, retrieving their subjective experiences of the work they do. It is a foregrounding of their subjectivity; it is also an attempt to not see them only as victims of exploitation by the powers of the state and capital, but more as agents vacillating between akrasia and enkrateia. Such an attempt is as politically driven as it is empirically grounded. Not only from what they actually say about their work, but also from how they do so—the lively gestures, the confident articulations, the well-coordinated clothes, and above all, the readiness to talk about their lives—these single women evoke a sense of doing OK, or at least no worse than many other working men and women

I come across in the same city. "When we undertake criticism, we presumably do so because of some kind of belief life might be made better," write Hesmondhalgh and Baker.[34] Morphing with their political thrust to democratize good work, I focus on how these single women manage to do precisely that; how they care for their work, for themselves, and for a better life, not always successfully, but they try, despite—and sometimes because of—all the challenges of precarity as presented earlier. One dominant way that I discern is: *chuangye* (创业).

Chuangye, or setting up a business, may correspond to the start-up culture elsewhere in the creative world. While the term, and its concomitant notion, is usually deemed a post-1990s product, it is also arguably rooted in traditional Chinese ways of valuing the entrepreneurial spirit.[35] At the same time, there are scholars who oppose this view, pinpointing the negative influence of Confucian thinking on the nurturing of a business mindset.[36] Intellectual discussions aside, the urge to *chuangye*, the tendency to see entrepreneurism above other modes of subsistence, is often part and parcel of the upbringing of children, particularly those growing up in a family with precarious living conditions. Typical of such an upbringing is the repetition of a well-known Chinese expression *gong zi bu chutou* (工字不出头). Referring to the Chinese character 工, denoting labour, the expression highlights the absence of any visual breakthrough in this character, stating that being a labourer, an employee, will never earn you a breakthrough in life; only by setting up your own business and becoming your own boss will you become somebody.

Among the 25 single women who spoke with me, 16 of them mention *chuangye* with various degrees of longing and stages of implementation. Skipper, Yang, and Lei, from three disparate generations of single women, introduced in Chap. 3, are all proponents and practitioners of *chuangye*; they have set up their own businesses using online platforms, for a porcelain workshop and merchandizing, as well as a new media platform centring on the theme of beauty. To illustrate how *chuangye* is connected to good creative work, I will introduce another woman.

C, born in 1983, Guangzhou, finished her undergraduate education majoring in commercial English. Her first job was copywriting for an advertising agency. After a year and a half, she quit and took up a government post arranged by her parents, both government officials themselves. Her parents were worried about the long working hours their daughter had to endure. In addition to an extreme work load, C had another issue with her advertising job: sexism. When they went on business trips, her male colleagues had their own hotel rooms while she was obliged to share with female colleagues. She earned 5000+ RMB a month while her male peers earned 8000+. On top of such inequality, C had to deal with a further gender-specific problem: sexual advances, if not downright harassment. On one business trip, her boss, a young CEO of her company, knocked on her door in the middle of the night and proposed to have an "intimate talk." She declined. Subsequently, she observed a radical change in the attitude of her boss. He rejected her copy as a rule, and she was no longer assigned to business trips.[37] Her following job with the government was stable and easy, a nine-to-five kind of routine. "I could see my life in 20 or 30 years' time if I stayed there," she says. Attributing it to the one-child policy of her *balinghou* generation, C describes herself as "independent." She quit and found a sales job with a major household products company, which required her to relocate to Wuhan, as well as make frequent trips to different parts of China. It dawned on her how much she liked travelling and being on her own: "This was the first time I had left my family and lived entirely on my own." It also dawned on her how she could integrate this new passion of hers with her creative aspirations: writing and photography. C started posting her photographic works and creative texts online, accumulating a massive fan base, of the order of millions. She was approached by a publisher, and on December 21, 2012, the day the world was supposed to end (the "Maya doomsday"), C published her first photo book. In 2013, she wanted to quit and move to her favourite city, Shanghai, to capitalize and build on her online popularity and launch a full creative career: "in my heart, I knew for a long time what I should do."

With what she calls "cultural enterprise," C believes she manages to strike a balance. On the one hand, she can dedicate herself fully to creative work; on the other, she has the autonomy to select, arrange, and juggle various kinds of projects to balance her creative autonomy and livelihood. Her company has six members: two designers, two salespeople, one employee targeting online matters, and herself. Spending a lot of time working and travelling, C overworks practically every day and has to sleep at her office very often. The upside is the closeness she has nurtured with her two designer colleagues. "We are almost 24 hours together, haha, except bed time," she says. In her description, they are like a family, eating together and going to cultural events together. Sometimes, their girlfriends would also join. Trading primarily on her online celebrity status and network, C's company forges collaboration projects with other creative platforms, and she makes paid appearances at events and in film clips as a KOL (key opinion leader). The highest fee she has received was 180,000 RMB for playing a major role in a 9-minute micro-film promoting a dating App. At the same time, she can continue doing what she likes—photographing women: "I just feel that every aspect of a woman is moving ... I only use natural light and natural setting, never studio work. I like to show a woman's natural state of being." The exhibition she is curating when we hold the interview is entitled *She*, and features six female photographers, including herself.[38]

C's account does not stand on its own. Motifs of this can be traced in the experiences of other single women who have started their own businesses, or in the imaginations of those who are contemplating doing so. As we can see, in C's life, her *chuangye* is both a symptom of all the negative dimensions of creative work and an antidote. It does not eradicate all the abuse, exploitations, and precarity, but it does give C and others like her a better sense, and perhaps a better chance too, of doing good creative work. Particularly for women who would like to have more control in arranging a work life that is relatively resilient against sexism and other patriarchal abuses, *chuangye* is often considered a solution. Zaizai was born in 1983, in Shenyang. Another post-1980s, she decided to start her own business in developing computer games after she, as an employee, experienced disadvantages in "this male-dominated industry."[39]

OTHER WAYS: MATCHING AND MIXING

To state the obvious, the qualities that configure good work are not necessarily a corollary of *chuangye*. Some women in this inquiry give a generally positive account of their work not as an entrepreneur, but as an employee. LIV, born in 1979, in a small town close to Shanghai, joined a men's fashion and lifestyle magazine when it was launched in China. Recounting her experiences over the past five years as the magazine's creative director, LIV says she enjoys the flexibility of the working hours, although she realizes that also means she has to continue working at home. She also enjoys the autonomy of deciding about feature topics and suitable writers: "it gives me a big space of possibilities." As an example, a colleague of hers happened to know a sailor and a captain involved in a Somali hijack incident. She proposed an idea to her boss, and in two days, she had fixed a budget for her colleague to take a crew and fly to Somalia to do a story. Directing her gaze at me, LIV tells me that if she considers me to be a good topic to write about, or a potential columnist myself, she can simply approach me. Her work thrives under the trust of her boss. Going through the trips she has made and the foreign shows she has covered—Chanel jewellery, Swiss watches, and so on—LIV becomes animated about the details of her work, her eyes sparking, her gestures captivating. She is especially elaborate when telling me how she made the decision to leave her stable and successful job with an important newspaper and join the new magazine. She had been with the newspaper for six years when the magazine invited her to help with the launch. It took her one full year to decide. "Newspaper work is text oriented, but magazines are very visual and require a lot of creativity. I was not sure if I was capable," LIV explains. At that point, she was 30. "I thought if I do not try something new now, I will be more inert when I am older." It transpired to be a good match. When she started her new job, she felt like a "country bumpkin" entering a big city with all the autonomy, all the resources that make it possible for her to realize what she wanted to do. After five years with the magazine, she says, "I am still very happy!"

Xiaoyan, born in 1976, grew up in the outskirts of Shanghai, where houses remained quaintly traditional and her family was well versed in the Chinese scholarly and artistic legacy. She developed a passion for classical literature and operatic arts. When she started her university education in Shanghai, Xiaoyan took up Kunqu, one form of Chinese opera. In Chap. 6, I will discuss the multiple connections between Kunqu and the single lives of women in Shanghai, including Xiaoyan's. For now, I would simply like to indicate how Xiaoyan negotiates her devotion to Kunqu and the precarity of Kunqu-related work, and maintains her sense of doing something good. In her case, it was not achieved by resorting to *chuangye*, but by managing a career path that is more stable and lucrative. As a "meaningful part of my life," Xiaoyan works as a Kunqu teacher for university students in Shanghai. She tells me she has just started learning to drive, to obtain greater mobility, so that she can reach more campuses more conveniently. She spends her afternoons and evenings on this teaching job, as Kunqu is not a major course in the university curriculum, and is thus assigned to less favourable timeslots. Xiaoyan enjoys this and feels a sense of achievement from what she is doing, and a sense of mission. She feels the urgency of doing this work, particularly when her own teachers, the Kunqu masters, passed away one after the other. But this teaching job is project-based, commissioned by the municipal authorities, and the pay is not good. For the past four years, Xiaoyan has also taken responsibility for managing her family business, which is not related to Kunqu or any other kind of creativity. As she is not required by her Kunqu job during the day, Xiaoyan can mix the two jobs well. "The management job pays much better than the Kunqu one," she says.

In Connection with Women

These are the ways the single women in this inquiry mobilize to persist. Their subjective accounts underline the multiple demands of creative work, as critiqued by many related studies, as much as the efforts, the resolve, and the ingenuity with which they attempt their version of good work. I hear them sigh, but I also observe their pride. "Single woman, *qilinghou*, and still doing creative work? They must be monsters." That was the remark made by the male designer. They may be seen as monsters, considering the struggles they have to go through; at the same time, they are deeply human, precisely because of the same struggles they are experiencing. Siqi, born in 1991, in Chengdu, talks about the stress of her journalistic work. One consequence was insomnia; however tired she was, she just could not fall asleep. She started to wonder if what she was doing was meaningful at all. She was also troubled by the question of why she was not capable of enduring what seemed to be normal to most of her fellow creative workers. Siqi says she would sit the whole day, not knowing what she was doing, feeling numb, as if she did not exist. After two months, she decided to quit. When she phoned from Shanghai and told her parents in Chengdu of her decision, she started crying for "the first time since seven or eight years ago." Siqi's mother says: "Girls should not do this kind of job. It's too tough!"

However, Siqi and all the other single women in this inquiry stay on. For the rest of this chapter, I will focus on the gendered dimension of creative work. More generally, this inquiry fills a research gap by connecting two fields of study. On the one hand, studies on the creative class are not focused on gender issues and—until recently, as noted earlier—affective dimensions. On the other, studies on single women often privilege the personal and leave behind issues of work. This missing connection is problematic, as there are a number of studies that do propose a closer cross-examination of single women and creative class. First, studies have demonstrated how work—and creative work in particular—has an impact on private lives. Second, studies have also demonstrated how women are especially attracted to—and suitable for—the kind of flexible, immaterial, communicative, and affective labour that is valued in contemporary society, whether it be labelled post-Fordist, knowledge, information, or the creative economy.[40] More specifically, I want to engage with two lines of gendered critiques: against inequalities, and against the increasing invasion of work into life.

First, inequalities. Located in this intersection between studies of creative work and studies of gender, one dominant body of investigations incorporates feminist struggles into a more "general" critique against the precarity of creative work at large. Equality, or the absence thereof, is the central concern of many studies on women workers in creative industries—for example, discrimination and gender segregation in the machismo advertising environment of Peru[41]; unpaid internship taken up by young Canadian women in the creative sectors of Toronto and New York[42]; and why women leave media work in the Irish context.[43] As McRobbie observes, the inclusion of women into creative industries does not automatically or necessarily lead to greater gender equality in the workplace.[44] While structural factors are identified and political economy scrutinized, a number of authors also observe a concomitant development that precisely seeks to erase the very existence of structural factors and political economy. Rosalind Gill, in a contribution to a special issue surrounding gender and creative labour, dissects the apparent paradox of "stark and growing inequalities" as well as "an ethos that celebrates openness, egalitarianism, and meritocracy" with the twin problems of post-feminist sensitivity and entrepreneurial subjectivity.[45] To begin with, the power of the current post-feminist complacency—namely, that there is nothing more to fight for and gender inequality belongs to the darker period of history—forecloses discussions and investigations. Further, to repudiate sexism and to render gender inequality unspeakable is to thrust forward a blanket promise of a meritocracy that assures individuals, men and women alike, of their fair share as long as they work hard and excel. This is what Gill calls the "entrepreneurial mindset" that is demanded of creative workers: "a new labouring subjectivity partly organized around individualism and the disavowal of structural power relations—whose gendered aspects remain under-explored."[46] In a lead article for another special issue on gender and creative labour, Gill cautions with Bridget Conor and Stephanie Taylor against persistent inequalities in creative industries.[47] The contributions to the special issue all address the gendered politics of this new labouring subjectivity, where the "creative" is flagged up to obfuscate issues of precarity, equality, and diversity.[48] Connecting the discussion to the immaterial, affective labour that is dominant in the digital economy, Kylie Jarrett similarly argues for "the (re)placing of feminist thinking and women's experience at the forefront of contemporary understandings of labour."[49]

The new labouring subjectivity is clearly embodied in many of the single women I talked to. They experience inequalities, but none of them speak of structural problems. After all, it is not easy, if not at all risky, for them to critique a political economy such as the contemporary Chinese one. They work on their own and rely largely on themselves. Not surprisingly, *chuangye*, setting up of their own business, is, for many of them, a preferred way to continue with their creative work. After all, becoming an entrepreneur seems to be a logical extension and manifestation of the entrepreneurial mindset. It is here that the empirical data from the Chinese case may be able to supplement international scholarship on creative work and women, which, seen from the narratives of the single women in this inquiry, may actually sound ironic. What I mean is, when creative workers are willing to sacrifice and subject themselves to less than desirable or blatantly unjust conditions of work with the celebratory overtone of DWYL, they will be cautioned about the romantic or the romanticized ethos of their work. At the same time, when they become more calculating and undertaking, they risk subsuming themselves under entrepreneurial subjectivity.

I call this ironic, not because I do not agree with it. I stand by the argument that as creative workers do what they love, they are prepared to do a lot in order to continue doing it. And they fight an individual battle, rather than fighting the structure, which, left to its own devices, will continue regenerating gender inequalities in creative work. Reverting to the "monster" reference, it is not individuals who are the monsters, but the structure. What I want to supplement is: the entrepreneurial drive of the single women in the Chinese context may not offer structural change to redress gender inequalities; it should be understood as their way to make changes and carve out a more personal space for themselves to do good work and have a good life. In other words, Gill is right in highlighting the repudiation of sexism, the absence of talk over structural problems, and in concluding that "[s]ubtle yet virulent forms of sexism are entrenched in 'creative' workplace cultures at precisely the moment when a critical vocabulary—let alone a political movement—for contesting them is being eroded and rendered unspeakable."[50] She and other feminist scholars should continue making this critique. Nonetheless, speaking with the single women in Shanghai, knowing the real danger of a critical vocabulary, let alone a political movement—think of the 2015 arrest of feminist activists, mentioned in Chap. 1—I am persuaded to see their *chuangye* and their entrepreneurial mindset *already* as their critical vocabulary, and as their political movement. No wonder, in a study on Australian creative aspirants, young women appear to be more equipped with "entrepreneurial savviness" and are more able to endure the vicissitudes of a creative career.[51] In a study on Chinese women entrepreneurs selling luxury goods online, their practices open up the space for these middle-class women to negotiate the multiple demands of being modern and being traditional.[52]

Which brings me to the second gendered line of critique I want to engage with: work endangers life. In her groundbreaking study on the affordances of new media technologies, Melissa Gregg observes a process of what she calls the "presence bleed" of contemporary office culture, where work is everywhere and anytime, facilitated by smartphones, the internet, and other online possibilities. Intrigued by the contemporary centrality of work amidst us, Gregg examines "the increasingly intimate relationship salaried professionals have with their work."[53] Particularly, women, she argues, are attracted to today's workplaces, which tend to offer them pleasure and achievements more readily than, say, remaining at home. The flexibility afforded by online technology, especially in creative work, is another woman-friendly feature of contemporary working culture. However, at the same time, Gregg finds cause for alarm. According to her empirical inquiry on online workers, "children, lovers and family are some of the intimate others that come and go in a larger narrative of achievement."[54] Put differently, workers "may withdraw from a range of more complex human relationships to focus on a proven source of personal esteem—their job—since its rewards are so openly celebrated in the dominant register for modern relationships: the capitalist marketplace."[55] Her fear is that if our capacities for intimacy are wont to professional and commercial purposes, we may fail to cherish intimacies for other purposes. Thus, for Gregg, there should be "a labour politics of love" to fight this corporatization of intimacy.

Again, I stand by such politics. However, the empirical data I collected from the single women doing creative work in Shanghai inform me to dissect the intricate connections between their creative work and life differently. Instead of, or in addition to, questioning the potential threat to women's personal lives, these women's narratives evince more complexity, at least when we intersect their professional identity with not only their womanhood, but more specifically, their life as a single woman. In other words, while this inquiry responds to the theoretical urge to insert a gendered dimension in discussing creative labour, it does so specifically with these women's singlehood. In the following sections, I will explicate three scenarios as narrated by the single women: first, some women report experiences of mutual constitution, that is, singlehood enables good creative work, while the demanding creative work necessitates and perpetuates singlehood; second, some choose creative work, particularly self-employment or entrepreneurship, and capitalize on its flexibility and autonomy to lead their lives as single women, particularly those who have to take care of family members; and finally, some are wrestling with the success of their creative work, making it more difficult for them to find compatible life partners, contributing to the typical (self-)accusation of success in work, failure in love—not unlike Andi in *Ode to Joy*, discussed in Chap. 2.

SCENARIO 1: "SINGLEHOOD IS GOOD FOR WORK, GOOD FOR LIFE, GOOD FOR DOING WHAT YOU WANT TO DO"

All of the single women I spoke with confirm the advantages of singlehood to their creative work. They do so in different wordings, with different degrees of intensity, approval, and resignation; in any case, being single makes it easier for them to do their creative work well. Jennifer, whom we met in the last chapter, recalls vividly her realization when she moved out of her marital home in 2009 and started living on her own. "I realized that singlehood is good for work, good for life, and good for doing what you want to do." Citing her long marital experience, Jennifer laments the persistent gendered thinking and gender inequality on the domestic front: women should and would care about their family, and thus, should be the only ones to take care of their family in addition to their work. Miss P, born in 1977, in Shanghai, now a creative director at an advertising agency, shares a similar *qilinghou* experience of her life as a married woman struggling with work. While she was aware of her role as a wife, and spent a lot of time and energy managing the household, Miss P felt that her husband continued living as a single man. "During that time, my career was practically on hold."

That singlehood functions as their tactic against inequality and towards good work is also illustrated by the narratives of women who have never married. Yvonne, born in 1987, left Shanghai for the first and only time to study at a drama academy in Beijing. She returned to her hometown after graduation and took up an internship position at a local television station. Two years later, Yvonne became a regular staff member, doing various creative writing jobs until she took up her current post as scriptwriter and director. It was a tough trajectory. Without any standard financial compensation or assurance of a future, Yvonne was the only one, among five, who survived the internship period. Still, "[t]his is the best job I have ever had," Yvonne concludes with a sense of contentment. While acknowledging the financial and emotional support her parents offer her, Yvonne also connects her relatively smooth career progress to her singlehood. "In our business, the management favours single employees, as they can contribute 100 per cent to their work." The week before our interview, Yvonne was busy preparing for an important television show. She had hardly had any sleep for the whole week. Miss P tells me she got her nickname, Panda, because of the dark circles constantly surrounding her eyes—a symptom of sleep deficiency. Due to her similar experience of devotion to work, Miss P, as a senior staff member of her company, underlines the management's preference for single employees. "Say, if you have two applicants, one male, one female, both 40, most companies would opt for the male as they would assume the female applicant, at her age, would either focus on her family, or would start thinking of building up a family." Skipper makes this observation bluntly: "Investors in China discriminate against women blatantly. Many famous people simply say: I won't invest in women." But somehow, she understands and echoes what Miss P says: "Women, due to love, due to family, due to kids, would destabilize the company."

For Yvonne and many of the other single women I spoke with, this easily becomes a cycle, vicious or not, a process of mutual constitution of singlehood and creative work. Remember Xiaoqian who, jokingly and tellingly, remarks that she is married to her job? Similarly, Yvonne says, "the management wants you to stay single, and the job keeps you single." What she insinuates is that only single people can afford the kind of devotion to the demanding creative work, which in turn, keeps the workers in certain conditions of living such that they are likely to stay single. Or, in some instances, to become single, again. A friend had called on Jennifer the day before our interview. She was filing for divorce; she found it difficult to combine the heavy burden of doing her work and taking care of her husband and child. Jennifer tells me it is quite a common development in her circle of friends.

It is not only the work itself that contributes to their singlehood; sometimes, it is the working environment as well. Those who work in the creative sectors are predominantly female, according to Jennifer. And those male colleagues who stay are usually more senior, and "they are either married or gay," according to Jin, born in 1982, in Shanghai, and working in the media. Or they are, as observed by Jennifer, "a bit weird." Indeed, a number of the single women confide in me about their involvements with married men, colleagues or not. Sometimes, the female creative workers do not want another creative worker as their potential partner. Yvonne, observing that creative people tend to be sentimental, follows with the remark that "our male colleagues are usually weak in their sense of responsibility and commitment," and hence, they are outside her imaginary of jointly building up a marital home. Miss P, however, cites another reason: there are too many good-looking men in the creative fields, making it difficult for her to fall in love again.

SCENARIO 2: "WE DON'T WANT TO SETTLE DOWN"

Next to mutual constitution, creative work and singlehood manifest their imbrication in another scenario. Some women in this inquiry narrate their preference or necessity to do creative work due to the flexibility and autonomy it offers. Especially as freelancers and working as their own bosses, they are more capable of leading their lives as single women, mostly for the sake of taking care of their family members, but also to continue pursuing their passions and interests. Lei is a vivid instance of the former. At the age of 40, she gave birth to a baby girl through artificial insemination. "A good female friend of mine had a pair of twins. She used artificial insemination and she suggested that I should consult a doctor." Lei used the sperm of the man she was having a relationship with at that point, but they broke up before the baby was born. She decided to bring up her daughter on her own, without involving the biological father. When she mentions another female friend who is following her example, I ask Lei if she knows of similar cases of single motherhood among her circle of friends. "Yes, a lot," she replies resolutely. "That's why the case of Xu Jinglei got so much attention."[56] Having been a single mother for 20 months, Lei explains the relative ease afforded by her creative work and entrepreneurship. She has, for instance, set up her office close to her home so that she can go and see her daughter regularly during the working day. Generally entrusting her daughter to an *ayi*, her domestic helper, Lei finds it reassuring that if something happens on the home front, she can be there swiftly. Similarly, Yang, who used to leave her child in the care of her parents in her hometown, decided to ask them to bring the child to Shanghai. They had arrived a few days before our interview took place. During the interview, Yang was checking her phone constantly. Noticing my inquisitive glance, she explained she was busy finding a nursery for her child. It takes time and energy to take care of a family, and the single mothers in my inquiry all positively mention the flexibility of creative work and entrepreneurship. "I will arrange my work in such a way that I have more time with my baby. I am sure I will regret it if I am not there and miss his important period of growing up." Yang is fully aware that her single motherhood will slow down the development of her porcelain workshop and online shopping business. As she is her own boss, Yang plans to keep the business running at a subsistence level. "When my child starts to go to school, I will have more time for my career."

For many other single women I spoke with, their account of creative work connects their singlehood to what a number of single women in this inquiry call "the beautiful things in life." Born in 1981, Shanghai, Vera mentions many beautiful things in her life, which, thanks to her creative work, she has opportunities to encounter as well as to experience. When working for a lifestyle magazine, Vera was assigned to do a feature on calligraphy. Touched by the beauty of this traditional art form, and encouraged by a master she interviewed, Vera started practising. She mentions having the same sentiments for porcelain making and Kunqu appreciation. In very similar discourse, Yvonne talks about practising calligraphy, going to Kunqu performances, reading, seeing a film, cooking, and taking a walk. She describes her current life as a "very stable triangle," consisting of work, family, and all her passions. Yvonne is thankful for her creative work, which allows her to lead her single life the way she wants. "If I had a boyfriend now, the triangle would be disturbed," she says.

Another group of single women mention travelling on their own as the advantage afforded by creative work. Anna, born in 1964, in Hong Kong, moved to Shanghai in 2010. A year earlier, she quit her advertising job to take care of her ailing mother. Her mother passed away at the end of 2009, and a few months later, Anna received an offer to relocate. During the interview, Anna describes emphatically one characteristic of creative people, herself included: "We don't want to settle down." Her advertising work keeps her from settling down; she particularly enjoys the in-between-jobs periods, which allow her to travel as a single woman. JM, born in 1973, in Shanghai, worked for a major advertising agency for some years before she decided to go to Spain to try to find a new life. A good female friend had migrated earlier and encouraged her to do so too. However, her visa application was rejected. We will discuss this incident further in Chap. 5; for the time being, let us note that JM still quit her job and started freelancing. She did her freelancing in such a way that she would be extremely busy for the duration of a project, and then, allow herself a relatively long interval of freedom to concentrate on her passion: painting.

SCENARIO 3: "MY CHOICES ARE LIMITED"

Finally, some single women report to me their struggles, not so much with creative work itself, but with its success, and the time they have spent to make it a success.[57] Ridiculed as the "3 high ladies," as mentioned earlier, those women with a high income, high education, and high age, are generally framed as problematic—compulsive, addicted to work, and emotionally incapable—and thus, destined to stay single.[58] Confronted with such negative framing, the single women in my inquiry articulate their dedication and passion for their work and one gender-specific price they are paying precisely for such good professional qualities: while "high quality" men would make desirable bachelors, "high quality" women find it difficult to have compatible life partners. Ultimately, it feeds into and sustains the cliché of success in work, failure in love, and the stigmatization of single women who enjoy a good creative career after spending years of their life achieving it.

Given the contours of this cliché, the single women I include here are, understandably, from the post-1970s and -1980s generations. Anna tells me the downside of being single, mature, and successful as a woman. "They talk behind your back, that you are perverted, a spinster and so on." Contrary to the workaholic bias against career women, Anna does have spare time and remains active on the dating front. However, she does notice the difficulty in finding the right guy who "is trying to improve their quality of life as much as us women." Underscoring what I reported earlier in Scenario 1, Anna and some other women working at a similar level of work and age seniority tell me of the greater likelihood of meeting someone at work who is already married, and thus, of their affairs or relationships with married men. Valerie shares a similar experience of the stigma of mature, single career women in her advertising world. When I ask her if she has anything to add, towards the end of our conversation, Valerie mentions age. Attributing it to a peculiar mainland cultural characteristic, Valerie observes how easily she is asked in Shanghai how old she is. While she will give a reply in Hong Kong, Valerie resists the imminent judgement and relocation of her to the role of a loser, when people know her age and start asking further questions. "They like to use age and marriage to judge if a life is successful or not." At first, when Valerie still replied straightforwardly, "they would continue asking me why I was not dating, why I was not married ... as if leading a single life is a crime."

Jennifer articulates this predicament using well-nigh identical wording. Resonating with the post-1970s generation, she says: "In the Chinese collective subconsciousness, especially in the eyes of my parents' generation, if a woman is single, she is a loser, however successful she is at work." In her position and at her age, the men who she would come across during work occasions are mostly married. "My choices are limited," thus summarizes Jennifer about her situation. Jennifer does meet men younger than her, but she finds this difficult to accept: "perhaps I am too conservative." Some other single women are more open to a relationship with someone younger and less senior in work positions; however, they have to withdraw once the issue of childbearing comes up, as in the case of Anna. Jennifer keeps trying, including using dating Apps. She describes her expectations of prospective life partners as emphatically as her insistence of such expectations. She looks for someone about her age, who will understand her, who is emotionally mature, who can communicate with her, and who will not disturb her way of life with incompatible habits.

Sometimes, it is not the intersection of career success and age that limits their choice of life partners and sustains their singlehood; it is their ambition, or dreams. Xiaoyan, who has been working on her Kunqu educational project among universities in Shanghai, tells me her plan to develop the project into a personal brand, ultimately securing her place in Kunqu as well as in top-tier theatres. "When I share this dream with men in Shanghai, they laugh at me," she says. "Men wish to push women back to the domestic sphere." Before we end the interview, Xiaoyan asks me if I know any other women like her, if I can introduce some to her, so that she can find or build up a supporting network. In any case, as with Jennifer, Xiaoyan will not lower her expectations. On the contrary, she remains "ambitious," and that may, in her view, actually help her encounter the right person. "I will try to climb higher, and then I will get to know more people, it will be good for me to find a boyfriend. The higher my platform, the better the people I will get in touch with, and perhaps some single men will be there."

I was not able to introduce more mature single women to Xiaoyan. As I noted earlier, it was not easy to find them, not so much because they were not there, I believe, but more because they remained invisible, reluctant to talk to about their singlehood. Regarding the kind of community that is constructed by single women, I will discuss this in greater detail in Chap. 6, in connection with one passion that many of the single women I spoke with share: Kunqu. But first, we will move on to talk about their love lives.

NOTES

1. David Hesmondhalgh and Sarah Baker, *Creative Labour: Media Work in Three Cultural Industries* (London: Routledge, 2011).
2. See, for instance, Melissa Gregg, *Work's Intimacy* (London: Polity Press, 2011); Brooke Erin Duffy, "The Romance of Work: Gender and Aspirational Labour in the Digital Culture Industries," *International Journal of Cultural Studies* 19, no. 4 (2016): 441–57.
3. Richard Florida, *The Rise of the Creative Class* (New York: Basic Books, 2002).
4. For historical reviews of governments adopting the creative agenda in the region, see Can-Seng Ooi and Birgit Stöber, "Creativity Unbound—Policies, Government and the Creative Industries," *Culture Unbound: Journal of Current Cultural Research* 3 (2011): 113–17; Chris Gibson and Lily Kong, "Cultural Economy: A Critical Review," *Progress in Human Geography* 29, no. 5 (2005): 541–61; Jo Foord, "Strategies for Creative Industries: An International Review," *Creative Industries Journal* 1, no. 2 (2009): 91–113.
5. See, for instance, Andrew Ross, *Nice Work If You Can Get It: Life and Labor in Precarious Times* (New York: NYU Press, 2009); Ann Markusen, "Urban Development and the Politics of a Creative Class: Evidence from a Study of Artists," *Environment and Planning A* 38, no. 10 (2006): 1921–40.
6. See, for instance, Ulrich Beck, *What Is Globalization* (Cambridge: Polity., 2000); Florida, *The Rise of the Creative Class*; John Hartley, "Creative Industries," in *Creative Industries*, ed. John Hartley (Oxford: Blackwell, 2005), 1–40; Paul Heelas, "Work Ethics, Soft Capitalism and the 'Turn to Life,'" in *Cultural Economy: Cultural Analysis and Commercial Life*, ed. Paul du Gay and Michael Pryke (London: SAGE, 2002), 78–96.
7. See, for instance, Axel Bruns, *Blogs, Wikipedia, Second Life, and Beyond: From Production to Produsage* (New York: Peter Lang, 2008); Henry Jenkins, *Convergence Culture: Where Old and New Media Collide* (New

York: NYU Press, 2006); Miya Tokumitsu, "In the Name of Love," *Jacobin Magazine*, January 12, 2014, http://jacobinmag.com/2014/01/in-the-name-of-love/.

8. While work–life balance appears to be a peculiarly contemporary term and problem, scholars trace its origin to the turn of the Industrial Revolution, where the hitherto separate components of life—work, life, and recreation—became jostled by the industrial demands for higher productivity and longer working hours, causing conflict between work and life, and resulting in strikes for 8-hour workdays in the United States as early as in 1889. For more, see Paula Brough et al., "The Ability of Work-Life Balance Policies to Influence Key Social/Organisational Issues," *Asia Pacific Journal of Human Resources* 46, no. 3 (2008): 261–74.

9. See Michael Curtin and Kevin Sanson, *Precarious Creativity: Global Media, Local Labor* (Oakland, CA: University of California Press, 2016); Rosalind Gill and Andy Pratt, "In the Social Factory?: Immaterial Labour, Precariousness and Cultural Work," *Theory, Culture & Society* 25, no. 7–8 (2008): 1–30; Hesmondhalgh and Baker, *Creative Labour*; Toby Miller, "From Creative to Cultural Industries," *Cultural Studies* 23, no. 1 (2009): 88–99; Gerald Raunig, *Factories of Knowledge, Industries of Creativity* (Los Angeles, CA: Semiotext(e), 2013); Andrew Ross, *No-Collar: The Humane Workplace and Its Hidden Costs* (Philadelphia: Temple University Press, 2004); Sabina Siebert and Fiona Wilson, "All Work and No Pay: Consequences of Unpaid Work in the Creative Industries," *Work, Employment and Society* 27, no. 4 (2013): 711–21.

10. Angela McRobbie, *Be Creative: Making a Living in the New Culture Industries*, 1 edition (Cambridge, UK ; Malden, MA: Polity, 2016): 14.

11. Duffy, "The Romance of Work."

12. See Christian Fuchs, "Labor in Informational Capitalism and on the Internet," *The Information Society* 26, no. 3 (2010): 179–96; Trebor Scholz, ed., *Digital Labor: The Internet as Playground and Factory* (New York: Routledge, 2013).

13. John Banks and Mark Deuze, "Co-Creative Labour," *International Journal of Cultural Studies* 12, no. 5 (2009): 419–31.

14. Hector Postigo, "America Online Volunteers: Lessons from an Early Co-Production Community," *International Journal of Cultural Studies* 12, no. 5 (2009): 451–69.

15. Kathleen Kuehn and Thomas F. Corrigan, "Hope Labor: The Role of Employment Prospects in Online Social Production," *The Political Economy of Communication* 1, no. 1 (2013).

16. Gina Neff, *Venture Labor: Work and the Burden of Risk in Innovative Industries* (Cambridge, MA: MIT Press, 2012).

17. Julian Kücklich, "Precarious Playbour: Modders and the Digital Games Industry," *Fibreculture Journal*, no. 5 (2005).

18. Ross, *Nice Work If You Can Get It.*
19. Guy Standing, *The Precariat: The New Dangerous Class* (London, UK; New York, USA: Bloomsbury Academic, 2011).
20. McRobbie, *Be Creative*, 14.
21. Banks and Deuze, "Co-Creative Labour"; Duffy, "The Romance of Work"; Scholz, *Digital Labor.*
22. See, for instance, Gregg, *Work's Intimacy*; Joke Hermes, ed., "Special Issue: Labour and Passion." Special issue, *European Journal of Cultural Studies* 18, no. 2 (2015); Arlie Russell Hochschild, *The Outsourced Self: Intimate Life in Market Times*, 1 edition (New York: Metropolitan Books, 2012).
23. Hermes, "Special Issue: Labour and Passion."
24. See, for instance, Jan Breman, "A Bogus Concept?," *New Left Review*, no. 84 (2013): 130–38; Ronaldo Munck, "The Precariat: A View from the South," *Third World Quarterly* 34, no. 5 (2013): 747–62.
25. See Lee Ching Kwan, "Precarization or Empowerment? Reflections on Recent Labor Unrest in China," *The Journal of Asian Studies* 75, no. 2 (2016): 317–33; Lee Ching Kwan and Zhang Yonghong, "The Power of Instability: Unraveling the Microfoundations of Bargained Authoritarianism in China," *American Journal of Sociology* 118, no. 6 (2013): 1475–1508.
26. Hesmondhalgh and Baker, *Creative Labour.*
27. Ibid., 2.
28. Ibid.
29. Private conversation on October 10, 2016.
30. Hesmondhalgh and Baker, *Creative Labour*, 8.
31. Ibid., 46.
32. Ibid., 47.
33. Ibid., 36.
34. Ibid., 49.
35. See, for instance, Liu Tian (刘天), "传统道德教育与大学生创业 [Traditional Moral Education and College Students' Entrepreneurship]," 中国青年研究 *[Zhongguo Qingnian Yanjiu]*, no. 11 (2008): 95–98; Li Yan (李艳) and Li Hefeng (李禾丰), "创业文化是传统客家文化的精髓 [Entrepreneurial Culture Is the Essence of Traditional Hakka Culture]," 江西农业大学学报:社会科学版 *[Jiangxi Nongye Daxue Xuebao: Shehuikexue Ban]* 8, no. 1 (2009): 147–50; Xie Wenqing (谢文庆), "儒家思想对大学生创业精神的积极影响—兼与胡友旺等先生商榷 [The Positive Influence of Confucianism on the Entrepreneurship of College Students—A Discussion with Mr. Hu Youwang et al.]," 湖南师范大学教育科学学报 *[Hunan Shifan Daxuae Jiaoyu Kexue Xuebao]* 12, no. 1 (2013): 116–19; Yang Xianmei (杨先梅), "中国传统文化在大学生创业精神培育中的价值研究 [A Study on the Value of Chinese Traditional Culture

in Cultivating College Students' Entrepreneurship]," 国网技术学院学报 *[Guowang Jishu Xueyuan Xuebao]* 18, no. 3 (2015): 73–76.

36. See, for instance, Hu Youwang (胡友旺), Sun Yanbao (孙艳宝), and Sun Xiaoyan (孙小燕), "儒家思想对大学生创业精神的消极影响及其对策 [The Negative Influence of Confucianism on the Entrepreneurship of College Students and Its Remedy]," 湖南师范大学教育科学学报 *[Hunan Shifan Daxuae Jiaoyu Kexue Xuebao]* 11, no. 5 (2012): 122–25; David A. Kirby and Ying Fan, "Chinese Cultural Values and Entrepreneurship: A Preliminary Consideration," *Journal of Enterprising Culture* 03, no. 03 (1995): 245–60.

37. For a recent study of working women with similar experiences of sexual harassment as C's, read Heather McLaughlin, Christopher Uggen, and Amy Blackstone, "The Economic and Career Effects of Sexual Harassment on Working Women," *Gender & Society* 31, no. 3 (2017): 333–58.

38. Partly as an attempt to tap the creativity of the single women in this book, I invited some of them to contribute visual works to represent themselves in Chap. 7. Unfortunately, C declined; she was "too busy."

39. In their study of young fashion designers in contemporary Russia, Olga Gurova and Daria Morozova observe a similar articulation of their entrepreneurial experiences in terms of autonomy and independence from the state. While acknowledging the need to address the ills of precarity, the authors also foreground the need to maintain this insistence on autonomy and independence. See Olga Gurova and Daria Morozova, "Creative Precarity? Young Fashion Designers as Entrepreneurs in Russia," *Cultural Studies* 32, no. 5 (2018): 704–26.

40. See Duffy, "The Romance of Work."; Gregg, *Work's Intimacy*; Hermes, "Special Issue: Labour and Passion."; Angela McRobbie, "Reflections on Feminism, Immaterial Labour and the Post-Fordist Regime," *New Formations*, no. 70 (2011): 60–76; Diane Negra and Yvonne Tasker, *Gendering the Recession: Media and Culture in an Age of Austerity* (Durham, NC: Duke University Press, 2014); Chow Yiu Fai, "The Aspiration, the Precarious, the Ethical: Hong Kong Creative Workers in Mainland China," *China Information* (forthcoming).

41. Marta Mensa Torras and Jean M. Grow, "Creative Women in Peru: Outliers in a Machismo World," *Communication & Society*, 2015, 1–18.

42. Leslie Regan Shade and Jenna Jacobson, "Hungry for the Job: Gender, Unpaid Internships, and the Creative Industries," *The Sociological Review* 63, no. 1 suppl (2015): 188–205.

43. Anne O'Brien, "'Men Own Television': Why Women Leave Media Work," *Media, Culture & Society* 36, no. 8 (2014): 1207–18.

44. McRobbie, "Reflections on Feminism, Immaterial Labour and the Post-Fordist Regime."

45. Rosalind Gill, "Unspeakable Inequalities: Post Feminism, Entrepreneurial Subjectivity, and the Repudiation of Sexism among Cultural Workers," *Social Politics* 21, no. 4 (2014): 509.
46. Gill, "Unspeakable Inequalities," 511.
47. Bridget Conor, Rosalind Gill, and Stephanie Taylor, "Gender and Creative Labour," *The Sociological Review* 63, no. 1_suppl (2015): 1–22.
48. Bridget Conor, Rosalind Gill, and Stephanie Taylor, eds., "Special Issue: Gender and Creative Labour," *The Sociological Review* 63, no. 1_suppl (2015).
49. Kylie Jarrett, "The Relevance of 'Women's Work': Social Reproduction and Immaterial Labor in Digital Media," *Television & New Media* 15, no. 1 (2014): 26. In a different take on gender and creative work, Seppo Poutanen and Anne Kovalainen have chosen to focus on women's inventions and innovations in the context of new economy and platform economy. Their book-length treatise examines women's role not only as innovators, but also as part and parcel of the innovative process. See Seppo Poutanen and Anne Kovalainen, *Gender and Innovation in the New Economy: Women, Identity, and Creative Work* (New York: Springer, 2017).
50. Gill, "Unspeakable Inequalities," 524.
51. George Morgan and Pariece Nelligan, "Labile Labour—Gender, Flexibility and Creative Work," *The Sociological Review* 63, no. 1 suppl (2015): 66–83.
52. Zhang Lin, "The Contradictions of 'Women's Work' in Digital Capitalism: A 'Non-Western'/Chinese Perspective," *Feminist Media Studies* 18, no. 1 (2018): 147–51.
53. Gregg, *Work's Intimacy*, 2.
54. Ibid., 174.
55. Ibid., xii.
56. A famous actress in China, Xu Jinglei joined a popular television talk show and told the female host about her experiences of freezing her eggs for future use. At the age of 43, single, Xu's candid disclosure surfed on the wave of single women discussions and led to heated debates in the Chinese media. For a "record" of her experience and an interview, read http://www.vistastory.com/a/201507/32961.html and http://www.vistastory.com/a/201507/30946.html. For a report of the controversy this incident caused, read http://health.people.com.cn/n/2015/0710/c14739-27282682.html. For an English-language report on Chinese women going abroad to freeze their eggs, read Alice Yan, "How a Ban Is Forcing China's Single Women to Put Their Fertility on Ice Overseas," *South China Morning Post*, August 20, 2017, http://www.scmp.com/news/china/society/article/2107287/how-ban-forcing-chinas-leftover-women-abroad-freeze-their-eggs.

57. For a study of the construction of "successful femininity" in the United Kingdom and its entanglement with post-feminism and neo-liberalism, especially in the new millennium, see Natalia Gerodetti and Martha McNaught-Davis, "Feminisation of Success or Successful Femininities? Disentangling 'New Femininities' under Neoliberal Conditions," *European Journal of Women's Studies* 24, no. 4 (2017): 351–65.

58. See the commentary on the popular Chinese search engine Baidu: "三高女人," 百度百科. http://baike.baidu.com/item/%E4%B8%89%E9%AB%98%E5%A5%B3%E4%BA%BA.

REFERENCES

Banks, John, and Mark Deuze. "Co-Creative Labour." *International Journal of Cultural Studies* 12, no. 5 (2009): 419–31.

Beck, Ulrich. *What Is Globalization*. Cambridge: Polity, 2000.

Branigan, Tania. "Five Chinese Feminists Held over International Women's Day Plans." *The Guardian*, March 12, 2015, sec. World news. http://www.the-guardian.com/world/2015/mar/12/five-chinese-feminists-held-international-womens-day.

Breman, Jan. "A Bogus Concept?" *New Left Review*, no. 84 (2013): 130–38.

Brough, Paula, Jackie Holt, Rosie Bauld, Amanda Biggs, and Claire Ryan. "The Ability of Work—Life Balance Policies to Influence Key Social/Organisational Issues." *Asia Pacific Journal of Human Resources* 46, no. 3 (2008): 261–74.

Bruns, Axel. *Blogs, Wikipedia, Second Life, and Beyond: From Production to Produsage*. New York: Peter Lang, 2008.

Chow, Yiu Fai. "Exploring Creative Class Mobility: Hong Kong Creative Workers in Shanghai and Beijing." *Eurasian Geography and Economics*, 2017, 1–25.

Chow, Yiu Fai. "The Aspiration, the Precarious, the Ethical: Hong Kong Creative Workers in Mainland China." *China Information*, Forthcoming.

Conor, Bridget, Rosalind Gill, and Stephanie Taylor. "Gender and Creative Labour." *The Sociological Review* 63, no. 1_suppl (2015a): 1–22.

Conor, Bridget, Rosalind Gill, and Stephanie Taylor, eds. "Special Issue: Gender and Creative Labour." *The Sociological Review* 63, no. 1_suppl (2015b).

Curtin, Michael, and Kevin Sanson. *Precarious Creativity: Global Media, Local Labor*. Oakland, CA: University of California Press, 2016.

Duffy, Brooke Erin. "The Romance of Work: Gender and Aspirational Labour in the Digital Culture Industries." *International Journal of Cultural Studies* 19, no. 4 (2016): 441–57.

Florida, Richard. *The Rise of the Creative Class*. New York: Basic Books, 2002.

Foord, Jo. "Strategies for Creative Industries: An International Review." *Creative Industries Journal* 1, no. 2 (2009): 91–113.

Fuchs, Christian. "Labor in Informational Capitalism and on the Internet." *The Information Society* 26, no. 3 (2010): 179–96.

Gibson, Chris, and Lily Kong. "Cultural Economy: A Critical Review." *Progress in Human Geography* 29, no. 5 (2005): 541–61.

Gill, Rosalind. "Unspeakable Inequalities: Post Feminism, Entrepreneurial Subjectivity, and the Repudiation of Sexism among Cultural Workers." *Social Politics* 21, no. 4 (2014): 509–28.

Gill, Rosalind, and Andy Pratt. "In the Social Factory?: Immaterial Labour, Precariousness and Cultural Work." *Theory, Culture & Society* 25, no. 7–8 (2008): 1–30.

Gregg, Melissa. *Work's Intimacy*. London: Polity Press, 2011.

Gurova, Olga, and Daria Morozova. "Creative Precarity? Young Fashion Designers as Entrepreneurs in Russia." *Cultural Studies* 32, no. 5 (2018): 704–26.

Hartley, John. "Creative Industries." In *Creative Industries*, edited by John Hartley, 1–40. Oxford: Blackwell, 2005.

Heelas, Paul. "Work Ethics, Soft Capitalism and the 'Turn to Life.'" In *Cultural Economy: Cultural Analysis and Commercial Life*, edited by Paul du Gay and Michael Pryke, 78–96. London: SAGE, 2002.

Hermes, Joke, ed. "Special Issue: Labour and Passion." *European Journal of Cultural Studies* 18, no. 2 (2015).

Hesmondhalgh, David, and Sarah Baker. *Creative Labour: Media Work in Three Cultural Industries*. London: Routledge, 2011.

Hochschild, Arlie Russell. *The Outsourced Self: Intimate Life in Market Times*. 1 edition. New York: Metropolitan Books, 2012.

Hu, Youwang (胡友旺), Sun Yanbao (孙艳宝), and Sun Xiaoyan (孙小燕). "儒家思想对大学生创业精神的消极影响及其对策 [The Negative Influence of Confucianism on the Entrepreneurship of College Students and Its Remedy]." 湖南师范大学教育科学学报 *[Hunan Shifan Daxuae Jiaoyu Kexue Xuebao]* 11, no. 5 (2012): 122–25.

Jarrett, Kylie. "The Relevance of 'Women's Work': Social Reproduction and Immaterial Labor in Digital Media." *Television & New Media* 15, no. 1 (2014): 14–29.

Jenkins, Henry. *Convergence Culture: Where Old and New Media Collide*. New York: NYU Press, 2006.

Kirby, David A., and Ying Fan. "Chinese Cultural Values and Entrepreneurship: A Preliminary Consideration." *Journal of Enterprising Culture* 03, no. 03 (1995): 245–60.

Kücklich, Julian. "Precarious Playbour: Modders and the Digital Games Industry." *Fibreculture Journal*, no. 5 (2005).

Kuehn, Kathleen, and Thomas F. Corrigan. "Hope Labor: The Role of Employment Prospects in Online Social Production." *The Political Economy of Communication* 1, no. 1 (2013).

Lee, Ching Kwan. "Precarization or Empowerment? Reflections on Recent Labor Unrest in China." *The Journal of Asian Studies* 75, no. 2 (2016): 317–33.

Lee, Ching Kwan, and Yonghong Zhang. "The Power of Instability: Unraveling the Microfoundations of Bargained Authoritarianism in China." *American Journal of Sociology* 118, no. 6 (2013): 1475–1508.

Li, Yan (李艳), and Li Hefeng (李禾丰). "创业文化是传统客家文化的精髓 [Entrepreneurial Culture Is the Essence of Traditional Hakka Culture]." *江西农业大学学报:社会科学版 [Jiangxi Nongye Daxue Xuebao: Shehuikexue Ban]* 8, no. 1 (2009): 147–50.

Liu, Tian (刘天). "传统道德教育与大学生创业 [Traditional Moral Education and College Students' Entrepreneurship]." *中国青年研究 [Zhongguo Qingnian Yanjiu]*, no. 11 (2008): 95–98.

Markusen, Ann. "Urban Development and the Politics of a Creative Class: Evidence from a Study of Artists." *Environment and Planning A* 38, no. 10 (2006): 1921–40.

McLaughlin, Heather, Christopher Uggen, and Amy Blackstone. "The Economic and Career Effects of Sexual Harassment on Working Women." *Gender & Society* 31, no. 3 (2017): 333–58.

McRobbie, Angela. *Be Creative: Making a Living in the New Culture Industries.* 1 edition. Cambridge, UK; Malden, MA: Polity, 2016.

McRobbie, Angela. "Reflections on Feminism, Immaterial Labour and the Post-Fordist Regime." *New Formations*, no. 70 (2011): 60–76.

Miller, Toby. "From Creative to Cultural Industries." *Cultural Studies* 23, no. 1 (2009): 88–99.

Morgan, George, and Pariece Nelligan. "Labile Labour—Gender, Flexibility and Creative Work." *The Sociological Review* 63, no. 1_suppl (2015): 66–83.

Munck, Ronaldo. "The Precariat: A View from the South." *Third World Quarterly* 34, no. 5 (2013): 747–62.

Natalia Gerodetti, and Martha McNaught-Davis. "Feminisation of Success or Successful Femininities? Disentangling 'New Femininities' under Neoliberal Conditions." *European Journal of Women's Studies* 24, no. 4 (2017): 351–65.

Neff, Gina. *Venture Labor: Work and the Burden of Risk in Innovative Industries.* Cambridge, MA: MIT Press, 2012.

Negra, Diane, and Yvonne Tasker. *Gendering the Recession: Media and Culture in an Age of Austerity.* Durham, NC: Duke University Press, 2014.

O'Brien, Anne. "'Men Own Television': Why Women Leave Media Work." *Media, Culture & Society* 36, no. 8 (2014): 1207–18.

Ooi, Can-Seng, and Birgit Stöber. "Creativity Unbound—Policies, Government and the Creative Industries." *Culture Unbound: Journal of Current Cultural Research* 3 (2011): 113–17.

Postigo, Hector. "America Online Volunteers: Lessons from an Early Co-Production Community." *International Journal of Cultural Studies* 12, no. 5 (2009): 451–69.

Poutanen, Seppo, and Anne Kovalainen. *Gender and Innovation in the New Economy: Women, Identity, and Creative Work.* New York: Springer, 2017.

Raunig, Gerald. *Factories of Knowledge, Industries of Creativity.* Los Angeles, CA: Semiotext(e), 2013.

Ross, Andrew. *Nice Work If You Can Get It: Life and Labor in Precarious Times.* New York: NYU Press, 2009.

Ross, Andrew. *No-Collar: The Humane Workplace and Its Hidden Costs.* Philadelphia: Temple University Press, 2004.

Scholz, Trebor, ed. *Digital Labor: The Internet as Playground and Factory.* New York: Routledge, 2013.

Shade, Leslie Regan, and Jenna Jacobson. "Hungry for the Job: Gender, Unpaid Internships, and the Creative Industries." *The Sociological Review* 63, no. 1_suppl (2015): 188–205.

Siebert, Sabina, and Fiona Wilson. "All Work and No Pay: Consequences of Unpaid Work in the Creative Industries." *Work, Employment and Society* 27, no. 4 (2013): 711–21.

Standing, Guy. *The Precariat: The New Dangerous Class.* London; New York: Bloomsbury Academic, 2011.

Tokumitsu, Miya. "In the Name of Love." *Jacobin Magazine,* January 12, 2014. http://jacobinmag.com/2014/01/in-the-name-of-love/.

Torras, Marta Mensa, and Jean M. Grow. "Creative Women in Peru: Outliers in a Machismo World." *Communication & Society,* 2015, 1–18.

Xie, Wenqing (谢文庆). "儒家思想对大学生创业精神的积极影响—兼与胡友旺等先生商榷 [The Positive Influence of Confucianism on the Entrepreneurship of College Students—A Discussion with Mr. Hu Youwang et al.]." *湖南师范大学教育科学学报 [Hunan Shifan Daxuae Jiaoyu Kexue Xuebao]* 12, no. 1 (2013): 116–19.

Yan, Alice. "How a Ban Is Forcing China's Single Women to Put Their Fertility on Ice Overseas." *South China Morning Post,* August 20, 2017. http://www.scmp.com/news/china/society/article/2107287/how-ban-forcing-chinas-leftover-women-abroad-freeze-their-eggs.

Yang, Xianmei (杨先梅). "中国传统文化在大学生创业精神培育中的价值研究 [A Study on the Value of Chinese Traditional Culture in Cultivating College Students' Entrepreneurship]." *国网技术学院学报 [Guowang Jishu Xueyuan Xuebao]* 18, no. 3 (2015): 73–76.

Zhang, Lin. "The Contradictions of 'Women's Work' in Digital Capitalism: A 'Non-Western'/Chinese Perspective." *Feminist Media Studies* 18, no. 1 (2018): 147–51.

CHAPTER 5

To Love, to Live

This chapter should be read in tandem with the previous one. While Chap. 4 examines single women's experience in creative work in general, and its intersection with being single in particular, Chap. 5 goes further, to explore their lives in domains of intimacy. It situates the exploration in studies on single women in China, which centre on urban-dwelling and middle-class categories, and largely report similar marginalization as reported in Western contexts. These women have to endure the demands to become a respectful, meaningful, and thus full woman, through matrimony and maternity, with various vectors of coercion including Confucian values, state propaganda, and parental pressure.[1] To underline the hegemony of matrimony, as noted in Chap. 1, about 30 to 40 per cent of Chinese people prefer a bad marriage to singlehood.[2] The divorce rate has doubled in the decade through 2016, increasing from 1.46 to 3 in every 1000 people in China.[3] If the invention and circulation of the derogatory term *shengnü* (leftover woman) is a mirror to reflect the indictment of this hegemony, it is certainly as harsh and chilling as any mirror on the wall meant to tell who is the fairest of them all.

This chapter builds on studies that consider such stigmatization of single women as part of a resurgence of male privilege in "post-socialist" China, that is, compared with the propagation of gender equality in the earlier, Maoist era.[4] It focuses on the lived experiences of single women, that point to a three-pronged approach in understanding the complexity with which they navigate and mitigate their "predicament," their lived

© The Author(s) 2019
Chow Y. F., *Caring in Times of Precarity*, Palgrave Studies in
Globalization, Culture and Society,
https://doi.org/10.1007/978-3-319-76898-4_5

replies to all the questioning, stigmatizing, and expectant gazes on them(selves) as Chinese women. First, there are negative accounts of anxiety and feelings of crisis, particularly when they are under pressure to get married. Parents, and sometimes peers, will arrange for single women to meet potential marriage candidates, a tradition or culture called *xiangqin* (相亲). At the same time, they also report ways to cope with such social and parental pressure to unsingle.[5] Second, an aversion to the pressure to get married is not to be conflated with an aversion to getting married. Some women articulate their wish to be romantically involved, and their tactics to find "the right one." They include attending courses offered by a "school" called Love Club—which trains single people, mostly female, to attain romantic success—as well as joining interest groups and cultural activities. Third, there are also more positive articulations of freedom and autonomy, lifestyle, and social support, underwriting single lives' potentials to open up spaces for alternative forms of relationships and cohabitation beyond the heteronormative. They do so often with a gesture towards global narratives of singlehood, of femininity, and ultimately, of what they consider to be a "good life." I will supplement the above analytical sections with an account of one group of women whose sexual preference already constitutes a challenge to the heteronormative regime. Here, in this inquiry, I will focus on the experiences of three self-proclaimed lesbian women. The chapter will end with a deliberation on their vicissitudes between the modern and the traditional in the realm of love and marriage.

SINGLE WOMEN

Some women prefer to be single. Some are forced by circumstances. Some just happen to be so … Whether as a matter of choice, an act of necessity, or somewhere between the two, ours is the time when they *can* lead a single life. While human beings are used to relying on clanship and family support to sustain their lives, they can now live on their own. The processes of urbanization and modernization are particularly conducive to single living. For example, for the basic need to eat, when someone lives in a modern city, she or he can use a microwave to heat up a ready-made meal bought at a supermarket, or simply call for food to be delivered. For the first time in human history, people do not need a family to sustain their daily lives, and individuals have become the basic unit of society.[6]

Despite the increasing number of people leading a single life, scholars have detected a persistent negative framing and experience of single people, from the 1970s to the present. As an extension of the gender bias in patriarchal societies (think of the different connotations of "bachelor" and "spinster"), single women are particularly prone to symbolic stigmatization, practical inconvenience, and often, downright discrimination. They are perceived as unnatural, unattractive, pathological, egocentric; in short, a lesser woman.[7] The persistence of these views indexes the ideology of marriage, family, and motherhood, or what Adrienne Rich calls "compulsory heterosexuality,"[8] which continues to be privileged, imbricating to structural and quotidian discrimination against single people, or, using Kinneret Lahad's shrewd formulation: "singlism."[9] Laconically put, despite decades of feminist critique, women continue to be expected to get married and become mothers.[10]

The persistent marginalization of single women coincides with the emergence and increasing influence of the "postfeminist discourse" in popular culture, as critiqued by, for instance, Angela McRobbie and Rosalind Gill.[11] Proclaiming a post-feminist era and proposing successful women as role models (think of the representations of the "happy single" such as Bridget Jones or in *Sex and the City*), such a discourse typically dissociates itself from feminist politics; instead, it allies with a neo-liberal understanding of personhood and emphasizes the personal choice, agency, and autonomy of female subjects. While women themselves—not state authorities, for instance—are considered to be personally responsible for their own well-being, happiness and livelihood, single women, for all their marginalization under the ideology of family, marriage, and motherhood, are still easy objects for a range of condescending reactions, from sympathy to accusations. Subsequently, studies usually focus on representations in popular culture. In Chap. 2, I have offered an account of such studies with an elaborate supplement of the Chinese case. Suffice it here to reiterate one persistent finding: since women themselves hold the keys to their own happiness, singlehood is often represented as being in need of repair, with therapeutic treatment as a panacea.[12] Another typical example is the portrayal of single women as overly ambitious, workaholic, and highly achieving in the workplace, but as losers in their private lives.[13]

There is also a line of research that connects women with precarious work. While these studies do not focus on single women or on creative work, they are of relevance to the current inquiry, particularly in demonstrating the power of "meta-narratives" on selfhood, family, and happiness for helping women survive the precarity of their lives. For instance, how the meta-narrative of a happy nation (Switzerland) demands women living there to narrate their own well-being, or how the meta-narrative of family- and self-appreciation subjects women to "mamapreneurialism" and to willingly endure the heavy burden of making a home and working at home.[14] It is in this body of scholarship that I will situate my empirical findings later in the chapter. The stories of the single women in this inquiry will tell us how they experience stigmatization and pressure; how they not only survive, but also manage to thrive in their own ways; and how they tell the stories of how they love, and live, or how they love to live, and how they live to love—in neo-liberal, post-feminist discourses, and more.

Single Women in China

Writers on Chinese singlehood generally agree on four waves of singlehood in modern, Communist Chinese history.[15] The first took place in the 1950s, after divorce laws were introduced into China in 1949. The second took place at the end of 1970s in the wake of the Cultural Revolution. While male intellectuals who were sent to rural areas usually got married to a local partner, their female counterparts refused to marry "down" to farming men, and returned to the cities as single women. The third wave was, again, related to divorce legislation. When the laws were revised in the 1990s to include emotional reasons as legitimate grounds to file for divorce, many couples broke up into singletons. In the fourth wave, which started in the new millennium and is ongoing, higher education and the financial independence of women, coupled with (post-)feminist influences, have been proposed as reasons for women to lead a single life.[16] Some of the women, the post-1970s and post-1980s women in this inquiry, have shared narratives of their singlehood with me that are reminiscent of the latter two waves.

Despite these "waves" of singlehood, single women in China continue to be marginalized and stigmatized, and struggle with the push to unsingle themselves. Zooming in on their plight, studies generally diverge. The first trajectory situates itself in the post-socialist period in China, and investigates the stigmatization of single women as part of a resurgence of male privilege compared with the propagation of gender equality in the earlier, Maoist era.[17] Leta Hong Fincher, for instance, in her book-length investigation of leftover women, demonstrates how urban professional women, in fear of being labelled *shengnü*, hastened to get married, and contributed their savings to the new homes, which were registered solely under the ownership of their husbands.[18] Another trajectory probes the lived experience of single women, from negative accounts of anxiety and feelings of crisis as well as mechanisms to cope with them, to more positive articulations of freedom and autonomy, subcultural lifestyle, social support, and opening up of space for same-sex relationships.[19]

Such studies point to two lacunae in existing scholarship on single women in China. First, their connections with working experiences. As far as the current inquiry is concerned, no other studies focus particularly on single women in the creative class. In the scholarship on "Creative China," existing studies show a preference for issues concerning political economy, for instance, creative policies and industry practices,[20] as well as concerning the nation itself, for instance, the promotion of freedom and the exercise of "soft power."[21] Second, corresponding to a similar gap in international scholarship, studies on the Chinese creative experience do not pay particular attention to women or to single women.

XIANGQIN AND OTHER WAYS OF MARITAL PERSUASION

Conforming to the academic and popular studies and discourses on contemporary Chinese women, the subjects in my inquiry generally report experiences of parental pressure against their singlehood. There are a few exceptions who are either relatively young (those born in the 1990s), thus not (yet) within the proper discursive domain of leftover women; or they have, in their own words, exceptionally understanding parents. The pressure manifests itself in many forms, most commonly when parents—usually mothers, as recounted by the single women—would privately enquire about their love life, with the more-or-less explicit mission of persuading or even coercing unmarried daughters into seeing someone. The most interventionist, often violent, manner is *xiangqin*. A term that finds its way into almost all of my conversations with the single women, *xiangqin* refers to practices involving gatherings arranged by parents, other family members, friends, or professional matchmakers, for single men and women to meet, hopefully leading to dating and marriage. In a time when even a masseuse would meddle in her client's love life (as experienced by Jennifer, one of the single women who spoke with me), *xiangqin*—a conventional form of marriage arranging prior to the introduction of "free love" to China—is enjoying a second life in contemporary Chinese societies. Nowadays, *xiangqin* has become commercialized and professionalized to the extent that single people can pay fees to obtain a *xiangqin* service.[22] While none of the single women I spoke with say that they tried such a service, Xiaoqian tells of two single friends of hers who spent 8000 RMB to join a *xiangqin* club.

My first round of fieldwork took place rather soon after Chinese New Year, a time when children return to their hometown for family reunions, and usually, the most challenging time of the year, when parents (and others) start probing into the status of their love lives. It has become especially burdensome and stressful for single women that, as noted earlier, another service has emerged in China: that of renting a boyfriend to bring home.[23] With their Chinese New Year experiences still fresh in their minds, many of the single women tell me how they survive the pressure with a weird mixture of annoyance, anguish, and guilt.

Xiaoqian expresses it using the most extreme wording. "They are pushing me to death!" As expected, her parents tried to arrange *xiangqin* gatherings for her. It was always trying. "I have no idea how to carry out a conversation with a total stranger," she says. For Xiaoqian, it is hard enough to spend a dinner sustaining some semblance of a conversation with someone from "another world," not to mention when it drags on. "Not so long ago, I met some guy who seemed to like everything about me. I told him it wouldn't work, but he said we could try. He even liked every message I posted on WeChat!" It was stressful, to Xiaoqian. Sometimes, when her parents push her hard, Xiaoqian would retort: "Getting married and having children is not the most important thing." Her parents would reply: "What is the most important thing then? You shouldn't be so selfish." Then, the conversation grinds to an end. To avoid the pressure, particularly from the extended family, Xiaoqian told her parents that she would only stay until a few days before the Spring Festival period, informing them that she would rather spend some quiet holidays on her own. In fact, Xiaoqian did spend her holidays in her hometown, but only with her friends.

The parents of Shanghai journalist Mi, born in 1989, have become more direct in urging her to marry, again using the interventionist form of *xiangqin*. "So far, about 10 times, but there's no spark at all," Mi recalls. "They were all very qualified, like PhD graduates in science disciplines from U.S. universities. My impression was, they were all pushed by their parents into the meeting." There might be no spark during the *xiangqin* meetings, but that does not mean they have no impact on the single women. "Even if you don't like the other guy, and you know the other guy doesn't like you too, you will still feel the negativity. When it happened several times, I started looking at myself in a negative way."

Jin, annoyed by the materialistic orientation of contemporary *xiangqin* practices in China, tells me: "The so-called *xiangqin* now, the first thing they mention is: how old is the man, what's his profession, how much does he earn, how tall is he. Just a series of figures." Jin says she would yield to one in five of her parents' *xiangqin* requests. She wanted to underwrite her feelings towards *xiangqin* by recalling a "terrifying" experience. The man who was supposed to be a suitable partner for Jin, called her up and fixed a dinner date. As the restaurant was in a remote location in Shanghai, he picked her up. After two hours' driving, the man received a phone call, and then, stopped the car. He told Jin the call was from someone who would very likely become his girlfriend and she had asked him to come over, right then. The man decided to do this, and so, asked Jin to leave his car and make her own way home. Xiaoyan reports a negative *xiangqin* experience at the instigation of her mother. Mentioning her mother's intellectual background, Xiaoyan says she started to feel pressure from her mother only when she was approaching 30. Selective in arranging *xiangqin* meetings for her daughter, Xiaoyan's mother was particularly enthusiastic about one candidate, a painter and university teacher. In the end, Xiaoyan was rejected. She knew her mother's feelings were hurt, and she herself was left in a state of anguish and grief.

Although the post-1990s women in my inquiry were not usually asked to participate in *xiangqin*, Weiwei reports otherwise. Born in 1990, she was 25 when we conducted the interview. She has experienced *xiangqin*, albeit only once. Describing her parents as "open and not urging me to get married," Weiwei tells me how her parents arranged for her to meet a relative of her father's colleague, from the same hometown. In Weiwei's case, no physical meeting was arranged; the parents only discreetly passed the digital contacts to each other's children. Not only do parents exert pressure; other family members, friends, friends' family members, and acquaintances, all show their eagerness to introduce prospective marriage candidates and propose *xiangqin* gatherings. Vera, born in 1981, tells me of two *xiangqin* occasions she remembers in particular. The first was initiated by her university tutor, the second by the mother of her friend. Valerie, likewise, recounts how her friends started cautioning her about singlehood. "My family is very good. No pressure at all. But my friends do put me under pressure, they tell me 'oh, you can't continue like this, you can't stay single for the rest of your life'."

Given all these *xiangqin* stories, and parental as well as social pressure, it is hardly surprising that quite a few single women in this inquiry succumbed and got married. Yang, who is building up a new life in Shanghai with her son as a divorced mother, tells me she attended more than 10 *xiangqin* gatherings the year she decided to get married. Miss P admits, "The pressure from society was too much! From friends, from parents. And I also had the feeling, like at this age [33], if I am still single, what will happen?" She subsequently married someone who, according to her, was equally unprepared. On the other hand, there are other single women in my inquiry who did not rush into marriage, despite persistent pressure. Vera narrates perhaps the toughest and most heartrending decision to resist the social urge to fulfil others' expectations. Pressurized by her parents, Vera started dating someone rather seriously at the early age of 21–22. She became pregnant, but in the end, decided to terminate the pregnancy in order not to continue with the expected marriage. "We almost got married," she contemplates.

More often, these single women seek to escape, to ignore, or, put less negatively, to find more meaningful reasons to empower themselves and to live in their own ways, which I will discuss later, when I talk about their notions of a good life. I will confine myself to four tactics often articulated by the single women in my inquiry. To begin with, living (far) away from their family. The distance works both physically and psychologically for the single women who were not born in Shanghai, in order to claim more autonomy, or, at any rate, to ward off the intervention of their parents residing in their hometowns. Shanghai, being another space, functions as a shelter.[24] As Lei explains: "The more they urged me to get married, the less I had the urge to see them. If we didn't talk, it became easier for me to escape and the pressure became less." Second, if nothing else changes, then eventually the passing of time helps. That is to say, when the single women stand their ground and become older, they are less susceptible to parental or peer pressure. As Vera summarizes it: "I haven't done *xiangqin* since I turned 30. It's not necessary at all." The third oft-cited "reason" for not rushing into marriage is, paradoxically, their understanding of what a relationship should be, which is both romantic and conservative. Typical of her fellow single women, Yvonne explicates her version of marital life with the romantic trope of "finding the right guy" and the traditional view that once married, the wife should take care of the home and the family: "[as a wife] I will make sure warm dinners are served when my husband comes home." It becomes logical for her and single women like her to explain their singlehood as "not yet finding the right guy to justify the sacrifice."

Finally, there are some very isolated and highly individualized ways to deal with the pressure. Lei chose to escape and avoid her parents, until something happened. It was during the time when her mother was suffering from a variety of health problems, culminating in a "shadow" in her intestines, the nature of which medical experts failed to ascertain. Lei returned to her hometown to visit her mother. She slept in the bedroom she had occupied as a teenage girl, even sleeping in between the same bed sheets she had used as a teenager. "They kept them clean and tidy, and whenever I paid a visit, they would fish them out for me." One night—"it must have been 3 or 4 am"—Lei woke up to find her mother sitting on one side of her bed. She was just sitting there, in total darkness, watching her daughter quietly. Then, she realized Lei was awake. She took hold of Lei's hand and said: "One day, when me and your dad are no longer here, what will happen to you?" Lei was shocked, speechless, and trembling. She was speechless since she knew that if she responded, she would start to cry. Trembling because she was confronted with the worries and wishes of an ailing, perhaps dying, mother—a form of parental pressure and expectation more subtle, but as emotionally coercive as the interventional tactic of *xiangqin*, if not stronger. Since that night, which Lei recounts to me in vividly intimate details, she started pondering seriously if she should continue her single life. "A writer friend of mine puts it this way: our parents are the only barrier between us and death," Lei says. She started ruminating on the scenario of her parents passing away, and her connection with the world. She did not rush into marriage; instead, her response to her mother's nocturnal persuasion was, finally, by giving herself a child, as recounted in the previous chapter.

FINDING "THE RIGHT ONE"

While the single women continue to employ a variety of tactics to deal with family and social pressure, some of them are trying another, sometimes concomitant, set of tactics to look for "the right one" for themselves. In other words, the annoyance, anguish, and guilt surrounding the pressure to get married does not mean that single women do not want to engage in a relationship. Put differently, while many of the single women articulate their enjoyment of the single life in various degrees and formulations, none of them proclaims the wish to stay single for the rest of their life. The tenacious centrality of relationship in one's intimate life corresponds with the findings of many studies on marital attitudes among contemporary Chinese populations[25] as well as in the East Asian region as a whole.[26] They would rather say they are open to relationships, again, in various degrees and formulations. At the same time, some of them, across different generations, articulate their ambivalence, if not reluctance to get married, even if they are willing to engage in a relationship. Vera, a post-1980s, is convinced when she says, after experiencing severe family pressure to get married, "Now, I would say, life is not about getting married." Siqi, a post-1990s, does not see the need for marriage: "I don't see why it is necessary, it's basically a transaction." She admits she is scared, although she adds, "I don't understand why I am scared. My parents have a good relationship … I fear that once you are married, the possibilities of life are reduced by half." Miss P, post-1970s, finds marriage "complicated." If she finds someone suitable, she is willing to accommodate any form of living arrangement, except getting married. "In China, marriage is a matter for the entire families of both the bride and the bridegroom, it's too complicated."

Mi's attitude is typical of many single women. She enjoys her single life, finds that it combines well with her work, and remains cautious about the prospect of relationships. To be involved in a relationship, in her conception, would mean a challenge to the status quo of her life, particularly her commitment to work; note the heavy demands of creative work described in Chap. 4. At the same time, she remains open to finding someone, to developing a relationship and getting married. Very quickly, Mi adds, "But if I get married, I would need to consider other things, like having a child." Echoing Yvonne's "sacrifice" discourse cited earlier, illustrating how many single women continue to imagine the possibility of a relationship in the context of an inevitable chain of heteronormative arrangements, such as getting married and forming a family with children. At times, it seems that the very idea of having a relationship is so entwined with additional familial responsibilities, that this has become a reason or excuse in itself not to have a relationship at all. Put differently, the heteronormative imaginary can and does become a means to refuse heteronormativity itself.

In addition to the generally open attitude, sometimes single women would tell me their specific tactics to find "the right one." Typically, it is the post-1980s and the post-1970s women who have more to say about their search for love, while the younger ones, understandably, sound more nonchalant about the prognosis of their love lives. The tactics they articulate include attending courses offered by the earlier-mentioned Love Club, which trains single people, mostly female, to achieve romantic success; using online possibilities; and joining interest groups and cultural activities. Such tactics, while pragmatic in nature, are at the same time, underpinned by something more conceptual: their understanding and expectations of what an intimate relationship should be, the concept of free love. In Liu Wenjia's study, "[t]hey all involve, to a greater or lesser degree, a courtship into which both parties enter freely. As in any 'modern' romance, these courtships are characterized by mutual admiration, misunderstanding, and, finally, expression of love and commitment."[27] In Khatjidja Chantler's analysis, it is the dominant Euro-American construction of intimate relationships, anchored to the individualization thesis put forward by Anthony Giddens and Beck and Beck-Gernsheim,[28] with the "assumption that it is both possible and desirable to act as autonomous agents outside of social processes that structure everyday lives and practices."[29]

The negative feelings surrounding *xiangqin* are the corollary when their longings for modern romance are frustrated by the burden of traditional arrangements, and their autonomy is disrupted by the social. The accent on individuality, autonomy, and equality, enshrined in the concept of free love, contrasts starkly with what Lee Haiyan, in her genealogy of love in China, calls: "the hypocrisy and tyranny of family, society and Confucian morality."[30] This modern concept of intimate relationships was arguably introduced into China and became popularized in the first half of the twentieth century; some observers have pinpointed the importance of the May Fourth Movement for campaigning for the ideal of modern womanhood.[31] The idea and ideal of free love, however, was largely repudiated and superseded by the other idea and ideal of revolutionary love—asexual and genderless—following the Communist Revolution and in the subsequent decades, only to enjoy a powerful comeback in the 1980s, when the reform policies opened the door to Freudian publications, women writer's works, and popular culture from elsewhere in the region.[32] At the same time, the history of free love is also complicated by recuperations from earlier literary sources in imperial China (for instance, the Mandarin Duck and Butterfly school of romantic fiction), which note that certain "traditional" sentiments predate and prelude the modern concept of romance.[33] Shelving a discussion of how modern or traditional the concept of free love is, suffice it to say that the single women in this inquiry have internalized the preference for finding romance and the right partner them-selves, not for relying on others. While their ideals are similar, they express it in a variety of practices.[34]

Xiaoyan talks passionately about her devotion to Kunqu, but with a hint of regret. She was eager to learn from the masters, but when they started to pass away, Xiaoyan realized she was already 30. "Perhaps it's my hormones, my biology, in any case, I started longing for a boyfriend." With her knowledge in Kunqu and other Chinese classics, Xiaoyan is sure of her attractiveness; it is more difficult for her to find attractive men. "First, they don't understand what I am talking about. Second, they don't understand my worth." Luckily, Xiaoyan says, she has the virtue of being curious and willing to learn. She reads books, mostly on psychology, in order to understand more about herself and about relationships. And dur-ing our conversation, she mostly talks about Wu Di and the Love Club she co-founded in Shanghai in 2011. Noting that increasing numbers of sin-gle people came to ask for her advice, Wu, a psychology consultant by training and a television specialist on intimate relationships, capitalized on the niche market and developed the idea of a training school in 2007, when the leftover women discourse was widely circulating in China. Although the Love Club, or *lian'ai xunlianying* 恋爱训练营 (literally, training camp for love), is not targeted exclusively at single women, the majority of Wu's clients who are willing to pay the fee of 4500 RMB (as of end 2014) for a three-month course are predominantly female, mostly with a university education, and in their mid-20s or mid-30s.[35] As noted by Xiaoyan, born in the 1970s, she is exceptional among the course participants.

"Wu Di has had a big big impact on my life," Xiaoyan says. Citing Wu's "theory of jumping out," Xiaoyan tells me how she learned from Wu about the importance of making oneself "jump out" in a group of people. "You have to be active, and introduce yourself actively." She is also empowered by Wu Di to travel on her own, for the first time in her life. When she showed the photos she took in Zhejiang to her mother, her mother asked why she had not taken her along. Inspired by Wu Di, the daughter replied, "If you want to go, I will give you money to go, both you and dad. But I wanted to travel on my own. I needed to be indepen-dent." Xiaoyan and her fellow students were learning a variety of tech-niques for connecting with other people. During one site visit to the Love Club, I witnessed students doing exercises—for that evening, they, male and female students, had to do groceries together in a supermarket, presumably for a party—and observed how Wu showed them intricate ways to communicate, including flirting.[36] While Xiaoyan is the only participant in my inquiry who mentioned to me her experience with the training school, her experience and my site visit gesture to a wider section of the population looking for similar assistance in their paths towards intimate relationships.

As Xiaoyan and others are intent on learning more techniques for attracting men in real-life situations, online platforms appear to be the most accessible route for them to continue their romantic search. Some of them mention the use of dating Apps, which have become a commonplace component of their social lives, indicating a substantial overlap of offline and online spaces for socialization. At the same time, single women have developed their own online tactics, either as a replacement for dating Apps, or as a supplement to them. Anna tells me she is not morally against online dating, but finds it generally too time-consuming and stressful in itself. "I am already very busy with my work, and if I am also required to market myself with an App, it's tiring. I only work hard for my job." Instead, she is more selective; Anna explains she visits a website targeted at expats in Shanghai. Besides visiting various sections offering information on nightlife, cultural events, and housing, Anna also surfs to a dating section, believing the "quality" of people there to be better. Dating an expat instead of a local Chinese man, to Anna, has an additional advantage, as local Chinese men would want to have children—which is not Anna's own plan. Digital spaces for people with common interests are another popular platform for meeting someone. Xiaoqian became acquainted with a man sharing the same fascination for the music of a Taiwanese singer-songwriter. They exchanged comments on a digital forum for fans, and entered into a relationship that is not readily classifiable. "We share many things in common. Sometimes we will chat … I like this," Xiaoqian says. Mi's tactic is proactively oriented to whatever social media platforms she subscribes to. She does not wait; rather, whenever she finds someone, perhaps a friend of a friend, posting something interesting, she takes the initiative to add him to her circle of friends. Such proactiveness is not common among Chinese women, according to Mi. "But I believe if you are not taking the initiative, you are limiting your choices to those who would take the initiative in choosing you. That's rather pointless." At the time of our conversation, Mi is dating "three to four men" and she does not mind them knowing about the existence of each other. "But they never ask, so I never tell."

Resonating with Xiaoqian's participation in the online forum surrounding the singer-songwriter, the single women in this inquiry behave similarly in their offline lives in the form of joining interest groups and participating in cultural activities. Xiaoqian talks profusely of her visits to Kunqu performances. Miss P tells me she has to rush off to a jazz festival after our interview. Jennifer plans to try out a workshop on fragrance blending. While these single women describe their leisure activities in the general context of fun and self-enrichment, such activities generate social occasions to meet people and make friends, and possibly more. The Love Club in Shanghai was established by Wu Di jointly with a salsa teacher, and the Club operates in his salsa house. Offline interest groups and cultural activities remain one avenue for single women to meet potential partners.

Finally, in their workplace. As noted in the previous chapter, most of the single women, especially those who are older or with a more senior professional position, note the scarcity of candidates for relationships. In the creative fields, they point to the high probability that their male colleagues are either married or gay. However, this does not mean that relationships do not develop at all in their workplaces. On the one hand, some of the single women in this inquiry articulate their hesitation—if not objection—to getting involved with work-related people, either because it may tarnish their professionalism, or because they are afraid of office gossip. On the other hand, at least four single women tell me that they did go ahead when they met someone at work. Yang met her current boyfriend while working on the same project. Anna started a long-term relationship with someone she met during a job interview, a married man. Given the social stigma, it is not unusual that besides Anna, only Valerie and LIV report similar extramarital involvement. However, more of such relationships must be going on, as Valerie observes it is "quite a common practice in Shanghai to have mistresses." LIV, additionally, also reports relationship experiences with her colleagues. For her, it was even an advantage to date someone from her own work circle: they could share their work experiences and problems. "He [a senior colleague she dated for a while] helped me a lot. He's good at writing, and sometimes he helped me with writing captions." Miss P mentions dating a colleague when she was 32.

To conclude this section on their aspirations and tactics surrounding love, I want to cite Xiaoqian, whose articulation echoes the words of many of the single women in this inquiry—hopeful about love's possibility, bewildered by its difficulty, and finally, comfortable with their singlehood even though "the right one" is not (yet) there. She says: "If I come across [the right guy], I am most willing to live a real life with him. I believe, like most people, that getting married and setting up a family, are necessary phases of one's life. But it is not up to me. If I do have it, I will be happy. Just like every winter, I always wish that it would be less cold, it would be nice to be in love. But then when winter is gone, I think, well, look, I survived on my own!"

The Good Life

Again, it may be some form of bias, inherent to this research project, that the single women who are willing to be interviewed may very well be those who feel rather comfortable with their lives as a single person. That said, under pressure to get married, while trying in their own ways to look for love, they report positive experiences of freedom and autonomy when they relate their lifestyles and social support. This recognition of what they are doing does not mean that they do not feel bad sometimes. Amidst the talk about their autonomy and freedom, some of the single women would make statements like Miss P: "Single life is freedom. But if you ask me if I am lonely? Well, sometimes." Regarding their various degrees of loneliness, Vera confides in me about a distressing period of her life. When I ask her about loneliness, Vera says: "I had depression. Can you believe it? It was not very serious, it was a light form. I thought of committing suicide." That was in 2005, when Vera had just started her university life in Shanghai. "I felt hopeless, and lonely. I was thinking, when I get up the next day, I need to pay the rent, I need to pay the utilities, I need to eat. However bad I felt, I still had to do so many things, to earn money. During the evenings, I felt lonely."

Michelle, who is living with her parents and has a good relationship with them, admits to thinking increasingly about the prospect of them passing away. "I am not afraid of being on my own, I am afraid of being lonely." This, she says, worries her more than her work now. "I think far ahead. Like, if I stay single for the rest of my life, who is going to take care of my funeral?" The feelings shared by Miss P, Vera, Michelle and their counterparts are, of course, real affects in their own right. However, at the same time, they are also reiterations of a certain representation of single womanhood, loneliness, and a desirable life: the "old maid who died alone" image.[37] Despite the worries, Michelle would not allow herself to rush into marriage. Referring to her interest in pop music, Michelle draws a comparison: "If I am now offered two options, one is to go to a concert on my own, and the other is to get married right away, I would certainly opt for the former." So, how does she deal with these worries? "For the time being, I try to make my life rich ... I fill it with work, and my interests. And I try to convince myself: it's ok, don't be afraid." This, for want of a better term—avoidance tactic—is employed by many single women in dealing with their experiences and imaginings of loneliness. Vera calls it her "Ah Q mentality." The protagonist of a well-known satirical novella, *The True Story of Ah Q*, penned by Lu Xun (first serialized in 1921–1922), "Ah Q" has become a catchphrase for anyone having an escapist mentality in dealing with—or some would say, avoiding to face—reality.

The following articulation is telling. Vera is handling two projects at the time we are having the interview. When asked whether she is worried about money, or tempted by the security of a regular job, Vera replies: "Not really, but I can't say I am not worried at all. There is pressure ... Now that I am running my own company, do I need to earn 500,000 RMB? Or if I earn only 50,000, is it shameful? I don't earn as much as when I was employed, but that doesn't matter." Acknowledging the freedom and autonomy she is enjoying and has become accustomed to, Vera says emphatically that she would never allow herself to re-enter salaried life. "We just need to support ourselves, to be independent, the rest doesn't matter." Apart from work, she likes spending time in markets buying food to prepare dinner at home for herself. She also likes to take photographs of the people who frequent the market. Recently, Vera has started practising calligraphy. She describes calligraphy as one of the "beautiful things in life" that enchant her. "It's probably in my genes. Whenever I see something beautiful, I will study it ... I am curious, and when I study these beautiful things, I feel that life is good."

This general sense of having a good life, or rather, having arranged a life more-or-less according to their own wishes, is often conveyed when we talk about their work—their talk of a good life is often referenced to the reasons why they opted for and stayed in creative work, as detailed in the previous chapter. What they talk about here is that how they spend their everyday life should be seen as a continuation of that expression of flexibility, freedom, and autonomy. JM arranges her life this way: occasionally, she will take up freelance jobs—by her definition, freelancing means taking up full-time jobs at advertising agencies for short periods of time—and will earn money, partly to save up for her travels and her non-working days in Shanghai. Most of the time, she does what she enjoys most: painting.

"Oil painting, water colours, and I am working on a book with my own illustrations." Sport is what Miss P enjoys in her single life. A few years ago, Miss P started going to the gym. By the time of our conversation, Miss P went three times a week. Other "solitary" pastimes are cited by the single women: reading, browsing the internet, watching films, and so on.

Besides sports, there are two other activities Miss P mentions in particular that resonate with the experiences of many other single women: socializing and travelling. First, socializing. "When I had a regular job, I would have gatherings with my friends every weekend," recalls Miss P. Now that she has more flexibility from freelancing, Miss P has become more spontaneous and available to her friends. "Now, whenever my friends need me, I will be there." Miss P says she has a lot of friends, of different ages and different personal statuses, including mothers and single women. The following chapter will discuss in greater length one specific case of sociality, where a number of the single women in this inquiry share their time, interest, and passion: Kunqu. For the time being, suffice it to note that friends, and the maintenance of a social network, are an integral part of their single life. Socially, the single women in this inquiry confirm findings elsewhere that single individuals maintain more social connections than the married.[38]

Second—and sometimes, relatedly—travelling. Miss P tells me she has just returned from a trip to Iceland with four female friends. In fact, among all the activities mentioned by the single women, travelling is undoubtedly the most cherished. As an extension and expression of their autonomy and freedom, single women of different generations have shared with me their travelling experiences. They put forward different motives. Miss P refers to it as a way of coping with her work stress. JM frames her travelling positively and creatively. "When I am away for some time, I get inspiration, some creative moments." Her longest trip was three months spent traversing Turkey, Iran, and Armenia, followed by a stay in Mongolia. The third motive is in its intertwining with work. Vera enjoys the business trips her branding work necessitates. Mi loves travelling so much that she has integrated her own travelling experiences into her work to launch a new App for fellow travellers. C turns her passion for travelling into her photography and online work, which, however, also caused the break-up with her erstwhile boyfriend. "I felt like every time I went on a work trip, I needed to explain or justify myself. I didn't like it." And finally, there is also the motive of self-enrichment, as in the case of Anna, who is planning a trip to Thailand for a yoga course.

Sometimes, it is not only travelling on a short-term basis that attracts them; some of the single women talk about their plans or dreams to leave Shanghai for a longer period of time for various reasons, from studying to migrating. *Chuguo*, 出国, literally leaving the country, is the term often mobilized, which is distinct from "travelling."[39] Captain Zoey, born in 1992, a native of Shanghai, works in an advertising agency. Her goal is to save enough money to study abroad as a postgraduate student of literature or philosophy. This prospective future seems to be aspired to by many of her contemporaries. Siqi, a fellow *jiulinghou*, plans to spend the coming two-to-three years preparing herself to study, most preferably, in France. Weiwei's plan is to study comparative literature outside mainland China. When they are articulating such plans or dreams, or a mixture of both, they are partly articulating their aspirations for freedom, at least for the years to come, when they are studying somewhere else beyond mainland China. Sometimes, they remark rationally on the curricula offered abroad. Often, they do not have a longer-term vision of what they would do or where they would go.[40]

With the older generation of single women, their aspiration of *chuguo* is quite different. For them, it is not only a question of continuing their education, but more a matter of radically changing their lives. Xiaoyan, a post-1970s, elaborates her scenario: "I actually want to *chuguo*. After so many years of struggling, I want to go to the United States. Even if I have to begin with serving coffee, I am fine. I will establish myself and then slowly enter their community, and find a job through their network. I feel that I will survive in the States." For the time being, she cannot actualize it; Xiaoyan is living with her parents, taking care of them. "I am still Chinese," she says. Echoing what Jennifer articulated earlier in this book, Xiaoyan adds, "But when they pass away, I will leave this country. Even if I just buy a ticket and stay wherever for a year, I will do it."

Among all of the women who express their longing to get away, to leave the country, to change their lives radically, only one actually gave it a try. JM, born in 1973, a native of Shanghai, was trained as a painter, but "accidentally" entered the advertising world as a designer. When I begin my interview by asking her to introduce herself, JM immediately tells me the following—in her words, "traumatic"—story in her life. After working for a 4A agency for some time, she started thinking of quitting. She had a dream plan of leaving Shanghai and moving to Spain "to learn more about art." JM had a female friend living in Spain, married to a Spanish man. JM tells me how she started learning the language, how she finally managed to submit her visa application in the Spanish language, and how the application was declined. In the absence of any official explanation—the authorities did not have to justify their decision—JM speculates, "I believe it's because I was single." When JM submitted the application, she was 35 or 36. "I believe they were afraid I wanted to go there simply because I wanted to find someone to get married to." Whether or not her plan to leave was thwarted by the reason she envisaged, single womanhood appears to be a problematic category, either to the authorities or to the self-perception of single women.

The Alternatives

JM continues to travel. In a general sense, all the single women in the inquiry continue to organize their lives—as to how they spend their time, and how they enjoy their freedom and autonomy—which also find their manifestations as alternative ways of conducting relationships and co-habiting. These ways are hugely diverse; to be single, in this sense, means to be capacitated or necessitated to imagine, to accommodate, and to find one's own way of living that is not always already scripted in the hetero-normative. I will outline some of them in the following sections, occasionally repeating what was written earlier, but in a different context. In terms of relationships, besides the majority who tell me they are not in any relationship at this point in time, some of them prefer keeping a distance, either physical or otherwise. Yang is dating someone, but maintains her life as a single mother. JM has a boyfriend, an artist like herself, but she is clear that she enjoys living separately. At times, the distance even goes beyond the confines of the same city. Lulu maintains a relationship with her boyfriend in Qingdao, the hometown where they started and conduct their relationship. Since she moved to Shanghai to take up her design job after graduation, she has relied on her mobile phone for daily contact, and occasional visits during holidays. "After some time, it can be tiring. But then the basis is still there, and it's hard to give it up. There is not much possibility in realistic terms. We are plodding on." While these women are conducting their relationships, departing from the heteronormative mode of living together, there are others who experiment with relationships that challenge the precept of monogamy. Skipper has two boyfriends, one in Shanghai and one in Beijing; she says she would not mind them knowing of the existence of each other. An "open relationship" is what Skipper is contemplating. There are also Anna and Valerie, who report long-term relationships with married men. Finally, there is a group of women who seek to further destabilize the naturalized connection between a relationship and marriage; they say affirmatively that they would never marry.

Regarding co-habitation, the forms taken by these single women are similarly diverse, collectively posing a question mark as to what a single life actually is, simultaneously offering alternatives and imaginaries of living together not necessarily as a couple, or as the nuclear family model upheld as the modern (Western) norm. For the native Shanghainese, the single women usually live with their parents, and sometimes with other family members as well. In the Chinese context, it is considered not only acceptable but desirable, if not mandatory, to live with your parents when you are not yet married. Especially in the case of daughters, who are charged with the responsibility for taking care of their aging parents. The case of Xiaoyan is a vivid example. Only occasionally, for practical reasons—for instance, due to the distance between home and work—would they live outside the family home. For those moving to the city, they either live on their own or in shared housing. Often, it is a function of financial possibility, which I will discuss in the last part of this chapter. The other cases defy generalization. Jiayin shares a flat with two lesbian couples and a gay man. Ocean, herself a self-proclaimed lesbian, lives with three lesbians, in her words: "one couple, and one tb [tomboy]." Weiwei's flatmate is a colleague of hers, while Siqi found her flatmate on Douban, a site for culturally inclined people. And C, while living on her own, says she spends a lot of time in her office, including making dinners, with her two male colleagues.

THE LESBIAN CASE

To avoid any misunderstanding, the fact that I am allocating a separate section to the experiences of the single women who are self-proclaimed lesbians, does not suggest any essential differences between heterosexual and homosexual women in matters of intimacy. On the contrary, the three women included here—Joy (born in 1981, growing up in Shanghai, independent music-maker); Ocean (born in 1990, Urumqi, graphic designer); and Zaizai (born in 1983, Shenyang, running a gaming start-up with partners)—all tell me different versions of the same social pressure to get married, tactics to negotiate their love lives, and general contentment with what they are doing. In the words of Joy, single women, whether heterosexual and homosexual, are "similar." Citing the straight women she knows, Joy says, "They are the same as me, waiting for the right moment, the right one, but we are leading a rich life on our own too."

At the same time, there are also experiences of their love lives, which are specific to those who fall for people of the same sex. Continuing with her reference to the similarity between homosexual and heterosexual single women, Joy adds: "The difference may well be: when straight women are desperate, they will do *xiangqin*, homosexuals won't." From here on, I will not reiterate the similarities of Joy, Ocean, and Zaizai to their straight counterparts; I will focus on two aspects of their love lives that are specific to their lesbian experiences: how to deal with family pressure, and how to find life partners. Both of these are premised on the contemporary Chinese context, where heterosexuality is largely taken for granted, naturalized, and propagated, as discussed in Chap. 1, particularly in connection with the derogatory term *shengnü*, the leftover women. Homosexuality, on the other hand, remains largely a social stigma, a practice confined to the realm of the private.

Like their straight counterparts, the three homosexual women in the inquiry invariably experience pressure to get married. Assuming or feigning to assume their heterosexuality, their parents urged them to find a man, and sometimes, offered to arrange *xiangqin* opportunities. Coming out is one of the tactics to deal with such pressure. Zaizai's mother kept asking her the same question every year that she visited her family until 2010. "I told them, I don't like men, I like women," says Zaizai. Her mother took a while to accept it, "or she hasn't entirely accepted it, and she would still like to talk about it." In any case, Zaizai was liberated from this particular marital demand. At the same time, Zaizai felt that she had hurt her family and admitted to a sense of guilt, which provided the drive for her to excel at her work, "in order to earn a stronger right to say things," both in the family and in society. Her articulation corresponded generally with the mutual constitution of one's love life and one's work life, as discussed in Chap. 1.[41]

Coming out is not the only tactic to speak of the homosexual difference in the face of heteronormative pressure to get married. Compared with their straight counterparts, homosexuals seem to be more ready to articulate to their family their hesitation about marriage, if not its explicit rejection. Joy did not come out to her family. She tries to, in her words, "brainwash" them. "I keep on telling them life is not about getting married. There are more meaningful things to do in life." And she also taught her mother how to use a smartphone to receive WeChat messages, so that she could forward messages to a similar effect. As a music-maker, she created a feminist song on International Women's Day and sent it to her mom. Ocean did try to tell her mom about her sexual orientation. "I was hinting to her that I might prefer girls. But she didn't seem to take notice, and avoided the topic." Ocean, still young and in her 20s, says her family is not yet pushing her and "my mom quite trusts me." But when her mom steers the conversation towards marriage, Ocean would say, "I won't get married, and that's that." The three women articulate their delight with the generally tolerant attitude of their families, especially when they compare themselves with some of their homosexual friends, male and female, who were compelled to get married and fulfil social expectations. The practice, known as *xinghun* (形婚)—literally, a formalistic marriage, or marrying someone for show—is a controversial technique that some Chinese homosexuals use in order to appease their families and escape from societal suspicion.[42] The three women state adamantly that they will not do this.

Again, like the other single women, the fact that they articulate negative reactions towards family pressure to get married, does not mean they do not wish to find love. All of them report having had long-term relationships that broke up for various reasons, and that they would like to have such relationships again. However, they are clear about what they would not do in their search to find a relationship. First, they are rather negative about dating Apps. A friend of Ocean's acted on her behalf and posted something on Douban, not exactly a dating App, but nonetheless, a social platform. She did start chatting with a woman there, but at the time of the interview, they were yet to meet face to face. "I don't really like to meet strangers." Second, they all say they do not *hunquanzi* (混圈子), emphasizing their disapproval of or at least distance from the homosexual scene.[43] While the accounts of these three women cannot claim to represent the lesbian population of mainland China, they do point to a certain negativity towards gay culture revolving around dating Apps, and commercialized as well as ghettoized scenes, which is worth further investigation.[44]

They do not frequent gay or gay-friendly clubs or bars, or other similar venues, but again, that does not mean they are hesitant about proclaiming their sexual orientation or identity. This aspect of their personal lives is known to the good friends and colleagues of Joy, Ocean and Zaizai. Underwriting the relative openness in the creative professions, they experience no problems in their workplace. Actually, as noted by their straight counterparts, they encounter a high density of homosexual colleagues.

Due to their relative openness in their own social circles, friends of theirs are sometimes enthusiastic in helping them find a partner. Often, it is out of well-meaning but misguided heterosexual prejudice; as Joy recounts her experience, "They will tell me, hey I also know a lesbian woman, should I introduce you?" Joy considers this a form of "misunderstanding and discrimination." As she puts it, "You wouldn't introduce every single heterosexual woman to a single heterosexual man either, right?" The three lesbian women in this inquiry share a similar aversion to such friendly offers. Ocean tells me about the Douban attempt in a lukewarm manner, and that she did not really pursue it. Joy urges her friends categorically not to do such things. Here, they might be expressing a common experience of another sort of pressure, from their peers, packaged as concern and friendliness. Declining is their tactic. In the end, Joy, of the many other single women in this inquiry, homosexual or heterosexual, articulates the most explicitly fatalistic attitude towards love: "I totally believe in *yuanfen* (緣分)." Roughly translated as destiny or fate, *yuanfen* refers to an allegedly Chinese way of explaining how, when, and why two people meet and develop a relationship. Necessarily illusive, this vernacular concept or term, according to one study, is popular among university graduates in Shanghai, both male and female, when they try to explain their choices of partner.[45] In another survey of young people in Shanghai and Chengdu, almost 80 per cent said they believe in *yuanfen*.[46]

"MONEY IS THE BEST GUARANTEE"?

The globalization and modernization of China brings with it globalization and modernization of love and marriage. This chapter can be read as a bottom-up investigation of how these processes are playing out in the lives of individuals living in the dynamics and crevices of transformations and disruptions. Extrapolating their experiences to one important perspective, to examine the politics of intimacy in contemporary China, my findings do not lend evidence to one school of thought—the "deinstitutionalization of marriage."[47] In their 2014 edited volume of collected studies from Hong Kong, Taiwan, and mainland Chinese cities, Deborah Davis and Sara Friedman argue in their introduction that late marriages, more divorces, and greater acceptance of premarital relationships signal "marital deinstitutionalization."[48] In other words, Chinese participation in the globalizing and modernizing processes would roughly follow the "second demographic transition," known in the Western model as increasing individualization in deciding on people's intimate lives. In Ron Lesthaeghe's analysis, the transition has been taking place in the West since the 1960s, manifesting itself in society's shift from material to non-material needs, such as individual autonomy and self-realization, which ushered in various forms of non-marital living arrangements, and the delinking of marriage from procreation.[49] The single women in this inquiry point me, instead, to the need to talk more appropriately of the "reinstitutionalization of marriage." As Henrik Donner and Gonçalo Santos analyse the cases of "pinnacles of Asian modernity," namely China and India,[50] in an editorial for a special issue on love, marriage, and intimate citizenship in these two contexts, "there is significant evidence for the growing importance of affective ties and partner choice, but a diminished centrality of (heteronormative) marriage in discourses about love or the decoupling of marriage from broader patrilineal family ideals cannot be assumed."[51] More is going on when we understand the experiences of single women not only in the binary of modernity or tradition, but something paradoxical.

Take Jennifer. When I see her enter the trendy café in a trendy shopping mall in Shanghai, she blends in perfectly. In her 40s, occupying a senior position in an international company, she strikes me as a modern professional in a designer dress, wearing up-to-date makeup, composed, assured, and knowing what she is doing. I would not have expected to see her weep when she articulates her complex feelings about the passing of her parents. She is both relieved and guilty, happy to be free at last, but not entirely prepared to admit to such feelings about her own life. This is a kind of paradox running through the accounts of the single women when they tell me their stories of love and life. A paradox of the modern *and* the traditional. On the one hand, they are using various versions of the meta-narrative of modern love to help them pursue their life choices; instead of staying in or rushing into a marriage that is not commensurate with the intimate relationship they have in mind, they divorced and became single, or they remain single. These single women also use the other dominant modern meta-narrative of autonomy and freedom to help them iterate their sense of doing fine. On the other hand, their *xiangqin* experiences, the parental pressure they intensely feel, and their largely overwhelming agreement with the heteronormative ideal of getting married, manifest the kind of weight, the pull of tradition on their lives, to such an extent that, not surprisingly, many of them desire to travel, to go away, to leave, whether for some brief respite, or for good.

This is something paradoxical about this paradox, too. Tradition, or what is known as tradition, is not only restraining their autonomy and freedom; sometimes, it also offers solace. I am referring in particular to their talk of *yuanfen*, or destiny. In so far as this is understood by these single women as something they retrieve from the so-called Chinese way of thinking, *yuanfen* and the nebulousness of such a concept or belief supply traditional resources for them to open up the predicament configured precisely by other aspects of the same set of traditions, at least presumably. Similarly, their maintenance of a modern single life of autonomy and freedom is, at the same time, never really that autonomous and free, definitely not free of charge. It requires money. As one may probably deduce from the accounts earlier, the tactics they employ to manoeuvre their way to a life to their liking is costly. All the travelling, cultural and recreational activities, alternative accommodation arrangements, Love Club courses and so forth necessitate a certain amount of income as well as subscription to the neo-liberal economy of work and consumer culture. No wonder Lei, speaking the most succinctly and explicitly on behalf of many of her fellow single women in Shanghai, utters: "Money is the best guarantee."

What else? In her close reading of the popular television drama *Chinese-Style Divorce*, Faye Xiao places the media texts and the narratives constructed on divorce and divorced women in the larger context of a neo-liberal market economy and the ongoing state-sponsored campaign to promote the "harmonious society" and its underpinning of traditional family values and patriarchy.[52] She takes issue with the state-capital nexus which, by translating the modern discourse of individual freedom into the consumerist form of free choice in lifestyle and lifestyle commodities, seeks to ensure the continuation of the political and economic situation desired by the nexus itself. According to Xiao, "[o]ne of the goals of this political project is to encourage the 'democracy of consumption' to divert people's attention from struggles for gender equality and social justice to economic gains and commodity consumption."[53] I stand by such political ideals, and I understand the frustration of those ideals, as expressed in this analysis, as well as by many other critics of post-feminist discourses. Like them, I do not want to see the replacement or displacement of such ideals by practices that merely help them deal with the lived reality, a sort of false consciousness that keeps these single women away from the "real" political project. Unlike them, however, I do not see these practices this way, at least not only this way. I cannot, when I am impressed by the hardship, the energy, the pain, the pleasure, the anguish, the ingenuity, in short, all the paradoxes embedded in their negotiation between the modern and the traditional, between the new and the old, and between what they aspire and what they can have. If they use money, consumption, and lifestyle as the resources to assert themselves, that is because they need to.

In the contemporary Chinese context, where fields of intimacy have become battle grounds where some people need to put up a front—it is tiring to put up a fight—yes, in the classic language of feminism and political activism in general, they may not be fighting the structure, be it patriarchy, the state that sanctions such patriarchy through the promotion of "harmonious society," or the neo-liberal practices that render collective struggles increasingly difficult; they are nonetheless showing their agency in managing their single lives in their personal, multiple ways, sometimes with fulfilment, sometimes not. It is their way to claim a different manner of loving and living. Like the single working mothers in Hong Kong in Evelyn Ng and Catherine Ng's study, the single women in Shanghai may not indicate any particular political interest "in seeing themselves as part of an evolving community that is an alternative to the conventional norm of the heterosexual couple."[54] Their very existence, as single women, living and relating in a multiplicity of forms, I argue, is always already a challenge to the heteronormative order.

I do not know how the paradoxical, in their experiences, and the confusing, if not conflicting, desires and aspirations stemming from the equally confusing and conflicting forces of modernity and tradition, will continue to play out. It may go on to destabilize family life in China in the years to come,[55] noting, on the one hand, the readiness of some of the women in this inquiry to divorce or remain single. Or it may not, noting, on the other, the readiness of the same group of women to enter into marriage in the first place, and those who allow themselves to do *xiangqin*—all under the power of what some call "retraditionalization" and "refamilialization" in post-socialist societies.[56]

NOTES

1. See Leta Hong Fincher, *Leftover Women: The Resurgence of Gender Inequality in China* (London, New York: Zed Books, 2014); Luo Wei and Sun Zhen, "Are You the One? China's TV Dating Shows and the Sheng Nü's Predicament," *Feminist Media Studies* 15, no. 2 (2015): 239–56; Wang Changfeng (王昌逢), "社会性别视角下的 [剩女] 现象分析 [An Analysis of the 'Leftover Women' Phenomenon in the Perspective of

Gender]," 中共山西省直机关党校学报 [ZhongGong Shanxisheng Zhi Jiguan Dangxiao Xuebao], no. 6 (2010): 46–47; Wang Haiping and Douglas A. Abbott, "Waiting for Mr. Right: The Meaning of Being a Single Educated Chinese Female Over 30 in Beijing and Guangzhou," *Women's Studies International Forum* 40, no. Supplement C (2013): 222–29; Jun Zhang and Peidong Sun, "'When Are You Going to Get Married?' Parental Matchmaking and Middle-Class Women in Contemporary Urban China," in *Wives, Husbands and Lovers: Marriage and Sexuality in Hong Kong, Taiwan, and Urban China*, ed. Deborah S. Davison and Sara L. Friedman (Stanford: Stanford University Press, 2014), 118–44; Sandy To, *China's Leftover Women: Late Marriage Among Professional Women and Its Consequences* (London, New York: Routledge, 2015).

2. Wei-Jun Jean Yeung and Hu Shu, "Coming of Age in Times of Change: The Transition to Adulthood in China," *The ANNALS of the American Academy of Political and Social Science* 646, no. 1 (2013): 149–71.

3. See Viola Zhou, "China's Marriage Rate Slumps as More Singles Say 'I Don't'," *South China Morning Post*, September 6, 2017, http://www.scmp.com/news/china/society/article/2109868/marriage-rate-down-divorce-rate-more-chinese-couples-say-i-dont.

4. Hong Fincher, *Leftover Women*; Luo and Sun, "Are You the One?"

5. Bella DePaulo, "Holiday Spirit, 21st Century Style: Kay Trimberger and I Share Our Vision," *Living Single* (blog), November 23, 2008, http://www.psychologytoday.com/blog/living-single/200811/holiday-spirit-21st-century-style-kay-trimberger-and-i-share-our-vision.

6. See Ulrich Beck and Elisabeth Beck-Gernsheim, *Individualization: Institutionalized Individualism and Its Social and Political Consequences* (London: Sage, 2002); Eric Klinenberg, *Going Solo: The Extraordinary Rise and Surprising Appeal of Living Alone*, 1 edition (London: Duckworth Overlook, 2014).

7. See, for instance, Tuula Gordon, *Single Women: On the Margins?*, Women in Society (Houndmills, Basingstoke, England) (Basingstoke: Macmillan, 1994); Peter J. Stein, "Singlehood: An Alternative to Marriage," *The Family Coordinator* 24, no. 4 (1975): 489–503.

8. Adrienne Rich, *Compulsory Heterosexuality and Lesbian Existence* (London: Onlywomen Press, 1980).

9. Kinneret Lahad, *A Table for One: A Critical Reading of Singlehood, Gender and Time* (Manchester: Manchester University Press, 2017).

10. See Bella M. DePaulo and Wendy L. Morris, "Singles in Society and in Science," *Psychological Inquiry* 16, no. 2–3 (2005): 57–83; Kinneret Lahad, "'Am I Asking for Too Much?' The Selective Single Woman as a New Social Problem," *Women's Studies International Forum* 40, no. Supplement C (2013): 23–32; Kinneret Lahad and Avi Shoshana,

"Singlehood in Treatment: Interrogating the Discursive Alliance between Postfeminism and Therapeutic Culture," *European Journal of Women's Studies* 22, no. 3 (2015): 334–49; Jill Reynolds, *The Single Woman: A Discursive Investigation* (London ; New York, NY: Routledge, 2008); Elizabeth A. Sharp and Lawrence Ganong, "'I'm a Loser, I'm Not Married, Let's Just All Look at Me': Ever-Single Women's Perceptions of Their Social Environment," *Journal of Family Issues* 32, no. 7 (2011): 956–80.

11. Angela McRobbie, "Post-feminism and Popular Culture," *Feminist Media Studies* 4, no. 3 (2004): 255–64; Rosalind Gill, "Empowerment/Sexism: Figuring Female Sexual Agency in Contemporary Advertising," *Feminism & Psychology* 18, no. 1 (2008): 35–60. See also Rachel E. Dubrofsky, *The Surveillance of Women on Reality Television: Watching The Bachelor and The Bachelorette* (Lanham: Lexington Books, 2011); Anthea Taylor, "Blogging Solo: New Media, 'Old' Politics," *Feminist Review* 99, no. 1 (2011): 79–97.

12. Lahad and Shoshana, "Singlehood in Treatment."

13. Stéphanie Genz and Benjamin A. Brabon, *Postfeminism: Cultural Texts and Theories* (Edinburgh: Edinburgh University Press, 2009); Taylor, "Blogging Solo."

14. See Ionela Vlase and Rebekka Sieber, "Narrating Well-Being in the Context of Precarious Prosperity: An Account of Agency Framed by Culturally Embedded Happiness and Gender Beliefs," *European Journal of Women's Studies* 23, no. 2 (2016): 185–99; Julie Ann Wilson and Emily Chivers Yochim, "Mothering Through Precarity," *Cultural Studies* 29, no. 5–6 (2015): 669–86.

15. See, for instance, Chen Yaya (陈亚亚), "孤单也可精彩:都市单身女性之生存状态考察 [Lonely Can Be Wonderful: An Investigation of the Living Status of Urban Single Women]," in *The Influence of Gender* (Shanghai: Shanghai Academy of Social Sciences, Gender and Development Centre, 2014), 148–59.

16. See Cui Xiaolu (崔小璐), "高知大龄未婚女性的婚恋问题浅析 [A Brief Analysis of the Love and Marriage Problems about the Older Educated Unmarried Women]," *Northwest Population Journal* 32, no. 5 (2011): 58–62, 68.

17. See Hong Fincher, *Leftover Women*; Luo and Sun, "Are You the One?"

18. Hong Fincher, *Leftover Women*.

19. See Su Xing (苏醒) and Tian Renbo (田仁波), ""城市剩女" 群体生存焦虑问题研究 [Research on Living Anxiety of the 3S Lady in Cities]," *Journal of Qujing Normal University* 31, no. 2 (2012): 116–20; Chen, "孤单也可精彩:都市单身女性之生存状态考察"; Su and Tian, ""城市剩女" 群体生存焦虑问题研究."; To, *China's Leftover Women*; Wang and Abbott, "Waiting for Mr. Right."

20. See Michael Keane, *Creative Industries in China: Art, Design and Media* (Malden: Polity, 2013); Winnie Wong, *Van Gogh on Demand: China and the Readymade* (Chicago ; London: University Of Chicago Press, 2014); Anthony Y. H. Fung and John Nguyet Erni, "Cultural Clusters and Cultural Industries in China," *Inter-Asia Cultural Studies* 14, no. 4 (2013): 644–56; Pang Laikwan, *Creativity and Its Discontents: China's Creative Industries and Intellectual Property Rights Offenses* (Durham: Duke University Press, 2012); Zhang Xiaoming (张晓明), Hu Huilin (胡惠林), and Zhang Jiangang (章建刚), eds., 文化蓝皮书:中国文化产业发展报告 *[Blue Book of China's Culture: Annual Report on the Development of China's Cultural Industries]* (Beijing: 社会科学文献出版社 [Social Sciences Academic Press], 2002); Niu Weilin (牛维麟) and Peng Yi (彭翊), 北京文化创意产业集聚区发展研究报告 *[Beijing Cultural Creative Industry Clusters Development Study Report]* (Beijing: 中国人民大学出版社 [People's University Press], 2009).

21. See Jeroen de Kloet, *China with a Cut: Globalisation, Urban Youth and Popular Music* (Amsterdam: Amsterdam University Press, 2010); Francois Jullien, *The Silent Transformations* (London; New York: Seagull Books, 2011); Keane, *Creative Industries in China*; Justin O'Connor and Xin Gu, "Shanghai: Images of Modernity," in *Cultures and Globalization: Cities, Cultural Policy and Governance*, ed. Helmut K. Anheier and Yudhishthir Raj Isar (London: Sage, 2012), 288–99; Jing Wang, "The Global Reach of a New Discourse: How Far Can 'Creative Industries' Travel?," *International Journal of Cultural Studies* 7, no. 1 (2004): 9–19.

22. For a report on such paid *xiangqin* services, see Fu Jian (傅坚) and Qu Fuqiang (屈富强), "国内顶级红娘:相亲收费最高超千万 Top Domestic Matchmaker: Blind Date Fees up to 10 Million]," 长江商报 *[ChangJiang Shangbao]*, December 30, 2015, http://news.sohu.com/20151230/n432980363.shtml. For a recent court ruling on fraudulent practices surrounding xiangqin services, see Bibek Bhandari, "Down to Fraud? Five Jailed for Scamming Singles," December 8, 2017, http://www.sixthtone.com/news/1001362/down-to-fraud%3F-five-jailed-for-scamming-singles].

23. Celia Hatton, "Boyfriends for Hire to Beat China's Wedding Pressure," *BBC News*, February 7, 2013, sec. China, http://www.bbc.com/news/world-asia-china-21192131.

24. We will talk more about the spatial dimension of their everyday life in Chap. 6.

25. See James Farrer, "Love, Sex, and Commitment. Delinking Premarital Intimacy from Marriage in Urban China," in *Wives, Husbands and Lovers: Marriage and Sexuality in Hong Kong, Taiwan, and Urban China*, ed. Deborah S. Davis and Sara L. Friedman (Stanford: Stanford University

Press, 2014), 62–96; Henrike Donner and Gonçalo Santos, "Love, Marriage, and Intimate Citizenship in Contemporary China and India: An Introduction," *Modern Asian Studies* 50, no. 4 (2016): 1123–46; Yeung and Hu, "Coming of Age in Times of Change."

26. Gavin W. Jones, Zhang Yanxia, and Pamela Chia Pei Zhi, "Understanding High Levels of Singlehood in Singapore," *Journal of Comparative Family Studies* 43, no. 5 (2012): 731–50.

27. Liu Wenjia, "The Dawn of 'Free Love': The Negotiation of Women's Roles in Heterosexual Relationships in Tanci Feng Shuang Fei," *Frontiers of Literary Studies in China* 9, no. 1 (2015): 98.

28. See Anthony Giddens, *The Transformation of Intimacy: Sexuality, Love, and Eroticism in Modern Societies*, 1st edition (Stanford: Stanford University Press, 1992); Beck and Beck-Gernsheim, *Individualization*.

29. Khatidja Chantler, "What's Love Got to Do with Marriage?" *Families, Relationships and Societies* 3, no. 1 (2014): 2.

30. Lee Haiyan, *Revolution of the Heart: A Genealogy of Love in China, 1900–1950* (Stanford: Stanford University Press, 2006). 106–107.

31. See Lee, *Revolution of the Heart*; Liu, "The Dawn of 'Free Love.'"

32. Xiao Hui Faye, "'Love Is a Capacity': The Narrative of Gendered Self-Development in Chinese-Style Divorce," *Journal of Contemporary China* 19, no. 66 (2010): 735–53.

33. Lee, *Revolution of the Heart*; Liu, "The Dawn of 'Free Love.'"

34. Chantler, "What's Love Got to Do with Marriage?"

35. Pi Chenying, "Fieldwork Report: Love Club," *HERA SINGLE* (blog), December 2, 2014, http://www.hera-single.de/love-club/. For a 2017 report on the Love Club, see http://www.kankanews.com/a/2017-02-13/0037878956.shtml?appid=141744. According to the report, the fee for the three-month course has increased to RMB 5000.

36. For a detailed account of the visit, see Pi Chenying's fieldwork report on Love Club (http://www.hera-single.de/love-club/). I joined Pi during one of her site visits.

37. Neta Yodovich and Kinneret Lahad, "'I Don't Think This Woman Had Anyone in Her Life': Loneliness and Singlehood in Six Feet Under," *European Journal of Women's Studies*, 2017, 1–15.

38. Natalia Sarkisian and Naomi Gerstel, "Does Singlehood Isolate or Integrate? Examining the Link between Marital Status and Ties to Kin, Friends, and Neighbors," *Journal of Social and Personal Relationships* 33, no. 3 (2016): 361–84.

39. See Chen Xiuming (陳秀明), "出国与抱负 [Leaving the Country and the Aspiration]," 出国与就业 *(Working and Going Abroad)*, no. 7 (2001): 25–27; Liu Haiming, "The Chinese Diaspora: Space, Place, Mobility, and

Identity (Review)," *Journal of Chinese Overseas* 20, no. 1 (2006): 150–53.

40. Fran Martin has embarked on a research project on the mobility of female Chinese students abroad. See, for instance, Fran Martin, "Intersections: The Gender of Mobility: Chinese Women Students' Self-Making through Transnational Education," *Intersections: Gender and Sexuality in Asia and the Pacific*, no. 35 (2014), http://intersections.anu.edu.au/issue35/martin.htm; Cpianalysis, "Overseas Study as 'Escape Route' for Young Chinese Women," *China Policy Institute: Analysis* (blog), June 22, 2016, https://cpianalysis.org/2016/06/22/single-and-mobile-overseas-study-as-escape-route-for-young-chinese-women/.

41. For a book-length empirical study of lesbian culture in Shanghai and urban China, see Lucetta Yip Lo Kam, *Shanghai Lalas: Female Tongzhi Communities and Politics in Urban China* (Hong Kong: Hong Kong University Press, 2012). The study reports and examines similar marital pressures in the larger context of lesbian communities and politics. For an inquiry on representations and imaginaries of female homoeroticism in contemporary China, see Fran Martin, *Backward Glances: Contemporary Chinese Cultures and the Female Homoerotic Imaginary* (Durham; London: Duke University Press, 2010).

42. In an analysis of the emergence of *xinghun*, Peng Tianxiao attributes it to the negativity surrounding homosexuality in contemporary China, in particular, the dominant filial norms governing the relationship between children and parents. See Peng Tianxiao (彭天笑), "浅析中国同性恋者选择形式婚姻的原因及影响 [On the Causes and Effects of 'Xinghun' Marriage by Chinese Homosexuals]," *中国性科学 [Zhongguo Xing Kexue]*, no. 8 (2014): 97–99. For an analysis of online ads looking for *xinghun* partners, see Liu Min, "Two Gay Men Seeking Two Lesbians: An Analysis of *Xinghun* (Formality Marriage) Ads on China's Tianya.Cn," *Sexuality & Culture* 17, no. 3 (2013): 494–511. Liu's study shows the complexity of such marital arrangements, in which traditional Chinese values function in tandem with modernistic requirement to be honest to oneself.

43. Literally, *hun* means "mix" and *quanzi* means "circles." The expression *hunquanzi* is usually used to refer to someone who spends time and effort entering social circles and frequenting social spaces, with clear goals of establishing contacts and networking.

44. Hu Xiaowen and Wang Ying, "LGB Identity Among Young Chinese: The Influence of Traditional Culture," *Journal of Homosexuality* 60, no. 5 (2013): 667–84; Tu Jia-Wei and Lee Tien-Tsung, "The Effects of Media Usage and Interpersonal Contacts on the Stereotyping of Lesbians and Gay Men in China," *Journal of Homosexuality* 61, no. 7 (2014): 980–1002.

45. Farrer, "'Love, Sex, and Commitment."
46. Li Yu (李煜) and Xu Anqi (徐安琪), 婚姻市场中的青年择偶 [*Youth Spousal Choices in the Marriage Market*] (Shanghai: Shanghai Academy of Social Sciences Press, 2004).
47. Andrew J. Cherlin, "The Deinstitutionalization of American Marriage," *Journal of Marriage and Family* 66, no. 4 (2004): 848–61.
48. Deborah S. Davis and Sara L. Friedman, eds., *Wives, Husbands and Lovers: Marriage and Sexuality in Hong Kong, Taiwan, and Urban China* (Stanford: Stanford University Press, 2014). 3.
49. Ron Lesthaeghe, "The Unfolding Story of the Second Demographic Transition," *Population and Development Review* 36, no. 2 (2010): 211–51.
50. Donner and Santos, "Love, Marriage, and Intimate Citizenship in Contemporary China and India," 1128.
51. Ibid., 1140.
52. Xiao, "'Love Is a Capacity.'"
53. Ibid., 750.
54. Evelyn G. H. Ng and Catherine W. Ng, "Single Working Women and Motherhood: The Personal and the Political," *Asian Journal of Women's Studies* 19, no. 1 (2013): 9–38. 9.
55. Yeung and Hu, "Coming of Age in Times of Change."
56. Steven Saxonberg and Tomáš Sirovátka, "Failing Family Policy in Post-Communist Central Europe," *Journal of Comparative Policy Analysis: Research and Practice* 8, no. 2 (2006): 185–202.

References

Beck, Ulrich, and Elisabeth Beck-Gernsheim. *Individualization: Institutionalized Individualism and Its Social and Political Consequences*. London: Sage, 2002.

Bhandari, Bibek. "Down to Fraud? Five Jailed for Scamming Singles," December 8, 2017. http://www.sixthtone.com/news/1001362/down-to-fraud%3F-five-jailed-for-scamming-singles].

Chantler, Khatidja. "What's Love Got to Do with Marriage?" *Families, Relationships and Societies* 3, no. 1 (2014): 19–33.

Chen, Xiuming (陳秀明). "出国与抱负 [Leaving the Country and the Aspiration]." 出国与就业 (*Working and Going Abroad*), no. 7 (2001): 25–27.

Chen, Yaya (陈亚亚). "孤单也可精彩:都市单身女性之生存状态考察 [Lonely Can Be Wonderful: An Investigation of the Living Status of Urban Single Women]." In *The Influence of Gender*, 148–59. Shanghai: Shanghai Academy of Social Sciences, Gender and Development Centre, 2014.

Cherlin, Andrew J. "The Deinstitutionalization of American Marriage." *Journal of Marriage and Family* 66, no. 4 (2004): 848–61.

Cpianalysis. "Overseas Study as 'Escape Route' for Young Chinese Women." *China Policy Institute: Analysis* (blog), June 22, 2016. https://cpianalysis. org/2016/06/22/single-and-mobile-overseas-study-as-escape-route-for-young-chinese-women/.

Cui, Xiaolu (崔小璐). "高知大龄未婚女性的婚恋问题浅析 [A Brief Analysis of the Love and Marriage Problems about the Older Educated Unmarried Women]." *Northwest Population Journal* 32, no. 5 (2011): 58–62, 68.

Davis, Deborah S., and Sara L. Friedman, eds. *Wives, Husbands and Lovers: Marriage and Sexuality in Hong Kong, Taiwan, and Urban China*. Stanford: Stanford University Press, 2014.

DePaulo, Bella. "Holiday Spirit, 21st Century Style: Kay Trimberger and I Share Our Vision." *Living Single* (blog), November 23, 2008. http://www.psychology today.com/blog/living-single/200811/holiday-spirit-21st-century-style-kay-trimberger-and-i-share-our-vision.

DePaulo, Bella M., and Wendy L. Morris. "Singles in Society and in Science." *Psychological Inquiry* 16, no. 2–3 (2005): 57–83.

Donner, Henrike, and Gonçalo Santos. "Love, Marriage, and Intimate Citizenship in Contemporary China and India: An Introduction." *Modern Asian Studies* 50, no. 4 (2016): 1123–46.

Dubrofsky, Rachel E. *The Surveillance of Women on Reality Television: Watching The Bachelor and The Bachelorette*. Lanham: Lexington Books, 2011.

Farrer, James. "Love, Sex, and Commitment. Delinking Premarital Intimacy from Marriage in Urban China." In *Wives, Husbands and Lovers: Marriage and Sexuality in Hong Kong, Taiwan, and Urban China*, edited by Deborah S. Davis and Sara L. Friedman, 62–96. Stanford: Stanford University Press, 2014.

Fu, Jian (傅坚), and Qu Fuqiang (屈富强). "国内顶级红娘:相亲收费最高超千万 [Top Domestic Matchmaker: Blind Date Fees up to 10 Million]." *长江商报 [ChangJiang Shangbao]*, December 30, 2015. http://news.sohu. com/20151230/n432980363.shtml.

Fung, Anthony Y. H., and John Nguyet Erni. "Cultural Clusters and Cultural Industries in China." *Inter-Asia Cultural Studies* 14, no. 4 (2013): 644–56.

Genz, Stéphanie, and Benjamin A. Brabon. *Postfeminism: Cultural Texts and Theories*. Edinburgh: Edinburgh University Press, 2009.

Giddens, Anthony. *The Transformation of Intimacy: Sexuality, Love, and Eroticism in Modern Societies*. 1st edition. Stanford: Stanford University Press, 1992.

Gill, Rosalind. "Empowerment/Sexism: Figuring Female Sexual Agency in Contemporary Advertising." *Feminism & Psychology* 18, no. 1 (2008): 35–60.

Gordon, Tuula. *Single Women: On the Margins?* Women in Society (Houndmills, Basingstoke, England). Basingstoke: Macmillan, 1994.

Hong Fincher, Leta. *Leftover Women: The Resurgence of Gender Inequality in China*. London, New York: Zed Books, 2014.

Hu, Xiaowen, and Ying Wang. "LGB Identity Among Young Chinese: The Influence of Traditional Culture." *Journal of Homosexuality* 60, no. 5 (2013): 667–84.

Jones, Gavin W., Zhang Yanxia, and Pamela Chia Pei Zhi. "Understanding High Levels of Singlehood in Singapore." *Journal of Comparative Family Studies* 43, no. 5 (2012): 731–50.

Jullien, Francois. *The Silent Transformations*. London; New York: Seagull Books, 2011.

Kam, Lucetta Yip Lo. *Shanghai Lalas: Female Tongzhi Communities and Politics in Urban China*. Hong Kong: Hong Kong University Press, 2012.

Keane, Michael. *Creative Industries in China: Art, Design and Media*. Malden: Polity, 2013.

Klinenberg, Eric. *Going Solo: The Extraordinary Rise and Surprising Appeal of Living Alone*. 1 edition. London: Duckworth Overlook, 2012.

de Kloet, Jeroen. *China with a Cut: Globalisation, Urban Youth and Popular Music*. Amsterdam: Amsterdam University Press, 2010.

Lahad, Kinneret. *A Table for One: A Critical Reading of Singlehood, Gender and Time*. Manchester: Manchester University Press, 2017.

Lahad, Kinneret. "'Am I Asking for Too Much?' The Selective Single Woman as a New Social Problem." *Women's Studies International Forum* 40, no. Supplement C (2013): 23–32.

Lahad, Kinneret, and Avi Shoshana. "Singlehood in Treatment: Interrogating the Discursive Alliance between Postfeminism and Therapeutic Culture." *European Journal of Women's Studies* 22, no. 3 (2015): 334–49.

Lee, Haiyan. *Revolution of the Heart: A Genealogy of Love in China, 1900–1950*. Stanford: Stanford University Press, 2006.

Lesthaeghe, Ron. "The Unfolding Story of the Second Demographic Transition." *Population and Development Review* 36, no. 2 (2010): 211–51.

Li, Yu (李煜), and Xu Anqi (徐安琪). 婚姻市场中的青年择偶 [*Youth Spousal Choices in the Marriage Market*]. Shanghai: Shanghai Academy of Social Sciences Press, 2004.

Liu, Haiming. "The Chinese Diaspora: Space, Place, Mobility, and Identity (Review)." *Journal of Chinese Overseas* 20, no. 1 (2006): 150–53.

Liu, Min. "Two Gay Men Seeking Two Lesbians: An Analysis of Xinghun (Formality Marriage) Ads on China's Tianya.Cn." *Sexuality & Culture* 17, no. 3 (2013): 494–511.

Liu, Wenjia. "The Dawn of 'Free Love': The Negotiation of Women's Roles in Heterosexual Relationships in Tanci Feng Shuang Fei." *Frontiers of Literary Studies in China* 9, no. 1 (2015): 75–103.

Luo, Wei, and Zhen Sun. "Are You the One? China's TV Dating Shows and the Sheng Nü's Predicament." *Feminist Media Studies* 15, no. 2 (2015): 239–56.

Martin, Fran. *Backward Glances: Contemporary Chinese Cultures and the Female Homoerotic Imaginary*. Durham; London: Duke University Press, 2010.

Martin, Fran. "Intersections: The Gender of Mobility: Chinese Women Students' Self-Making through Transnational Education." *Intersections: Gender and Sexuality in Asia and the Pacific*, no. 35 (2014). http://intersections.anu.edu. au/issue35/martin.htm.

McRobbie, Angela. "Post-feminism and Popular Culture." *Feminist Media Studies* 4, no. 3 (2004): 255–64.

Ng, Evelyn G. H., and Catherine W. Ng. "Single Working Women and Motherhood: The Personal and the Political." *Asian Journal of Women's Studies* 19, no. 1 (2013): 9–38.

Niu, Weilin (牛维麟), and Peng Yi (彭翊). 北京文化创意产业集聚区发展研究报告 *[Beijing Cultural Creative Industry Clusters Development Study Report]*. Beijing: 中国人民大学出版社 [People's University Press], 2009.

O'Connor, Justin, and Xin Gu. "Shanghai: Images of Modernity." In *Cultures and Globalization: Cities, Cultural Policy and Governance*, edited by Helmut K. Anheier and Yudhishthir Raj Isar, 288–99. London: Sage, 2012.

Pang, Laikwan. *Creativity and Its Discontents: China's Creative Industries and Intellectual Property Rights Offenses*. Durham: Duke University Press, 2012.

Peng, Tianxiao (彭天笑). "浅析中国同性恋者选择形式婚姻的原因及影响 [On the Causes and Effects of 'Xinghun' Marriage by Chinese Homosexuals]." 中国性科学 *[Zhongguo Xing Kexue]*, no. 8 (2014): 97–99.

Pi, Chenying. "Fieldwork Report: Love Club." *HERA SINGLE* (blog), December 2, 2014. http://www.hera-single.de/love-club/.

Reynolds, Jill. *The Single Woman: A Discursive Investigation*. London: Routledge, 2008.

Rich, Adrienne. *Compulsory Heterosexuality and Lesbian Existence*. London: Onlywomen Press, 1980.

Sarkisian, Natalia, and Naomi Gerstel. "Does Singlehood Isolate or Integrate? Examining the Link between Marital Status and Ties to Kin, Friends, and Neighbors." *Journal of Social and Personal Relationships* 33, no. 3 (2016): 361–84.

Saxonberg, Steven, and Tomáš Sirovátka. "Failing Family Policy in Post-Communist Central Europe." *Journal of Comparative Policy Analysis: Research and Practice* 8, no. 2 (2006): 185–202.

Sharp, Elizabeth A., and Lawrence Ganong. "'I'm a Loser, I'm Not Married, Let's Just All Look at Me': Ever-Single Women's Perceptions of Their Social Environment." *Journal of Family Issues* 32, no. 7 (2011): 956–80.

Stein, Peter J. "Singlehood: An Alternative to Marriage." *The Family Coordinator* 24, no. 4 (1975): 489–503.

Su, Xing (苏醒), and Tian Renbo (田仁波). ""城市剩女"群体生存焦虑问题研究 [Research on Living Anxiety of Shengnü in Cities]." *Journal of Qujing Normal University* 31, no. 2 (2012): 116–20.

Taylor, Anthea. "Blogging Solo: New Media, 'Old' Politics." *Feminist Review* 99, no. 1 (2011): 79–97.

To, Sandy. *China's Leftover Women: Late Marriage Among Professional Women and Its Consequences*. London, New York: Routledge, 2015.

Tu, Jia-Wei, and Tien-Tsung Lee. "The Effects of Media Usage and Interpersonal Contacts on the Stereotyping of Lesbians and Gay Men in China." *Journal of Homosexuality* 61, no. 7 (2014): 980–1002.

Vlase, Ionela, and Rebekka Sieber. "Narrating Well-Being in the Context of Precarious Prosperity: An Account of Agency Framed by Culturally Embedded Happiness and Gender Beliefs." *European Journal of Women's Studies* 23, no. 2 (2016): 185–99.

Wang, Changfeng (王昌逢). "社会性别视角下的 [剩女] 现象分析 [An Analysis of the 'Leftover Women' Phenomenon from the Perspective of Gender]." *中共山西省直机关党校学报 [ZhongGong Shanxisheng Zhi Jiguan Dangxiao Xuebao]*, no. 6 (2010): 46–47.

Wang, Haiping, and Douglas A. Abbott. "Waiting for Mr. Right: The Meaning of Being a Single Educated Chinese Female Over 30 in Beijing and Guangzhou." *Women's Studies International Forum* 40, no. Supplement C (2013): 222–29.

Wang, Jing. "The Global Reach of a New Discourse: How Far Can 'Creative Industries' Travel?" *International Journal of Cultural Studies* 7, no. 1 (2004): 9–19.

Wang, Yanjun. "Spouse Selection Amongst China's Post-1980 Generation." Master's Thesis, Central European University, 2012.

Wangyi nüren pingdao (网易女人频道). *我知女人心:70后、80后、90后女性情感大调查 [I Know a Woman's Heart: 70/80/90 Female Emotional Survey]*. Zhejiang: 浙江大学出版社 [Zhejiang daxue chubanshe], 2011.

Wilson, Julie Ann, and Emily Chivers Yochim. "Mothering Through Precarity." *Cultural Studies* 29, no. 5–6 (2015): 669–86.

Wong, Winnie. *Van Gogh on Demand: China and the Readymade*. Chicago ; London: University Of Chicago Press, 2014.

Xiao, Hui Faye. "'Love Is a Capacity': The Narrative of Gendered Self-Development in Chinese-Style Divorce." *Journal of Contemporary China* 19, no. 66 (2010): 735–53.

Yeung, Wei-Jun Jean, and Shu Hu. "Coming of Age in Times of Change: The Transition to Adulthood in China." *The ANNALS of the American Academy of Political and Social Science* 646, no. 1 (2013): 149–71.

Yodovich, Neta, and Kinneret Lahad. "'I Don't Think This Woman Had Anyone in Her Life': Loneliness and Singlehood in Six Feet Under." *European Journal of Women's Studies*, 2017, 1–15.

Zhang, Jun, and Peidong Sun. "'When Are You Going to Get Married?' Parental Matchmaking and Middle-Class Women in Contemporary Urban China." In *Wives, Husbands and Lovers: Marriage and Sexuality in Hong Kong, Taiwan, and Urban China*, edited by Deborah S. Davis and Sara L. Friedman, 118–44. Stanford: Stanford University Press, 2014.

Zhang, Xiaoming (张晓明), Hu Huilin (胡惠林), and Zhang Jiangang (章建刚), eds. 文化蓝皮书:中国文化产业发展报告 [*Blue Book of China's Culture: Annual Report on the Development of China's Cultural Industries*]. Beijing: 社会科学文献出版社 [Social Sciences Academic Press], 2002.

Zhou, Viola. "China's Marriage Rate Slumps as More Singles Say 'I Don't.'" *South China Morning Post*, September 6, 2017. http://www.scmp.com/news/china/society/article/2109868/marriage-rate-down-divorce-rate-more-chinese-couples-say-i-dont.

CHAPTER 6

Living with Us—The Case of Kunqu

Richard Sennett quotes the famous reply that Freud gave when he was asked what constituted a good life: love and work. This formulation, Sennett observes, misses one important dimension of our lives: community. Building on the third category of community discussed by Sennett— one that is constructed and maintained by what he calls informal sociality[1]—this chapter offers a case study of such community evolving and revolving around a particular creative practice: Kunqu (昆曲). Originating in the late Yuan dynasty, Kunqu is generally considered one of the oldest forms of operatic arts in China. In contradistinction with the northern, officially and nationally endorsed Peking Opera, Kunqu continues to enjoy popularity in the more "southern" localities surrounding and including Shanghai.

During my attempt to recruit subjects through snowballing, it transpired that quite a number of single women in Shanghai's creative industries were active in the Kunqu scene, as fans, as apprentices, as teachers, as organizers, or as promoters. And very often, they knew one another. This chapter investigates this particular form of creative pursuit and seeks to map out what exactly they do regarding Kunqu; how and why this community of informal sociality came into being; and what the passion, friendships, and contacts they share with regard to its creative practice mean to these single women. For these purposes, I have supplemented what I have learned from Kunqu lovers during the rounds of individual interviews with fieldwork that places the social context centrally in the inquiry. I refer

© The Author(s) 2019

Chow Y. F., *Caring in Times of Precarity*, Palgrave Studies in
Globalization, Culture and Society,
https://doi.org/10.1007/978-3-319-76898-4_6

to participant observation in four Kunqu performances at three different venues in Shanghai. I also refer to four focus groups where participants were facilitated to talk about their shared interest. In other words, if the previous chapters try to understand single women primarily as individuals, Chap. 6 offers another lens to examine their everyday lives more collectively—as groups. In total, 10 single women joined the group discussion, ranging in age from 24 to 39 years, and working in a variety of creative sectors.[2] While three of them were identified from the earlier individual interviews, the rest were recruited from Kunqu circles and through mutual friends or acquaintances. To ensure an amiable atmosphere and ease of sharing views and experiences, focus groups were arranged in such a way that at least some members, if not all, were already friends. I have used this method in my other research projects; the advantage of such an arrangement over a group of total strangers is that it is more "effective in tapping in group life and understanding group meanings, processes and norms as in their everyday life practices."[3] Except for one group, which was organized to meet online, the meetings were conducted face-to-face.

I will begin with a discussion engaging with three lines of scholarship: first, as inspired by Sennett's work, deliberations on (imagined) community and citizenship; second, creative labour studies that often frame "sociality" among creative workers in professional terms; and finally, fandom studies as well as audience research, which attempt to redefine what fans and audiences are in our time. It will be followed by a brief history of Kunqu, especially regarding its development and current situation in Shanghai. The core of this chapter will consist of a presentation of the subjects' practices in connection with Kunqu, individually as well as socially, imbricated with the ways of and reasons for such community formation. Finally, I will discuss what the practices surrounding Kunqu mean to these single women, for their work, their loves, and their lives.

FROM CREATIVE WORKERS, FANS TO COMMUNITY

Even if we are able to distinguish between fans and audiences, it would be difficult to tell which group the single women in this inquiry belong to. Only a few of them use the language of fandom and talk of their favourite Kunqu performers as *aidou* (爱豆, a phonetic translation of "idol"), and of themselves in a variety of fan-related neologisms.[4] Most do not readily call themselves fans—not surprisingly when fans have long been stigmatized and pathologized[5]; particularly female fans, who have often been perceived by the wider society as fanatical, hysterical, and immature.[6] Popular images of female pop music fans as "groupies," or girls screaming at their idols, are just some examples of such stereotyping.[7] After all, the word "fan" has its roots in the Latin *fananticus*, carrying with it the connotation of being fanatic, mad, and possessed by the gods.[8] Most of the women in this inquiry would be happy to say they like or love Kunqu, from nonchalantly to effusively. They are, at any rate, far more than the conventional understanding of an audience. I am not only referring to the notion of "active audience," where they construct meaning actively from the media texts.[9] They *do* things with Kunqu, as we shall see later. Taking fans as a form of audienceship, perhaps the most "visible" one[10] or the most "adoring" kind,[11] I will situate the inquiry of these Kunqu aficionados in the continuum of fandom and audienceship studies, particularly in its engagement with two threads of thinking: convergence culture and feminist fandom.

In 2006, Henry Jenkins published an influential book deliberating on the developments of media cultures and practices, particularly those of the "new" media and their interactions with the "old." In his *Convergence Culture*, Jenkins puts forward convergence as a keyword to understand the contemporary mediascape, "a paradigm shift—a move from medium-specific content toward content that flows across multiple media channels, towards the increased interdependence of communications systems, toward multiple ways of accessing media content, and toward ever more complex relations between top-down corporate media and bottom-up participatory culture."[12] It is particularly the last remark that helps usher succeeding generations of fandom and audienceship studies into a trajectory where the "recipients" of media content and cultural products are no longer recipients only; they are consumers and participants, users and producers. Axel Bruns coined the hybrid term "produser" precisely to capture and encapsulate the blurring boundaries between what used to be the two poles of media and cultural production.[13]

Given the prominent intervention of new media into old media, studies on fans and audiences morph into a field of participation and production practices, particularly by means of online possibilities.[14] Zhang Weiyu and Mao Chengting's study on online translation communities in China is illustrative of such investigations. It probes into how fan groups interested in foreign comics, games, movies, and television dramas constitute fan labour and fan activism when they offer translated subtitles in Chinese cyberspace.[15] Among the critics of convergence culture, Elizabeth Bird raises a similar question, or rather remark, on the tendency of the newer generations of studies on fans and audiences to perhaps exceedingly embrace new media practices. Titling her commentary rhetorically "Are We All Producers Now?" she pleads for more attention to non-web-based practices, especially in non-Western contexts.[16] This chapter, an inquiry into lovers of Kunqu, responds to this appeal. It notices the participatory dimension of these Kunqu-watching women; it also notices their online practices. Above all, the inquiry is sensitized to the everyday lives of people who articulate their affection for something that is, first and foremost, embedded in physical space: Kunqu performance.

This inquiry is about physical space and practices; it is also about female fandom. Given the stereotypes that are imposed on female fans, whether in scholarly or popular discourses, an important line of work takes issue with such stereotyping and adopts a feminist perspective to revisit female fandom. Adrienne Trier-Bieniek, for instance, has inserted in the field of fandom studies a collection of essays in the book *Fan Girls and Media*, which "attempts to demonstrate the gendered aspect of fandom while also exploring the ways different forms of media are challenging stereotypical ideals of how gender and culture are consumed."[17] Contributors recuperate a multiplicity of fan practices to challenge these stereotypes—"an explosion of feminist fandom," as Trier-Bieniek calls them.[18] In a general sense, this chapter on Kunqu fandom aligns with the fundamental drive of feminist fandom studies—that female fans should not continue to be framed in such a prejudicial manner—and its radical concern with how marginalized populations are given the space to live their lives. It does so differently: it is not immediately concerned with the marginalization of female identities in cultural outlets. Trier-Bieniek looks at the female fans of *Orange Is the New Black*, and their discussions on themes of race, class, gender, sexual orientation, and the underpinning problematic of power and control as shown in the American television series. My inquiry on the female fans of Kunqu directs itself not so much to how the fans perceive this operatic form as to what they do with it. Instead of taking identity politics as its premise, the primary goal of Chap. 6 is to tease out the female fans' sense of being together, of sharing something, of a community, imagined or real, in the physical performance venues and classrooms, and online. In short, Matt Hills' seminal work *Fan Cultures* is my point of departure, in its persistent reminder of the complexity of fandom, and appeal to take the everyday lives of fans seriously, by finding out "what fandom does culturally."[19]

It is easy to compartmentalize studies according to similar compart-mentalization of one's life. In other words, when we study fan or audience practices, we take them primarily in the context of leisure, seldom in tan-dem with what these fans and audiences do for work. Similarly, when we study a certain profession or employment, we frame the investigations largely in the context of work, sidestepping leisurely or after-work pur-suits. For the present inquiry, how creative workers spend their leisurely or after-work time has largely escaped research attention. Most investigations focus on their work or work-related practices. Quite understandably, as creative work is predominantly conceptualized in economic terms, whether in the upbeat prognosis of its flexibility, autonomy, and presumably, humane way of working and living, or in the critical tradition of addressing exploitation, power imbalances, and job insecurity. Researchers want to find out more about what creative workers actually experience and encoun-ter in their work, not after-work, lives. In the Floridian version of a cool city populated by creative workers and teeming with cultural events, that the former would participate in the latter is often assumed, rather than empirically evidenced.

The few studies that do examine creative workers' social lives tend to understand it from a professional—or what I would describe as func-tional—perspective. That is to say, how they socialize remains framed as an inflection of, and eventually contribution to, their work. Lily Kong's study of the Hong Kong film industry is exemplary. Through interviews with practitioners, Kong demonstrates the importance of social networks, interpersonal relationships, and above all, trust in their film work. Studies on the social lives of creative workers employ a similar framing of social network analysis in the context of professionalism and functionality.[20] Gino Cattani and Simone Ferriani aim their empirical study on the Hollywood film industry from 1992 to 2003 to explicate the complex impact of social networks on individual creative performance.[21] Focusing on Australia, Emma Felton's research team relocates inquiries from the cities, the usual hub of creative industries, and examines networking and sociality in outer-suburban locations.[22] Lee Minha, tapping into the expe-riences of a group of entrepreneurs in a creative incubation space in Seoul, confirms the contribution of physical proximity to social networking, knowledge exchange, and interactive learning.[23] In that sense, this chap-ter, informed by the empirical findings of a group of creative workers shar-ing an interest in Kunqu, serves as a supplement to, and a radical departure from, the aforementioned line of social network studies. It examines the social life of creative workers without presupposed remit to understand its relationship with their creative work. Rather, it seeks to understand their social life in its own right, that is, primarily as leisure, as pleasure, as something they do when they are not working. It may help them deal with the multiple demands of life and work, or not, as we will see later, but not necessarily make them work better, professionally and functionally speaking. This brings us back to the opening of this chapter, where Sennett supplements the Freudian conception of a good life—"work and love"—with "community." My curiosity is piqued, in particular, by the ways the latter interacts with the former, lending support and sustainability to the lives of these single women in their entirety. Many thinkers have deliberated on the notion of community. The founding figures of sociology, such as Max Weber, Ferdinand Tönnes, and Emile Durkheim, have put forward their distinction of *Gemeinschaft-Gesellschaft*, where the former, community, is anchored in subjective feelings, while the latter, society, is formed by rational agreement.[24] While these thinkers debated on the European progression from *gemeinschaft* to *gesellschaft*, the Chicago School reflected on the experience in the United States and held up a pessimistic view on urbanization's negative effects on community building.[25] In the field of community studies that followed, three key ideas were identified: "the rural-urban continuum, community lost and community found."[26] Sennett's sensitivity to the importance of community can be understood as a continuation of such a concern with community lost and found in the urbanizing and modernizing society.

However, he wants more; informed by his own childhood experience in a deprived neighbourhood, he wants "to imagine, instead, community as a process of coming into the world" and its promises of "pleasures of a serious sort."[27] While Sennett's experience and concern is with the poor and the marginalized in a materialistic sense, I extend it to the single women in this inquiry who may not exactly be poor, but are definitely subject to a multiplicity of areas of duress—work, love, and otherwise—configured by the larger society. It is about how they use Kunqu to construct a community, either through face-to-face relationships as foregrounded by Sennett, or through an imaginary act of co-existence and sharing—itself a twist on Benedict Anderson's notion of "imagined community" in the sense that these Kunqu fans do see known and unknown fellow fans in physical venues and online platforms, *as well as* imagine more beyond.[28] It is about how such community helps them lead their lives as single women, as creative workers, as themselves. To probe into such experience, we will end with a feminist understanding of such community formation, but we will start with the physical form of Kunqu.

KUNQU AND SHANGHAI

The Yu Zhen-fei Kun Opera House, located on 9th Shaoxing Road, is the place where the Shanghai Kun Opera Troupe holds its weekly performances. Just like all the other residential buildings on this old street, this three-storied, Western-style house with beige walls and bronze doors is nested quietly in the shadow of the trees. On almost every Saturday, however, Kunqu lovers from different parts of Shanghai gather here, expecting traditional or contemporary Kunqu works to be performed on the Lanxin Stage on its second floor. Although only 100 metres away from Huaihai Road, one of the busiest commercial areas in Shanghai, the small Kunqu stage is a refraction of the old times, bringing classical operatic art back to the modern Shanghai of today.

Honoured by UNESCO as a "masterpiece of the oral and intangible heritage of humanity," Kunqu stands as one of the oldest, as well as the most representative forms of musical theatre that exist in China today. The history of Kunqu, or Kun Opera, can be traced back to the late Yuan dynasty (fourteenth century), when its predecessor, Kunshan Qiang (昆山腔), the folk music of the district of Kunshan (now a city in Jiangsu province near Shanghai), began to prevail in the Suzhou area. Around 1530, this regional music was standardized by the theatre musician Wei Liangfu in terms of its tune, language, enunciation, and instrumentation, to retain its delicate style while, at the same time, drawing on the merits of theatrical forms, both from the north and the south. Wei's reform proved a success. When the refined Kunshan Qiang was later adopted by the Ming dramatist Liang Chenyu as the foundation for his renowned play *Huansha Ji* (浣纱记), it was a sensation among both the populace and the intelligentsia, positioning what is known as Kunqu today as the prime choice for the dramatists of the time. The period from the mid-sixteenth century to early eighteenth century witnessed the heyday of Kunqu. Starting from the regions south of the Yangtze River, Kunqu spread; the expanding audience and the creation of increasingly sophisticated dramatic texts gave rise to a league of folk troupes, who were commissioned by the literati for entertainment at family gatherings or banquets. For nearly two centuries, Kunqu was established as the official theatrical form of the Imperial Court, and its dominance over the operatic world paled only with the rise of the

Peking Opera in the eighteenth century. Two characteristics persist in the vicissitudes of this operatic form: the sophistication of its performance, and its integration of traditional Chinese art and literature—as is often claimed by contemporary Kunqu lovers, including the women in this inquiry.

Turning to Shanghai, the area surrounding the ancient Songjiang, located right beside Kunshan, was among the very first to ride the wave of Kunqu. According to archival records, formal Kunqu performances in Shanghai can be traced back to 1578, when *Huansha Ji* was performed in Shanghai in the Qingpu region. The new Qing dynasty brought new impetus to Kunqu in Shanghai, with the adoption of dramatic texts by local writers as well as the influx of operatic troupes into the city. The metamorphosis of the city into an open port, as decreed by the 1841 Treaty of Nanking, fundamentally changed the power balance of the Shanghai theatre industry in Late Imperial China. The increasing commercial prosperity contributed to a population boom and a concomitant hike in the entertainment needs of the city. By the early years of the Xianfeng period, four veteran Kunqu troupes—*Hongfu* (鴻福), *Dazhang* (大章), *Daya* (大雅), and *Quanfu* (全福)—had made their entrée into the Shanghai market. At the same time, Kunqu experienced fierce competition from emerging folk operas, in particular the Hui and Peking Operas. As Peking Opera finally gained the upper hand and rose to become the nation's most coveted operatic genre, Kunqu troupes in Shanghai had to wrestle with dwindling market demand and artistic supply, and sometimes, ironically, with Kunqu troupes being summoned to support performances of Peking Opera. Efforts were made by modern industrialists to rescue Kunqu, but these were ineffective. As the Sino-Japanese war waged in the 1930s and 1940s, Kunqu artists were forced to change career, and the operatic form entered the most trying period in its history.

Surviving through decades of wars and social unrest, Kunqu returned to the stage in Shanghai with a graceful gesture. The Shanghai Kun Opera Troupe was founded in 1978. As a key performance organization, under the aegis of the state, the Troupe has housed some of the most senior artists, and has established itself as one of the most star-studded of all Kunqu troupes nationwide. Since 2014, when the Troupe moved back to its restored home on Shaoxing Road, performances have been held nearly every weekend. Compared with troupes elsewhere, the tickets, at RMB 100, are probably not the cheapest, but are certainly affordable for most of its target audience. Pedagogically, the Troupe has opened classes for laypeople, offering professional training so that even beginner-level students are able to perform on stage after a one-semester course. Besides the Shanghai Kun Opera Troupe, various "unofficial" organizations have been set up in the city to promote Kunqu and its practices. Groups of a similar nature have emerged in major universities in Shanghai, as Kunqu was gradually introduced into higher education institutions and was generally well received.[29]

Doing Kunqu

Despite its grounding in Chinese history and literature, Kunqu has not received much academic attention. The limited number of publications I have located assume, by and large, a historical perspective. There are Chinese-language book-length treatises that explore its historical development and current transformations.[30] There are also English-language studies that delve into the interplay between history and stage, as well as the loss of Kunqu's centrality to Peking Opera.[31] While no studies specifically engage with the gender dimension of Kunqu fandom, Joseph Lam chooses one Kunqu masterpiece, *Jingniang* (*Escorting Lady Jing Home*) and its performances over five decades to illustrate how the opera opens up space for Chinese men and women to reflect on gender issues.[32] I will supplement these studies on Kunqu by inserting a gender perspective specifically in the realm of fandom.

This scant academic interest in gender, fandom, and Chinese operatic art is particularly remarkable as *xiqu* (戏曲, the generic term for operatic arts in Chinese) audiences are predominantly female. According to a questionnaire survey launched during the national tour of a Fujian operatic group, two-thirds of its audiences are women.[33] While the researchers of this quantitative study primarily aimed at investigating the future of *xiqu*, I position my qualitative inquiry as one way to fathom out the present *xiqu* audiences themselves, and my particular case is Kunqu. During our participant observation exercise, women occupied most of the seats. They looked between 30 and 40, dressed in ways that suggested an educated, middle-class background—not unlike the single women in this inquiry. There were also men and younger women among the audience. During the shows, those who would applaud and yell enthusiastically were mostly women. Turning to online activities, the gender ratio mirrors offline participation. According to Zheng, one of the focus group participants, her encounters with online circles of friends show that they "seem to be predominantly female." Similarly, those who take Kunqu classes are overwhelmingly female. Xiaoyan told her focus group mates of her Kunqu teaching experience at one university in Shanghai where the gender ratio is a "big problem." Almost all of her Kunqu students were female, roughly "10 females to 1 male." To which, Michelle, her group mate, responded with a joke: "Just like the *xiangqin* market!"[34] They all laughed. Very quickly, their conversation flowed to other domains where they also observed a gender ratio problem; even basketball societies are recruiting more female members than male, not to mention their work spaces, where the creative sectors seem to be dominated similarly by women.

Indeed, resonating with Xiaoyan's teaching experience, the majority of the women we interviewed came into contact with Kunqu during their university years. To be precise, they would have seen some performances of Chinese opera, Kunqu or otherwise. However, it was usually when they became university students that they had the determination and the opportunity to join Kunqu classes and become serious fans. In other words, while Western conventions of operatic art are typically embedded in connoisseur and adult culture,[35] Kunqu operates not only as a gendered practice, but also as part and parcel of youth culture. Zhang, for instance, was initially interested in Yueju, another form of Chinese operatic art.[36] When she was in her second year at university, she heard of Kunqu classes being offered by the Shanghai Kun Opera Troupe. After confirming a total absence of similar training in Yueju in the city, Zhang decided to enrol. Since then, she was increasingly exposed to Kunqu and became increasingly a fan.

In this context, it should be noted that—as some of the Kunqu fans also pointed out during the focus group conversations—their increasing involvement with Kunqu is not only a bottom-up affair; it is also a result of promotional efforts conducted in a more top-down manner. Next to the availability of Kunqu classes, evidently facilitated by official sponsorship, as illustrated by the university programme championed by Xiaoyan, quite a number of the female fans mentioned the name Pai Hsien-yung (Bai Xianyong 白先勇).[37] A renowned writer and a Kunqu connoisseur, Pai calls himself "a volunteer for Kunqu" and has dedicated much of his life to promoting his favoured operatic form, especially in the new millennium. Besides writing on Kunqu, Pai has also championed the staging of traditional Kunqu performances aimed to be attractive to younger audiences. In 2004, under his leadership, the Kunqu classic *Peony Pavilion* was refashioned into *Peony Pavilion: The Young Version* with a younger cast. After the premiere in Taiwan, more than 200 shows followed in different parts of the world, including Shanghai. Pai and this groundbreaking—and controversial—work was often cited by participants in the group discussions as a milestone in their personal involvement with Kunqu. Here, I do not aim to continue with a full-fledged discussion of the importance of top-down promotional efforts in constituting a certain youth culture. Suffice it to say that both official sponsorship as well as celebrity endorsement do play an important role in the case of Kunqu, as evidenced by the experiences of the women in this inquiry.

While quite a number of these Kunqu lovers trace their relationship with Kunqu to their university time and the promotional efforts of Pai, others offer rather diverse narratives of their first encounters. Xiaoyan alludes to family influence and became interested in traditional Chinese culture, including Kunqu, when she was a child. At the other "extreme," Jin made her entrée into the Kunqu world when she was already working. It was pure coincidence, according to her, that she heard of an after-work Kunqu class catering to "the white-collared" in Shanghai. As diverse as their first encounters are their continued engagements with Kunqu. A heated argument in one focus group is telling. While Xiaoyan, as someone having dedicated years of her life to Kunqu education, talks elaborately about her mission to carry on the tradition, her fellow Kunqu lovers in the group are equally intent on explaining their simple enjoyment of something beautiful and entertaining. Yvonne's words represent one common sentiment of their engagement with Kunqu: "For me it's more like what Kunqu can offer me, than what I can offer Kunqu." Like many others, Yvonne would not wish to add more stress to her life, when life itself is already stressful enough. And yet, just when her utterance may be taken as an indication of her treating Kunqu merely as entertainment, Yvonne also tells us how seriously she takes Kunqu: she followed her favourite Kunqu performers as far as to Cologne, Germany.

In the first instance, they watch and enjoy Kunqu performances. Sometimes, they mention their favourite Kunqu performers as stars, as *aidou*. Quite a few continue to take Kunqu classes. While Xiaoyan may be the most outspoken defender of her operatic form, she is hardly exceptional in allocating her time and efforts to promoting Kunqu. Most of them contribute fan labour towards a variety of goals, from writing reviews, to coordinating logistical matters for Kunqu performances. Finally, we also have fans who turn their passion into a profession. Yi brought the Kunqu exposure and experience she gathered during her university years to her job as a radio producer, making programmes not only on Kunqu, but *xiqu* in general. Xiaoyan, after securing funding from the authorities, started promoting and practising Kunqu education on various campuses in Shanghai, organizing Kunqu performances, as well as releasing recordings of Kunqu masters—a job she considers more important than the family business where she works for the sake of necessity, both in terms of family expectations and for financial reasons.

Once we start explicating what the single women in this inquiry are doing with Kunqu, it becomes apparent that conceptions seeking to embrace developments in fan culture are lacking. The interest, the passion, the love may be common, but the practices are diverse. Some of them indeed fulfil the classic understanding of fans; they proclaim that they just want to appreciate and to enjoy it. And yet, some offer what may be generalized as fan labour, for instance, in mediating the arrangement of Kunqu events. At the same time, at least a couple of these Kunqu lovers go "further," in the sense that they are not only offering fan labour as such—they turn their fandom *into* labour, which is paid and career-oriented. They have embarked on a creative career driven by their enthusiasm for Kunqu. Even the latest theorization of produsers falls short of explaining what some of them are doing. Very often, indeed, they not only consume; they also produce. When they are learning to play Kunqu or when they are helping to organize events, they are delivering Kunqu products too. Again, they do more. They are producing not only Kunqu itself, but also new generations of Kunqu lovers—by teaching, for instance. My intention here is not to conceive of another term to embrace these; to me, the inevitably and incredibly diverse and messy manifestations of how people articulate and cultivate their creative penchants and pursuits is intriguing. I am amazed by the manifestations themselves, to the extent that perhaps the best theorization, if there must be one, is not, at least not only, to describe what fans do, but to acknowledge that what they do always surpasses description. It is not only that what they love is creative, their love itself is creative.

TOGETHER, THEY...

While the fans have their own practices and engagements with Kunqu, that they often do these together is evident. Resonating with the togetherness so successfully dramatized with the five single women neighbours in the hit series *Ode to Joy* (see Chap. 2), the single women in the Kunqu inquiry share their neighbourhood not in a geographical sense, but by partaking in the same collectivity of something in which they are passionately involved. In what ways it can be understood as community will be discussed in greater detail in the following section. Here, I will first outline how they get to know each other, and what they do when they are together.

The first way these women became friends was through a complex interaction of online and offline practices, of physical presence and smartphone communication. Michelle and Yvonne's experience is typical:

Michelle: When it started, we were just familiar faces that we often came across during performances. It might take some time before a real opportunity presents itself. For instance, if I am supposed to distribute tickets, then I must have the contact details of other people and they would have my details. Now, we have WeChat, and with WeChat, we can form a "circle of friends." Then, I would probably know what you are doing, what kind of interests you have. We may not be very familiar with each other. But if all of a sudden, I find out that she is watching Kunqu at Tianchan [a Kunqu venue in Shanghai], then we would say hello during the intermission. Gradually, we become closer. But is it really a circle of friends? I don't really know. To me, it's more like people meeting each other under very specific circumstances, very specific timing. Are we really a group? Sometimes, I don't think so. We are just –

Yvonne: I am somewhat better. In my case, if I know we are watching the same show, I would ask if they would like to have dinner together. If we go to Tianchan, then we find a restaurant close by. Dining together and having a chat. It's quite nice.

Here is an instance of Kunqu fans getting familiar at least with each other's presence. Such familiarity is built up in a physical space, that of a Kunqu venue, and finds its possibility for amplification, and actualization, into a "real" friendship through the omnipresence of smartphone technology. In contemporary China, it is the WeChat platform that offers the digital space and convenience to string people into a circle of friends, waiting to be mobilized into more and stronger social acts and ties. Another platform that functions similarly is Douban, a website popular among younger generations of Chinese interested in art and culture. Siqi introduced a few friends to join our focus groups from her Douban group on Kunqu. Vera refers to the older possibility of BBS as her first platform to reach out to fellow Kunqu lovers. Before we attach too readily, and too much, importance to their smartphones for such socializing, I want to flag up their experience of the physical venue as a vital site of feeling together. To begin with, the cosy, intimate, and in-crowd atmosphere felt in the theatres during our participant observations testifies to the conduciveness of physical space transforming itself into social space. As if to corroborate such necessity of the physical, sometimes they would even insist on building up familiarity not only with the venue itself, but very specifically with the seats. To them, it is not even just to be in the same theatre; they want to, they need to, be in the same seats, relating to each other with the same familiarity.

Michelle: We are not herds of animal. We can to go to Kunqu on our own, and we can go to Kunqu as a group. We always say: every one of us has our own eccentric insistences. I like a particular seat in the venue. Every time, I must book the same seat. This is my insistence.
Yvonne: Yes, we all do this.
Michelle: We all have our own particular seats. So? So, every time we go to see a performance, suddenly you turn around and you will see the same people. It doesn't mean that we know each other. It's just our everyday kind of habit. I like that seat, and I sit there every time. Slowly and surely there is some tacit understanding among us: a group of strangers, and yet whenever there is a performance, this group of strangers will be in the same place, in the same seats, expecting.

The second way for Kunqu fans to become friends has nothing to do with Kunqu venues or WeChat groups, but with contingency. That is to say, if Kunqu venues and WeChat groups are always already expected bases for people who like Kunqu to gather and get to know each other, sometimes friendly encounters take place on unlikely occasions. Michelle and Yvonne knew of each other from a Kunqu group on Douban. They did not become friends, at least not in the offline sense, until they were both at the Shanghai Book Fair in 2010, carrying out their respective duties. They were there for four days and they talked for four days, embarking on something that developed into regular contact and friendship. It should be noted that the encounter at the book fair might be contingent and unexpected, but the fact that it was at a creative space such as a book fair underlines the premise of that encounter, that they share an interest in things artistic and cultural. Yi and Zhang's story is even more "distant" from Kunqu. They attended the same party. At the end of this, Yi asked Zhang if she also planned to take the subway. Yes, she did. On their way to the station, they started chatting about the usual things, such as where you live, and what kind of work you do. Radio. What kind of programmes? Chinese operas. Oh, I like Kunqu! And the two immediately shared a lot about Kunqu, the same "informal social currency," and became friends.[38]

This experience is radically different from what Yi usually encounters. Usually, when Yi tells people she is working for the radio, they become curious and excited. But when she continues to tell them she is working for programmes on Chinese opera, their interest subsides instantly. While Yi experiences Kunqu as something that fulfils "all my expectations of art," others usually, if not mostly, do not feel the same. Yi's as well as other Kunqu fans' similar articulations point to the typical mechanism of group formation: internal recognition and external distinction. On the one hand, they share something they recognize as vital, as a group; on the other, such recognition, perceived as unique and distinct to the group, serves as a marker of distance—or some would say, demarcation—from those who do not subscribe to the same. Sometimes, it works on the personal level:

Zhang: I feel that all those in the Kunqu classes are of a similar type. Maybe we have different interests, but we are still similar. We all have a strong personality, insistent on what we are interested in, having a certain sophistication in thinking. We can echo each other, especially those of a similar age.

Other times, it works on the artistic level:

Gu: Kunqu is rather demanding to anyone who's trying it out. You need to have a certain cultural background, otherwise you won't be able to understand it. You may listen to it the whole day, and yet, you don't know what they are singing about. Compared to Yueju, well you listen to Yueju and you will understand right away what it's about. I believe Kunqu imposes that kind of demand on its audience.

Zheng: Yes. I think we can describe Kunqu as a grand lady, while a girl next door is more appropriate for Yueju.

Jin: Precisely because of this special appeal of Kunqu, many people
                who learned Kunqu with me, well, I know them for years and
                Kunqu is part and parcel of their growing up. Now, they are
                married, and are mothers. They bring their young children to
                the rehearsals. Even the post-70s and post-80s generations,
                they bring their children with them, trying to hand over the
                Kunqu culture to the next generation.

Together, they share Kunqu information through WeChat and Douban. They make appointments and go to the same performances. Siqi recalls fondly how they, a group of Kunqu fans-cum-university students, would rush together for the last subway train to return to their campus dormitories after a show. Some of them take Kunqu classes together. And it is not only Kunqu that brings them together. Many of them mention dining out, drinking coffee, and going to the cinema. In particular, they talk about travelling together as one major activity they would do with their Kunqu friends, travelling within Shanghai as well as outside the city, or even outside the country.[39] Sometimes, they would get together to do something loosely considered artistic or creative. One day, Yvonne noticed that the chinar trees, well known for their scenic presence in Shanghai's French Concession neighbourhoods, were shedding leaves. She decided to take a day off, and she planned to go to a particular area to take photographs of the trees. Yvonne asked Michelle to accompany her, and off they went.

A footnote to the intimacy of the Kunqu community should be inserted on the relative difficulty of finding women willing to join the focus groups. In addition to the heavy workload imposed by their creative jobs, the explanation they put forward was also related to Kunqu itself. On the one hand, some of the women who agreed to join the investigation did help us further by introducing fellow Kunqu lovers. It often turned out that they had already been approached. On the other hand, many of the Kunqu lovers we approached indicated their interest, to the extent that they would ask us many questions regarding why we were doing the investigation and what we had found out so far. They would even ask us to stream the focus group discussions live online, as they were curious how fellow Kunqu lovers talked about their common passion. However, most of them would want to think about it, and ultimately, declined joining. They hinted at acquaintances with Kunqu performers and promoters, as well as their circle of Kunqu friends. One group member who did agree to join requested to use a pseudonym. It was the everybody-knows-everybody sense of not only intimacy, but also anxiety that comes with the life of community.

COMMUNITY: YOU ARE NOT ALONE

In Sennett's discussion on community, he resorts to his childhood in a disenfranchised neighbourhood in Chicago, where he crystallizes three dimensions of a community from his experience: morale, conviction, and co-operation. I will focus on the first in this section. Not that the single women do not show conviction to Kunqu, or co-operate with each other. They do. As noted earlier, they demonstrate their commitment through years of spending their time and other resources attending Kunqu classes, going to Kunqu performances, and helping arrange Kunqu events. One dedicated her graduation thesis to Kunqu. Some even take it as their "vocation," to use Sennett's word, or profession to contribute to and keep the operatic art and its community alive. Some would definitely find it difficult, if not impossible, to contemplate a life outside this art form and community. As regards co-operation, these single women did not mention much in addition to mundane problems in their everyday lives, friendly undertakings such as taking care of others' pets—probably because these are all professional people who are wont to live independently. Their experiences must be different, for instance, from those of the single women in *Ode to Joy*, who are living together in the same building, or in the same apartment. They must also be different from the physical community Sennett is referring to where people, marginalized and threatened (by gangsters), work together to carve out a safer time and space. In that sense, it would also be misguided to look for the same kind and level of conviction and co-operation as in Sennett's notion of community.

I want to focus on morale, "the matter of keeping one's spirits up in difficult circumstances,"[40] as this seems to be what the single women are experiencing from being together. The following conversation in one focus group is revealing.

He: Those who enjoy Kunqu belong to the intellectual circle. Their upbringing and temperament are rather good. Those people I got to know through Kunqu usually became good friends, because we have respect for each other... I also observe one thing, that is those who love Kunqu generally like to lead a slow life, and they have better tempers... I believe

	that people who like creative and artistic things can't help being somewhat idealistic. We like to get in touch with things related to art. We love them, stubbornly, crazily.
Yue:	Yes. Like me, when I think about these last six months, I was working a lot, and when I wasn't working, I was reading. At least I did something in my after-work life.
He:	Because we place aesthetics as our top priority. Life itself is a sort of aesthetics. Aesthetics, I feel, is huge, and we need to spend our whole life to practise it. I like to get in touch with anything related to aesthetics...
Yue:	Yes, yes, yes. I like to make my life more elegant... As a matter of fact, we are attracted to Kunqu also because of its elegance.
He:	It's just beautiful.

Such corroboration of a certain way of life, a certain norm, is evident in many focus group conversations. It nods to two sentiments at the same time. First, it is their affirmation of their cultural taste, their priorities for slowness and beauty. Second, it is also a tacit acknowledgement of a larger social context—one outside their Kunqu community—that cares less for art, culture, and beauty, that requires them to work and work fast. This context underlines the importance of the Kunqu community to uphold their morale and their resolve to continue living the way they like. Zhang compares her work life with her Kunqu life using vivid, perhaps biased, operatic imagery. For her, work life is like a Western opera, requiring "high tempo, and its general direction is height, efficiency, and strength"; it expects her and people like her to become a "diva," a strong woman. Luckily, she has Kunqu that asks her to slow down. Zhang describes her after-work time with other Kunqu fans as categorically and refreshingly distinct from her working hours. "I always feel such a transition, when I go to attend Kunqu classes after work. From one state of being to another state of being." The transition can be difficult too, a "kind of personality split haha," she says. In any case, Zhang echoes many others about the morale-building effect that Kunqu, as community, imparts on her life. As cited earlier, Zhang feels that they belong to a similar type: having a strong personality, insistent on their interests, sophisticated.

Such a morale building effect is achieved largely without recourse to verbal communication. In fact, they usually do not talk about work; nor do they talk about love or any other issues that exude what they call "negative energy." This term is used frequently by these single women, undergirding a paradox in their lives, namely, they do experience negativity as single women and they tend to file it away as such. In other words, they usually choose not to talk about it. If need be, they would use more instant ways to communicate their negativity, not aiming at sharing, seeking feedback and finding a way out, but simply for the possibility of venting it, releasing it. They articulate a strong sense of individualism in dealing with their problems, and do not see any point in seeking more collective wisdom and solutions. Somehow, they believe rather firmly that if it is inevitable to be confronted with negative energy in their single lives, at least they should cultivate their group life with positive fun.

Yvonne: We won't really talk about our work, or about our emotional life. More often, it's about anything. What actually do we talk about when we meet?
Xiaoyan: It's all about food, drinks, and having fun!
Yvonne: Basically that. If you ask me whether I have friends who can talk about emotional stuff or about families, friends who can talk about things with negative energy, I guess I do have. But sometimes, when I feel I am not happy about something, I will call her up, or text her. Just release myself, that's it. When we are actually having an appointment, I want us to be happy... When we are meeting, why should I pass on my unhappiness to you? When I am unhappy, I ask you for a date, and we sit down and have dinner, why should we still be talking about my unhappiness? ... I know it very well. I can find ways to release my feelings, but after that, I still have to deal with the problems by myself. No one can help me. My problems are still mine.
Michelle: We make an appointment so that we can do something fun together, or something we cannot do on our own.
Xiaoyan: That's why I don't really talk about problems with friends.

This does not mean that they never talk about things. Yi and Zhang mention the fact that they would confide in each other about problems at work or when they are not feeling good. The way they do it is, in their words, *jishi tucao* (即时吐槽), or instantaneous venting, that is to shoot it out right away on WeChat or by calling, at the moment of grievance, not making appointments or waiting for the occasion to meet and to talk. For most of the time, they would simply make use of their togetherness for pleasure, for positivity, for confirmation. The same tactic applies to their singlehood. They seldom talk about emotional issues concerning their love lives, or the pressure to marry that they feel from their families or peers. This particular group of peers whom they got to know through Kunqu offer a platform for them to stay where they stand in terms of their single lives. It keeps up their morale when the wider society does not condone either their singlehood or their passion for Kunqu. In defending their Kunqu, they are defending their singlehood at the same time. It is a defence of choosing the unlikely, the marginalized.

Zheng: As regards my singlehood, [my mother] has always been very worried. She feels that she must get me married away, like she would owe me a great deal if she failed to find me a good husband. She had sleeping problems because of this worry. But in the past couple of years, I don't know why, perhaps they feel that this life of mine is quite OK. And they slowly have accepted it, that it's OK like this, my way of life.

Gu: My parents don't really intervene in my life, such as in my interest in Kunqu. Well, they don't understand it, so they won't talk to me about it. Even when I try to, they are not interested... My mother's only worry is that if I get too involved with Kunqu, maybe I will find it more difficult to find a partner. This is her only worry. Well, I think she's got a point.

From their conversations, it is clear that they have to deal with the kind of pressure to marry, not unlike what we have discussed in the previous chapter. However, they usually do not complain to each other, or seek advice. They brush it aside with humour[41]—such as Xiaoyan, who says, "Well they failed to get me away from Kunqu, they won't manage to force me into marriage"—and chit-chat not meant to be serious and weighty, yet grounded in their shared state of living. They talk about, for instance, if their ideal partners would need to share the same interest in Kunqu. Opinions diverge. Some say yes, it would be better for communication. Some say no, "there can't be two Kunqu fanatics in one household." And some do not really care. Among all the single women in this inquiry, only Vera actually tried to form a relationship with a male Kunqu fan. They communicated online for three years. When he finally made plans to visit

Shanghai, she decided not to see him. Vera could not articulate exactly why. Most importantly, what transpires from their conversations is the feeling that there are others like themselves, who are unlike the rest. They have found their "soul mates" through the love of their life: Kunqu; they are not alone and it is morale building—sometimes, even when they do not actually go to performances any more.

Gu: Although I haven't been to Kunqu performance for some time, it feels a bit remote now, and yet, it remains always by my side.

Zheng: Haha, soul mate. This is probably a choice by us, single women.

Gu: I actually think that as long as I can go and see Kunqu, it doesn't matter if I have a partner or not.

Jinzhou: I would say it's quite impossible to spend large chunks of time every week or every month on Kunqu. It's more like fragmentation. Like what both of you said, it integrates into our everyday life as fragments.

Zheng: I don't have much expectation. The only one I have is to live more beautifully. I feel that after so many years as a single woman, I don't think I can tolerate or adapt to another person. I wouldn't want him to make compromises, and I don't want myself to make compromises. I'd better stay on my own. Me and Kunqu, we live together very well.

While dominant, Western discourse of friendship, particularly the female form, would equate intimacy, closeness, and trust with heart-to-heart talks, soul baring, and searching, as well as an eagerness to express and share what is happening to them, especially the associated feelings,[42] the Kunqu community has its own ways to cultivate their friendships. It offers a case that is different from the dominant framing of female relations in terms of emotional femininity and private, domestic space.[43] That it does not subscribe to the dominant personalized, emotionalized, and confessionalized way of conducting friendships, does not mean it is less affective and cherished. By the same token, that their issues in life are not articulated and elaborated, does not mean that they do not understand and share. The single women who are talking about Kunqu and about their way of relating to each other, are also narrating a basis of their getting along and getting together that barely requires being spoken: they know they all have their share of difficulties in terms of work demands, marriage pressure, difficulty to find the right partner, and a myriad of other problems, big and small. And they do it through a heavily gendered, feminized practice in a heavily gendered, feminized space. It is Michelle who expresses it so poignantly, "every one of us knows, very clearly, that all the problems are your own." This tacit understanding, at once individualistic and collective, of the toughness of life makes them keep the issues and the negative energy to themselves instead of allowing them to flow and bleed into their circle of friends. After all, such understanding may offer the most endearing comfort and reassurance; in Michelle's words: "It is not easy, for all of us."

CLARIFICATIONS AND DISCLAIMERS

I would like to conclude with some clarifications. The experiences of these Kunqu lovers as presented in this chapter, I am aware, may lead to some impressions regarding Kunqu and single women. First, they tend to enjoy Kunqu as a group of friends. Second, Kunqu forms an important part of their lives. And third, those women who enjoy Kunqu are mostly, if not all, single. I need to make these clarifications as I am often reminded by the women themselves.

In the first instance, Yvonne calls herself and people like her a "solo connoisseur," stressing their ability to enjoy life, including Kunqu, on their own. Michelle, in the same conversation, responds with her own history of solo Kunqu viewing since 2003. In other words, they do not always enjoy Kunqu as a group. Besides, they have groups of friends beyond those of Kunqu. As He stresses: "Everybody has many circles of friends, it's normal." Regarding the importance of Kunqu, Michelle puts it in perspective with the following: "Those who don't really know us would think that we are spending 100 per cent of our leisure time on Kunqu. But we know, well, if we watch 100 shows a year, perhaps 60 are Kunqu." Again, some of them, definitely Xiaoyan, would attach prime importance to Kunqu, but most of them would qualify this like Michelle. During focus group discussions, when they are touching on issues of relationships and marriage, very often they would articulate some sort of disclaimer to the effect that there are all sorts of women enjoying Kunqu, including married women. In Yvonne's words, "I want to say that we should not stereotype, that those mature single women who go to Kunqu are invariably reluctant to get married. It's not like that." Jin mentions fellow Kunqu students who got married, became mothers, and brought their children to rehearsals. Our observation at the venues corroborate the presence of audience members who come to the shows as mothers and daughters.

Another disclaimer is mine. To make way for the primary goal of this inquiry, I have not covered the textual—when Zheng, for instance, refers to the difficulty to find the same kind of man in real life as in the opera she saw. I am also not exploring how they, as individuals, are making use of Kunqu—when Vera, for instance, confides in me how Kunqu helps her survive periods of depression. Instead, I focus on what they do together, physically and symbolically, privately and publicly, online and offline. Indeed, I have probed into the experiences of togetherness when these single women get involved through their common interest in Kunqu. Sometimes, they do that in real physical spaces, such as Kunqu venues. In many ways, these women may be leading a single life, but they are not really single. Above all, the inquiry is on how they relate to each other. In the following chapter, we move on to examine how they relate to physical space at large.

NOTES

1. Richard Sennett, *Together: The Rituals, Pleasures and Politics of Co-operation* (New Haven: Yale University Press, 2012).
2. There is one exception, who works in the financial sector.
3. Chow Yiu Fai, "Martial Arts Films and Dutch–Chinese Masculinities: Smaller Is Better," *China Information* 22, no. 2 (2008): 331–59.
4. They include those associated with "fans" such as *fenxi* (粉丝, a sound translation of "fans") and *naocanfen* (脑残粉, literally braindead fans), those associated with *mi* (迷), meaning obsessed, admiring, such as *ximi* (戏迷, an admirer of *xiqu*, 戏曲) and *mimei* (迷妹, literally an admiring girl) as well as a term peculiar to Kunqu fans: *kunchong* (昆虫, literally insect, a hybrid sound play with the *kun* in Kunqu).
5. See, for instance, Janice A. Radway, *Reading the Romance: Women, Patriarchy, and Popular Literature* (London: Verso, 1987); Karen R. Scheel and John S. Westefeld, "Heavy Metal Music and Adolescent Suicidality: An Empirical Investigation," *Adolescence* 34, no. 134 (1999): 253; Lyn Thomas, *Fans, Feminisms and "Quality" Media* (Hove: Psychology Press, 2002).
6. See Barbara Ehrenreich, Elizabeth Hess, and Gloria Jacobs, "Beatlemania: Girls Just Want To Have Fun," in *The Adoring Audience: Fan Culture and Popular Media*, ed. Lisa A. Lewis (London: Routledge, 2002), 84–106;

Anna Fishzon, *Fandom, Authenticity, and Opera: Mad Acts and Letter Scenes in Fin-de-Siècle Russia* (Basingstoke: Palgrave Macmillan, 2013); Stephen Hinerman, "Beatlemania: Girls Just Want To Have Fun," in *The Adoring Audience: Fan Culture and Popular Media*, ed. Lisa A. Lewis (London: Routledge, 2002), 107–34; Adrienne Trier-Bieniek, *Feminist Theory and Pop Culture* (Rotterdam: Sense Publishers, 2015).

7. Male fans, on the other hand, "tend to be typed as 'aggressive' and are often the target for most media markets." See Trier-Bieniek, *Feminist Theory and Pop Culture*, xii.

8. Tanya R. Cochran, "The Browncoats Are Coming! Firefly, Serenity, and Fan Activism," in *Investigating Firefly and Serenity: Science Fiction on the Frontier*, ed. Rhonda V. Wilcox and Tanya R. Cochran (London: I.B. Tauris, 2008), 239–240.

9. See Stuart Hall, "Encoding/Decoding," in *Culture, Media, Language: Working Papers in Cultural Studies*, ed. Centre for Contemporary Cultural Studies (London: Hutchinson, 1980).

10. Chow Yiu Fai and Jeroen de Kloet, *Sonic Multiplicities: Hong Kong Pop and the Global Circulation of Sound and Image* (Bristol, UK; Chicago, USA: Intellect Books, 2013), 44.

11. Lisa A. Lewis, *The Adoring Audience: Fan Culture and Popular Media* (Hove: Psychology Press, 1992).

12. Henry Jenkins, *Convergence Culture: Where Old and New Media Collide* (New York: NYU Press, 2006), 243.

13. Axel Bruns, *Blogs, Wikipedia, Second Life, and Beyond: From Production to Produsage* (New York: Peter Lang, 2008).

14. See, for instance, Kristin M. Barton and Jonathan Malcolm Lampley, eds., *Fan CULTure: Essays on Participatory Fandom in the 21st Century* (NC: McFarland, 2014); Elizabeth Evans, *Transmedia Television: Audiences, New Media, and Daily Life* (London: Routledge, 2011).

15. Zhang Weiyu and Mao Chengting, "Fan Activism Sustained and Challenged: Participatory Culture in Chinese Online Translation Communities," *Chinese Journal of Communication* 6, no. 1 (2013): 45–61.

16. S. Elizabeth Bird, "Are We All Produsers Now?," *Cultural Studies* 25, no. 4–5 (2011): 502–16. See also James Hay and Nick Couldry, "Rethinking Convergence/Culture," *Cultural Studies* 25, no. 4–5 (2011): 473–86.

17. Trier-Bieniek, *Feminist Theory and Pop Culture*, xii.

18. Ibid., xi.

19. Matt Hills, *Fan Cultures* (Hove: Psychology Press, 2002), xii.

20. Lily Kong, "The Sociality of Cultural Industries," *International Journal of Cultural Policy* 11, no. 1 (2005): 61–76.

21. Gino Cattani and Simone Ferriani, "A Core/Periphery Perspective on Individual Creative Performance: Social Networks and Cinematic

Achievements in the Hollywood Film Industry," *Organization Science* 19, no. 6 (2008): 824–44.

22. Emma Felton, Christy Collis, and Phil Graham, "Making Connections: Creative Industries Networks in Outer-Suburban Locations," *Australian Geographer* 41, no. 1 (2010): 57–70.

23. Lee Minha, "Fostering Connectivity: A Social Network Analysis of Entrepreneurs in Creative Industries," *International Journal of Cultural Policy* 21, no. 2 (2015): 139–52.

24. See Max Weber, "The Distribution of Power Within the *Gemeinschaft*: Classes, Stände, Parties," in *Weber's Rationalism and Modern Society: New Translations on Politics, Bureaucracy, and Social Stratification*, ed. Tony Waters and Dagmar Waters (New York: Palgrave Macmillan, 2015), 37–58. See also Ferdinand Tönnies, *Gemeinschaft Und Gesellschaft* (Leipzig: Fues's Verlag, 1887); Emile Durkheim, "A Review of Ferdinand Tönnies's Gemeinschaft Und Gesellschaft: Abhandlung Des Communismus Und Des Socialismus Als Empirischer Culturformen," *American Journal of Sociology* 77 (1972): 1193; Joan Aldous, Emile Durkheim, and Ferdinand Tonnies, "An Exchange Between Durkheim and Tonnies on the Nature of Social Relations, with an Introduction by Joan Aldous," *American Journal of Sociology* 77, no. 6 (1972): 1191–1200. For a critique of Weber's conception of *gesellschaft* being more progressive than *gemeinschaft*, see Jean-Luc Nancy, *The Inoperative Community* (Minnesota: U of Minnesota Press, 1991).

25. See, for instance, Robert Park, "The City: Suggestions for the Investigation of Human Behavior in the Urban Environment," in *Classic Essays on the Culture of Cities*, ed. Richard Sennett (Englewood Cliffs: Prentice-Hall, 1916).

26. Tony Blackshaw, *Key Concepts in Community Studies* (London: SAGE Publications, 2010): 5.

27. Sennett, *Together*, 273.

28. Benedict Anderson, *Imagined Communities: Reflections on the Origin and Spread of Nationalism* (London: Verso, 1991).

29. This brief account of Kunqu and its connection with Shanghai is based on the following selection of works: Feng Yun (冯芸), "苏州的昆曲传承:昆曲曲社的历史变迁 [Suzhou Kunqu de Chuancheng: Kunqu Qushe de Lishi Bianqian]," *中国音乐 [Zhongguo Yinyue]*, no. 3 (2010): 47–53; Gu Duhuang (顾笃璜), "苏州昆曲曲家与道和曲社 [Suzhou Kunqu Qujia Yu Daohe Qushe]," *文匯报 [Wenhui Bao]*, May 18, 2015; Guo Yingde (郭英德), *明清传奇史 [Mingqing Chuanqi Shi]* (Nanjing: Jiangsu guji chuban-she, 1999); Qian Nanyang (钱南扬), "南词引正校注 (Nanci Yinzheng Jiaozhu)," *戏剧报 [Xiju Bao]*, no. 2 (1961): 60–61; Zheng Chuanjian (郑传鉴), "昆剧传习所纪事 [Kunju Chuanxisuo Jishi]," *中国戏曲网*

[*Zhongguo Xiqu Wang*] (blog), November 6, 2006, http://www.chinaopera.net/html/2006-11/606p3.html;   中国戏曲志全国编辑委员会 [Zhongguo xiquzhi quanguobianji weiyuanhui], *中国戏曲志上海卷 [Chinese Xiqu Records Shanghai volume]* (Beijing: Zhongguo, 1999).

30. Zhao Shanlin (赵山林), "试论昆曲观众的历史变迁与现状 [On the Historical Vicissitude and Current Situation of Kunqu]," *东南大学学报(哲学社会科学版) [Journal of Southeast University (Philosophy and Social Science)]* 16, no. 1 (2014): 96–165; Yu Weimin (俞为民), "昆曲的现代性发展之可能性研究 [Study on the Possibility of the Modern Development of Kunqu]," *文化艺术研究 [Wenhua Yishu Yanjiu]*, no. 1 (2011): 133–55.

31. See Josh Stenberg, "Three Relations between History and Stage in the Kunju Scene Slaying the Tiger General," *Asian Theatre Journal* 32, no. 1 (2015): 107–35; Chen Chaochen, "How Beijing Opera Eclipsed Kun Opera in Chinese Sociocultural and Sociopolitical Contexts" (California State University, 2011).

32. Joseph Sui Ching Lam, "Escorting Lady Jing Home: A Journey of Chinese Gender, Opera, and Politics," *Yearbook for Traditional Music* 46 (2014): 114–39.

33. Josh Stenberg and Jason J. P. Cai, "Mostly Young Women with Quite Traditional Tastes: Empirical Evidence for National Contemporary Audiences of Xiqu," *Theatre Journal* 69, no. 1 (2017): 43–59.

34. For a discussion on *xiangqin* practices, see Chap. 5.

35. John Storey, "The Social Life of Opera," *European Journal of Cultural Studies* 6, no. 1 (2003): 5–35.

36. For a book-length treatise on a particular form of Yueju—all-female cast— see Jiang Jin (姜进), *诗与政治: 20世纪上海公共文化中的女子越剧 [Poetry and Politics: Female Yue Opera in 20th Century Shanghai Public Culture]* (Beijing: 社会科学文献出版社 [Social Sciences Academic Press], 2015).

37. Born in Guangxi province in 1937, Pai moved to Taiwan with his family when he was a teenager. His works enjoy persistent popularity among literary youth in the Chinese-speaking world. See Wang Yan (王焱), "现代主义与传统文化的璧合——白先勇小说创作概论 [The Combination of Modernism and Traditional Culture — An Introduction to Bai Xianyong's Novel Creation]," *天中学刊 [Tianzhong Xuekan]*, no. 1X (1995): 66–69. Bai Xianyong is the rendition of Pai's name in the mainland Chinese pinyin system.

38. In her study on teenage girl smokers, Fin Cullen uses the term "informal social currency" to describe how smoking practices are mobilized and shared as a way to initiate relationships. See Fin Cullen, "'Two's up and Poncing Fags': Young Women's Smoking Practices, Reciprocity and Friendship," *Gender and Education* 22, no. 5 (2010): 491–504.

39. See Chap. 5 for an account of their travelling practices.

40. Sennett, *Together*, 248.
41. On the use of humour in managing young women's lives, see Akane Kanai, "On Not Taking the Self Seriously: Resilience, Relatability and Humour in Young Women's Tumblr Blogs," *European Journal of Cultural Studies*, 2017, 1–18.
42. For a deliberation of the rise of emotional culture and the making of capitalism, see Eva Illouz, *Cold Intimacies: The Making of Emotional Capitalism* (Cambridge: Polity, 2007).
43. Kate Themen and Jenny van Hooff, "Kicking against Tradition: Women's Football, Negotiating Friendships and Social Spaces," *Leisure Studies* 36, no. 4 (2017): 542–52.

References

Aldous, Joan, Emile Durkheim, and Ferdinand Tonnies. "An Exchange Between Durkheim and Tonnies on the Nature of Social Relations, with an Introduction by Joan Aldous." *American Journal of Sociology* 77, no. 6 (1972): 1191–1200.

Anderson, Benedict. *Imagined Communities: Reflections on the Origin and Spread of Nationalism*. London: Verso, 1991.

Barton, Kristin M., and Jonathan Malcolm Lampley, eds. *Fan CULTure: Essays on Participatory Fandom in the 21st Century*. NC: McFarland, 2014.

Bird, S. Elizabeth. "Are We All Produsers Now?" *Cultural Studies* 25, no. 4–5 (2011): 502–16.

Blackshaw, Tony. *Key Concepts in Community Studies*. London: SAGE Publications, 2010.

Bruns, Axel. *Blogs, Wikipedia, Second Life, and Beyond: From Production to Produsage*. New York: Peter Lang, 2008.

Cattani, Gino, and Simone Ferriani. "A Core/Periphery Perspective on Individual Creative Performance: Social Networks and Cinematic Achievements in the Hollywood Film Industry." *Organization Science* 19, no. 6 (2008): 824–44.

Chen, Chaochen. "How Beijing Opera Eclipsed Kun Opera in Chinese Sociocultural and Sociopolitical Contexts." Master's Thesis, California State University, 2011.

Chow, Yiu Fai. "Martial Arts Films and Dutch–Chinese Masculinities: Smaller Is Better." *China Information* 22, no. 2 (2008): 331–59.

Chow, Yiu Fai, and Jeroen de Kloet. *Sonic Multiplicities: Hong Kong Pop and the Global Circulation of Sound and Image*. Bristol, UK; Chicago, USA: Intellect Books, 2013.

Cochran, Tanya R. "The Browncoats Are Coming! Firefly, Serenity, and Fan Activism." In *Investigating Firefly and Serenity: Science Fiction on the Frontier*, edited by Rhonda V. Wilcox and Tanya R. Cochran, 239–50. London: I.B. Tauris, 2008.

Cullen, Fin. "'Two's up and Poncing Fags': Young Women's Smoking Practices, Reciprocity and Friendship." *Gender and Education* 22, no. 5 (2010): 491–504.

Durkheim, Emile. "A Review of Ferdinand Tönnies's Gemeinschaft Und Gesellschaft: Abhandlung Des Communismus Und Des Socialismus Als Empirischer Culturformen." *American Journal of Sociology* 77 (1972): 1193.

Ehrenreich, Barbara, Elizabeth Hess, and Gloria Jacobs. "Beatlemania: Girls Just Want To Have Fun." In *The Adoring Audience: Fan Culture and Popular Media*, edited by Lisa A. Lewis, 84–106. London: Routledge, 2002.

Evans, Elizabeth. *Transmedia Television: Audiences, New Media, and Daily Life*. London: Routledge, 2011.

Felton, Emma, Christy Collis, and Phil Graham. "Making Connections: Creative Industries Networks in Outer-Suburban Locations." *Australian Geographer* 41, no. 1 (2010): 57–70.

Feng, Yun (冯芸). "苏州的昆曲传承:昆曲曲社的历史变迁 [Suzhou Kunqu de Chuancheng: Kunqu Qushe de Lishi Bianqian]." *中国音乐 [Zhongguo Yinyue]*, no. 3 (2010): 47–53.

Fishzon, Anna. *Fandom, Authenticity, and Opera: Mad Acts and Letter Scenes in Fin-de-Siècle Russia*. Basingstoke: Palgrave Macmillan, 2013.

Gu, Duhuang (顾笃璜). "苏州昆曲曲家与道和曲社 [Suzhou Kunqu Qujia Yu Daohe Qushe]." *文匯報 [Wenhui Bao]*, May 18, 2015.

Guo, Yingde (郭英德). *明清传奇史 [Mingqing Chuanqi Shi]*. Nanjing: Jiangsu guji chubanshe, 1999.

Hall, Stuart. "Encoding/Decoding." In *Culture, Media, Language: Working Papers in Cultural Studies*, edited by Centre for Contemporary Cultural Studies. London: Hutchinson, 1980.

Hay, James, and Nick Couldry. "Rethinking Convergence/Culture." *Cultural Studies* 25, no. 4–5 (2011): 473–86.

Hills, Matt. *Fan Cultures*. Hove: Psychology Press, 2002.

Hinerman, Stephen. "Beatlemania: Girls Just Want To Have Fun." In *The Adoring Audience: Fan Culture and Popular Media*, edited by Lisa A. Lewis, 107–34. London: Routledge, 2002.

Illouz, Eva. *Cold Intimacies: The Making of Emotional Capitalism*. Cambridge: Polity, 2007.

Jenkins, Henry. *Convergence Culture: Where Old and New Media Collide*. New York: NYU Press, 2006.

Jiang, Jin (姜进). *诗与政治: 20世纪上海公共文化中的女子越剧 [Poetry and Politics: Female Yue Opera in 20th Century Shanghai Public Culture]*. Beijing: 社会科学文献出版社 [Social Sciences Academic Press], 2015.

Kanai, Akane. "On Not Taking the Self Seriously: Resilience, Relatability and Humour in Young Women's Tumblr Blogs." *European Journal of Cultural Studies*, 2017, 1–18.

Kong, Lily. "The Sociality of Cultural Industries." *International Journal of Cultural Policy* 11, no. 1 (2005): 61–76.

Lam, Joseph Sui Ching. "Escorting Lady Jing Home: A Journey of Chinese Gender, Opera, and Politics." *Yearbook for Traditional Music* 46 (2014): 114–39.

Lee, Minha. "Fostering Connectivity: A Social Network Analysis of Entrepreneurs in Creative Industries." *International Journal of Cultural Policy* 21, no. 2 (2015): 139–52.

Nancy, Jean-Luc. *The Inoperative Community*. Minnesota: U of Minnesota Press, 1991.

Park, Robert. "The City: Suggestions for the Investigation of Human Behavior in the Urban Environment." In *Classic Essays on the Culture of Cities*, edited by Richard Sennett. Englewood Cliffs: Prentice-Hall, 1916.

Qian, Nanyang (钱南扬). "南词引正校注 (Nanci Yinzheng Jiaozhu)." 戏剧报 *[Xiju Bao]*, no. 2 (1961): 60–61.

Radway, Janice A. *Reading the Romance: Women, Patriarchy, and Popular Literature*. London: Verso, 1987.

Scheel, Karen R., and John S. Westefeld. "Heavy Metal Music and Adolescent Suicidality: An Empirical Investigation." *Adolescence* 34, no. 134 (1999): 253.

Sennett, Richard. *Together: The Rituals, Pleasures and Politics of Cooperation*. New Haven: Yale University Press, 2012.

Stenberg, Josh. "Three Relations between History and Stage in the Kunju Scene Slaying the Tiger General." *Asian Theatre Journal* 32, no. 1 (2015): 107–35.

Stenberg, Josh, and Jason J. P. Cai. "Mostly Young Women with Quite Traditional Tastes: Empirical Evidence for National Contemporary Audiences of Xiqu." *Theatre Journal* 69, no. 1 (2017): 43–59.

Storey, John. "The Social Life of Opera." *European Journal of Cultural Studies* 6, no. 1 (2003): 5–35.

Themen, Kate, and Jenny van Hooff. "Kicking against Tradition: Women's Football, Negotiating Friendships and Social Spaces." *Leisure Studies* 36, no. 4 (2017): 542–52.

Thomas, Lyn. *Fans, Feminisms and "quality" Media*. Hove: Psychology Press, 2002.

Tönnies, Ferdinand. *Gemeinschaft Und Gesellschaft*. Leipzig: Fues's Verlag, 1887.

Trier-Bieniek, Adrienne. *Feminist Theory and Pop Culture*. Rotterdam: Sense Publishers, 2015.

Wang, Yan (王焱). "现代主义与传统文化的璧合——白先勇小说创作概论 [The Combination of Modernism and Traditional Culture — An Introduction to Bai Xianyong's Novel Creation]." 天中学刊 *[Tianzhong Xuekan]*, no. 1X (1995): 66–69.

Weber, Max. "The Distribution of Power Within the Gemeinschaft: Classes, Stände, Parties." In *Weber's Rationalism and Modern Society: New Translations on Politics, Bureaucracy, and Social Stratification*, edited by Tony Waters and Dagmar Waters, 37–58. New York: Palgrave Macmillan, 2015.

Yu, Weimin (俞为民). "昆曲的现代性发展之可能性研究 [Study on the Possibility of the Modern Development of Kunqu]." 文化艺术研究 [*Wenhua Yishu Yanjiu*], no. 1 (2011): 133–55.

Zhang, Weiyu, and Chengting Mao. "Fan Activism Sustained and Challenged: Participatory Culture in Chinese Online Translation Communities." *Chinese Journal of Communication* 6, no. 1 (2013): 45–61.

Zhao, Shanlin (赵山林). "试论昆曲观众的历史变迁与现状 [On the Historical Vicissitude and Current Situation of Kunqu]." 东南大学学报(哲学社会科学版) *[Journal of Southeast University (Philosophy and Social Science)]* 16, no. 1 (2014): 96–165.

Zheng, Chuanjian (郑传鉴). "昆剧传习所纪事 [Kunqu Chuanxisuo Jishi]." 中国戏曲网 *[Zhongguo Xiqu Wang]* (blog), November 6, 2006. http://www.chinaopera.net/html/2006-11/606p3.html.

中国戏曲志全国编辑委员会 [Zhongguo xiquzhi quanguobianji weiyuanhui]. 中国戏曲志上海卷 *[Chinese Xiqu Records Shanghai Volume]*. Beijing: Zhongguo, 1999.

CHAPTER 7

Living with the City

The English writer Virginia Woolf opens her novel *The Years*, which traces the lives of a family for half a century from the 1880s to the mid-1930s, not with an expected family tree, but with a map of London.[1] The novel was published in 1937. Almost 80 years later, in 2015, American writer, Vivian Gornick, published her collection of essays *The Odd Woman and the City*, offering a document of her experience wandering through New York.[2] In an interview, Gornick connects her urban experience with her single womanhood: "I have no children, not married, live on my own. If I feel hurt somewhere, I don't immediately call someone to say: I am angry, I am depressed. I go out, to the streets. There I am liberated from the loneliness and dark thoughts."[3] Gornick's experience not only resonates with what the single women in this inquiry say in the previous chapter about their disapproval of confessional culture and the concomitant primacy of emotionalizing problems in dominant Western discourse, it also points to the complexity of living as a single woman in a big city.

London, New York, and what about Shanghai? So far, this book has sought to understand how single women in Shanghai do their creative work, how they deal with love, marriage, and the pressure associated with it, or with its absence, as well as the community constructed from one creative interest, Kunqu. Amidst all the common—and different—experiences, something remains fundamentally shared by all of the study participants: living in Shanghai. Chapter 7 is about these women's relationships with the city, and I will scrutinize this, as inspired by the map and the

© The Author(s) 2019

Chow Y. F., *Caring in Times of Precarity*, Palgrave Studies in
Globalization, Culture and Society,
https://doi.org/10.1007/978-3-319-76898-4_7

walks of the two creative women who opened this chapter, with the lens of mobility. After all, as Michel de Certeau argues, cities become cities only when their dwellers move, from one site to another site, linking up spaces otherwise distant and disparate, not experienced as one entity called city.[4] For female urban dwellers, mobility is a rather recent possibility. Put very succinctly, mobility defines modern women as public space was virtually monopolized by men until less than a century ago. In China, to cite an almost clichéd but nonetheless telling instance, footbinding, that brutally reduced female feet to a "three-inch-golden-lotus"—and, with them, female mobility—only began to disappear in the Republican time during early twentieth century.[5] In the 1930s, portraying women as mobile subjects was common practice to promote modern commodities in China, and representations of women in "glossy images of a mobile, globalized citizenry" were visible everywhere in Chinese cities.[6]

Informed by the "spatial turn" in the humanities—the increasing interest in the interaction between place and human beings—Chap. 7 uses methods of mapping to recuperate mobile narratives of such interactions, to probe and collect data on subjects' geographical presence in, and their spatial experiences of, the city. Questions concerning sense of belonging, security, convenience, choice, and freedom are all addressed. Why do they move to Shanghai? Why do they stay? Where do they stay? Once in Shanghai, how do they make it home? Where do they go? How do they go? This chapter seeks to understand the mobile relations of people and place in the lives of single female creative workers. While cities, with their potentials for the three T's—talent, technology, and tolerance—have been put forward as the ideal place to attract and keep creative workers,[7] the present inquiry intervenes in this dominant line of thought on creative cities and creative class mobility with empirical insights from Shanghai, ultimately to offer one reply to the fundamental issue of how people make a place of their own, of who owns the city.

WOMEN: PLACE, WORK, MOBILITY

Earlier in this chapter, I wrote: mobility defines modern women. Ironically or not, human beings have been defined by their immobility for a long time. What I refer to is a well-entrenched understanding of who we are by where we are: rooted, stable, and secure. As Jon Anderson and Kathryn Erskine remind us, "[i]n the humanist and phenomenological tradition, concepts of people and place have been commonly understood as static and stable in nature."[8] Such a fixed and fixating way of looking at the relations between people and place has its own historical and empirical background.[9] "Thinking of the world as rooted and bounded"[10] is, however, as understandable as it is problematic; understandable as it corresponds to certain conceptions of home, and problematic as it has the potential to feed into various exclusivist and nativist claims generated in the name of home. Thinkers on migration, diaspora, and multicultural and postcolonial societies have alerted us to the importance of, using James Clifford's nomenclature—"routes" rather than "roots."[11] Mobility, intertwined with processes of modernization, poses productive challenges to traditional investigations of people and place. In an increasingly urbanized and globalized world, we move increasingly, from country to country, from rural areas to the urban, from home to work, simply, from places to places. For observers of what is happening, mobility—and its partners of urbanization and globalization—may be threatening to certain expectations of home: constant, defying change, secure; it has also become a fertile ground to examine contemporary conditions of life, of experience, of territoriality, of all things changed and unchanged amidst all the mobility.[12]

It is here into the more general examination of the relations between people and place that a third axis must be inserted: work. Given the centrality of work in contemporary life, it is essential to fathom how work plays a role in moving and moulding people's experience of place. Considering the work the women in this inquiry are doing, this chapter brings in one particular line of studies on mobility, that of the creative class. The interest in creative class mobility, and the scholarship associated with it, finds its roots in the global policy initiative in developing and promoting cities as being "creative" to vie for the presence of creative people. Underpinning such phenomena, as I point out elsewhere, "is a two-pronged belief: on the one hand, creative workers, unlike many other resources for growth, can be and are indeed mobile; on the other, certain places bear particular appeal to them and they respond by moving there."[13]

Richard Florida is often named for his influential "creative class thesis," which proposes that a tolerant, diverse, and culturally thriving city attracts hip and talented workers, forming a healthy ecology of place and people sustained by and sustaining creativity.[14] While more than a decade earlier, thinkers on the economic future of cities, such as Edward Glaeser, proposed a similar perspective on place and human capital movement,[15] Florida's publication succeeded in putting at the core of creative class mobility what he calls "quality of place." By this, he means: what is there—

"a proper setting for pursuit of creative lives"; who is there—diversity of people and making of community life; and what is going on—"vibrancy of street life, café culture, arts, music and people engaging in outdoor activities."[16] In this triangulation of people, place, and work, empirical inquiries on creative class mobility have delivered mixed results.[17] On the one hand, there are studies that confirm the validity of the "creative class thesis," that is, cool places do attract creative talents, but usually with cautions for nuances and complexities.[18] On the other hand, there are also studies that confirm otherwise, that work remains the primary consideration when creative workers move, questioning if the mobility of the creative class is any different from that of other professionals.[19]

Chapter 7 converses with this line of scholarship, adding empirical insights from the single women in Shanghai. Its intervention is fourfold. First, it contributes to the continual questioning of the dominant thought in creative city initiatives: are cool places indeed attracting cool people? In other words, the inquiry is aiming to help us understand, in this case, "the primary push and pull mechanisms behind migration of talent and the creative class."[20] Second, its Chinese embedding supplements existing research on creative class mobility, which is largely based on experiences in the United States, Europe, and Australia, save for the study of Dai Juncheng's research team on animation workers moving to Beijing and Shanghai,[21] and the mobility research project I have just concluded on Hong Kong creative workers, also in these two Chinese cities.[22] I will discuss these works later. Third, this inquiry on the mobility experience of single women serves to fill a much larger lacuna in the research on creative workers: "the lack of explicit engagement with gender relations and subjectivities."[23] Finally, while work on creative class mobility focuses on mobility from city to city, often across national borders, I extend it to include how they move when they are "settled" in a city.

In the analytical sections to come, I will present their mobility along three dimensions: the macro, or migratory movements from one city to another; the meso, or relocation movements within the same city; and the micro, or everyday movements in Shanghai. Elsewhere, Sonja van Wichelen, Jeroen de Kloet, and I have edited a special issue on the notion of home in the Asian Century. In its lead article, we explicate our biographies, our movements and our mixed feelings towards what would be conventionally called "home." For us, "it is constructed out of contradictions, ruptures and anxieties."[24] We disagree with, and thus, deconstruct the opposition between home and mobility, citing Magdalena Nowicka's study on transnational professionals to underline a possible line of inquiry on the relation between people and place despite or because of movement: how people make the place their own *in* their mobility. In Nowicka's formulation, "mobile individuals achieve security, stability and familiarity under conditions of temporality, flexibility and anxiety characteristic of a mobile lifestyle."[25] We conclude by making a plea to recognize alternative experiences of people about the place they are at. It is a process of place-making, not always belonging, but flexible and shifting. While both the special issue and our plea are grounded in the Asian context, our aim is not to essentialize the "Asian"; rather, we want to use "Asia as method"[26] to re-enter notions on home that are so often based in Western experiences, but claim to be universal.[27] This chapter hopes to contribute in a similar manner. It seeks to find out what these single women have to tell us about their mobility and place-making practices, the dynamics between moving and mooring; this Chinese case, to me, may help us rethink one claim, David Harvey's understanding of the right to the city. I will do this towards the end of this chapter.[28] For now, I need to offer an explanatory note on methods.

Methodological Note

I begin with an admission. I admit that after practicing more conventional, qualitative research methods, I was fascinated by the possibilities that modern tracking technology seemed to be able to offer to mobility and cartographical research. I was curious, particularly about Geographic Information Systems, or GIS, ubiquitous and powerful software which, as argued by its practitioners, lies at the heart of the spatial turn in humanities.[29] So, I decided to give it a try. Immediately, my research assistants and I came across difficulties, as many of the tracking systems were blocked or not supported in mainland China. Finally, we managed to find a suitable one. We asked our mobile subjects to download the App and keep it open 24 hours a day for seven days, in order to generate the mobile data required for further spatial analysis. In the end, the results were disappointing, but illuminating. Some said they forgot. Some complained that the App used up too much energy of their phones. Some said signals sometimes disappeared. One woman's response urged me to change my mind altogether. She declined categorically as she did not want to spend her time and effort being tracked.

This personal response evokes the entire politics of methods.[30] On the one hand, mobilities researchers are cautioned if they should employ GIS and compete with the powerful corporate and governmental agencies that are likely to dominate future mobilities research. On the other hand, researchers should also reflect on the distancing effect of high technology on their subjects.[31] Urged by the response cited earlier, I decided to revert to a low-tech and perhaps more personal way of probing into the relation between people and place: drawing a mattering map. I asked the single women who agreed to join this round of the inquiry to draw a map of Shanghai with sites that mattered to them. The term "mattering map" was borrowed from Lawrence Grossberg's alert to the affective sensitivity of fans, when he writes "affect is also organized; it operates within and, at the same time, produces maps which direct our investments in and into the world."[32] With this as a general guideline, we asked half of the single women we have already come across in the first round of in-depth interviews to join this mapping exercise and to tell us their mobile narratives based on the maps they created.[33] Hopefully, we would be able to track, as put forward by Grossberg, the "sites at which we can, at least temporarily, find ourselves 'at home' with what we care about."[34] In the end, we received the mattering maps from 10 of the women we asked: elaborate, well-considered, generally a product of memory, as Joy, one of the women in this inquiry, tells us: "When I drew this map, I really made an effort in remembering."

MACRO MOBILITY: INTO THE BIG CITY

Why Shanghai? Such a question, a major one that underlines scholarship on creative city, creative class, and their mobility, lays bare immediately another question: to whom is the question addressed? As far as the 10 women in this exercise of mobile methods are concerned, one factor is as decisive as it is contingent. It depends on where one was born. For those born outside Shanghai, who grew up with the possibility, if not necessity, to move to the big city to study and/or to work, they were wont to wonder not if, but when they would be moving. It is a powerful assumption or imagination that one has to leave the provincial towns or villages for first-tier cities, from the margins to the centres of the nation, to have serious career prospects. While sites connected to creative vibrancy and lifestyle, such as book stores, cafés, galleries, museums, and organic food stores, fill the mattering maps drawn up by the women in this inquiry, those who

moved to Shanghai did so primarily due to work, or to study that pre-
ceded and prepared them for work. This migratory move remains central
in the way they map their lives.

Weiwei moved from Anhui to Shanghai to study.[35] She marks down the
university she enrolled in as the second significant site on her map, after
her current home. She spent four years in this university area. Majoring in
English language, Weiwei was keen on working in the media. Her choice
of university was influenced by geographical proximity as well as the media
scene of Shanghai. "In 2009, when I started my undergraduate study, it
was a golden period for print media." If print media were the pull factor
for Weiwei, animation was Zaizai's. Her migratory narrative is typical for
its running thread of a job. On her map, she puts Zhongshan Park as her
starting point: "When I first moved to Shanghai, the company was located
near Zhongshan Park. I found a place to live there too." Coming from
Shenyang, Zaizai recalls vividly how she took the train ride on her own to
Suzhou, where she started her first job at an animation studio. She was 21,
a fresh graduate. She did not stay there long, as "for our profession, it's
either Beijing or Shanghai." Before Shanghai, Zaizai was living in Beijing.
She was earning little money, but working extremely hard. In less than a
year, she moved again: "There were many more work opportunities in
Shanghai." More specifically, Zaizai was thinking to move not only geo-
graphically but also creatively, from animated films to gaming, which was
the job located close to Zhongshan Park.

LIV marks on one edge of her map the area of Xujiahui with a special
note: "In 2002, came to Shanghai on my own, to work." A Jiangxi girl,
LIV recalls how she envied those who left earlier and sent back letters
mentioning "the life outside." One day, her father was enjoying an after-
noon nap. On the spur of the moment, she shook him awake and said,
"Dad, I am going to Shanghai."

> He asked, "Have you found a job there?" "No, I'll just resign here, and
> go there to find one … Is it ok?" "Yes." And then, her father said, "Then,
> you go."

On her first day in Shanghai, carrying just a single bag, LIV went straight
to a job fair in an arena capable of hosting 80,000 people—not unlike the
one Qiuyin goes to in *Ode to Joy*. The move to Shanghai was obviously less
impulsive than it sounded; for people intent on making a career in the
media, "it's either Beijing or Shanghai, and Shanghai is closer to my
hometown," LIV says.

What these single women tell us about their move to Shanghai resonates with the "personal trajectory" thesis introduced by Dai et al. in their
study on mobility of animation workers relocating from various places to
Shanghai and Beijing. By personal trajectory, they include "hometown,
place of residence and graduate university."[36] The primacy and the prospect of work in urging them to leave and go, in this case to Shanghai, is
also found in my other creative class mobilities research project, from
Hong Kong to Shanghai and Beijing.[37] What is not foregrounded in all
these investigations is the singlehood of the migrants and its affordance.
Even when work, and relatedly, study seem to be the determining pull factor for these creative workers to move to Shanghai, LIV's epitaph "on my
own" lays bare how their singlehood affords all the above migratory possibilities. This, interestingly, seems to be what affirms, not only affords, the
migratory moves of those who have to leave Shanghai, as we shall see later.

On the other hand, those who were born in Shanghai seem to take their
continuous residence in Shanghai for granted. Xiaoyan, Michelle, and
Captain Zoey have *not* noted down anything regarding outward migration. Another native Shanghainese, Xiaoqian puts Hangzhou on the edge
of her map, a city where she spent eight years of her working life, commuting frequently, if not every weekend, to Shanghai where her home and
circle of friends remained. "Hangzhou is close by ... if I told my parents I
would move to Beijing, they would definitely object." The Shanghai-born
women, unlike the women who grew up in smaller and more marginal
localities, did not need to move to look for better opportunities and futures.
Even if they do accept an offer, the locality seems to be close enough that
they can simply keep their base in Shanghai. The centre is Shanghai, but
then not only in terms of work and career—also in terms of culture, at least
to many local Shanghainese. Reverting to the importance of work or place
in creative workers' choice of where they are, it seems that place has its
strongest impact on people who *already* perceive the place to be vibrant,
cool, and culturally superior, not on people who are located elsewhere.[38]

It follows that those Shanghainese who eventually moved out, did so
not for work. If this inquiry serves as any indication, research on creative
class mobility should be inserted with a factor of "centrality." What I mean
is: the pull and push mechanism involved in creative class mobility may be
fundamentally different, depending on the direction of the movement:
from the centre, or towards the centre. Even when it is about movement
from one centre to another centre, it seems to be more complex than the
work-first narrative of the migration stories outlined earlier. Mi's case is

telling. Born and bred in Shanghai, Mi never thought of leaving Shanghai. Her journalistic work for the cultural section of a national newspaper did not find Shanghai wanting. She met someone in Guangzhou, one of "three or four men" she was dating at the point we did our earlier interview (see Chap. 5). "Then he moved to Beijing, and I was in Shanghai. We had this long-distance relationship for more than a year. Well, at a certain point, I thought, OK, let me move to Beijing too." When we met the first time, Mi was still living in Shanghai; a year later, she had moved. However, Mi hesitated to attribute her migratory decision entirely to her boyfriend. "Probably 50 per cent because of him," she says. The other 50 per cent was "career development." Incidentally, her newspaper decided to scrap the cultural section and "within one month, I moved."

This complexity, however, is not only found in the migration biography of local Shanghainese. The narrative of Valerie should serve as a reminder that decisions about leaving and going to a city may be often due to more than work or place. Coming from Hong Kong, Valerie puts Pudong International Airport in the centre of her map, and from there, she draws a line to Huaihai Zhonglu, where the hotel for her first night in Shanghai was situated. This was three years ago, when her advertising agency in Hong Kong closed for business, and she was offered a job in Shanghai. While work seems to be the determining factor, like the other women who moved to Shanghai, she adds something personal. Valerie also wanted to make use of the geographical move to terminate a relationship. More recently, Valerie decided to move out of Shanghai. She made the decision, partly because her new boyfriend, someone she had met at work, moved back to Taiwan, and partly because of her grandmother. "She is 93, and I want to spend more time with her."[39] Here, singlehood inflects creative class mobility in different ways. In Mi's case, she moves out of Shanghai, at least partly, to be in the same city as her new boyfriend. In Valerie's case, her singlehood makes it both possible and necessary to move—a single granddaughter's obligation and intimate longing to spend more time with her family member. It would have been quite different if she were married.[40]

Meso Mobility: In the City

That they moved to Shanghai, or continued to stay in Shanghai, does not mean a life characterized by fixity and inactivity. They move around *within* the city. I will discuss this intra-city movement, often ignored in creative class mobility studies, with its usual focus on cross-border movement, in two sections. First of all, they move, rather immediately and mundanely, as directed by their everyday needs, longings, or impulses. Second, they move, rather generally and fundamentally, as their primary areas of living move. I will start with this.

Regarding such movement at the meso level, the maps and the associated narratives have two things in common. On the one hand, all the women have marked down their various homes as what matters in their lives. For Michelle, Xiaoyan, Captain Zoey, Zaizai, and Weiwei, their current place of residence offers them the centrality of living. For Xiaoqian, Mi, Joy, and Valerie, they show the strongest attachment to where they first lived, whether it be their childhood homes in Shanghai or their first base upon migrating to the city. Underwriting the significance of home ownership, LIV puts neither her first nor her current home as the centre of her mattering map, but the first property she purchased in the city. On the other hand, they move frequently. For those growing up in Shanghai, it is hardly surprising that they have not stayed in the place they were born. For the later-comers, they also moved a lot, actually more if we take frequency—that is how much time spent on one residence—into account. Zaizai, as an exception, moved only once in her eight years in Shanghai—within the same neighbourhood, as she did not want to get used to a new locality again—while she changed jobs four times. Weiwei mentions a rented place where she stayed for only three months.[41]

Juxtaposing the two common features, the significance of where they live is apparent. In other words, however frequently they move, their homes certainly matter to them. The native dwellers come up with many childhood memories; they become enlivened when tracing through the map as if traversing back through time. Mi recalls, "the road leading to my granny's place, the road I took when I finished class." She moved three times in Shanghai, but "all the areas surrounding my homes, several kilometres around them, they feel like where I belong."[42] For the relative newcomers, the home areas marked down on their maps also evoke strong memories. Joy, in the campus area where she first settled in Shanghai, found a music store where she went every day. The boss, a senior university student, played metal guitar while Joy played acoustic. "I asked him a lot of things," she says. Finally, she moved to live above the store, a home that was "totally empty, only one mattress … It was 15 years ago, when the first music production software was launched. It was magical. I started learning how to arrange music … I was very happy, time passed quickly." Joy, now a singer-songwriter, stayed there for a year.

Stories like those recollected by Mi and Joy abound. On the other hand, while intimacy, passion, and a sense of nostalgia seep through these stories, the movement associated with their place of residence is more often a mundane affair concerning money and control, understood as shrewdness with the capitalist logic dominant in the housing market. Xiaoyan marks her current home as the centre of her map, with lines linking it to other significant places, including her older homes, as well as where she was born. Xiaoyan's trajectory offers a prime example of how someone negotiated the housing market and tried to arrange the best home for herself and her family within the confines configured by her own means and the dramatic property price hikes in a city such as Shanghai. It is an example of geographical mobility with upward mobility, fuelled by canny property investment. Xiaoyan did this together with another woman, her mother; the two continued to buy and sell. Now, they are living in a villa complex, which Xiaoyan is clearly proud of. "Let me tell you, this [pointing to the spot of her current home on the map] is happiness."

Most of the women in this inquiry, however, do not articulate the same kind of control over where they live. Michelle, at one point, moved with her parents to a place from which she needed to spend two hours to get to her workplace. She did that for almost six years. Michelle did think of renting a place closer to work, but money remained an issue. Xiaoqian did rent her own place to live closer to work, but after six months, she moved back to her parents' place—even though she had to survive their nagging over when she would get married. "But my rent took half of my salary, it was not worth it." With her parents' financial support, LIV was able to buy her own property in the city she moved to. However, when it became too small for her, she could not follow Xiaoyan's example. Instead of selling and buying, LIV rented out her property and rented a bigger place for herself. During our conversation over her mattering map, LIV received a phone call. It was from her friend, who, after years of remaining single, had decided to marry a man she had met five months earlier. LIV knew her friend's place and asked if she would sublet it to her when her friend started living with her husband. "Coming Friday, my friends will have dinner with me, as Saturday is my birthday. On Sunday, I will move." The phone call was to confirm the arrangement. Reminiscent of Xiaoqian's financial calculation, LIV stressed the cheaper rent of the new place compared with where she had been living: a beautiful and spacious duplex in an old neighbourhood, very central in Shanghai. She had to pay a lot—

10,000 RMB to be precise—for "a bit more attention to style." Now, she thinks, "On Saturday, I will turn 38. Single. No boyfriend. I guess I am going through some change in my life. I guess my life so far has been too unrealistic." It will be her twelfth home in Shanghai.

LIV's narrative also foregrounds an aspect integral to many of these women's movement histories: support offered by fellow women, single or otherwise. It offers a different understanding of women and housing, from what Leta Hong Fincher, as noted earlier, observes as a dominant phenomenon in contemporary China. According to her study, Chinese women, subjected to the discourse of leftover women and the angst of possibly becoming one themselves, run the risk of giving away their accumulated wealth for the property bought as marital homes. Due to the conventions shaped by the patriarchal system, the property is usually registered in the name of the husband, even when it is partly or fully financed by the wife.[43] As far as the single women in this inquiry are concerned, they support each other to seek the housing they want or need. In Xiaoyan's case, she does so together with her mother. LIV is helped by her female friend. The apartment Valerie lived in before she left Shanghai was, similarly, vacated by her close female friend. Sometimes, it is not only womanhood that buttresses the mutual support, but also a common interest in art and culture, which configures a platform that quite a few of the single women visit for their housing arrangements: Douban. Captain Zoey got to know her flatmate on Douban. Weiwei narrates a similar experience. Initially, she tried a "regular" housing platform, but found a lot of fake notices. "It was by chance that I came across the big renting community on Douban." There, Weiwei can see the photos of her potential flatmates, and she finds the information to be reliable. The support offered by fellow women with similar creative interests, however handy this is, does not make them immune to the turmoil of moving, physical, psychological, or above all, a mixture of the two. In Valerie's account: "I feel lonely when I need to move, when I don't have a man by my side to help. For most of the time, I am very independent, but at occasions like this, I feel a tiny little bit helpless."

MICRO MOBILITY: QUOTIDIAN PRACTICES

While work does not seem to be an important factor in how these women choose to find their home, it features prominently on their maps as areas that they frequent and have strong memories associated with. Michelle, a native Shanghainese, maps a major part of her movement history as being dictated by work. Next to "home," Michelle marks down two major points on her map, both related to her work. Mi mentions the galleries she visited and other cultural events she covered when she started her job as a cultural reporter. Weiwei talks endearingly of a small alley in the neighbourhood of her publishing house where she and her colleagues would have lunch: "We would order something good at the beginning of the month when we just received our salary, and something fast-food-like by the end of the month."

The sites cited indicate three spatial nodes as far as their relationships with the city are concerned: creative spaces (galleries); everyday spaces (restaurants); affective spaces (social gathering). Considering the creative work these women have been doing, it is hardly surprising that spaces connected to art and culture feature prominently on their maps. The Kunqu lovers highlight their Kunqu-related venues; they talk eloquently about places associated with the masters and theatres that are special to them. In Michelle's case, "in Shanghai, the theatre I visit the most is in People's Park, called Tianchan." In her fond description, "[in] such an old theatre, housed in the bustling city centre, that has not been destroyed, you feel a sense of humanity." Captain Zoey marks down a theatre for dramatic arts, where she often goes, to the extent that she once applied for a writing job at the company. There are also cinemas, and the Shanghai Film Festival, in particular, is significant to many of these women with an affinity for creativity. LIV adds: "Also because it takes place in summer, and I like summer." The creative district Red Town is a favourite for many of the women. For Joy, it occupies a unique place on her map, as it was there that she, as a singer-songwriter, staged her first solo show since her return to Shanghai. Another favourite is a bookstore that many women mention: Jifeng Shuyuan.[44] On Captain Zoey's map, she writes "my kind of book collections": poetry, philosophy, literature. "It's a very small book store, just at the exit of a subway station, very convenient." We will go back to this notion of convenience later; suffice it here to note how much creative spaces mean to these women.

Many of these creative sites, as marked on their mattering maps, show an importance of food at the same time. Michelle visits the Shanghai Film Festival every year. She says she is fully aware of the existence of Starbucks, McDonald's, Kentucky Fried Chicken and the likes in the area. For LIV, it is not only the films, but also food. She marks a "yummy food street" in the vicinity. More often, sites of restaurants, bars, karaokes, spas, supermarkets and markets, shops, and 24-hour convenience stores are highlighted. Fewer put down doctor's clinics and hospitals as being significant. One interesting feature of many of these quotidian sites is the Japanese influence on the city. Captain Zoey marks down a Japanese eatery with good alcoholic concoctions. Weiwei talks vividly of a Japanese supermarket, when supplementing the fact that the clips her company has produced are heavily influenced by "Japanese style": slow, beautiful, quiet. She watched a lot of Japanese television dramas when she was at university.

Just as many creative spaces are not only creative spaces, but are also associated with food and drink, many spaces of food and drink are also something more. They are affective spaces. Valerie elaborates on a Japanese Teppanyaki restaurant close to her work place. Her colleague brought her there. Working in the advertising industry, "We work overtime frequently. Usually we would leave our offices later than 10 pm," she explains. "Basically, we are there seven days a week." The restaurant is not only a place to satiate their hunger, but a site of sociality. Valerie shows a snapshot taken shortly before she left Shanghai. "They are all friends I got to know through the restaurant." They were mostly single, like Valerie, coming from different parts of the world. "It feels a bit like home." When she was ill, they would make congee and bring it to her home. LIV marks a street in the French Concession Area, with the words "all my good friends are here." She is referring to the friends she made, all from the literary circle, some of whom have become established writers. "We were all single, and young ... We hung out together every day ... somewhat like in *Ode to Joy*" (see Chap. 2). But now they do not really see one another anymore. "I am the only one still single," she explains.

While friends form the most cited group of people on their maps, a few of the women also mention their relationship, and for those not born in Shanghai, their hometown. Valerie adds her boyfriend's residential area on her map. Joy marks down the area where her first girlfriend lived, and also, she adds, where a store was selling *dakou* CDs.[45] Zaizai, likewise, marks down the neighbourhood of her current girlfriend. Weiwei marks down the long-distance coach station on her map where she used to embark on the trip back to her hometown. The location of Valerie's home is at the centre of her map: Pudong International Airport. Joy now usually splits her week between two homes: one her own; the other, her grandmother's. The McDonald's that she marks down near to the latter indicates the complexity of space: in this case, the intertwining of the affective and the everyday. Pointing to the fast food restaurant, Joy says: "If I am with my granny, I go there every day."

What connects all the aforementioned sites is the term all of them use to describe their relationship with the city: convenience or *fangbian* (方便). Mi marks down a shopping mall in the centre of the city because she knows she can charge her phone there. Captain Zoey mentions cinemas, live music venues, and galleries, and concludes with her feeling about Shanghai: "it's particularly convenient." She also marks down her favourite supermarkets, particularly because they offer "fruits sliced and served in portions for one person. So convenient." Valerie's strongest impression of Shanghai is its "convenience." While their movements within the city can be analysed into different trajectories connected by different kinds of spaces, what binds them together into one life, one central gratitude towards the city they are living in is its convenience. For these working single women, it has to be convenient.

Extrapolating this to the discussion on creative class mobility, we can see the complexity involved. While work seems to be the most decisive factor for these women to move to and stay in Shanghai, what the city has to offer remains vital for their everyday lives, and to their continual attachment to where they are living. It could be galleries and theatres; it could also be restaurants, cafés, and McDonalds, as well as places where they meet friends, go to their hometowns, or see their boyfriend or girlfriend. In the end, they all admire the convenience they can find in this big city of Shanghai. While Florida and his followers propose a place and its vibrancy— often abbreviated as a creative city—as a paramount form of appeal to the creative class, something more mundane and quotidian should be added. I am not contesting the important attraction of cultural and culinary resources as part and parcel of the city's vibrancy; it would, however, be remiss not to include this mundane and quotidian dimension of urban living: convenience, as it is perceived and experienced.

MOBILITY AND TRANSPORT

Transport is one important element that enables the perception and experience of convenience described earlier. The women in the study draw and talk a great deal about various modes of transport that convey them through the city. Among them, the Shanghai subway system features most prominently in what makes their lives easier in the city. Michelle connects it with her work. "I would take any job, as long as the workplace is reachable by subway." She used to spend two hours in buses, commuting from her home to work, for five to six years. The importance of the subway and its accessibility is particularly salient when the movement of the work place itself is taken into account. Michelle's office, a website for cultural promotion, moved often. "When your company decides to move, what can you do? Nobody would come and ask me if I wanted to move." Her current job is only 15 minutes away by subway. "This is one reason why I care about my current job, it's the closest to home of any in my work history."

The subway not only makes life easier, it also makes it better. To continue with Michelle: "One Friday evening, I did not have any appointments. I worked overtime, 'till 8.30 p.m. Then, I got a message around 8.15 p.m. from a friend, asking if I would like to join for a drink." Thanks to the convenience of line number 9 of the subway, Michelle went. Her home is on line number 9 as well. "The shopping and entertainment sites along the line are my circle of after-work activities." Sometimes, in addition to being a means of transport, bringing them from A to B, the subway system and the travelling itself can be a form of enjoyment. Captain Zoey marks down line number 10. "It's not a crowded line," she says, and it takes her to places she likes, besides which, "its stations are refreshingly pretty."

Only a few women mark down other modes of public transport. If they do, they do so negatively. Pointing to the centre of her map, Pudong Dadao, where her first point of settling was, Joy says: "It was such a broken place, so dusty. It's only accessible by public buses." She recalls the inconvenience: "Everywhere was dusty, as a lot of infrastructural constructions were going on there. The buses were so crowded, and traffic jams were severe." In other cases, when they no longer can catch the subway, they would rather not travel, and so, cease to be mobile. Once, Captain Zoey went to a gig at Mao, a live music venue. It was too late for her to go back to her dormitory. She and a friend rented a hotel room, which was better than another time, Captain Zoey recalls jokingly, when she spent the night in a 24-hour KFC. For her as a student, a taxi was obviously too expensive. Some of the women do mention taxis, especially the latest taxi App, Didi Dache. Compared with the subway, taxis do not seem to mean much to them, probably due to their infrequent and haphazard nature. They do not function the same way as the subway, which is a service most of them use on a structural basis, for example, to commute between home and work.

For the rest, there are singular instances of mobility. During the conversations, Xiaoyan talks proudly of the mobility afforded by her driver's licence, particularly in connection with various activities she does for Kunqu, her passion. Biking is Zaizai's passion, and for her, also a socializing platform. Four years ago, she joined a "vintage ride" group, requiring her to dress in old-style costumes and bike through the city. The group became friends. But usually, Zaizai prefers biking on her own. Zaizai also marks down her favourite biking route. "With the chinar trees along the sides, and then, when it's spring, you can smell the flying willow seeds. I love biking here." She even has a bike tattoo designed by herself: a bike in the middle, on two sides are two wings, one angelic, one demonic. "I believe we all have two sides, good and bad … where you go depends on where you want to take yourself to." On her map, Valerie marks down several streets close to her place that she can walk to. "Actually I do like walking in Shanghai. I feel that in a city you don't know that well, walking helps you understand the city better." She walks, and then, sits down at a café, to enjoy the city.

Finally, many of the women mark down sites on the map that indicate their mobility outside of Shanghai (see the section on travelling in Chap. 5). Pudong International Airport, as noted earlier, is the centre point of Valerie's map. Xiaoyan marks down hiking in India on her map. For Zaizai, it is Jeju island in South Korea: "I see it as my backyard. I go there often, to the extent that I would spend weekends there." After Michelle left her entertainment company, she went to Beijing and then Chuanzhou, her current favourite city, for a month. Michelle marks down various cities outside her map of Shanghai. All the mobility surrounding the airport points to the often articulated interest in travelling as well as the convenience afforded by Shanghai. As reflected by how they draw their mattering maps—they are never confined to only one or two areas, but expand and extend to many disparate, far-flung places in the city, as well as outside it, all made possible by the transport linkages—the Shanghai as perceived and experienced by these women is a paradox: convenient despite and because of its vastness.

MOBILITY AND DISTANCE

Shortly after LIV moved to Shanghai, she would sometimes sit by a shopping mall, watching people passing by, wanting to shout to the city: "Shanghai is so big." That is such a big, vast, huge—or whatever semantic term they employ—place is often articulated by these women. Amidst such an expanse of space, their feelings are mixed. To begin with, they often feel estranged. Michelle marks down a "longest work place," and after that, in parentheses, "the most familiar strange place." What does that mean? "No feelings," she explains. "It's a commercial space. Many people. I went there for work, then I went home. Why no feelings? I suppose anyone else who has stayed in one work place for nine years would have some stable colleagues? I didn't. My company had a lot of staff movement." And many women report a sense of distance and anonymity in their neighbourhood. Far from the neighbourly intimacy as portrayed in *Ode to Joy*, the more common experience among these women is that they do not know or even come across their neighbours. Captain Zoey says: "My immediate neighbour is supposed to be a French lady, but I have never met her."

The women may not be forging connections with their neighbours, but they are, however, rather skilful in minimizing other distances, and maintaining other forms of affective bonding. Against the expected, presumably strong, interpersonal ties offered by family, friends, colleagues, and relationship partners, these women have marked down on their maps a dazzling inventory of what would be called "weak ties": casual, contingent, non-structural connections between human beings that develop not because they must, or not in any obligatory manner such as kinship or friendship. Weak ties do not function with the same strength and intensity as strong ties, but they are, nonetheless, ties. It may not be a matter of trust, commitment, and shared history, but it is essential for one to feel anchored, familiar, known, and recognized in an ontological sense.[46] In other words, while the big city often makes one feel anonymous, there are ways urban dwellers employ to allow themselves to enjoy the anonymity without necessarily resorting to conventional forms of bonding. Volunteer work is frequently mentioned. Michelle works as a volunteer at Kunqu performances. Valerie, during her last year in Shanghai, joined a group to care for stray dogs and cats, and got to know her fellow volunteers. Joy marked down a local residents' committee, where she is helping with a theatre play that is raising awareness of cancer survivors. LIV does not join any voluntary groups, but got to know someone who introduced her to badminton, and consequently, a WeChat group with more than 100 badminton friends. "Sometimes when I take a taxi home, they will ask in the WeChat group: is LIV home? When I am home, I will write: I'm home, good night. It's really sweet."

If these ties still conjure or require some form of commitment and trust, other ties are even weaker, but nonetheless significant in the women's experience of the city. Their maps are dotted with sites signifying ties with people who are not exactly friends, and yet, not strangers. On her map, Mi notes down, near the Shanghai Library—also a significant space for many other women in this inquiry—a hair salon. After narrating how she used to visit the library very regularly, Mi, in the same breath, moves to the salon that she started visiting five years ago. It is a Japanese-style salon, recommended by a friend. "I immediately got connected to the stylist." Even now, after moving to Beijing, Mi still patronizes the same stylist whenever she returns to the city. "I don't get my hair cut in Beijing," she says. On LIV's map, just next to her yet-to-move-into place is a store she writes, "buying DVDs there for 15 years." Affectionately, she mentions how the store owner would give her viewing advice and she describes vividly how this prospective "neighbour" of hers lost weight and turned "from a fat guy to a thin guy." Valerie remembers the porters at her residence and the masseuses at the spa she frequented.

Sometimes, it does not even need to be someone they are acquainted with. A fan of Kunqu, Michelle explains her habit of ordering the same seat at theatres, a practice that seems to be shared by many other Kunqu goers. As she says, "I started to notice, at several performances, the same group of people sitting around me" (see Chap. 6). Contrasting with how Michelle describes the workplace where she stayed the longest as "the most familiar strange place," it is amazing how, in spaces other than work, she turns strangers into affects of familiarity. More than a year ago, she noticed the absence of a man who used to tout tickets, illegally, outside the theatre. One day, another man took over his place and job, telling Michelle that the previous ticket scalper had had an acute attack of something related to diabetes and had passed away. "It's like, every time you go there, you will see the same group of people. And then, one day, someone's gone. You would wonder why you care, why you care about a stranger. But it happens when you go to a place a lot and see the same group of people a lot." Then, a stranger is no longer a stranger.

Sometimes, these women travel in this big city full of strangers and succeed in not feeling like a stranger themselves. At other times, they simply enjoy being anonymous, being a stranger themselves. Very often, these single women would point to the space surrounding us when we were having our conversations, spaces such as cafés, which are anonymous. It is, however, not only the feeling of being anonymous that makes them feel free. This sense of freedom is also constituted in what makes such cafés appealing to women like them: they ooze modernity, cosmopolitanism, internationality, or whatever other terms these women would use to similar effect. The vastness of Shanghai is not only confined to the geographical space, but is open to include an imaginary quintessence of the world. While they sometimes do go to Pudong International Airport and fly away, they do not need to, as the world is already present in their city. Together, the real journeys and the cosmopolitan imaginary of Shanghai make the city even bigger and more spacious. Such an experience of an individual in a vast space, anonymous and strange, is articulated by these women when they talk about their relationships with the city; they feel free. More specifically, they feel free as women, as single women, divorcees, single mothers, and as strangers. The city, for all its vastness, openness, and space, tolerates strangers, or people who are strange. They usually and literally refer to an imaginary group of single women in their midst: "This is such a big city, there must be a lot of single people, and single women." A common sigh of relief is that no one bothers about their marital status.

What can be added here is how the lesbian women in this inquiry report the possibility opened up by a city such as Shanghai to this particular group of strangers, the queer ones. Joy talks briefly but openly about how she came across her current girlfriend when she is recalling a music festival in a creative district in Shanghai. On the other hand, Zaizai met her current girlfriend in a gathering specifically for LGBT professionals in Shanghai. Zaizai narrates her participation in opening parties or receptions of exhibitions, and also, the Shanghai Pride event. "You flirted with people, people flirted with you." However, Zaizai's earlier relationship shows the limits of a so-called open and tolerant city. When she first moved to Shanghai, she was in a relationship. They came from the same hometown. "She followed me to Shanghai," Zaizai says. "Only her and me when we started our lives in Shanghai. No circle of friends. Slowly, we built up." They split up after seven years together, as her girlfriend decided to get married, "due to her family situation," she says, insinuating the pressure on single daughters.

RIGHT *IN* THE CITY

In an overview article on mobilities research, Anthony D'Andrea's research team discusses various methodological challenges and innovations, their aspirations and limitations, delivered not only by the methods themselves, but also by what they call "the usually messy, unpredictable and serendipitous nature of empirical realities."[47] This messiness, unpredictability, and serendipity must be the ultimate caveat for all the data collected in this analysis of the relations between people, place, and work through the lens of mobility. And this is a time of accelerated mobility, as we have witnessed in the maps and mobile narratives of the 10 single women. In this chapter, I have tried to trace their place-making processes, across space and time, into and out of, and within a city.

From what they have drawn and narrated, their mattering maps tell us bits and pieces of what matters to them when they were invited to participate in this methodological exercise and revisit Shanghai through a journey of multiple purposes, configured by necessity and longing, sometimes contingency. Necessity is largely driven by work and money, itself sometimes an inflection of work. I say inflection because work is not always money, as many of the single women do attach value to the creative work they do, not only about the money they earn. However, by and large, these women relate where they live and/or spend their time to work and money to the need to find work opportunities, and the limits of the money they earn and have. Longing, on the other hand, seeps through their everyday lives, when they lay bare the myriad of ways they navigate the city for pleasure, for a good way of living: browsing in a bookstore, chilling in a café, biking and walking, shopping, drinking or playing badminton with friends, doing groceries for solo home cooking—ways generally of their own choosing. In the end, it may also be contingency, or what D'Andrea et al. call "serendipity" that configures their relationship with the city. Why would Captain Zoey come across her flatmates through the Douban platform? Why would LIV get to know someone who brought her to a new world of badminton? And Mi, who finally left Shanghai for Beijing, did so partly due to a new love. "It's just so coincidental. Those I didn't continue dating remain in Shanghai, and those who continued having a relationship with me were all from outside," she says, half complaining.

In the meantime, they mention, profusely and proficiently, how convenient Shanghai is for them. Sometimes, the convenience is writ small on their life as a single woman, as someone with creative work and interests. Sometimes not, or not in particular. The convenience, both within the city and out of the city, is in turn, mapped onto the vastness of the city, which, literally and figuratively, includes the world beyond. They travel to and with their creative work. They go to see international films at a festival, or visit an international exhibition in a gallery in Shanghai, and they can also fly to see a film or visit an exhibition somewhere else—provided their work and money allow them to do so. More intimately, the vast city finds these single women trying, in their own ways, not to be a stranger, and at the same time, enjoying being one. The anonymity is both alienating, when they do not know who lives next door, and liberating, when they do not have to worry if someone next door will start enquiring about their marital status.

At the start of this chapter, I cited my co-authored deliberation on "home" which, for the authors, "is constructed out of contradictions, ruptures and anxieties."[48] These 10 single women doing creative work in Shanghai have told us their contradictions, ruptures, and anxieties in their mattering maps and mobile narratives. And the question probably remains: do they consider Shanghai "home"? I do not venture an answer, but I offer three rejoinders.

First, they seldom talk about their spatial experiences in Shanghai in terms of home, at least not with all the underpinning notions, such as stability, permanence, and a sense of belonging. After all, they move, and they move a lot. When they express some sentiments akin to the conventional understanding of "home sweet home," they do so nostalgically, that is when they talk about where they were. It is as if home can only be constructed in the past tense, not in the present or the future. They know they will move again, whether it is the everyday hecticness, the relocation of dwelling, or even, especially for those non-native Shanghainese, moving to another city.

Second, almost ironically, I must add that they are not only mobile. As cautioned by Peter Merriman, mobilities research, by putting mobility, movement, and motility in a central position, runs the tautological risk of producing "an overanimated mobile subject."[49] Here, I recall what all of the mobile subjects in this inquiry mention: that they are actually very *zhai* (宅), and they like it. *Zhai*, an archaic word referring to home, dwelling, and residence has been revitalized, and in vernacular currency, evokes a form of domesticity reminiscent of the English term "couch-potato," not necessarily glued to the screen, just at home, doing nothing significant, usually on one's own.[50] Michelle, after talking about all the cities she has been to, including early that year to Hong Kong to see a show by her favourite music group, says, "I can be very *zhai*." Jia's way is: "At the weekend, if I go out on Saturday, I will stay home the whole day on Sunday." She would spend the whole *zhai* day playing games, and watching television shows on streaming sites. It seems that they like to be more passive and static precisely because they move so much, that they desire to do nothing, save that of their own accord precisely because they do a lot according to other dictates. Translated into the moving-mooring binary underpinning mobilities research in its examination of the relation between people and place, these women show the complexity of contemporary mobile life. In Anderson and Erskine's study of lifestyle travellers, they introduce a neologism "tropophilia," vis-à-vis topophilia, to refer to "the new ways in which the relations between people and place can be understood—not a love of rooted and static geographical relations, but a love of mobility, movement and change in terms of the coingredient constitution of identity and geography."[51] The single women in this inquiry show that tropophilia can feed back to topophila, that moving is often a constituent of mooring. In mobility, they desire to be at home. And this at-homeness may, but does not necessarily, morph to the more ontological kind; it is literally at home, there, physically, bodily, more mundane, nonetheless enlivening and sacred, a practice of the hermit, the singleton.

Finally, I want to go back to money, and the "right to the city," quite simply because the mobile narratives of these single women seem to share one common understanding, in various articulations and degrees of precarity: money is one major way for them to claim their right to the city. First put forward by Henri Lefebvre, the term and his rather sketchy concept "right to the city" has subsequently informed intellectual discussion and activist movements surrounding the problematic of space and justice.[52] Amidst the multiplicity of thinking and practices, there is a consensus that something is fundamentally wrong in the arrangement of urban space, such that many dwellers feel helpless, trapped, and deprived of what David Harvey considers a precious but neglected human right: our collective power and freedom to reshape processes of urbanization.[53] To Harvey, the urgency of this deprivation is not only an intellectual concern, but above all, is already manifested in the streets, in the neighbourhoods, in the "rebel cities," the title of his 2012 book. To claim the right to the city, Harvey reminds us, is "to claim some kind of shaping power over the process of urbanization, over the ways in which our cities are made and remade, and to do so in a fundamental and radical way."[54]

The experience of the educated, middle-class single women in this inquiry does not speak against these urban politics; they demand more, an acknowledgement. Of the 10 single women talking to us about their relations with Shanghai, Xiaoqian was the one without a job at that point.

Echoing Fanjie's lengthy monologue in *Ode to Joy* (see Chap. 2), Xiaoqian tells us: "It's not easy to live as a single woman in Shanghai, as the living standard is demanding." A Shanghai native, Xiaoqian lives with her family, and she thinks that women who come to Shanghai to work would find it even tougher. "I feel that the women who live in Shanghai must be very strong, very independent, fearless about being single." In a mixture of condemnation and admiration, sadness and pride, Xiaoqian is acknowledging the importance of money as much as single women's strength, skills, and capabilities in remaining, if not in control, simply there, in the demanding city. Introducing the right to the city, Harvey reiterates a list of questions commentators pose on urbanization: "Has this dramatic urbanization contributed to human well-being? Has it made us into better people, or left us dangling in a world of anomie and alienation, anger and frustration? Have we become mere monads tossed around in an urban sea?"[55] If these questions are meant to be rhetorical, the empirical sections of this chapter compel us to reply not necessarily or absolutely in a negative manner, but at least with hesitation and nuances. These women have not done poorly.

In his comparative reading of what Peter Marcuse and Edward Soja understand as the right to the city, Kurt Iveson draws attention to two of their convergences: that wider processes and relations that generate injustices in the city, including the spatial, must be dismantled; and that the right to the city can serve as a common rally for thinkers and activists on spatial injustice, despite their differences.[56] On this front, much needs to be done. The fundamental choice of cities for the people, or cities for the capital-state nexus, in contemporary China, must be remade in favour of the former. For the time being, the single women in this chapter tell us what they are doing to find and make their place in Shanghai. For LIV, she realizes she feels something now that she did not earlier: *tashi* (踏实). Literally meaning "standing on solid ground," this Chinese term is often invoked to insinuate the kind of achievement that these single women want to have acknowledged. They may not be claiming the right to the city; they are claiming they are right *in* the city, standing there. It is, to me, a necessary nod to the experience of women, particularly single women, who meander their way through the city. Not so long ago, they were used to be confined, domesticated, immobile; now, they can and do travel—or they can and do stay *zhai*. They can go far, when they stand on firm ground.[57]

NOTES

1. Virginia Woolf, *The Years* (London: Hogarth Press, 1937).
2. Vivian Gornick, *The Odd Woman and the City: A Memoir* (New York: Farrar, Straus and Giroux, 2015).
3. See Simone van Saarloos, "'Op Straat, Tussen de Mensen, Kom Je Jezelf Pas Echt Tegen,'" *NRC*, February 3, 2017, https://www.nrc.nl/nieuws/2017/02/03/op-straat-tussen-de-mensen-kom-je-jezelf-pas-echt-tegen-6534397-a1544348.
4. See Chapter VII "Walking in the City," in Michel de Certeau, *The Practice of Everyday Life* (Berkeley: University of California Press, 2011).
5. For a historical account of footbinding, see Dorothy Ko, *Cinderella's Sisters: A Revisionist History of Footbinding* (Berkeley: University of California Press, 2005); see also Angela Zito, "Bound to Be Represented: Theorizing/Fetishizing Footbinding," in *Embodied Modernities: Corporeality, Representation, And Chinese Cultures*, ed. Fran Martin and Larissa Heinrich (Honolulu: University of Hawaii Press, 2006), 21–41; Yang Jianli's Chinese-language account in Yang Jianli (杨剑利), 女性与近代中国社会 *[The Female and Modern China Society]* (Beijing: 中国社会出版社 [China Society Press], 2007).
6. See Megan M. Ferry, "Advertising, Consumerism and Nostalgia for the New Woman in Contemporary China," *Continuum* 17, no. 3 (2003): 277–90.
7. See Richard Florida, *The Rise of the Creative Class* (New York: Basic Books, 2002).
8. Jon Anderson and Kathryn Erskine, "Tropophilia: A Study of People, Place and Lifestyle Travel," *Mobilities* 9, no. 1 (2014): 130.
9. See Lewis Holloway and Phil Hubbard, *People and Place: The Extraordinary Geographies of Everyday Life* (Harlow: Pearson Education, 2001); Paul J. Cloke, Phil Crang, and Mark A. Goodwin, eds., *Introducing Human Geographies* (London: Hodder Arnold, 2005).
10. Tim Cresswell, *Place: A Short Introduction* (Oxford: Blackwell, 2004): 110.
11. James Clifford, *Routes: Travel and Translation in the Late Twentieth Century* (Cambridge: Harvard University Press, 1997).
12. See Jon Murdoch, *Post-Structuralist Geography: A Guide to Relational Space* (London: Sage, 2005); Doreen Massey, "Landscape as a Provocation: Reflections on Moving Mountains," *Journal of Material Culture* 11, no. 1–2 (2006): 33–48; Mimi Sheller and John Urry, "Places to Play, Places in Play," in *Tourism Mobilities: Places to Play, Places in Play*, ed. Mimi Sheller and John Urry (London: Routledge, 2004), 1–10; Peter Adey, *Mobility* (London: Routledge, 2009); Anderson and Erskine, "Tropophilia."

13. Chow Yiu Fai, "Exploring Creative Class Mobility: Hong Kong Creative Workers in Shanghai and Beijing," *Eurasian Geography and Economics*, 2017, 4–5.

14. Florida, *The Rise of the Creative Class*.

15. See Edward L. Glaeser, "Cities, Information, and Economic Growth," *Cityscape* 1, no. 1 (1994): 9–47; Edward L. Glaeser, "Are Cities Dying?," *The Journal of Economic Perspectives* 12, no. 2 (1998): 139–60; Robert E. Lucas, "On the Mechanics of Economic Development," *Journal of Monetary Economics* 22, no. 1 (1988): 3–42.

16. Florida, *The Rise of the Creative Class*, 232.

17. Lily Kong, "Transnational Mobilities and the Making of Creative Cities," *Theory, Culture & Society* 31, no. 7–8 (2014): 273–89.

18. See Tony Bennett et al., *Culture, Class, Distinction* (London: Routledge, 2009); Mark Boyle, "Culture in the Rise of Tiger Economies: Scottish Expatriates in Dublin and the 'Creative Class' Thesis," *International Journal of Urban and Regional Research* 30, no. 2 (2006): 403–26; Ann Markusen, "Urban Development and the Politics of a Creative Class: Evidence from a Study of Artists," *Environment and Planning A* 38, no. 10 (2006): 1921–40.

19. See also Høgni Kalsø Hansen and Thomas Niedomysl, "Migration of the Creative Class: Evidence from Sweden," *Journal of Economic Geography* 9, no. 2 (2009): 191–206; Enda Murphy and Declan Redmond, "The Role of 'Hard' and 'Soft' Factors for Accommodating Creative Knowledge: Insights from Dublin's 'Creative Class,'" *Irish Geography* 42, no. 1 (2009): 69–84; Madeleine Verdich, "Creative Migration? The Attraction and Retention of the 'Creative Class' in Launceston, Tasmania," *Australian Geographer* 41, no. 1 (2010): 129–40.

20. Hansen and Niedomysl, "Migration of the Creative Class," 193.

21. Dai Juncheng et al., "Mobility of the Creative Class and City Attractiveness: A Case Study of Chinese Animation Workers," *Eurasian Geography and Economics* 53, no. 5 (2012): 649–70.

22. See Chow, "Exploring Creative Class Mobility"; Chow Yiu Fai, "Hong Kong Creative Workers in Mainland China: The Aspirational, the Precarious, and the Ethical," *China Information* 31, no. 1 (2017): 43–62.

23. Brooke Erin Duffy, "The Romance of Work: Gender and Aspirational Labour in the Digital Culture Industries," *International Journal of Cultural Studies* 19, no. 4 (2016): 444. See also Angela McRobbie, *Be Creative: Making a Living in the New Culture Industries*, 1 edition (Cambridge, UK; Malden, MA: Polity, 2016).

24. Chow Yiu Fai, Sonja van Wichelen, and Jeroen de Kloet, "Introduction: At Home in Asia? Place-Making, Belonging and Citizenship in the Asian Century," *International Journal of Cultural Studies* 19, no. 3 (2016): 243.

25. Magdalena Nowicka, "Mobile Locations: Construction of Home in a Group of Mobile Transnational Professionals," *Global Networks* 7, no. 1 (2007): 70.

26. Chen Kuan-Hsing, *Asia as Method: Toward Deimperialization* (Durham, NC: Duke University Press, 2010).

27. Chow, van Wichelen, and de Kloet, "Introduction."

28. For a book-length treatise on the intricate relationships between mobility and the Chinese state, see Pál Nyíri, *Mobility and Cultural Authority in Contemporary China* (Seattle and London: University of Washington Press, 2011). In this comprehensive examination of migration and tourism, the author argues, on the one hand, for the contribution of Chinese mobility to discourses of Chinese modernization, and on the other, for the successful state control over its mobile populations and national image. The inquiry in Chap. 7, in its insertion of work and gender and in its empirical grounding, can be taken as a departure from and supplement to Nyíri's focus on the state with the subjective and everyday accounts of a particular group of mobile subjects: single women doing creative work.

29. David J. Bodenhamer, Trevor M. Harris, and John Corrigan, "Deep Mapping and the Spatial Humanities," *International Journal of Humanities and Arts Computing* 7, no. 1–2 (2013): 170–75.

30. Mike Savage and Roger Burrows, "The Coming Crisis of Empirical Sociology," *Sociology* 41, no. 5 (2007): 885–99.

31. For the discussion of employing GIS and the politics of methods, see Bodenhamer, Harris, and Corrigan, "Deep Mapping and the Spatial Humanities"; Monika Büscher, John Urry, and Katian Witchger, "Introduction: Mobile Methods," in *Mobile Methods*, ed. Monika Büscher, John Urry, and Katian Witchger (London: Routledge, 2010), 1–19; Peter Merriman, "Rethinking Mobile Methods," *Mobilities* 9, no. 2 (2014): 167–87; Jo Vergunst, "Technology and Technique in a Useful Ethnography of Movement," *Mobilities* 6, no. 2 (2011): 203–19. For a discussion specifically of the politics of big data visualization, see Helen Kennedy and Rosemary Lucy Hill, "The Feeling of Numbers: Emotions in Everyday Engagements with Data and Their Visualisation," *Sociology*, 2017, 1–19.

32. Lawrence Grossberg, "Is There a Fan in the House? The Affective Sensibility of Fandom," in *The Adoring Audience: Fan Culture and Popular Media*, ed. Lisa A. Lewis (London: Routledge, 1992), 57.

33. Roughly speaking, those more familiar with visual arts were "reserved" for the visual methods for Chap. 8.

34. Grossberg, "Is There a Fan in the House," 60.

35. Before we discuss further their migratory narratives, it should be added that the single women in this inquiry moved in a rather straightforward manner, from somewhere else to Shanghai. As I argue elsewhere, sometimes creative workers follow circuitous routes before they become based

in a certain city (see Chow, "Hong Kong Creative Workers in Mainland China"). In the preface to her collection of interviews with "singles in the city," Wu Shuping also points to intense mobility of Chinese women. "These days people tend to lead mobile lives so it is not easy to define where they are from." See Wu Shuping, *Single in the City: A Survey of China's Single Women* (Beijing: Long River Press, 2012): 5–6.

36. Dai et al., "Mobility of the Creative Class and City Attractiveness," 667.
37. See Chow, "Exploring Creative Class Mobility"; Chow, "Hong Kong Creative Workers in Mainland China." Shanghai, or mainland China in general, attracts not only Chinese from other parts of the country, but also Chinese from the diaspora. Elsewhere, I have studied Diana Zhu, a young Dutch-born woman, who moved from her hometown in the Netherlands to Shanghai, where her parents came from, to pursue her musical dream. See Chow Yiu Fai, "Hope Against Hopes: Diana Zhu and the Transnational Politics of Chinese Popular Music," *Cultural Studies* 25, no. 6 (2011): 783–808.
38. This intra-racial, inter-regional demarcation, some would say discrimination, is articulated by most of these women, both "outsiders" (*waidiren*, 外地人), and the "locals." As yet, there has been no academic study on the alluded xenophobic or nativist sentiment of Shanghai people, while online discussions abound.
39. Anna, another single woman in this inquiry, made a similar move with a similar reason. She wants to spend more time with her aging father.
40. Among those who were not covered in this mobile inquiry, three moved out of Shanghai. Anna and Lulu returned to their respective hometowns, Hong Kong and Qingdao, to take care of their aging or ailing fathers. Siqi moved to Beijing for a mixture of personal and work reasons, and subsequently, returned to Shanghai for a film project.
41. Lulu, not included in this chapter but in the following one, has taken the opportunity of showing an image underlining a similar narrative of constantly moving. See Chap. 8.
42. For a book-length account from a personal, historical perspective (from 1910s) of living in an alley neighbourhood in Shanghai, see Li Jie, *Shanghai Homes: Palimpsests of Private Life* (New York: Columbia University Press, 2014). For an ethnographic study of residents living in alley neighbourhoods preserved by the Shanghai government as part of its city branding, see Non Arkaraprasertkul, "Traditionalism as a Way of Life: The Sense of Home in a Shanghai Alleyway," *Harvard Asia Quarterly* 15, no. 3/4 (2013): 15–25.
43. Leta Hong Fincher, *Leftover Women: The Resurgence of Gender Inequality in China* (London, New York: Zed Books, 2014).

44. As if to underscore the spatial fluidity of Shanghai, both Red Town and Jifeng Shuyuan ceased to exist after our interviews.

45. *Dakou* CDs refer to the discs dumped by the West to China during the 1990s, intended for recycling. To avoid them from entering the market as good CDs, these discs suffered a small cut from within, thus *dakou*, literally meaning "a cut." However, as the small cut only made the last part of the recording non-playable, they found their way into the illegal market. For the impact of *dakou* CDs on early generation of rock musicians and youth culture in China, see Jeroen de Kloet, *China with a Cut: Globalisation, Urban Youth and Popular Music* (Amsterdam: Amsterdam University Press, 2010).

46. See Mark S. Granovetter, "The Strength of Weak Ties," *American Journal of Sociology* 78, no. 6 (1973): 1360–80; D Krackhardt, "The Strength of Strong Ties: The Importance of Philos in Organizations," in *Networks and Organizations: Structure, Form, and Action* (Boston, MA: Harvard Business School Press, 1992), 216–39; Melinda Blau and Karen L. Fingerman, *Consequential Strangers: Turning Everyday Encounters into Life-Changing Moments* (New York: W. W. Norton & Company, 2009).

47. Anthony D'Andrea, Luigina Ciolfi, and Breda Gray, "Methodological Challenges and Innovations in Mobilities Research," *Mobilities* 6, no. 2 (May 1, 2011): 154–155.

48. Chow, van Wichelen, and de Kloet, "Introduction," 243.

49. Merriman, "Rethinking Mobile Methods," 177.

50. Note that the common Chinese word for home (家) also carries the multiple references including dwelling and residence, plus the possible reference to family.

51. Anderson and Erskine, "Tropophilia," 131.

52. Henri Lefebvre, *Writings on Cities*, ed. Eleonore Kofman and Elizabeth Lebas (Cambridge, Massachusetts: Wiley-Blackwell, 1996).

53. David Harvey, "The Right to the City," *New Left Review*, II, no. 53 (2008): 23–40.

54. David Harvey, *Rebel Cities: From the Right to the City to the Urban Revolution* (London; New York: Verso Books, 2012). 5.

55. Ibid., 4.

56. Kurt Iveson, "Social or Spatial Justice? Marcuse and Soja on the Right to the City," *City* 15, no. 2 (2011): 250–59.

57. For a commentary that claims the right to the city from the perspective of migrant workers in China, see Carlo Inverardi-Ferri, "Commons and the Right to the City in Contemporary China," *Chinoiresie* (blog), September 28, 2017, http://www.chinoiresie.info/commons-and-the-right-to-the-city-in-contemporary-china/.

References

Adey, Peter. *Mobility*. London: Routledge, 2009.

Anderson, Jon, and Kathryn Erskine. "Tropophilia: A Study of People, Place and Lifestyle Travel." *Mobilities* 9, no. 1 (2014): 130–45.

Arkaraprasertkul, Non. "Traditionalism as a Way of Life: The Sense of Home in a Shanghai Alleyway." *Harvard Asia Quarterly* 15, no. 3/4 (2013): 15–25.

Bennett, Tony, Mike Savage, Elizabeth Bortolaia Silva, Alan Warde, Modesto Gayo-Cal, and David Wright. *Culture, Class, Distinction*. London: Routledge, 2009.

Blau, Melinda, and Karen L. Fingerman. *Consequential Strangers: Turning Everyday Encounters into Life-Changing Moments*. New York: W. W. Norton & Company, 2009.

Bodenhamer, David J., Trevor M. Harris, and John Corrigan. "Deep Mapping and the Spatial Humanities." *International Journal of Humanities and Arts Computing* 7, no. 1–2 (2013): 170–75.

Boyle, Mark. "Culture in the Rise of Tiger Economies: Scottish Expatriates in Dublin and the 'Creative Class' Thesis." *International Journal of Urban and Regional Research* 30, no. 2 (2006): 403–26.

Büscher, Monika, John Urry, and Katian Witchger. "Introduction: Mobile Methods." In *Mobile Methods*, edited by Monika Büscher, John Urry, and Katian Witchger, 1–19. London: Routledge, 2010.

de Certeau, Michel. *The Practice of Everyday Life*. Berkeley: University of California Press, 2011.

Chen, Kuan-Hsing. *Asia as Method: Toward Deimperialization*. Durham, NC: Duke University Press, 2010.

Chow, Yiu Fai. "Exploring Creative Class Mobility: Hong Kong Creative Workers in Shanghai and Beijing." *Eurasian Geography and Economics*, 2017a, 1–25.

Chow, Yiu Fai. "Hong Kong Creative Workers in Mainland China: The Aspirational, the Precarious, and the Ethical." *China Information* 31, no. 1 (2017b): 43–62.

Chow, Yiu Fai. "Hope Against Hopes: Diana Zhu and the Transnational Politics of Chinese Popular Music." *Cultural Studies* 25, no. 6 (2011): 783–808.

Chow, Yiu Fai, Sonja van Wichelen, and Jeroen de Kloet. "Introduction: At Home in Asia? Place-Making, Belonging and Citizenship in the Asian Century." *International Journal of Cultural Studies* 19, no. 3 (2016): 243–56.

Clifford, James. *Routes: Travel and Translation in the Late Twentieth Century*. Cambridge: Harvard University Press, 1997.

Cloke, Paul J., Phil Crang, and Mark A. Goodwin, eds. *Introducing Human Geographies*. London: Hodder Arnold, 2005.

Cresswell, Tim. *Place: A Short Introduction*. Oxford: Blackwell, 2004.

Dai, Juncheng, Shangyi Zhou, Michael Keane, and Qian Huang. "Mobility of the Creative Class and City Attractiveness: A Case Study of Chinese Animation Workers." *Eurasian Geography and Economics* 53, no. 5 (2012): 649–70.

D'Andrea, Anthony, Luigina Ciolfi, and Breda Gray. "Methodological Challenges and Innovations in Mobilities Research." *Mobilities* 6, no. 2 (May 1, 2011): 149–60.

Duffy, Brooke Erin. "The Romance of Work: Gender and Aspirational Labour in the Digital Culture Industries." *International Journal of Cultural Studies* 19, no. 4 (2016): 441–57.

Ferry, Megan M. "Advertising, Consumerism and Nostalgia for the New Woman in Contemporary China." *Continuum* 17, no. 3 (2003): 277–90.

Florida, Richard. *The Rise of the Creative Class.* New York: Basic Books, 2002.

Glaeser, Edward L. "Are Cities Dying?" *The Journal of Economic Perspectives* 12, no. 2 (1998): 139–60.

Glaeser, Edward L. "Cities, Information, and Economic Growth." *Cityscape* 1, no. 1 (1994): 9–47.

Gornick, Vivian. *The Odd Woman and the City: A Memoir.* New York: Farrar, Straus and Giroux, 2015.

Granovetter, Mark S. "The Strength of Weak Ties." *American Journal of Sociology* 78, no. 6 (1973): 1360–80.

Grossberg, Lawrence. "Is There a Fan in the House? The Affective Sensibility of Fandom." In *The Adoring Audience: Fan Culture and Popular Media*, edited by Lisa A. Lewis, 50–65. London: Routledge, 1992.

Hansen, Høgni Kalsø, and Thomas Niedomysl. "Migration of the Creative Class: Evidence from Sweden." *Journal of Economic Geography* 9, no. 2 (2009): 191–206.

Harvey, David. *Rebel Cities: From the Right to the City to the Urban Revolution.* London; New York: Verso Books, 2012.

Harvey, David. "The Right to the City." *New Left Review*, II, no. 53 (2008): 23–40.

Holloway, Lewis, and Phil Hubbard. *People and Place: The Extraordinary Geographies of Everyday Life.* Harlow: Pearson Education, 2001.

Hong Fincher, Leta. *Leftover Women: The Resurgence of Gender Inequality in China.* London, New York: Zed Books, 2014.

Inverardi-Ferri, Carlo. "Commons and the Right to the City in Contemporary China." *Chinoiresie* (blog), September 28, 2017. http://www.chinoiresie.info/commons-and-the-right-to-the-city-in-contemporary-china/.

Iveson, Kurt. "Social or Spatial Justice? Marcuse and Soja on the Right to the City." *City* 15, no. 2 (2011): 250–59.

Kennedy, Helen, and Rosemary Lucy Hill. "The Feeling of Numbers: Emotions in Everyday Engagements with Data and Their Visualisation." *Sociology*, 2017, 1–19.

de Kloet, Jeroen. *China with a Cut: Globalisation, Urban Youth and Popular Music*. Amsterdam: Amsterdam University Press, 2010.

Ko, Dorothy. *Cinderella's Sisters: A Revisionist History of Footbinding*. Berkeley: University of California Press, 2005.

Kong, Lily. "Transnational Mobilities and the Making of Creative Cities." *Theory, Culture & Society* 31, no. 7–8 (2014): 273–89.

Krackhardt, D. "The Strength of Strong Ties: The Importance of Philos in Organizations." In *Networks and Organizations: Structure, Form, and Action*, 216–39. Boston, MA: Harvard Business School Press, 1992.

Lefebvre, Henri. *Writings on Cities*. Edited by Eleonore Kofman and Elizabeth Lebas. Cambridge, Massachusetts: Wiley-Blackwell, 1996.

Li, Jie. *Shanghai Homes: Palimpsests of Private Life*. New York: Columbia University Press, 2014.

Lucas, Robert E. "On the Mechanics of Economic Development." *Journal of Monetary Economics* 22, no. 1 (1988): 3–42.

Markusen, Ann. "Urban Development and the Politics of a Creative Class: Evidence from a Study of Artists." *Environment and Planning A* 38, no. 10 (2006): 1921–40.

Massey, Doreen. "Landscape as a Provocation: Reflections on Moving Mountains." *Journal of Material Culture* 11, no. 1–2 (2006): 33–48.

McRobbie, Angela. *Be Creative: Making a Living in the New Culture Industries*. 1 edition. Cambridge, UK; Malden, MA: Polity, 2016.

Merriman, Peter. "Rethinking Mobile Methods." *Mobilities* 9, no. 2 (2014): 167–87.

Murdoch, Jon. *Post-Structuralist Geography: A Guide to Relational Space*. London: Sage, 2005.

Murphy, Enda, and Declan Redmond. "The Role of 'Hard' and 'Soft' Factors for Accommodating Creative Knowledge: Insights from Dublin's 'Creative Class.'" *Irish Geography* 42, no. 1 (2009): 69–84.

Nowicka, Magdalena. "Mobile Locations: Construction of Home in a Group of Mobile Transnational Professionals." *Global Networks* 7, no. 1 (2007): 69–86.

Nyíri, Pál. *Mobility and Cultural Authority in Contemporary China*. Seattle and London: University of Washington Press, 2011.

van Saarloos, Simone. "'Op Straat, Tussen de Mensen, Kom Je Jezelf Pas Echt Tegen.'" *NRC*, February 3, 2017. https://www.nrc.nl/nieuws/2017/02/03/op-straat-tussen-de-mensen-kom-je-jezelf-pas-echt-tegen-6534397-a15 44348.

Savage, Mike, and Roger Burrows. "The Coming Crisis of Empirical Sociology." *Sociology* 41, no. 5 (2007): 885–99.

Sheller, Mimi, and John Urry. "Places to Play, Places in Play." In *Tourism Mobilities: Places to Play, Places in Play*, edited by Mimi Sheller and John Urry, 1–10. London: Routledge, 2004.

Verdich, Madeleine. "Creative Migration? The Attraction and Retention of the 'Creative Class' in Launceston, Tasmania." *Australian Geographer* 41, no. 1 (2010): 129–40.

Vergunst, Jo. "Technology and Technique in a Useful Ethnography of Movement." *Mobilities* 6, no. 2 (2011): 203–19.

Woolf, Virginia. *The Years*. London: Hogarth Press, 1937.

Wu, Shuping. *Single in the City: A Survey of China's Single Women*. Beijing: Long River Press, 2012.

Yang Jianli (杨剑利). 女性与近代中国社会 [*The Female and Modern China Society*]. Beijing: 中国社会出版社 [China Society Press], 2007.

Zito, Angela. "Bound to Be Represented: Theorizing/Fetishizing Footbinding." In *Embodied Modernities: Corporeality, Representation, And Chinese Cultures*, edited by Fran Martin and Larissa Heinrich, 21–41. Honolulu: University of Hawaii Press, 2006.

CHAPTER 8

Living with Themselves, Creating Themselves

While this book opens with a discussion of how single women in contemporary China are represented, it ends with their self-representation. Fundamentally, this chapter is an attempt, the most explicit among the chapters, to let the women speak. More empirically, since the women in this inquiry are working in the creative fields, and have vested interest in creative practices, it occurs to me to be an opportune occasion whereby their creativity can be mobilized as part of the inquiry.

Inspired by visual methodology in general and image-elicitation techniques in particular, I invited the subjects to produce visual materials that best represent themselves as single woman in Shanghai.[1] These "cultural probing" materials are used in two ways. First, they are documented in the book as materials generated directly by the subjects. They offer the reader immediate glimpses of the worlds the women are living in. Second, the materials were used for discussions between the subjects and the investigator. In addition to the attempt to give the women more freedom to come up with their own materials, the self-generated images lend themselves to opening up areas for examination otherwise unexamined, overlooked, and finally, erased from any understanding of their lives.

Visual Methods

I have never used visual methods before, but have read much about them. I am attracted to the "easy and fun" parts, not only for the researched, but

© The Author(s) 2019
Chow Y. F., *Caring in Times of Precarity*, Palgrave Studies in
Globalization, Culture and Society,
https://doi.org/10.1007/978-3-319-76898-4_8

also, I believe, for the researcher.[2] It would not be exactly accurate to describe what has been happening in recent decades in qualitative research as a "visual turn," as Andrew Clark and Lisa Morriss do in their overview of visual methods and social work research.[3] After all, empirical inquiries that involve human subjects are still dominated by interviews, focus groups, and other talk-based methods, as is the case for the book you are reading. It would be, however, equally inaccurate if we fail to note the increasing deployment of visual methods, and their contribution to research projects, which has reached the extent that Clark and Morriss, in the same review article, propose the emergence of a "visual canon": the seminal works by Marcus Banks, Sarah Pink, and Gillian Rose.[4] This is in addition to all the individual articles, special issues, journals, and handbooks dedicated to visual methodology and published during the same period.[5]

Whichever way the history of visual methods is written, its development gestures to the limitations of talk-based methods, and on the flip side, to what visual methods are able to achieve. On the one hand, talk-based methods are criticized for their reliance on the verbal ability of the subjects, which is inclined, like textual language itself, to a higher level of rationality and (self-)consciousness. Given the context where the researcher usually takes the lead vis-à-vis the researched, in asking, probing, and largely deciding the pace, flow, and termination of the conversations, talk-based methods are found wanting in the power relationships between the two parties, and the researched are largely placed in a passive role. On the other hand, visual methods are believed to be less logocentric, more neutral, and more capable of tapping into something non-verbal, even the subconscious or the unconscious, allowing "their voice" to speak.[6] In that sense, they are also more egalitarian, collaborative, and participatory, with less interference from the researcher. The process includes the participant in the research process as an active contributor and "expert" in his or her own life, rather than as a passive subject of the study.[7] This explains why visual methods are often used in investigations concerning children, youth,[8] people with mental health issues,[9] and for generally marginalized and stigmatized groups.[10] In this sense, they are also called "inclusive" research. Sometimes, visual methods are stretched beyond the conventional realms of research, into the field of intervention, for instance to empower,[11] and to achieve pedagogical goals.[12]

Meanwhile, we have to be cautious. Critics, while not disapproving of visual methods per se, pose questions as to their presumably unique value and draw attention to the complexities of doing visual research.[13] David Buckingham warns against the uncritical celebration of visual methodology's privileged assumption to yield an objective, authentic voice or story, of what he calls "naïve empiricism." Recalling the reminder raised by the three canonizers, Buckingham emphasizes the equally constructive nature of visual representations. In Rose's words, "[i]nterpreting images is just that, interpretation, not the discovery of their 'truth'."[14] For this inquiry, I decided to use visual methods not because I consider them neutral or empowering or pedagogical. And I do not consider them essentially better than talk-based methods; after all, I have conducted the entire research project primarily with interviews and focus groups. If I am naïve, I am naïve in succumbing to the, as previously mentioned, easy and fun appeal for myself and the women in this inquiry. I am also naïve in the sense that, instead of mistrusting their abilities in verbal research approaches, I am actually assuming their creative savviness and expecting them to make good use of this invitation, if visual methods are used. For me, it is a three-pronged response to this particular group of participants in the visual inquiry. First, it acknowledges what they are supposed to be interested, trained, and experienced in; they have been working in creative fields. Second, this visual exercise may also offer glimpses of how they would use their creative skills to insert what they think into their creative products. And third, I want to present the visual data they offer not only as data, but also as creative products in themselves (reproduced here invariably in black and white).

I performed this part of my inquiry as follows. After the selection of subjects, as explained in the previous chapter, I sent invitations to 10 of the women involved in the first round of research who suggested a more immediate affinity with visual culture, asking them if they would agree to participate by sending image(s) they find representative of themselves as single women. One declined. As the Chinese language does not need to specify if the word "image" is singular or plural, they were given the liberty to produce more than one image. The invitation also did not specify the format or the origin of the visual materials.[15] After receiving the images, we—that is, my research assistants and I—discussed them, and came up with some rough and initial observations, or rather, visual dimensions, presumably of interest that would need to be probed into.

The session usually started with the "factual" aspects of the images, that is when, where, and under what circumstances they were created, and by whom, followed by their accounts of why these images were selected. Sometimes, the single women in the inquiry would come up suddenly or incidentally with other images, which would also be included in the conversation. In line with image-elicitation techniques, the images they provided served as "visual stimuli … to 'trigger' more projective information with the respondents."[16] In other words, what I wanted to achieve with this particular deployment of visual methods was not only to decipher the inherent meanings in the visual materials created or presented in the inquiry.[17] If Rose, by arguing that visual methodology is visual culture par excellence, also argues that "images tend to be deployed much more as communicational tools than as representational texts," I wanted to use them as both.[18] The following accounts of their images will be a crisscrossing of the communicational and the representational.

To me, the insistence on the representational is essential, when the politics of representation are still at stake. In that sense, Chap. 8 also intersects with the scholarship on visual self-representation, as the practice itself has proliferated with the development and popularization of digital technology and of social network culture. From the earlier avatar studies[19] to the more recent investigations of selfies, arguably the most popular means of representing the self in social networks,[20] one central theme is the imagination and construction of the self in such representative acts and symbolic— nonetheless, social—spaces. As far as these investigations concern gender politics, they yield mostly disappointing findings. Most of the studies on visual self-representation detect a similar tendency to other forms of mediated representation: persistent (self-)objectification of women, gender stereotyping, and exacerbation of surveillance and control.[21] Only a few studies show the possibilities of resistance.[22] The study of Chang Jiang et al. is noteworthy as it is a rare case engaging squarely with gender politics amidst a handful of studies that consider social media as a possible platform for resisting cultural norms in China.[23] It examines profile pictures that young women post on their WeChat accounts, identifying a tactic of self-empowerment not directly connected with the conventional understanding of feminist struggles against patriarchy and gender inequality, empowering nonetheless.[24] I will respond to this finding when concluding the chapter.

Most of the images presented by the women here were chosen specifically for this inquiry. As we will read from the accounts to follow, some are or have been the women's profile pictures. The discrepancy, that is to say, the fact that not *all* of these images that are supposed to represent them have been posted on social networks, is interesting. It shows the enabling and disabling dimensions of such self-representation: enabling in the sense of having the power to choose what they prefer to present to the world at large; disabling in the sense that perhaps such choice is always already entrenched in caution, convention, and calculation. The "social" of the network is wrestling with the "self" in representation. I have to make it clear here: I am not suggesting that the act of choosing, showing, and talking about the images proffered by the single women in this inquiry is less performative, communicative, and meditated. It is different. The women in this inquiry may want to impress the researchers in question, but it is different from trying to impress their immediate and mediated circles of friends. I conceive this research context as a platform not of consequence, but of significance. In so far as they take the participation and contribution seriously—their seriousness is articulated by some and insinuated by others in their willingness to offer time and energy to participate—and in so far as they are rich in creative resources, the question is: what do they want to use this platform, the academic one, to say about themselves?[25]

Vera (Born in 1981): Rebellious Monkey

Vera brings with her an image she also uses as her current WeChat portrait: a monkey, "primarily in the tones of red and green, don't you notice?" Such a combination of colours, Vera says, is not the taste of most people, but it shows the skills of the artist who made it, as well as being the reason she likes it. The artist is Chen Jianzhou, and this particular work belongs to a series with the Monkey King as its theme. "The green occupies the most of the image, giving it some sort of stability and quiet," is how Vera analyses the image, "but the red clothes and yellow scarf in the centre jump out, and the colours of the hair. It's bright." She summarizes her feeling about the image as "not suppressive," as she does not like suppressive things. "It is lively! And its facial expression is a bit silly, perhaps this is the kind of state I aspire to."

Another reason Vera offers for the choice of this image is because she was born in the Year of the Monkey, and she finds that she looks like a monkey—perhaps less now, as she has put on weight. "When I was a child, I was very skinny. We lived in a rural area, and I loved climbing trees and jumping into the water," Vera recalls. Yet, she has changed with age, "as you can't really stay like a child, that whenever you want to cry, you cry, whenever you want to make a mess, you make a mess." That is why when she looks at her favourite monkey image, she sees "a little bit of cunningness, of wittiness, but for most of the time it's hidden." Recalling the theme of Chen's work series, Vera narrates the mythical story well known to Chinese children. It tells of the Monkey King storming through the heavenly palace, rebelling against the powerful gods. However, in real life, the Monkey King would become the monkey in the image, keeping the rebellious spirit behind a normal face, a normal societal role. "It has to balance things out … It's the usual state of being for most people and it's not vulgar," Vera says. The moments of rebellion, whether in the past or in the future, seem to have placed the monkey beyond vulgarity.

Resonating with Fanjie in the television series *Ode to Joy*, Vera recalls, in painful detail, how unfairly she was treated by her parents. "They were hysterical with their children," Vera says, "They indoctrinated me that I should remain indebted to them, for ever. And they had bad tempers." Her mother showed a clear preference for her son. While she received hardly any support from her family, they would come to her for help whenever they were in trouble. With all the family burden on her shoulders, Vera had her first "breakdown" three years after she started working. She wanted to quit. When Vera talked to her mother on the phone, her mother said: "What other jobs can someone like you find?"

Through the years, through more breakdowns and "a light form of depression," as diagnosed by the doctor, Vera says she has learned something about herself, about her life. "Maybe I am that Monkey King: so stubborn, so rebellious, only hoping to last till a critical point." That critical point, Vera says, is the realization that "I don't need anyone." Such realization, hard gained by being stubborn and rebellious, helped Vera to become, in her words, "more relaxed and tranquil." She stopped seeing her family;

she decided not to proceed with a "relationship" with a colleague who clearly wanted more; and she recalls her recent start-up with another creative worker who is, likewise, a little bit stubborn, a little bit rebellious, and with a strong sense of self-realization. "At my age, we are sort of stuck. If I want a further promotion, I'll need to work on my English. But I am too old for that. So, if I stay in my job, well it's OK for me to earn 200,000 RMB a year now. But what about later?" She does not find it easy running her start-up, but she tells herself to keep trying, or where else would she like to go? "I hate 9-to-5 work. I am a monkey," Vera says. For now, her concern is not making a career, but making money. Maybe, Vera says, one day when her "conditions of life" are better, that is when she is financially more stable, Vera will go and buy one of Chen's original works.

MISS P (BORN IN 1977): AT THE CROSSROADS

The image Miss P presents is a technologically manipulated one. The original photo was taken during one of her advertising projects four years ago. Miss P made two changes. First, she cut the photo as if precisely half of the panda stands there. She subsequently duplicated and combined the two halves into the image we see now. The one wearing the panda outfit was not herself, although "Panda" has been what people call her, dating back to the beginning of her work life. She worked hard and she always had black circles around her eyes, to the extent that her Taiwanese boss joked: "You were born to be an advertising person, you look like a panda." Since then, Panda has become her nickname.

Miss P's choice of making up this "artificial" image this way is because, "I want to show the kind of crossroads I was facing at that point in my life." The panda in the photograph is "made" into facing two paths ahead of the zebra crossing, instead of one. "On the opposite side are many common people, on Huaihai Road." It shows what Miss P feels like; that she has to face a lot of people, strangers or not; she, on her own, vis-à-vis the multitude, the expectations of the common people, and of society. "That was when both my work and my life were in a bottleneck."

In terms of work, Miss P says, "I knew I had reached the top of what I could achieve in that company. If I left and started my own business, there were realistic issues. I was anxious. The image shows the state of my anxiety." After more than a decade of employment, Miss P realized that the kind of achievement and honour are no longer the same as when you started. Moreover, however hard one works, "In the end, the aura belongs to the company you work for." In terms of her private life, Miss P says, with tears in her eyes, "That was also the time that I had just got divorced. Another kind of crossroads." The divorce was not her choice and she found that it was hard not to let her work be affected by her private life. "Well, any normal woman when facing the same situation would have difficulty in doing her work. You started to wonder, I am going to lose my marriage, and then, I continue to come across unpleasant things at work. It was during this time that I decided to leave the company."

Why only the panda's back? "Because that's my subjective state, facing a group of people. At that point, I want to keep some distance from the people, or I want to keep them away, so that I can see from a distance and see my own position. In the midst of two paths, I don't know which to choose." Contrary to Vera's accent on colours, Miss P made another change to the original photo: she turned the colourful image into black and white. Remarking how Huaihai Road is very colourful in the evening, she says, "I wanted to make it simpler, purer. I think black and white is simpler." In other words, the simplicity lies in erasing the hustle and bustle of the city, of the common people. There, on her own, the panda is waiting not only for the choice of which path to take, but more fundamentally, "for the green light," she says. Ironically, by turning the image black and white, she also renders it impossible to detect the colours of the traffic lights at all. It becomes more understandable when Miss P looks at the image she made, and says of her current life: "Now the green light seems a bit too bright. Wherever I go, the light is always green."

Resonating with Vera's superficially normal, but essentially rebellious monkey, Miss P feels that the panda at the crossroads image represents her present equally well. At that point, the path she finally took is essentially the same advertising one, with one major change, she thought: "I won't ever join a 4A firm," as "once I am back in that environment, I will feel suppressed, uncomfortable." Since then, Miss P has been running her own freelance business, arranging her own work and life. "I am more relaxed, feeling calmer ... Now I feel like I am choosing work, not working to please. I feel a lot happier." Nevertheless, if "hesitation" is the word Miss P uses to describe herself then, now she says, "I am hesitating again. My current mode of work-life should expire by the end of the year. And there is a family reason ... Perhaps I need to take up more pressure." Reverting to her earlier resolve, Miss P says, "I am hesitating if I should look for a job with a 4A firm. Or I should find a partner, and run a start-up."

She is less hesitant regarding her private life. "I don't demand too much, and I don't give myself any deadlines. I have passed the age of 30, and I wouldn't say something like I must get married and have a kid by 30! No, not any more. It's just being realistic. At this moment in life, I don't want to choose. If I come across it, I come across it. If not, then not." Her pressure is more the financial sort; she needs to support her mother. Miss P connects her financial pressure to the way freelancing is paid: while the project is still underway, the freelancer is yet to be paid.

In the end, Miss P contrasts the waiting panda image with what is forever moving: time. "Slowly, time will change everything. Time can cure everything. There is nothing much I can say regarding how I came through the crossroads, but time." And it is also time that seems to give her consolation and confidence. "The image represents then and now. When I look back, I feel, oh I was so tired then! It's fine now."

Jin (Born in 1982): Cat and Books

The third image is also that of an animal, but this time a real one. It is, according to Jin, about the cat and the books as shown in her chosen image, a photograph taken by her at her home. Jin starts with the central part of the image: her cat—and her family that she seems to draw a line with by keeping the cat. Corresponding with the familial complexity articulated by Vera, when she talks about her image, Jin says, "My parents and parents of my friends all believe that cats carry viruses and parasites with them. They are not clean, and we have to stay away from them. Our generation usually has this kind of memory, and most of us do not have experience growing up with animals." She expresses her independence and autonomy this way: "I live on my own, and I have my own place. I realize I am independent, and now I can make my own decisions." Defiantly, she adds: "My parents cannot intervene anymore."

Jin compares herself with many friends of her age, who live with their parents, and would still be forbidden to keep cats, even if they love cats. At the same time, many others have done so even when their parents do not like it. Jin was encouraged. Still, it was not an impulsive decision; she thought about it for some time, but she always considered her life to be too "shaky," especially for "renters like us." In the end, it is precisely the sense of responsibility that Jin feels the most about keeping her cat. "When I first owned this cat, I started to realize: for a long, long time, I didn't get the chance to deal with a life on my own, a life that is totally dependent on me." It is like taking care of a child, she explains. "When I am with my cat, I can't help feeling like I am with a child. And I talk gently to the cat … and I realize: oh, I still have this side of myself!"

For her as a single woman, taking care of a cat is even more demanding, and she takes it even more seriously. "It's not like taking care of a cat as a couple. In that case, you always have someone else to share the responsibility." Every morning when Jin wakes up and realizes the cat relies so much on her, she acknowledges the grown-up part of herself, that is "you can't always look for help, you need to deal with things on your own." Paradoxically, if the dependence of the cat makes her singlehood more prominent, it also makes it less so. She and her cat have developed a relationship, more "pure" than personal ones. And it helps her deal with the difficulties of creative work. She will go and play briefly with the cat every hour when she is busy writing. "For people like us who write in the middle of the night, you feel that you are the only person left over in the world, very quiet. And then, you realize there is also this cat, and it's alive. The sense of company is very nice." Jin articulates clearly her preference for this kind of company. "I find it difficult to live with other people." Jin finds it complicated between human beings, such as when they are in love: "How close can two people be? How loose?" Human beings need a sense of security, but cats just have to follow the one who has chosen them. It is as simple as: "If you are with someone, you can't wake that someone up when you fail to fall asleep. But you can with a cat."

Why did Jin take the photo from below? "Purely by chance," she says. But the round face, accentuated by the perspective, makes the cat cuter. "When I posted this photo on my WeChat, my friends said it looked like me." What does she see of herself in that image? "It's slightly timid, slightly gentle, slightly curious." Reverting to the incidental nature of the snapshot, Jin says she actually does not find it important to read the image; she just likes it, also the background, the shelves with books. "I am already 35. What I look for now is quietness. I am no longer interested in things that make me high. The best is to hold a cat, and read." Jin simply feels good when she looks at the bookshelves. "When you are home, you have to choose a pleasant corner, then of course it's by the book shelves." She quickly adds: "But then if you ask me whether anything is at all important, I would say nothing." That is why Jin does not look for perfection in her life anymore. "I don't think we need to have perfection. Well, perfection is perhaps: the cat can go to toilet on its own." And a cat will not deceive you, or scheme against you. "I want to have another cat."

Siqi (Born in 1991): Incidentally There

"I thought of drawing something myself, but I couldn't think of myself in any gesture or expression. I felt that I would strike a vague image in this society, in this world." Siqi explains why she, in the end, has chosen a film still to represent herself, from *Dogville*. "Actually I am very much like the main character." Siqi outlines the plot of the film, where a young woman comes to a small town and finds that the inhabitants transform from kindness to hostility against this outsider. Siqi cites a conversation between the woman and her gangster-boss father. Her father says: "Now you know what the so-called goodness, kindness, and simplicity actually is." She says: "Because they are like that, they are ignorant, they haven't seen the larger world. When everyone tells them I am a bad person, they treat me like that. But I know what this is about, so I can forgive them." Then, her father says: "You know what you are doing is not virtuous, it's arrogance. Because you place yourself on higher ground, so you think you can forgive them. In fact, you don't have the right to forgive them. You are just like them. To some extent, you are depriving them of the chance to realize their own wrongs, their capacity to seek salvation and forgiveness."

This conversation has left a big impact on Siqi. "For a long time, my way of dealing with people, looking at the world, has been like that female protagonist." Referring to the emptiness of the image, Siqi calls it "without any direction ... It's my state of being, whether it's the choice of work, or of life ... nothing is really possible or impossible. Directions are everywhere, and nowhere." The female protagonist, Siqi points out, actually does not have any real connections with the world. Against this vast, empty background, she is incidentally there, small and faceless. This is, she says, her experience in any city. "I feel that it wouldn't matter if I vanished." The image only shows the back of the young woman in the film—a choice reminiscent of Miss P's panda's back. "It's quite enough. It's the totality of my self-recognition. I feel like I'm in a vast emptiness, just a back and no one knows who she is."

It is also the reason why Siqi says she never uses photos of herself on social networks. She describes herself as "quiet," not "lost." "I don't feel lost. First, I am sharply conscious of where I am going. Second, I know very clearly that I can give up this path at any time." Siqi explains that she can give up her work, the future of her work, as well as "other things, like my interests." Such as going to Kunqu performances, watching films, reading, and going to theatre. Recently, she has fallen for online gaming. Eagerly, she describes two games that fascinate her. One is set in an enclosed space, with only the player in the scene. The other requires the player to follow the guidance of a voice-over, presumably guiding the player to the heart of someone who is determined to shut himself off from the outside world. In the end, the voice-over breaks down, as it realizes what it says is determined by the game producer, not by what it really wants to say.

Both games centre around a single person, existentially contemplative, questioning; just what Siqi often seems to be doing herself. A small figure facing a vast emptiness, as in the image. This can also be liberating. "I don't insist on anything; it's also my way towards love matters." When she recalls her love experiences, Siqi says she has no right to forgive, as inspired by *Dogville*. Concerning work, Siqi says she has hesitated about leaving her music-related job, as music is what she loves. "But then it is not so important that I must keep my work with music for ever." While she would insist on nothing in matters of love, work, and the future, the only thing Siqi cannot give up is writing. And she is quick to admit that she takes it far too seriously, and she procrastinates. "When you are used to reading great writers' work such as Marquez, you know you are not writing well enough. But when you know you fail to write what you ideally want to, that's painful."

Jiayin (Born in 1990): Eyes on Me

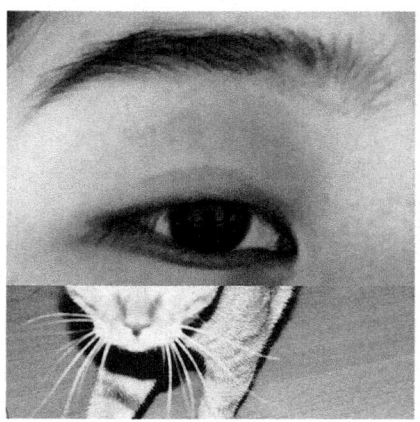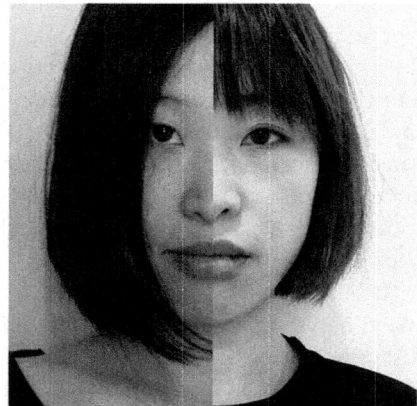

While Miss P brings one pastiche image, Jiayin presents a pair, made up of four different photos, taken by different persons, from different perspectives, including that of the cat—like Jin.

First, the cat-plus-Jiayin image. The photo of the cat was taken by Jiayin's boyfriend, who posted it after they split up, when they had lost contact for a year and a half. "When I was travelling in Istanbul, I saw this photo posted by him. I saved it, as some memento of us." Recalling her relationship with the cat, not with her boyfriend, Jiayin returned to four years ago, when she was a university student. It was a stray cat she came across in her neighbourhood. While Vera reminds me of Fanjie in *Ode to Joy*, Jiayin acts not unlike Xiaoqu in the drama series. She fed the cat for three months before she decided to take it home. "He was abandoned, which made him different from other cats. Some neighbours said the cat was kept by a Korean student and when the student returned home, the cat was left behind. I felt that the cat was hurt emotionally. That's why he was very close to me." Jiayin calls it "mutual healing" between the hurt cat and herself. "When I took him home, I was living on my own. We kept each other company." The cat's photo represents her lonely moments in Shanghai; only the cat was there. "The cat witnessed all the emotional changes of mine. He saw me cry, he saw me laugh." To Jiayin, as much as to Jin, it did feel like having a child, and it helped her become softer. She felt that the cat and her became alike, particularly the eyes. That is why Jiayin decided to paste her own eyes onto the cat's face.

The other image is a combination of Jiayin's portraits at different times in her life. She refers to our last interview when she was in a relationship. "One of the portraits was taken when I was applying for a visa with a plan to travel with my boyfriend. I was jobless at that point." Jiayin wanted to travel and relax, to readjust her life. This portrait, like the cat photo, was taken by her boyfriend. "My last job was not very nice. I was lost." Jiayin's "workshop" [a small-scale creative business] had financial problems, and was disbanded suddenly, shortly after it started up. "My previous job was with a publishing house, for three years. I had never experienced such sudden change in working conditions." Jiayin also remembers the time when she decided to quit the publishing house job as she had become too familiar with it. She wanted to look for challenges out of her "comfort zone." But then, after the brevity of the new job, Jiayin was left at home, with nothing to do. It so happened that her boyfriend had some time off at that point, so they decided to go on vacation. "But then, I really didn't know what would happen in the future."

The other portrait was taken by Jiayin's current colleague, for her trip with her mother, their very first after she started working. Both portraits were taken for visa applications, no make-up, same size. "But this one was taken last year, when I had found a job I liked. Although the salary was not that high, I liked my boss' vision and concept of work." After saving up some money, and when her mom mentioned her wish to travel, Jiayin proposed making a trip. She put the two portraits together because she wants to highlight her change. Recall how Miss P put the two halves of the panda together similarly to highlight her wish to change? "I can sense the change in my eyes … I feel that I like my current state better. I'm probably more determined. So I want to use this to represent some crossover." It is not only about her work. "Now that me and my boyfriend are no longer together, I feel that I am doing quite good." Compared with the period when Jiayin was still with him, "I'm more certain of what I want."

Jiayin names these images "Eyes on Me," after her favourite song performed by Faye Wong, a Chinese pop diva, known for her eccentricity in both her vocal and lifestyles. "I am a designer, I have to work overnight all the time. There are always black circles around my eyes." Jokes aside, Jiayin explains: "I was attracted to eyes even as a child. And my current work is also connected to eyes [designing spectacles]. I find it coincidental."

OCEAN (BORN IN 1990): KING OF THE PACK

The image was created by Ocean herself, in 2013, when she first started working. "I like drawing things. At that point, I wanted to draw myself as a 'king' in a pack of playing cards. So, I drew this." The image shows two different versions of the same person. Unlike the pastiche works of Miss P and Jiayin, with the motif of change, Ocean's drawing shows, rather, the core complexity of herself. "It's like who I usually am. Sometimes, I am very quiet, not talking much. But sometimes, I can be very crazy." This is how Ocean describes the two sides of herself. "During fun time, I want to be loud, I want to have fun with friends, becoming mad, getting high." Like going to music festivals, drinking, and dancing; she elaborates with expansive gestures. "During quiet moments, I want to talk to myself, not to others. Sometimes you just need to talk to yourself. And stay home, reading, drawing." The shapes of the shirt necks in the images are telling: the upper figure wears something with a V-neck while the lower one has a round neck. "I feel that roundness is more casual and friendly, and the V shape is more loud and outstanding." The two hair styles are also different, both hers. "When I go to work, I will keep my hair down. When I go to have fun, I want to be a bit loud, and I will use gel to push it up." According to Ocean, the bob hair style gives her a sense of security, say, when she is with strangers. Nevertheless, the bob in the image does not cover the entire forehead, which Ocean explains as a characteristic of her hair: somewhat unkempt.

Ocean explains the difference between photography and drawing, which is her favourite. She always carries a notebook with her, so that she can draw whenever she fancies. "Photos are taken for fun. Like selfies. It's about the moment." And photo taking is configured by the circumstances, the context. "I went to an exhibition today. I took some photos. But they were confined by the exhibition context." Drawing is categorically different. "If I draw, I can draw the inside of my heart, the complexity, the different sides." Ocean found it difficult to select one image to represent herself. In the end, she chose this playing card image, which is her own work. She has used this image as her portrait for quite some time.

The playing card idea and image came to her when she, a designer, came across a pack of cards, and it immediately appealed to her. "At first, I wanted to draw more than the faces, at least also the torsos. But then I realized I didn't have the space. So, I decided to put an H there, the short form of my [Chinese] name." And the wavy patterns and the symbols used are associated with "ocean," her English name as well as the English equivalent of her family name. What would be the images in her mind if she was to draw the torsos? Equally split. "I would make the upper one more rock-and-roll like, say, wearing a denim jacket with holes, and a T-shirt, and the lower one with a more sentimental old T-shirt, or linen shirt, that sort of thing." Why black and white? "Laziness," Ocean replies simply. "I have a notebook. When I have nothing else to do, I will draw something like this. It's like making a record of my life, a bit like a diary. That's why I don't use colours. Black and white is faster."

To illustrate the spontaneity of her drawing practice, Ocean produces a couple of images from her phone (which are not printed here). One is based on a group of six beer-drinking photos. One shows her in the snow. Ocean's desire is to draw better, and differently. If she has to draw another image of herself, perhaps it would be more abstract, probably because she has started to realize that her appearance may not always reflect reality; she may use something more abstract, perhaps the ocean itself.

Her wish remains to draw the rest of the pack, her own pack of playing cards.

JENNIFER (BORN IN 1976): FROM HUMAN TO HORSE

Jennifer brings two images. Again, an animal; the horse image was something she did for a psychology course. The teacher asked: which animal best represents you, or, which animal do you want to become? Jennifer asked a friend of hers to draw a horse. "Horses are good looking, and flexible. It's not the kind of cunning flexibility, but the carefree kind." And, "You can't tell if it's male or female." Particularly its eyes, according to Jennifer, show good-heartedness. She used it as her social media portrait for a couple of days, but then, took it down. "Too girlish. I am no longer that kind of age." The image represents at least part of her, Jennifer says. "The truthful part. I was rather lost for a while." What is truthfulness to her? "Well, you think you know something, but when you try to communicate and articulate it, you find you don't really know it. So now when I try to say something, I ask myself, if I truly understand what it means. For instance, when I say: I want love, do I truly know what love is?" That, to her, is truthfulness.

"Love is when two souls can communicate, and are sexually integrated." Has she experienced the kind of love she now believes in? "No. I only know better now." While discovering the knowing in not knowing, Jennifer also finds a certain sense of liberation. She cites a Chinese saying: Life is precious, love has more value, but both can be discarded, for freedom. "Everybody has heard of this, but we are not doing it." For her, "I just go ahead, step by step, and see. No one knows what tomorrow brings." But we should remember who we are. Looking at the horse image again, Jennifer clarifies that she does not like animation, except the works of Japanese master Hayao Miyazaki, particularly the Oscar-winning *Spirited Away*. She remembers the scene when the girl in the film is told: "This is your name, no matter what, you never forget your name, never forget who you are."

The other image, also drawn by a friend, is based on a photo sent by Jennifer. Like Ocean and Jiayin, Jennifer draws connection between the image and her appearance: "The woman in the image is sharp, capable, modern, and her feminine features are pronounced. That is what I looked for at a certain stage of my life." Before 2012, Jennifer says, she was rather masculine, wearing sombre colours, hiding her feminine characteristics, so that she might look capable, fierce. It was partly because of the demands of work, and partly because she was on her own in Shanghai. There was also another reason. "I was used to being the eldest child, being the pillar of the family. I was trained to feel like a man. I even used the word 'sissy' to ridicule other people, including women." After her divorce, she realized it would be difficult for her to survive with a masculine, strong-woman image. "Suddenly, I realized I must return to the femininity market." She lost weight, going from 65 kg to 55 kg. She lost weight since she decided she should walk to work. With her weight loss, the curves of her body reappeared, and so did her confidence. And she also started to wear sexy clothes, with more colours.

With the passing of both of her parents within the space of a year, Jennifer says, "I thought things through, and I started to look for something that would make me feel at peace." She used to live for someone else, and at the same time, she knows, it was a wish to control that someone. After all, you contribute, say, your money, so you want something back. Now, her parents are no longer there, she also feels there is no particular demand, or urge, in her life. Jennifer says she should be content with her current life, but she is not. Turning to her work, Jennifer reflects on the 10 years at the European luxury brand she has been working for. "Well, at my age, I know what I am capable of, and what I am not. My biggest headache is: I don't know what I want. I am still trying to find out what kind of life I want." She remained, as the job was well paid, and was sufficient for her to support her family. Now, she stays because she does not know which type of job she really wants, a conundrum not unlike Miss P's when she talks about the image of herself she created.

Jennifer brings two images, one of a human, and one of an animal. "I think they show my change: from searching for outward things to caring more for inward things." She is learning *guqin*, a Chinese musical instrument. And indeed, she has joined the fragrance workshop that she said she would try at the end of our last interview, a year earlier.

LULU (BORN IN 1990): LOOKING FOR A PLACE

Distinct from the other images that readily evoke work, Lulu's image concerns home-making. It is a photo taken when she was looking for a place to rent for the second time in Shanghai. "When I first rented a place in Shanghai, I didn't realize I could be kicked out any time. I thought we could stay longer. But then, the first year expired, our landlord told us he would sell the place. And then, the new landlord didn't want to continue the lease." Lulu was a student when she did her first home search in Shanghai. She had more time. This second time, she was working. She and her flatmate could only do the viewings after work. They saw a lot of places, but in the end, they failed to find one that was suitable. It was depressing, especially when it was close to the end of the year and they planned to return to their home towns for Spring Festival holidays. If they could not find a new place in time, it would be complicated. "We thought of taking a walk along Suzhou River. That was the first time I had been there that late. And then, suddenly, we turned back and saw how beautiful it was!" They became cheerful: "Oh what the heck, it's so beautiful. Let's take a photo!" The two women went onto a footbridge and tried out all sorts of poses for snapshots. Since both of them were foodies, they made use of the good mood to put aside the renting problem and look for something good to eat.

In the end, they found a place to rent, a bit far out. And they moved further and further away due to the continuous hike of property prices in Shanghai. "Since my working hours were flexible, I didn't have to fight the crowds. It was OK. But it was challenging for my flatmate." Lulu was working for a multimedia company centred around an influential blogger-writer. In November 2016, her father got ill. She went to Qingdao, her hometown, to take care of him. He passed away in July 2017. She decided to stay there, to keep her mother company, and also, to take care of her. Her image, however, is of her in Shanghai, trying to find a home. The move from Shanghai to Qingdao, and the changes in the last year, mean "growth" to Lulu. Regarding work, her old colleagues continue to send her design projects, and her old company keeps her on as a part-timer. Slowly, she has developed into a more mature freelancer. Regarding her private life, Lulu has experienced the death of a dear one.

When she had decided to stay in Qingdao, she and her mother did some improvement work on the family house. "Mainly to accommodate my books, my tools," the essentials of her design work. "I really like my work, actually more and more." But when she first moved back to Qingdao, she was struggling. She is Scorpio, and "somewhat introvert." Lulu realized she did not have any friends in Qingdao. So was her social life in Shanghai when she first moved there. However, when she got her second job, at the multimedia company, her colleagues were her contemporaries. They got along very well. "I have actually never experienced the kind of harsh working environment people talk about. I would say my working life was happier than my study life." She gradually overcame her homesickness. As she saw "progress" in her work, she grew to cherish her job.

Lulu calls her colleagues-cum-friends *guimi*, a popular term referring to intimate friends, particularly female. Her boss, born in the 1980s, is one of them. She says, there was "No competition among us. If there was, it was only the positive kind." They had dinners at weekends, throwing parties together, playing "truth or dare," and occasionally *tucao*, airing grievances, to one another. Lulu was particularly touched by one episode in her work and social life. Her father was ill and Lulu had to fly back to Qingdao. Before she returned to Shanghai, she told her colleagues her arrival information. "They set up a secret WeChat group. They waited for me at the airport. They even made a banner, to receive me. I wasn't a crying person, but I was deeply touched."

Qingdao, Lulu observes, does not have an active creative scene, unlike Shanghai. Still, she is determined to work as a designer with a stronger accent on creativity, and less on commerciality. She calls it "spiritual mysophobia." Luckily, she has the support of her colleagues. "I am very grateful that clients keep coming along. Whenever I get anxious about the next client, thinking that I may be running out of projects, there comes a new client. I really think I am lucky." Lulu has thought of starting her own workshop, but probably not yet. "Anyway, I am quite determined never to have a real job." Lulu connects character traits of people to what she is learning: astrology. "Gradually, I have come to understand that it's not superstitious at all. Before learning astrology, I found it difficult to come to terms with some people. Now, with astrology, I can see people more objectively."

This year, a year of change and growth, Lulu also broke up with her boyfriend. And back in Qingdao, there are "no opportunities" at all to try something new, Lulu says. As a freelancer, she stays home often. Recently, she started jogging. "You don't have to think of anything while jogging. Just listening to music. It's nice." Initially, she resisted jogging, as much as she resisted trying watercolours—a good supplement to her design, she knows. "But then, I remembered what one friend said to me: you should always do the things you don't want to." In Qingdao, Lulu misses friends who can offer her such advice. "I am quite lonely," she says. In the image, Lulu's face is almost totally covered, striking a pose symbolically, reminiscent of Siqi's woman with her back to the viewer. "I have a nickname: big face cat. So, when I take photo, I usually cover a bit of my face. That day, when my flatmate wanted to take my photo, I instinctively covered it."

Lulu did not only cover her face; she had also draped a scarf over her body, not against the camera, but against the cold. It was an exceptionally cold day, she remembers.

YVONNE (BORN IN 1987): THREE PARTS OF MY LIFE

Yvonne brings four images with her, to represent the "three parts of my life." The first one she talks about was taken shortly before the interview, in April 2017. She was making a wish in Lamma Temple, Beijing. Yvonne had travelled to Beijing for a Kunqu performance. "Everyone knows I love Kunqu," she says, as passionately as when Ocean talks about her drawing. That trip, however, was rather complicated. For her television work, Yvonne was supposed to make a site visit to Eastern Europe around that time. "But then I thought, no way. First of all, I am not 100 per cent needed for the visit. Also, I don't want to travel more than once a year." Another visit had been scheduled for May. The Beijing performance, starring her favourite master, was one she had missed several times. She could not allow herself to miss it again. The day before the performance, Yvonne heard that the master had tripped during rehearsal. "He's over 70. Everyone was worried." That day, she happened to have an appointment with friends close to the Lama Temple; on the spur of the moment, she decided to go there to pray for the master. "Basically, whichever statue I came across, I made a wish that the show would be all right."

Both this photo and the panda one were taken by a female friend who, as she says, "always takes nice photos of me … our 'revolutionary friendship' is about having fun together." It was the day after Yvonne returned from the Eastern European trip that they met up. They went to a shopping mall, planning to have dinner together. There, they saw the huge panda. "It looks like you," her friend said, "Want to take a photo with it?" Yvonne also recalled her "idol," another Kunqu master, who was often referred to as a national treasure, just like the panda. "The panda looks like your idol. It looks like you. You should take a photo!" So she did. Talking about having idols, Yvonne's own idols are mostly late Kunqu masters. "You know, that evening, the Beijing performance did go smoothly. If I could learn anything from it, it's this: what I like is getting more and more scarce. What I like to see, to touch, to experience, is getting more and more scarce." There, in the shopping mall, next to the huge panda, Yvonne struck a pose she described as *maimeng*, a vernacular Chinese term suggesting cuteness, usually associated with young women. "I take cuteness as a form of relaxation. Perhaps it's because during work I don't really have any opportunity to be cute." Yvonne's work requires her to be strong. "Our profession is like this: women are used as men, and men as beasts." She needs to be strong during work, but then in her after-work life: "I can do this *maimeng* too!" At almost 30, she continues collecting "sonny angels"—a cute boy angel figure created in Japan. "I have about 60 of them." And she likes taking photos with cute figures. "I am Libra, I am the kind of person who would do such a pose."

A Libra hates to choose. "I am afraid of making choices," Yvonne says, "If somehow, the choice is made for me, I can blame the gods." She would rather do things impulsively. Like how she ended up enrolling in her university in Beijing, rather than staying in Shanghai, her home town. Born to unusual family circumstances, Yvonne grew up not with her parents but with her grandmother. An educated woman herself, granny did not impose restrictions on the young Yvonne. As the only girl in the family, Yvonne was actually pampered. It was granny who told her about the alternative in Beijing and Yvonne got her place "through ignorance and fearlessness." Her impulsive entrance into this line of creative education led to her television job, which delivers the other two images Yvonne shows of herself. One was taken during a Spring Festival show in 2016, her second time, when she was much less anxious than the year before. "I remember one big problem during the first. The backstage was huge." Her job was to make sure all the performers would be ready and she had to run around all the time. "I kept on running." The image she brings represents a more relaxed Yvonne at work. They were shooting a fragment written by her. It was the last shoot for her, the last day of work, also the last time she worked with the retiring chief director. She flashed a bright smile. "I am happy, and relaxed … It was a good stage of my work, I travelled with the wind. Things were under my control."

The other image is quite the opposite. We only see her back, sitting, waiting—waiting for a vehicle. "It was a hapless situation, in Innsbruck, our first day of shooting." It was the Eastern Europe trip Yvonne mentioned earlier. "My first reality show. I had always been doing variety shows, never reality shows. And it was on site: even more complicated." The person in charge of the shooting was a new collaborator of hers. "He never listened to me," Yvonne says. The artists involved were also new to her, and their accommodation was poor. "We stayed in a youth hostel. Bunkbeds. The four of us. We used their lobby to have work meetings." That was the first time Yvonne felt so helpless during her television work. She thought, "Is this my show? Is this who I have become?" After leading a smooth working life for six years, she felt a full stop at that point—the sense of being lost also articulated by Miss P and Jennifer. "I needed to face a new start." Subsequently, Yvonne took various courses, including scriptwriting and Kunqu performance.

Thus are the three parts of Yvonne: her fan life, her "normal" everyday life, and her work life. What she has not brought are images from her non-work-related trips. Yvonne travels a lot. "It feels like I'm charging myself up," she compares herself to her smartphone. During her trips, she would ask herself: "Should I continue the way I do? Is this strange way of life good?" She is quick to add: "Perhaps the point is not to look for a correct answer. I just want to confirm myself again, reminding myself not to forget why I am doing what I am doing." In the end, "it's important to be happy."

After All

Nine sets of images. Nine women. They responded positively to the invitation to join this exercise in visual methodology, telling us, explicitly or not, how they would treat this invitation. Yvonne tells us that when she received the invitation, she thought about it, and decided to confine her choices to images taken this year, which, to her, would be the best to represent her. Miss P assures us she did not choose her images casually or perfunctorily: "Why would I? It's not like I am obliged to do this." This exercise in visual methodology confirms, above all, their familiarity and adroitness with visual culture in particular, and with creative practices in general. They offer lucid accounts of their thinking processes before deciding on the images. They are also sharply aware of the participatory and collaborative nature of such an act of meaning production. Time and again, Vera iterates to the researcher, "If you didn't ask me, I would have never thought about it." They have also volunteered to tell us the transitional, momentary aspect of their choosing, to the extent that some of them do give the impression that if they take a lot of pictures, their goal is not so much a "documenting of the self" or a narcissistically directed practice,[26] but to underline precisely the transitional, momentary aspects of their everyday life, of who they are. After all, one of the strongest claims formulated by the single women about their images is the difficulty, if not utter impossibility, to represent themselves. In Jin's words, "It's actually difficult to find an image that really represents me. It's too difficult. First, we don't really know ourselves. And you are changing all the time, and it takes a long, long time to know oneself. I find it too difficult."

With this caveat in mind, they do present images to us; some, more than one. In so far as the visual data collected and the narrative accounts thus constructed can be understood as their active contribution and their manner of representing themselves not so much to the world at large, but to the academic world embodied in the researchers they encountered, these single women want to tell us something. First, there are the things I may have overlooked. I could think of, for instance, the relationship between single womanhood and animals. Quite a few bring with them images of animals and talk readily about their relationships with them. I could also think of a more in-depth investigation—in addition to what has been covered or uncovered in earlier rounds of interviews—of their growing-up and their familial backgrounds, not only with their parents, but also with siblings and grandparents. I could think of their belief systems. I refer to *yuanfen* (also mentioned in Chap. 5), when they talk about their love lives. At the same time, they frequently mention horoscopes and astrological knowledge in connection with the paths they take in their lives. I could think of charting their creative trajectory or biography, taking hints from their citations of films, books, theatre plays, and authors. And I feel indebted particularly to those who created the images for this methodological exercise. I could think of focusing on the aesthetics of their creative works, instead of, or in addition to, treating them as essentially representational. These works can be taken in their own right as objects of aesthetic analysis, and the creators as creators.[27]

At the same time, I could also try to read these images and accounts in the analytical frameworks discussed in Chap. 2. By and large, their lives do demonstrate the tension between subscription to the norms of modernity and subservience to the demands of tradition, between the wish to be an independent, autonomous woman and the ties of the family, as well as the social pressures that make this difficult. Yes, their lives can be understood in those terms. However, for now, I want to suspend such reading and framing, precisely to affirm the singularity of these single women, to foreground their personal narratives as a way to complicate, if not to interrogate, the grand narratives circulated about them. It is a different way to present the feminist struggle and empowerment from the argument that Chang's research team makes in their study on the profile pictures that young Chinese women post on their WeChat accounts. In their study, "middle-class" women opt for a moderate, non-confrontational tactic to "realize self-empowerment and self-identification by choosing and editing their profile pictures."[28] Drawing attention to the importance of Confucian values and the state-driven campaign to promote a harmonious society, the authors note that "all of our interviewees, despite their various ways of 'resisting' gender norms, eventually fell back on their desire to create a more harmonious social reality for themselves where they could handle their life and the world with more ease."[29]

The single women in Chap. 8 mobilize different images and narrations to show their aspirations to be happy, quiet, relaxed, and similar states of being, but using slightly different terminology. They may be collectivized into an aspiration to handle their lives and the world with more ease. At the same time, what is remarkable about this exercise of self-representation is precisely a concomitant refusal to be represented, at least not in the sense of being fixated on any understanding of their lives and themselves. In the paradoxical seriousness of choosing the images, and thus, the narratives to be constructed, and the recalcitrant clarification that no image can represent themselves, that the images are inevitably transitional and momentary—in such paradox, they articulate not so much a longing for a harmonious social reality, but precisely the very element that such harmony may be disturbed: change, and the insistence on as well as possibility for this. Whatever they were, they became different. Whatever they are, they would again transform. Jennifer's dual image of herself and the horse, and her articulation of the change from an appearance-dependent way of managing her life to a state of being anchored to inner attributes is perhaps the most explicit, but by no means exceptional statement. They know they will change, inevitably. They may not have articulated, as the young women in Chang et al.'s study, the Western articulation of gender equality, but I hesitate to call it pro-harmony, neo-liberal, and post-feminist. Instead, I want to highlight this: they embrace change, with struggles and content, pain and pleasure, precarity and caring. And therein, lies their politics.

Notes

1. See Gillian Rose, *Visual Methodologies: An Introduction to Researching with Visual Materials,* 2001. Reprint, 3rd edition (London: Sage, 2012); Luc Pauwels, "Visual Sociology Reframed: An Analytical Synthesis and Discussion of Visual Methods in Social and Cultural Research," *Sociological Methods & Research* 38, no. 4 (2010): 545–81.
2. Gillian Rose, "On the Relation between 'Visual Research Methods' and Contemporary Visual Culture," *The Sociological Review* 62, no. 1 (2014): 24–46.
3. Andrew Clark and Lisa Morriss, "The Use of Visual Methodologies in Social Work Research over the Last Decade: A Narrative Review and Some Questions for the Future," *Qualitative Social Work* 16, no. 1 (2017): 29–43.
4. See Marcus Banks, *Visual Methods in Social Research* (London: Sage, 2001); Sarah Pink, *Doing Visual Ethnography,* 3rd Edition (London:

SAGE, 2013); Rose, *Visual Methodologies*. Note also that Gillian Rose prefers the term "visual research methods" or VRM (2014).

5. See Caleb Gattegno, *Towards a Visual Culture* (New York: Dutton, 1969); James Agee, *Let Us Now Praise Famous Men: Three Tenant Families* (Boston: Houghton Mifflin, 1941); Gregory Bateson and Margaret Mead, *Balinese Character, a Photographic Analysis* (New York: The New York Academy of Sciences, 1942).

6. See Banks, *Visual Methods in Social Research*; David Gauntlett, *Creative Explorations: New Approaches to Identities and Audiences* (London: Routledge, 2007); Caroline Knowles and Paul Sweetman, "Introduction," in *Picturing the Social Landscape: Visual Methods and the Sociological Imagination*, ed. Caroline Knowles and Paul Sweetman (Routledge, 2004), 1–17.

7. See Joseph Wherton et al., "Designing Assisted Living Technologies 'in the Wild': Preliminary Experiences with Cultural Probe Methodology," *BMC Medical Research Methodology* 12 (2012): 188; Linda Liebenberg, "The Visual Image as Discussion Point: Increasing Validity in Boundary Crossing Research," *Qualitative Research* 9, no. 4 (2009): 441–67; Dawn Mannay, "Making the Familiar Strange: Can Visual Research Methods Render the Familiar Setting More Perceptible?," *Qualitative Research* 10, no. 1 (2010): 91–111; Kim Rasmussen and Søren Smidt, "Children in the Neighbourhood: The Neighbourhood in the Children," in *Children in the City: Home Neighbourhood and Community*, ed. Pia Christensen and Margaret O'Brien (London: Routledge, 2003), 82–100; Allen White et al., "Using Visual Methodologies to Explore Contemporary Irish Childhoods," *Qualitative Research* 10, no. 2 (2010): 143–58.

8. See Alisha Ali, Emily Sharp, and Shira Meged, "Youth Empowerment and the Digital Representation of Self: Lessons from the PhotoCLUB Project," *Journal of Art for Life* 7, no. 1 (2016); Martin Lindstrom, *BrandChild: Remarkable Insights into the Minds of Today's Global Kids and Their Relationship with Brands* (London: Kogan Page, 2004); James U. McNeal, *The Kids Market: Myths and Realities* (New York: Paramount, 1999).

9. See Judit Fullana, Maria Pallisera, and Montserrat Vilà, "Advancing towards Inclusive Social Research: Visual Methods as Opportunities for People with Severe Mental Illness to Participate in Research," *International Journal of Social Research Methodology* 17, no. 6 (2014): 723–38; Victoria J. Palmer, Christopher Dowrick, and Jane M. Gunn, "Mandalas as a Visual Research Method for Understanding Primary Care for Depression," *International Journal of Social Research Methodology* 17, no. 5 (2014): 527–41.

10. Claudia Mitchell, *Doing Visual Research* (London: Sage, 2011).

11. Ali, Sharp, and Meged, "Youth Empowerment and the Digital Representation of Self"; Mitchell, *Doing Visual Research*.

12. Nigel Meager, "Children Make Observational Films—Exploring a Participatory Visual Method for Art Education," *International Journal of Education Through Art* 13, no. 1 (2017): 7–22.

13. See Buckingham, "'Creative' Visual Methods in Media Research"; Clark and Morriss, "The Use of Visual Methodologies in Social Work Research over the Last Decade."

14. Rose, *Visual Methodologies*, xviii.

15. Luc Pauwels distinguishes two kinds of visual materials: pre-existing visual materials and researcher-instigated visuals. For the purpose of this inquiry, I do not consider it necessary to confine the participants in their choice of what to represent them. See Luc Pauwels, *Reframing Visual Social Science: Towards a More Visual Sociology and Anthropology* (Cambridge: Cambridge University Press, 2015).

16. Pauwels, *Reframing Visual Social Science*, 27.

17. Knowles and Sweetman, "Introduction."

18. Rose, "On the Relation between 'Visual Research Methods' and Contemporary Visual Culture," 2.

19. See Béatrice S. Hasler and Doron A. Friedman, "Sociocultural Conventions in Avatar-Mediated Nonverbal Communication: A Cross-Cultural Analysis of Virtual Proxemics," *Journal of Intercultural Communication Research* 41, no. 3 (2012): 238–59; Zhong Zhi-Jin and Mike Zhengyu Yao, "Gaming Motivations, Avatar-Self Identification and Symptoms of Online Game Addiction," *Asian Journal of Communication* 23, no. 5 (2013): 555–73; Paolo Gerbaudo, "Protest Avatars as Memetic Signifiers: Political Profile Pictures and the Construction of Collective Identity on Social Media in the 2011 Protest Wave," *Information, Communication & Society* 18, no. 8 (2015): 916–29.

20. See Jesse Fox and Margaret C. Rooney, "The Dark Triad and Trait Self-Objectification as Predictors of Men's Use and Self-Presentation Behaviors on Social Networking Sites," *Personality and Individual Differences* 76, no. Supplement C (2015): 161–65; Yasmin Ibrahim, "Self-Representation and the Disaster Event: Self-Imaging, Morality and Immortality," *Journal of Media Practice* 16, no. 3 (2015): 211–27; Derek Conrad Murray, "Notes to Self: The Visual Culture of Selfies in the Age of Social Media," *Consumption Markets & Culture* 18, no. 6 (2015): 490–516.

21. See Ana Sofia Elias and Rosalind Gill, "Beauty Surveillance: The Digital Self-Monitoring Cultures of Neoliberalism," *European Journal of Cultural Studies*, 2017, 1–19; Ursula Oberst, Andrés Chamarro, and Vanessa Renau, "Gender Stereotypes 2.0: Self-Representations of Adolescents on Facebook," *Estereotipos de Género 2.0: Auto-Representaciones de Adolescentes En Facebook*. 24, no. 48 (2016): 81–89; Dian A. de Vries and Jochen Peter, "Women on Display: The Effect of Portraying the Self Online on Women's

Self-Objectification," *Computers in Human Behavior* 29, no. 4 (2013): 1483–89; Betsy Emmons and Richard Mocarski, "She Poses, He Performs: A Visual Content Analysis of Male and Female Professional Athlete Facebook Profile Photos," *Visual Communication Quarterly* 21, no. 3 (2014): 125–37.

22. Chang Jiang, Ren Hailong, and Yang Qiguang, "A Virtual Gender Asylum? The Social Media Profile Picture, Young Chinese Women's Self-Empowerment, and the Emergence of a Chinese Digital Feminism," *International Journal of Cultural Studies*, 2016, 1–16; Murray, "Notes to Self."

23. See Lu Ye and Chu Yajie, "Media Use, Social Cohesion, and Cultural Citizenship: An Analysis of a Chinese Metropolis," *Chinese Journal of Communication* 5, no. 4 (2012): 365–82; Liu Tzu-kai, "Minority Youth, Mobile Phones and Language Use: Wa Migrant Workers' Engagements with Networked Sociality and Mobile Communication in Urban China," *Asian Ethnicity* 16, no. 3 (2015): 334–52; Lian Hongping, "The Resistance of Land-Lost Farmers in China," *Asia Pacific Journal of Public Administration* 36, no. 3 (2014): 185–200; Jeroen de Kloet and Anthony Y. H. Fung, *Youth Cultures in China* (Cambridge: Polity, 2017).

24. Chang, Ren, and Yang, "A Virtual Gender Asylum?"

25. The images are reproduced with the subjects' consent.

26. Edgar Gómez Cruz and Helen Thornham, "Selfies beyond Self-Representation: The (Theoretical) f(r)Ictions of a Practice," *Journal of Aesthetics & Culture* 7, no. 1 (2015): 1–10.

27. Yvette Wong, in her master's thesis on *wenyi qingnian* (文艺青年), roughly translated as literary youth, points to the same lacuna: studies on creative workers tend to overlook the aesthetic aspects of their work. Put crudely, creative workers are often taken more as workers and less as creative. See Wong Lok Yee, "The Poetics and Politics of Hong Kong *Wenyi Qingnian*" (Hong Kong Baptist University, 2017).

28. Chang, Ren, and Yang, "A Virtual Gender Asylum?" 13.

29. Ibid., 12.

REFERENCES

Agee, James. *Let Us Now Praise Famous Men: Three Tenant Families*. Boston: Houghton Mifflin, 1941.

Ali, Alisha, Emily Sharp, and Shira Meged. "Youth Empowerment and the Digital Representation of Self: Lessons from the PhotoCLUB Project." *Journal of Art for Life* 7, no. 1 (2016).

Banks, Marcus. *Visual Methods in Social Research*. London: Sage, 2001.

Bateson, Gregory, and Margaret Mead. *Balinese Character, a Photographic Analysis*. New York: The New York academy of sciences, 1942.

Buckingham, David. "'Creative' Visual Methods in Media Research: Possibilities, Problems and Proposals." *Media, Culture & Society* 31, no. 4 (2009): 633–52.

Chang, Jiang, Hailong Ren, and Qiguang Yang. "A Virtual Gender Asylum? The Social Media Profile Picture, Young Chinese Women's Self-Empowerment, and the Emergence of a Chinese Digital Feminism." *International Journal of Cultural Studies*, 2016, 1–16.

Clark, Andrew, and Lisa Morriss. "The Use of Visual Methodologies in Social Work Research over the Last Decade: A Narrative Review and Some Questions for the Future." *Qualitative Social Work* 16, no. 1 (2017): 29–43.

Cruz, Edgar Gómez, and Helen Thornham. "Selfies beyond Self-Representation: The (Theoretical) f(r)Ictions of a Practice." *Journal of Aesthetics & Culture* 7, no. 1 (2015): 1–10.

Elias, Ana Sofia, and Rosalind Gill. "Beauty Surveillance: The Digital Self-Monitoring Cultures of Neoliberalism." *European Journal of Cultural Studies*, 2017, 1–19.

Emmons, Betsy, and Richard Mocarski. "She Poses, He Performs: A Visual Content Analysis of Male and Female Professional Athlete Facebook Profile Photos." *Visual Communication Quarterly* 21, no. 3 (2014): 125–37.

Fox, Jesse, and Margaret C. Rooney. "The Dark Triad and Trait Self-Objectification as Predictors of Men's Use and Self-Presentation Behaviors on Social Networking Sites." *Personality and Individual Differences* 76, no. Supplement C (2015): 161–65.

Fullana, Judit, Maria Pallisera, and Montserrat Vilà. "Advancing towards Inclusive Social Research: Visual Methods as Opportunities for People with Severe Mental Illness to Participate in Research." *International Journal of Social Research Methodology* 17, no. 6 (2014): 723–38.

Gattegno, Caleb. *Towards a Visual Culture*. New York: Dutton, 1969.

Gauntlett, David. *Creative Explorations: New Approaches to Identities and Audiences*. London: Routledge, 2007.

Gerbaudo, Paolo. "Protest Avatars as Memetic Signifiers: Political Profile Pictures and the Construction of Collective Identity on Social Media in the 2011 Protest Wave." *Information, Communication & Society* 18, no. 8 (2015): 916–29.

Hasler, Béatrice S., and Doron A. Friedman. "Sociocultural Conventions in Avatar-Mediated Nonverbal Communication: A Cross-Cultural Analysis of Virtual Proxemics." *Journal of Intercultural Communication Research* 41, no. 3 (2012): 238–59.

Ibrahim, Yasmin. "Self-Representation and the Disaster Event: Self-Imaging, Morality and Immortality." *Journal of Media Practice* 16, no. 3 (2015): 211–27.

de Kloet, Jeroen, and Anthony Y. H. Fung. *Youth Cultures in China*. Cambridge: Polity, 2017.

Knowles, Caroline, and Paul Sweetman. "Introduction." In *Picturing the Social Landscape: Visual Methods and the Sociological Imagination*, edited by Caroline Knowles and Paul Sweetman, 1–17. Routledge, 2004.

Lian, Hongping. "The Resistance of Land-Lost Farmers in China." *Asia Pacific Journal of Public Administration* 36, no. 3 (2014): 185–200.

Liebenberg, Linda. "The Visual Image as Discussion Point: Increasing Validity in Boundary Crossing Research." *Qualitative Research* 9, no. 4 (2009): 441–67.

Lindstrom, Martin. *BrandChild: Remarkable Insights into the Minds of Today's Global Kids and Their Relationship with Brands*. London: Kogan Page, 2004.

Liu, Tzu-kai. "Minority Youth, Mobile Phones and Language Use: Wa Migrant Workers' Engagements with Networked Sociality and Mobile Communication in Urban China." *Asian Ethnicity* 16, no. 3 (2015): 334–52.

Lu, Ye, and Yajie Chu. "Media Use, Social Cohesion, and Cultural Citizenship: An Analysis of a Chinese Metropolis." *Chinese Journal of Communication* 5, no. 4 (2012): 365–82.

Mannay, Dawn. "Making the Familiar Strange: Can Visual Research Methods Render the Familiar Setting More Perceptible?" *Qualitative Research* 10, no. 1 (2010): 91–111.

McNeal, James U. *The Kids Market: Myths and Realities*. New York: Paramount, 1999.

Meager, Nigel. "Children Make Observational Films—Exploring a Participatory Visual Method for Art Education." *International Journal of Education Through Art* 13, no. 1 (2017): 7–22.

Mitchell, Claudia. *Doing Visual Research*. London: Sage, 2011.

Murray, Derek Conrad. "Notes to Self: The Visual Culture of Selfies in the Age of Social Media." *Consumption Markets & Culture* 18, no. 6 (2015): 490–516.

Oberst, Ursula, Andrés Chamarro, and Vanessa Renau. "Gender Stereotypes 2.0: Self-Representations of Adolescents on Facebook." *Estereotipos de Género 2.0: Auto-Representaciones de Adolescentes En Facebook*. 24, no. 48 (2016): 81–89.

Palmer, Victoria J., Christopher Dowrick, and Jane M. Gunn. "Mandalas as a Visual Research Method for Understanding Primary Care for Depression." *International Journal of Social Research Methodology* 17, no. 5 (2014): 527–41.

Pauwels, Luc. *Reframing Visual Social Science: Towards a More Visual Sociology and Anthropology*. Cambridge: Cambridge University Press, 2015.

Pauwels, Luc. "Visual Sociology Reframed: An Analytical Synthesis and Discussion of Visual Methods in Social and Cultural Research." *Sociological Methods & Research* 38, no. 4 (2010): 545–81.

Pink, Sarah. *Doing Visual Ethnography*. 3rd Edition. London: SAGE, 2013.

Rasmussen, Kim, and Søren Smidt. "Children in the Neighbourhood: The Neighbourhood in the Children." In *Children in the City: Home Neighbourhood and Community*, edited by Pia Christensen and Margaret O'Brien, 82–100. London: Routledge, 2003.

Rose, Gillian. "On the Relation between 'Visual Research Methods' and Contemporary Visual Culture." *The Sociological Review* 62, no. 1 (2014): 24–46.

Rose, Gillian. *Visual Methodologies: An Introduction to Researching with Visual Materials.* London: Sage, 2012.

de Vries, Dian A., and Jochen Peter. "Women on Display: The Effect of Portraying the Self Online on Women's Self-Objectification." *Computers in Human Behavior* 29, no. 4 (2013): 1483–89.

Wherton, Joseph, Paul Sugarhood, Rob Procter, Mark Rouncefield, Guy Dewsbury, Sue Hinder, and Trisha Greenhalgh. "Designing Assisted Living Technologies 'in the Wild': Preliminary Experiences with Cultural Probe Methodology." *BMC Medical Research Methodology* 12 (2012): 188.

White, Allen, Naomi Bushin, Fina Carpena-Méndez, and Caitríona Ní Laoire. "Using Visual Methodologies to Explore Contemporary Irish Childhoods." *Qualitative Research* 10, no. 2 (2010): 143–58.

Wong, Lok Yee. "The Poetics and Politics of Hong Kong Wenyi Qingnian." MPhil thesis, Hong Kong Baptist University, 2017.

Zhong, Zhi-Jin, and Mike Zhengyu Yao. "Gaming Motivations, Avatar-Self Identification and Symptoms of Online Game Addiction." *Asian Journal of Communication* 23, no. 5 (2013): 555–73.

CHAPTER 9

Epilogue

To change, and to keep on changing. There, I pin my hope. As long as they want to change, look for change, and fear unchanging, there is hope for change.

This is a book about single womanhood and creative work. If this book, and the experiences of the women who have lynchpinned this book, has prompted the reader to start rethinking single womanhood, creative work, and the overcoded language of stigmatization, marginalization, insecurity, and precarization, I would consider myself as having achieved something. I would consider that I have not wasted the time of the women who agreed to speak with me, and trusted me. In Chap. 1, I mentioned my chance encounters with single women in China doing creative work. I mentioned my curiosity. But curiosity is one thing, researching it is another. What troubled me at the inception of this research project, and what guided me throughout my fieldwork, as well as this writing challenge, is the question: how dare I speak on *their* behalf? I am not a single woman. This question has never been resolved, but it morphed into a resolve to be cautious, careful, and to speak not for them, but *with* them. I rely on my own experience in creative work; I have been writing lyrics and prose, participating in art projects, and doing an assortment of other creative work, since the end of the 1980s. I also rely on my personal experience as someone who has been wrestling with issues of "Chineseness"— all the dominant heteronormative, familial, Confucian, state-sanctioned values that the so-called Chinese should subscribe to.[1] Listening to all of

© The Author(s) 2019
Chow Y. F., *Caring in Times of Precarity*, Palgrave Studies in
Globalization, Culture and Society,
https://doi.org/10.1007/978-3-319-76898-4_9

the single women I have come across, seeing them, feeling what they feel, I often think of the following quotation.

> Ours is essentially a tragic age, so we refuse to take it tragically. The cata-clysm has happened, we are among the ruins, we start to build up new little habitats, to have new little hopes. It is rather hard work: there is now no smooth road into the future: but we go round, or scramble over the obsta-cles. We've got to live, no matter how many skies have fallen.

These are the opening lines from *Lady Chatterley's Lover*.[2] D.H. Lawrence was outlining the position of the heroine of his novel, published in 1928, just a few years before Lu Xun described the "Shanghai Girls", cited in Chap. 1, as being between danger and glory. [3] It is despair, it is also hope-fulness. Such ambiguity, such complexity is what I have learned and intended. So, they *refuse*. They may have different accounts of discontent, different grievances, and negative experiences as single women doing cre-ative work in Shanghai, but taken in their entirety, they refuse to live oth-erwise. They take care of themselves; they are positive about themselves, about living their lives the way they are. Reverting to the politics of precar-ity this book has been engaging with, these single women do not assume otherwise; perhaps for these Chinese women, precarity is a human condi-tion known to them, suitable for them, and available to them. If I pose, as I did in Chap. 1, the question if "precarity" is a male-centric and Western-centric notion, I must reiterate that I do not mean to ignore the down sides of all these precarious lives of our time. I do not mean to ignore other experiences from women with other backgrounds. What I want to do is to foreground the gender and cultural specificities of the notion. Perhaps, for a lot of women, in a lot of different, but all profoundly globalized cultural contexts, precarity is what constitutes their very being. Perhaps for them, they cannot afford the kind of security, certainty, and predictability that men, particularly those in a more privileged context, can.

Again, I must stress that I am not trying to trivialize the pain, the suf-fering, and the huge amount of energy that these (as well as other) women need to negotiate their everyday lives, but I wonder if I can or should turn them into victims while, of course, resisting the temptation to treat them as heroes. The book takes as its fundamental mission, to seek alternative, if not better, ways to understand these women's lives in the context of contemporary China amidst a critique of global neo-liberalization and precarization of our times, to reformulate a possible politics with—not on behalf of—these women who may not experience themselves as part of the precariat. From this empirical scrutiny, from this group of women with their very specificities—single, doing creative work, living in Shanghai—I propose to revitalize the politics of recognition alongside the politics of redistribution, to recognize what the women in this book have done, and are capable of. They refuse what is expected of them, and they take care of themselves, but not always and not always successfully. It inspires, nonetheless, an ethics of care, a plea for more people to refuse what is expected of them, to live differently, to be more sure of their capacity to take care of themselves, despite and because of all the struggles. After all, they love *zheteng*. More precarity, more individuals, until something shakes, trembles, topples. As I said, I am not sure if this is better politics, but it is, at least, an alternative.

PRECARIOUS 摇摇欲坠

I cited the above Chinese translation of precarious in Chap. 1. Shortly after we decided on the term for our exhibition in Shanghai, I was having tea with three Chinese single female friends, all doing creative work. I asked them what they thought about the translation. With dazzling speed and wit, they played with the sound of the Chinese term *yaoyao yuzhui*—one said, "I want *yaoyao yuzui*," another said, "I want *yaoyao yushui*," and the third woman said, "I want *yaoyao yutui*." While *zhui* denotes toppling, collapsing, *zui* (醉), *shui* (睡), and *tui* (退) refer, respectively, to getting drunk, going to sleep, and retiring.[4] In this book, I have cited, I think substantially, the stress and anxiety of their lives, work and love lives, and the ways they take care of themselves: the *zui* and *shui* dimensions of their lives. I have not enquired into or written enough about *tui*, and the related thematic of aging. This is what I am going to do for my next project: to study the intersection of age with single womanhood and creative work.[5]

Talking about what I am going to do urges me to think of what I have failed to do. I want to flag up two fronts: activism and creativity.

Throughout this book, I have argued that singlism is not only about the marginalization, and stigmatization of single women, but also about the reductionist way of seeing them as marginalized and stigmatized; and from the politics of precarity, I have attempted a move towards an ethics of care. It begs, I must admit, the question of whether such ethics can be translated into activist practices, and if yes, how. When the women in this inquiry demonstrate to us their myriad of ways of taking care of themselves in times of precarity—as singletons and as creative workers—they do so, by and large, as individuals, not necessarily or consciously as part and parcel of a social movement. I have explained why in Chap. 1. But then, in that case, one may wonder if any ethics of care can constitute, or collectivize these individual practices into any moment or momentum of feminist activism in contemporary China, and if yes, how. As much as I have failed to address the activism issue, I have also left an important dimension of their work largely unexamined. I tried marginally, in the previous chapter, to mobilize their creativity and to reproduce their creative outputs as a component of visual methodology. There, I have noted a research lacuna—that studies on creative workers tend to focus on "workers" rather than "creative"; they generally do not seek to understand the aesthetics of their creative work, for instance. In this study of single female creative workers, I have inherited this bias. My primary concern has been to recuperate their subjective accounts of work, particularly good work, and I have sought to converse with discussions on precarity, not on creativity. Subsequently, little attention has paid to their creative works, and their conception of creativity itself. Let me then end this book with a common, but nonetheless important appeal to knowledge co-production: I hope this articulation of what I have failed to do may somehow morph into further studies in the future.

NOTES

1. For a methodological reflection on me as a man doing research on diasporic Chinese women and beauty pageants, see Chow Yiu Fai, "Moving, Sensing Intersectionality: A Case Study of Miss China Europe," *Signs: Journal of Women in Culture and Society* 36, no. 2 (2011): 411–36. For an autographical essay on me as a creative practitioner, vis-à-vis issues of Chineseness, see Chow Yiu Fai, "Me and the Dragon: A Lyrical Engagement with the Politics of Chineseness," *Inter-Asia Cultural Studies* 10, no. 4 (2009): 544–64.
2. David Herbert Lawrence, *Lady Chatterley's Lover*, 1928. Reprint, New edition (Ware, Herfordshire: Wordsworth Editions, 2005).
3. See, again, Lu Xun, "Shanghai Girls," in *Lu Xun: Selected Works*, trans. Xianyi Yang and Gladys Yang, vol. 3 (Beijing: Foreign Languages Press, 1980), 332–33.
4. I used this episode to write a Chinese-language essay musing on the condition of contemporary Chinese women when I was invited by Fangsuo, a major bookstore chain in China, to contribute to their magazine feature on the said theme. See Chow Yiu Fai, "周耀辉:欲醉,欲退,欲睡 [Chow Yiu Fai:

To Drunk, to Retire, to Sleep]," 方所刊 *[Fangsuo Kan]*, March 8, 2015, https://site.douban.com/122554/widget/notes/15607165/note/487340549/.

5. For a book-length study on single womanhood from the perspective of time, see Kinneret Lahad, *A Table for One: A Critical Reading of Singlehood, Gender and Time* (Manchester: Manchester University Press, 2017). While Lahad's book takes texts primarily as its object of study, my following project (sponsored by the Hong Kong Research Grant Council, project number 12613117) will again be based on qualitative research tools tapping experiences from single women of different ages. See also Kinneret Lahad and Haim Hazan, "The Terror of the Single Old Maid: On the Insolubility of a Cultural Category," *Women's Studies International Forum* 47, no. Part A (2014): 127–36.

References

Chow, Yiu Fai. "Me and the Dragon: A Lyrical Engagement with the Politics of Chineseness." *Inter-Asia Cultural Studies* 10, no. 4 (2009): 544–64.

Chow, Yiu Fai. "Moving, Sensing Intersectionality: A Case Study of Miss China Europe." *Signs: Journal of Women in Culture and Society* 36, no. 2 (2011): 411–36.

Chow, Yiu Fai. "周耀辉:欲醉,欲退,欲睡 [Chow Yiu Fai: To Drunk, to Retire, to Sleep]." 方所刊 *[Fangsuo Kan]*, March 8, 2015. https://site.douban.com/122554/widget/notes/15607165/note/487340549/.

Lahad, Kinneret. *A Table for One: A Critical Reading of Singlehood, Gender and Time*. Manchester: Manchester University Press, 2017.

Lahad, Kinneret, and Haim Hazan. "The Terror of the Single Old Maid: On the Insolubility of a Cultural Category." *Women's Studies International Forum* 47, no. Part A (2014): 127–36.

Lawrence, David Herbert. *Lady Chatterley's Lover*. New edition. Ware, Herfordshire: Wordsworth Editions, 1928.

Lu, Xun. "Shanghai Girls." In *Lu Xun: Selected Works*, translated by Xianyi Yang and Gladys Yang, 3: 332–33. Beijing: Foreign Languages Press, 1980.

Appendix I

Anna	Born 1964, Hong Kong. Graduated from a local university, majoring in Business Management and Psychology. Joined the advertising industry upon graduation. Relocated to Shanghai in 2010 for work. Around the time of the interview, resigned from her senior position at an advertising firm. Returned to Hong Kong in 2016. Had a short-lived marriage. Single.
C	Born 1983, Guangzhou. Studied Business English at a local university, and has worked as a copywriter and editor. In 2010, started her own business, and in 2012, moved to Shanghai for work. Photographer. Single at the time of the interview, currently in a stable relationship.
Captain Zoey	Born 1992, Shanghai. Studied Broadcasting at a local university. Joined the advertising industry after a short internship in the broadcasting field. Currently, working as a copywriter in advertising. Single.
Jennifer	Born 1976, Wuhan. Received technical education at college. Relocated to Shanghai in 2000 with husband and daughter. Had worked as a brand designer for various foreign companies before joining a luxury label as senior designer. Divorced in 2011. Single.
Jiayin	Born 1990, Zhejiang Province. A graduate in Visual Communication at an art academy. Has worked for various publishing houses as well as design firms. At the time of the interview, was working on a branding project for a coffee shop, and was in a stable relationship. After breaking up with her boyfriend, is currently single, and working as an art director at an advertising firm.
Jin	Born 1982, Shanghai. Studied Communication at a local university, and has worked in print media and at a media agency as an editor and copywriter. At the time of the interview, was working as a journalist. Currently, a magazine journalist and running her own online platform. Single.

© The Author(s) 2019   293
Chow Y. F., *Caring in Times of Precarity*, Palgrave Studies in
Globalization, Culture and Society,
https://doi.org/10.1007/978-3-319-76898-4

JM   Born 1973, Shanghai. Studied Art in college. Joined an advertising firm as a
            designer after graduation. After resignation, has been dividing her time
            between freelancing for a 4A advertising agency and indulging in her own
            pursuits. Has a boyfriend, but has no plans to get married or live together.

Joy   Born 1981, Anhui Province. Completed her Maritime Studies in Shanghai.
            Started learning guitar and writing music after her university time. After
            graduation, took up different jobs before becoming an indie singer. Since
            2012, has released two albums. Currently, a singer-songwriter and artist.
            Single.

Lei   Born 1975, Xi'an. Studied Chinese at a local university, and has worked as
            programme host and reporter for various media companies in Xi'an and
            Beijing. Moved to Shanghai in 2008, and worked as TV talk-show host. In
            2016, resigned and started her current media platform business. Single, with a
            daughter.

LIV   Born 1979, Jiangxi Province. Studied Chinese at university. In 2002, resigned
            from her job at a local TV station, and moved to Shanghai to seek
            development. Has worked at various print media companies as a culture
            reporter. Currently, holding a senior position at a well-known fashion
            magazine. Single.

Lulu   Born 1990, Qingdao. Studied Interior Design at a university near her home
            town. After graduation, started working in Shanghai as an art editor and
            graphic designer. Moved back to Qingdao for personal reasons shortly after
            the interview. Currently, a freelance designer. At the time of the interview, had
            a boyfriend. Now single.

Mi   Born 1989, Shanghai. Received Master's degree in Journalism at a university
            in London. Has worked for different media platforms as a reporter and editor.
            At the time of the interview, was a reporter. Currently, a freelance writer. Was
            single then, but married in 2017.

Michelle   Born 1983, Shanghai. Studied Business English at a local university. Has
            worked as an editor for a video-streaming platform and as an entertainment
            news reporter. At the time of the interview, was working at an educational
            institution, responsible for new media management and brand-building.
            Currently, working in advertising and new media management. Single.

Miss P   Born 1977, Shanghai. Studied Packaging Design, and joined a 4A advertising
            agency as designer upon graduation. Had a short-lived marriage. At the time
            of the interview, was working as an art director at an advertising company.
            Currently, a freelance designer. Single.

Ocean   Born 1990, Urumqi. Studied Publishing and Printing, and had taken up jobs
            related to graphic and platform design. At the time of the interview, was
            working as a graphic designer for a music website. Now working as branding/
            graphic designer for a design studio. Single.

Siqi   Born 1991, Sichuan Province. Studied Translation at a university in Shanghai.
            Has worked for various media companies as a reporter and editor. Around the
            time of the interview, resigned from her journalist position at a financial
            newspaper. In 2016, moved to Beijing and worked for a music-related
            platform. In 2017, moved back to Shanghai to join a film project. Single.

Skipper   Born 1991, grew up in various Chinese cities. Studied Game Design at an art academy in Chicago. During the last year of her study, returned to China to work on her start-up in Shanghai, which she is currently managing. At the time of the interview, was single. Still single, but with a son.

Valerie   Born 1979, Hong Kong. Completed tertiary education in the United States before working in the local advertising industry. Returned to Hong Kong in 2003, and moved to Shanghai in 2014. Still in advertising. Single.

Vera   Born 1981, Shanghai. Studied Chinese at university. Has worked for various media companies as a copywriter, reporter, and editor. At the time of the interview, was embarking on a start-up of a branding business. Now, running a cultural media company. Single.

Weiwei   Born 1990, Anhui Province. Studied English at a university in Shanghai. Upon graduation, became an English language tutor. At the time of the interview, was working at a new media company as an editor. In 2017, moved to digital marketing. Single.

Xiaoqian   Born 1982, Shanghai. Studied Journalism at a local university. Has worked in various positions such as magazine editor, promotion director for a theatre company, and radio programme host. At the time of interview, was the content manager for a major online music platform, dividing her time between Hangzhou and Shanghai. Currently, Shanghai-based as a freelancer promoting music-makers and copywriting for music projects. Single.

Xiaoyan   Born 1976, Shanghai. Started learning Kunqu at home at a young age. Studied Japanese at a local university. In 2009, was hired to teach Kunqu at universities. Currently, dividing her time between Kunqu education and working for her family business. Single.

Yang   Born 1984, Hubei province. Studied Advertising at a university in Xiamen. Has worked in the media industry. In 2013, made use of her pottery training to start a related business. Divorced in the same year. At the time of the interview, was starting a new life with her son and transforming her pottery business into an online pottery information platform that aims at education and promotion of pottery art. Currently, in her second marriage.

Yvonne   Born 1987, Shanghai. Studied Television and Film at a drama school in Beijing. Since graduation, has been working in the television industry, responsible for large-scale variety shows, as well as creative writing. Single.

Zaizai   Born 1985, Shenyang. Studied Design at a local art college. Has worked as an animator and art director. In 2009, relocated to Shanghai to work in game development. Currently working on a VR project. Single.

Note: All names were suggested by the subjects themselves, and the biographical notes were updated in December 2017

Appendix II

Individual

Name	First Interview		Second Interview	
	Date/Time	Venue	Date/Time	Venue
Anna	19/03/15, 17:30	Anna's home	13/05/17, 10:00	Jiaotong University (Dong Chuan Road)
C	21/03/15, 12:00	Costa Coffee (iapm)	N/A	N/A
Captain Zoey	28/02/15, 16:30	Emi's Family Coffee by illy (Zhaojiabang Road)	16/03/17, 19:30	Marienbad Cafe (Wukang Road)
Jennifer	16/10/16, 11:00	Paras Coffee (South Shanxi Road)	25/03/17, 13:00	Starbucks (Hua Shan Road)
Jiayin	27/02/15, 16:00	Costa Coffee (iapm)	07/01/17, 13:00	Wages (South Huangpi Road)
Jin	27/02/15, 13:30	Costa Coffee (iapm)	16/01/17, 14:00	Wages (South Huangpi Road)
JM	16/10/16, 14:00	Starbucks (MetroCity)	N/A	N/A
Joy	09/03/15, 14:00	Costa Coffee (iapm)	13/03/17, 16:00	New York University Shanghai Cafe (Century Avenue)
Lei	18/10/16, 10:00	Email Coffee (Lianhua Road)	N/A	N/A

© The Author(s) 2019

Chow Y. F., *Caring in Times of Precarity*, Palgrave Studies in Globalization, Culture and Society, https://doi.org/10.1007/978-3-319-76898-4

Name	First Interview		Second Interview	
	Date/Time	Venue	Date/Time	Venue
LIV	17/10/16, 13:00	Costa Coffee (iapm)	17/04/17, 14:00	Bakerspice Restaurant (K11)
Lulu	10/03/15, 12:00	Costa Coffee (iapm)	12/12/16, 10:00	Jiaotong University (Dong Chuan Road)
Mi	28/02/15, 12:30	Emi's Family Coffee by illy (Zhaojiabang Road)	06/03/16, 12 noon	New Element, restaurant (near Jingan Temple)
Michelle	13/11/16, 14:00	Costa Coffee (iapm)	24/04/17, 20:00	Starbucks (People's Park)
Miss P	15/10/16, 14:00	Paras Coffee (South Shanxi Road)	11/05/17, 13:00	Starbucks (Hua Shan Road)
Ocean	16/03/15, 12:30	Spinelli Coffee (North Sichuan Road)	26/12/16, 14:00	Jiaotong University (Dong Chuan Road)
Siqi	10/03/15, 14:30	Costa Coffee (iapm)	11/03/17, 14:00	Wages (South Huangpi Road)
Skipper	02/03/15, 12:30	Emi's Family Coffee by illy (Zhaojiabang Road)	N/A	N/A
Valerie	17/03/15, 16:30	Costa Coffee (iapm)	10/06/17, 11:00	Skype interview
Vera	28/02/15, 14:30	Emi's Family Coffee by illy (Zhaojiabang Road)	18/01/17, 14:00	South Bridge (Zhenjiang Haixin District)
Weiwei	01/03/15, 16:00	Costa Coffee (iapm)	22/03/17, 19:30	Starbucks (Xingguo Road)
Xiaoqian	01/03/15, 13:30	Costa Coffee (iapm)	29/04/17, 15:00	Seesaw Cafe (iapm)
Xiaoyan	02/03/15, 15:00	Emi's Family Coffee by illy (Zhaojiabang Road)	27/03/17, 14:00	Seesaw Cafe (Century Avenue Bailian Mall)
Yang	26/02/15, 13:30	Villa Hut Kafe (West Nanjing Road)	26/09/17, 15:00	Jiaotong University (Dong Chuan Road)
Yvonne	26/02/15, 16:00	Villa Hut Kafe (West Nanjing Road)	15/01/17, 15:00	Wages (South Huangpi Road)
Zaizai	11/03/15, 12:30	Costa Coffee (iamp)	22/04/17, 12 noon	Little Catch, poke restaurant (near Nanjing West Road)

GROUP

Name	Time	Venue
Yue, He	04/03/17, 10:00	Nana's Green Tea (Century Avenue)
Jinzhou, Gu, Zheng	05/03/17, 21:00	Voice Call
Zhang, Yi	01/05/17, 19:30	SML Center (Xujiahui Road)
Yvonne, Xiaoyan, Michelle	12/11/16, 15:00	Costa Coffee (iamp)

BIBLIOGRAPHY

"2016年全国新闻出版业基本情况 [Overview of the National Press and Publication Industry in 2016]." 国家新闻出版广电总局 [State Administration of Press, Publication, Radio, Film and Television], 2017. http://www.sapprft.gov.cn/sapprft/govpublic/6677/1633.shtml.

Adey, Peter. *Mobility*. London: Routledge, 2009.

Agee, James. *Let Us Now Praise Famous Men: Three Tenant Families*. Boston: Houghton Mifflin, 1941.

Aldous, Joan, Emile Durkheim, and Ferdinand Tonnies. "An Exchange Between Durkheim and Tonnies on the Nature of Social Relations, with an Introduction by Joan Aldous." *American Journal of Sociology* 77, no. 6 (1972): 1191–1200.

Ali, Alisha, Emily Sharp, and Shira Meged. "Youth Empowerment and the Digital Representation of Self: Lessons from the PhotoCLUB Project." *Journal of Art for Life* 7, no. 1 (2016).

Allison, Anne. *Precarious Japan*. Durham: Duke University Press, 2013.

Anderson, Benedict. *Imagined Communities: Reflections on the Origin and Spread of Nationalism*. London: Verso, 1991.

Anderson, Jon, and Kathryn Erskine. "Tropophilia: A Study of People, Place and Lifestyle Travel." *Mobilities* 9, no. 1 (2014): 130–45.

Arkaraprasertkul, Non. "Traditionalism as a Way of Life: The Sense of Home in a Shanghai Alleyway." *Harvard Asia Quarterly* 15, no. 3/4 (2013): 15–25.

Banks, John, and Mark Deuze. "Co-Creative Labour." *International Journal of Cultural Studies* 12, no. 5 (2009): 419–31.

Banks, Marcus. *Visual Methods in Social Research*. London: Sage, 2001.

© The Author(s) 2019
Chow Y. F., *Caring in Times of Precarity*, Palgrave Studies in Globalization, Culture and Society,
https://doi.org/10.1007/978-3-319-76898-4

Banks, Mark, and Justin O'Connor. "After the Creative Industries." *International Journal of Cultural Policy* 15, no. 4 (2009): 365–73.

Barton, Kristin M., and Jonathan Malcolm Lampley, eds. *Fan CULTure: Essays on Participatory Fandom in the 21st Century*. NC: McFarland, 2014.

Bateson, Gregory, and Margaret Mead. *Balinese Character, a Photographic Analysis*. New York: The New York academy of sciences, 1942.

Beck, Ulrich. *What Is Globalization*. Cambridge: Polity, 2000.

Beck, Ulrich, and Elisabeth Beck-Gernsheim. *Individualization: Institutionalized Individualism and Its Social and Political Consequences*. London: Sage, 2002.

Bennett, Tony, Mike Savage, Elizabeth Bortolaia Silva, Alan Warde, Modesto Gayo-Cal, and David Wright. *Culture, Class, Distinction*. London: Routledge, 2009.

Berlant, Lauren. *Cruel Optimism*. Durham: Duke University Press, 2011.

Berry, Chris. "Representing Chinese Women: Researching Women in the Chinese Cinema." In *Dress, Sex and Text in Chinese Culture*, edited by Antonia Finnane, 198–211. Clayton: Monash Asia Institute, 1999.

Berry, Chris, and Mary Ann Farquhar. *China on Screen: Cinema and Nation*. New York, NY: Columbia University Press, 2006.

Bhandari, Bibek. "Down to Fraud? Five Jailed for Scamming Singles," December 8, 2017. http://www.sixthtone.com/news/1001362/down-to-fraud%3F-five-jailed-for-scamming-singles.

Bird, S. Elizabeth. "Are We All Produsers Now?" *Cultural Studies* 25, no. 4–5 (2011): 502–16.

Blackshaw, Tony. *Key Concepts in Community Studies*. London: SAGE Publications, 2010.

Blau, Melinda, and Karen L. Fingerman. *Consequential Strangers: Turning Everyday Encounters into Life-Changing Moments*. New York: W. W. Norton & Company, 2009.

Blecher, Marc. *China Against the Tides: Restructuring Through Revolution, Radicalism and Reform*. New York: Continuum, 2003.

Bodenhamer, David J., Trevor M. Harris, and John Corrigan. "Deep Mapping and the Spatial Humanities." *International Journal of Humanities and Arts Computing* 7, no. 1–2 (2013): 170–75.

Boyle, Mark. "Culture in the Rise of Tiger Economies: Scottish Expatriates in Dublin and the 'Creative Class' Thesis." *International Journal of Urban and Regional Research* 30, no. 2 (2006): 403–26.

Bragg, Melvyn. *Grace and Mary*. London: Sceptre, 2014.

Branigan, Tania. "Five Chinese Feminists Held over International Women's Day Plans." *The Guardian*, March 12, 2015, sec. World news. http://www.theguardian.com/world/2015/mar/12/five-chinese-feminists-held-international-womens-day.

"Breaking Out: China's Youth Finally Dare to Be Different." *Time*, February 2, 2004.

Breman, Jan. "A Bogus Concept?" *New Left Review*, no. 84 (2013): 130–38.

Bristow, Jennie. *The Sociology of Generations: New Directions and Challenges.* London: Palgrave Macmillan, 2016.

Brough, Paula, Jackie Holt, Rosie Bauld, Amanda Biggs, and Claire Ryan. "The Ability of Work—Life Balance Policies to Influence Key Social/Organisational Issues." *Asia Pacific Journal of Human Resources* 46, no. 3 (2008): 261–74.

Bruns, Axel. *Blogs, Wikipedia, Second Life, and Beyond: From Production to Produsage.* New York: Peter Lang, 2008.

Buckingham, David. "'Creative' Visual Methods in Media Research: Possibilities, Problems and Proposals." *Media, Culture & Society* 31, no. 4 (2009): 633–52.

Büscher, Monika, John Urry, and Katian Witchger. "Introduction: Mobile Methods." In *Mobile Methods*, edited by Monika Büscher, John Urry, and Katian Witchger, 1–19. London: Routledge, 2010.

Butler, Judith. "Merely Cultural." *New Left Review*, no. 227 (1998): 33–44.

Butler, Judith. *Precarious Life: The Powers of Mourning and Violence.* London: Verso, 2004.

Cai, Shenshen. *Television Drama in Contemporary China: Political, Social and Cultural Phenomena.* London; New York: Routledge, 2016.

Carr, D. Jasun, Melissa R. Gotlieb, Nam-Jin Lee, and Dhavan V. Shah. "Examining Overconsumption, Competitive Consumption, and Conscious Consumption from 1994 to 2004: Disentangling Cohort and Period Effects." *The ANNALS of the American Academy of Political and Social Science* 644, no. 1 (2012): 220–33.

Casas-Cortés, Maribel. "A Genealogy of Precarity: A Toolbox for Rearticulating Fragmented Social Realities in and out of the Workplace." *Rethinking Marxism* 26, no. 2 (2014): 206–26.

Cattani, Gino, and Simone Ferriani. "A Core/Periphery Perspective on Individual Creative Performance: Social Networks and Cinematic Achievements in the Hollywood Film Industry." *Organization Science* 19, no. 6 (2008): 824–44.

de Certeau, Michel. *The Practice of Everyday Life.* Berkeley: University of California Press, 2011.

Chang, Jiang, Hailong Ren, and Qiguang Yang. "A Virtual Gender Asylum? The Social Media Profile Picture, Young Chinese Women's Self-Empowerment, and the Emergence of a Chinese Digital Feminism." *International Journal of Cultural Studies*, 2016, 1–16.

Chantler, Khatidja. "What's Love Got to Do with Marriage?" *Families, Relationships and Societies* 3, no. 1 (2014): 19–33.

Chen, Chaochen. "How Beijing Opera Eclipsed Kun Opera in Chinese Sociocultural and Sociopolitical Contexts." Master's Thesis, California State University, 2011a.

Chen, Guiqin (陈桂琴). "试论女性时尚杂志中的女性角色问题 [Discussions on the Issues of Female Characters in Women Fashion Magazines]." 新闻学硕士论文 [MA thesis of Journalism], 暨南大学 [Chi Nan University], 2003.

Chen, Jian, and Rong Lian. "Generational Differences in Work Values in China." *Social Behavior and Personality: An International Journal* 43, no. 4 (2015): 567–78.

Chen, Kuan-Hsing. *Asia as Method: Toward Deimperialization.* Durham, NC: Duke University Press, 2010.

Chen, Siyu. "Disciplining Desiring Subjects through the Remodeling of Masculinity: A Case Study of a Chinese Reality Dating Show." *Modern China* 43, no. 1 (2017): 95–120.

Chen, Xiuming (陳秀明). "出国与抱负 [Leaving the Country and the Aspiration]." *出国与就业 (Working and Going Abroad)*, no. 7 (2001): 25–27.

Chen, Yaya (陈亚亚). "孤单也可精彩:都市单身女性之生存状态考察 [Lonely Can Be Wonderful: An Investigation of the Living Status of Urban Single Women]." In *The Influence of Gender*, 148–59. Shanghai: Shanghai Academy of Social Sciences, Gender and Development Centre, 2014.

Chen, Zhou. "The Embodiment of Transforming Gender and Class: Shengnü and Their Media Representation in Contemporary China." Thesis, University of Kansas, 2011b.

Cheng, Hong, and Guofang Wan. "Holding up Half of the 'Ground': Women Portrayed in Subway Advertisements in China." In *Commercializing Women: Images of Asian Women in the Media*, edited by Katherine Toland Frith and Kavita Karan. USA: Hampton Press, 2008.

Cherlin, Andrew J. "The Deinstitutionalization of American Marriage." *Journal of Marriage and Family* 66, no. 4 (2004): 848–61.

Chew, Matthew. "Contemporary Re-Emergence of the Qipao: Political Nationalism, Cultural Production and Popular Consumption of a Traditional Chinese Dress." *The China Quarterly* 189 (2007): 144–61.

Chong, Gladys Pak Lei. *Chinese Subjectivities and the Beijing Olympics.* London: Rowman & Littlefield International, 2017.

Chow, Rey. "Fetish Power Unbound: A Small History of 'Woman' in Chinese Cinema." In *The Oxford Handbook of Chinese Cinemas*, edited by Carlos Rojas and Eileen Chow. Oxford Handbooks. Oxford, New York: Oxford University Press, 2013.

Chow, Yiu Fai. "Exploring Creative Class Mobility: Hong Kong Creative Workers in Shanghai and Beijing." *Eurasian Geography and Economics*, 2017a, 1–25.

Chow, Yiu Fai. "Hong Kong Creative Workers in Mainland China: The Aspirational, the Precarious, and the Ethical." *China Information* 31, no. 1 (2017b): 43–62.

Chow, Yiu Fai. "Hope Against Hopes: Diana Zhu and the Transnational Politics of Chinese Popular Music." *Cultural Studies* 25, no. 6 (2011a): 783–808.

Chow, Yiu Fai. "Martial Arts Films and Dutch–Chinese Masculinities: Smaller Is Better." *China Information* 22, no. 2 (2008): 331–59.

Chow, Yiu Fai. "Me and the Dragon: A Lyrical Engagement with the Politics of Chineseness." *Inter-Asia Cultural Studies* 10, no. 4 (2009): 544–64.

Chow, Yiu Fai. "Moving, Sensing Intersectionality: A Case Study of Miss China Europe." *Signs: Journal of Women in Culture and Society* 36, no. 2 (2011b): 411–36.

Chow, Yiu Fai. "Subcultures: Role of Media." In *The International Encyclopedia of Media Effects*. New Jersey: John Wiley & Sons, Inc., 2017c.

Chow, Yiu Fai. "The Aspiration, the Precarious, the Ethical: Hong Kong Creative Workers in Mainland China." *China Information*, Forthcoming.

Chow, Yiu Fai. "周耀辉:欲醉,欲退,欲睡 [Chow Yiu Fai: To Drunk, to Retire, to Sleep]." 方所刊 *[Fangsuo Kan]*, March 8, 2015.

Chow, Yiu Fai, and Jeroen de Kloet. *Sonic Multiplicities: Hong Kong Pop and the Global Circulation of Sound and Image*. Bristol, UK; Chicago, USA: Intellect Books, 2013.

Chow, Yiu Fai, Sonja van Wichelen, and Jeroen de Kloet. "Introduction: At Home in Asia? Place-Making, Belonging and Citizenship in the Asian Century." *International Journal of Cultural Studies* 19, no. 3 (2016): 243–56. https://site.douban.com/122554/widget/notes/15607165/note/487340549/.

Chumley, Lily. *Creativity Class: Art School and Culture Work in Postsocialist China*. Princeton: Princeton University Press, 2016.

Clark, Andrew, and Lisa Morriss. "The Use of Visual Methodologies in Social Work Research over the Last Decade: A Narrative Review and Some Questions for the Future." *Qualitative Social Work* 16, no. 1 (2017): 29–43.

Clifford, James. *Routes: Travel and Translation in the Late Twentieth Century*. Cambridge: Harvard University Press, 1997.

Cloke, Paul J., Phil Crang, and Mark A. Goodwin, eds. *Introducing Human Geographies*. London: Hodder Arnold, 2005.

Cochran, Tanya R. "The Browncoats Are Coming! Firefly, Serenity, and Fan Activism." In *Investigating Firefly and Serenity: Science Fiction on the Frontier*, edited by Rhonda V. Wilcox and Tanya R. Cochran, 239–50. London: I.B. Tauris, 2008.

Conor, Bridget, Rosalind Gill, and Stephanie Taylor. "Gender and Creative Labour." *The Sociological Review* 63, no. 1_suppl (2015a): 1–22.

Conor, Bridget, Rosalind Gill, and Stephanie Taylor. eds. "Special Issue: Gender and Creative Labour." *The Sociological Review* 63, no. 1_suppl (2015b).

Corré, Anne. "Ik Wil Er 't Allerbeste van Maken." *NRC Handelsblad*, April 8, 2017, sec. E14–E15.

Cpianalysis. "Overseas Study as 'Escape Route' for Young Chinese Women." *China Policy Institute: Analysis* (blog), June 22, 2016. https://cpianalysis.org/2016/06/22/single-and-mobile-overseas-study-as-escape-route-for-young-chinese-women/.

Cresswell, Tim. *Place: A Short Introduction*. Oxford: Blackwell, 2004.

Cruz, Edgar Gómez, and Helen Thornham. "Selfies beyond Self-Representation: The (Theoretical) f(r)Ictions of a Practice." *Journal of Aesthetics & Culture* 7, no. 1 (2015): 1–10.

Cui, Xiaolu (崔小璐). "高知大龄未婚女性的婚恋问题浅析 [A Brief Analysis of the Love and Marriage Problems about the Older Educated Unmarried Women]." *Northwest Population Journal* 32, no. 5 (2011): 58–62, 68.

Cullen, Fin. "'Two's up and Poncing Fags': Young Women's Smoking Practices, Reciprocity and Friendship." *Gender and Education* 22, no. 5 (2010): 491–504.

Curtin, Michael, and Kevin Sanson. *Precarious Creativity: Global Media, Local Labor.* Oakland, CA: University of California Press, 2016.

Dai, Jinhua. "Imagined Nostalgia." Translated by Judy T. H. Chen. *Boundary 2* 24, no. 3 (1997): 143–61.

Dai, Jinhua (戴锦华). "不可见的女性:当代中国电影中的女性与女性的电影 [Invisible Women: Women and Female Films in Contemporary Chinese Cinema]." 当代电影 *[Contemporary Cinema]*, no. 6 (1994): 37–45.

Dai, Jinhua (戴锦华). "性别与叙事:当代中国电影中的女性 [Gender and Narration: Women in Contemporary Chinese Films]." 天涯 *[Tianya]* 11, no. 5 (2003).

Dai, Juncheng, Shangyi Zhou, Michael Keane, and Qian Huang. "Mobility of the Creative Class and City Attractiveness: A Case Study of Chinese Animation Workers." *Eurasian Geography and Economics* 53, no. 5 (2012): 649–70.

Dai, Wei (戴维). "《欢乐颂》大结局了 我们和神秘的作者阿耐聊了聊 ["Ode to Joy" Finale: Chatting with the Mysterious Author A-Nai]." 都市快报 *[Dushi Kuaibao]*. May 15, 2016. http://hzdaily.hangzhou.com.cn/dskb/html/2016-05/15/content_2263672.htm.

Dales, Laura. "Ohitorisama, Singlehood and Agency in Japan." *Asian Studies Review* 38, no. 2 (2014): 224–42.

Dales, Laura. "Single Women and Their Households in Contemporary Japan." In *The Global Political Economy of the Household in Asia*, edited by Juanita Elias and Samanthi J. Gunawardana, 110–126. Basingstoke: Palgrave Macmillan, 2013.

D'Andrea, Anthony, Luigina Ciolfi, and Breda Gray. "Methodological Challenges and Innovations in Mobilities Research." *Mobilities* 6, no. 2 (May 1, 2011): 149–60.

Das Gupta, Monica, Ethan Jennings Sharygin, and Avraham Ebenstein. "China's Marriage Market and Upcoming Challenges for Elderly Men." The World Bank, 2010. http://documents.worldbank.org/curated/en/948771468212988136/Chinas-marriage-market-and-upcoming-challenges-for-elderly-men.

Davis, Deborah S., and Sara L. Friedman, eds. *Wives, Husbands and Lovers: Marriage and Sexuality in Hong Kong, Taiwan, and Urban China.* Stanford: Stanford University Press, 2014.

Department of Culture, Media, and Sport. "Creative Industries Mapping Documents." London: DCMS, 2001.

DePaulo, Bella. "Holiday Spirit, 21st Century Style: Kay Trimberger and I Share Our Vision." *Living Single* (blog), November 23, 2008. http://www.psychologytoday.com/blog/living-single/200811/holiday-spirit-21st-century-style-kay-trimberger-and-i-share-our-vision.

DePaulo, Bella M., and Wendy L. Morris. "Singles in Society and in Science." *Psychological Inquiry* 16, no. 2–3 (2005): 57–83.

Donald, Stephanie Hemelryk, Yin Hong, and Michael Keane, eds. *Media in China: Consumption, Content and Crisis.* London; New York: Routledge, 2014.

Donner, Henrike, and Gonçalo Santos. "Love, Marriage, and Intimate Citizenship in Contemporary China and India: An Introduction." *Modern Asian Studies* 50, no. 4 (2016): 1123–46.

Dou, Wenyu, Guangping Wang, and Nan Zhou. "Generational and Regional Differences in Media Consumption Patterns of Chinese Generation X Consumers." *Journal of Advertising* 35, no. 2 (2006): 101–10.

Du, Yaquan (杜亚泉). "个人之改革 [Reforming the Individual]." In 杜亚泉卷(中国近代思想家文库) [*Du Yaquan Volume (Chinese Modern Thinkers Collection)*]. Beijing: 中国人民大学出版社 [People's University Press], 1914.

Dubrofsky, Rachel E. *The Surveillance of Women on Reality Television: Watching The Bachelor and The Bachelorette.* Lanham: Lexington Books, 2011.

Duffy, Brooke Erin. "The Romance of Work: Gender and Aspirational Labour in the Digital Culture Industries." *International Journal of Cultural Studies* 19, no. 4 (2016): 441–57.

Durkheim, Emile. "A Review of Ferdinand Tönnies's Gemeinschaft Und Gesellschaft: Abhandlung Des Communismus Und Des Socialismus Als Empirischer Culturformen." *American Journal of Sociology* 77 (1972): 1193.

Ehrenreich, Barbara. *Nickel and Dimed: On (Not) Getting By in America.* New York: Holt Paperbacks, 2010.

Ehrenreich, Barbara, Elizabeth Hess, and Gloria Jacobs. "Beatlemania: Girls Just Want To Have Fun." In *The Adoring Audience: Fan Culture and Popular Media*, edited by Lisa A. Lewis, 84–106. London: Routledge, 2002.

Elias, Ana Sofia, and Rosalind Gill. "Beauty Surveillance: The Digital Self-Monitoring Cultures of Neoliberalism." *European Journal of Cultural Studies*, 2017, 1–19.

Emmons, Betsy, and Richard Mocarski. "She Poses, He Performs: A Visual Content Analysis of Male and Female Professional Athlete Facebook Profile Photos." *Visual Communication Quarterly* 21, no. 3 (2014): 125–37.

Ettlinger, Nancy. "Precarity Unbound." *Alternatives* 32, no. 3 (2007): 319–40.

Evans, Elizabeth. *Transmedia Television: Audiences, New Media, and Daily Life.* London: Routledge, 2011.

Evans, Harriet. *The Subject of Gender: Daughters and Mothers in Urban China.* Maryland: Rowman & Littlefield, 2008.

Fan, Lu (范璐). "江苏卫视下战书:《非诚勿扰》不怕模仿 [Jiangsu Television Welcomes Competition: 'If You Are the One' Is Not Afraid to Be Imitated]." *Shanxi Wanbao [山西晚报]*, May 27, 2010. http://media.people.com.cn/GB/40724/11715400.html.

Fan, Shenggen, Xibao Zhang, and Arjan de Haan. *Narratives of Chinese Economic Reforms: How Does China Cross the River?* Singapore; Hackensack, NJ: World Scientific, 2010.

Fan, Yali (樊亚丽). "电视剧《欢乐颂》的人物形象塑造与时代美学精神 [The Construction of Character Image and the Spirit of Contemporary Aesthetics in TV Series 'Ode to Joy']." 当代电影 *[Contemporary Cinema]*, no. 7 (2016): 13–19.

Fang, Hanming, Quanlin Gu, Wei Xiong, and Li-An Zhou. "Demystifying the Chinese Housing Boom." *NBER Macroeconomics Annual* 30, no. 1 (2016): 105–66.

Farrer, James. "Love, Sex, and Commitment. Delinking Premarital Intimacy from Marriage in Urban China." In *Wives, Husbands and Lovers: Marriage and Sexuality in Hong Kong, Taiwan, and Urban China*, edited by Deborah S. Davis and Sara L. Friedman, 62–96. Stanford: Stanford University Press, 2014.

Felton, Emma, Christy Collis, and Phil Graham. "Making Connections: Creative Industries Networks in Outer-Suburban Locations." *Australian Geographer* 41, no. 1 (2010): 57–70.

Feng, Yun (冯芸). "苏州的昆曲传承:昆曲曲社的历史变迁 [Suzhou Kunqu de Chuancheng: Kunqu Qushe de Lishi Bianqian]." 中国音乐 *[Zhongguo Yinyue]*, no. 3 (2010): 47–53.

Ferguson, Marjorie. *Forever Feminine: Women's Magazines and the Cult of Femininity.* Exeter, NH: Heinemann, 1983.

Ferry, Megan M. "Advertising, Consumerism and Nostalgia for the New Woman in Contemporary China." *Continuum* 17, no. 3 (2003): 277–90.

Feuchtwang, Stephan, and Athar Hussain, eds. *The Chinese Economic Reforms.* London: Croom Helm, 1983.

Fishzon, Anna. *Fandom, Authenticity, and Opera: Mad Acts and Letter Scenes in Fin-de-Siècle Russia.* Basingstoke: Palgrave Macmillan, 2013.

Florida, Richard. *The New Urban Crisis: How Our Cities Are Increasing Inequality, Deepening Segregation, and Failing the Middle Class and What We Can Do About It.* New York: Basic Books, 2017.

Florida, Richard. *The Rise of the Creative Class.* New York: Basic Books, 2002.

Foord, Jo. "Strategies for Creative Industries: An International Review." *Creative Industries Journal* 1, no. 2 (2009): 91–113.

Foucault, Michel. "On the Genealogy of Ethics: An Overview of Work in Progress." In *The Foucault Reader*, edited by Paul Rabinow, 340–72. New York: Pantheon, 1984.

Foucault, Michel. "The Subject and Power." *Critical Inquiry* 8, no. 4 (1982): 777–95.

Fox, Jesse, and Margaret C. Rooney. "The Dark Triad and Trait Self-Objectification as Predictors of Men's Use and Self-Presentation Behaviors on Social

Networking Sites." *Personality and Individual Differences* 76, no. Supplement C (2015): 161–65.

France, Alan, and Steven Roberts. "The Problem of Social Generations: A Critique of the New Emerging Orthodoxy in Youth Studies." *Journal of Youth Studies* 18, no. 2 (2015): 215–30.

Fraser, Nancy. "A Rejoinder to Iris Young." *New Left Review*, I, no. 223 (1997): 126–29.

Fraser, Nancy. "From Redistribution to Recognition? Dilemmas of Justice in a 'Post-Socialist' Age." *New Left Review*, no. 212 (1995): 68–93.

Fu, Jian (傅坚), and Qu Fuqiang (屈富强). "国内顶级红娘:相亲收费最高超千万 Top Domestic Matchmaker: Blind Date Fees up to 10 Million]." 长江商报 *[ChangJiang Shangbao]*, December 30, 2015. http://news.sohu.com/20151230/n432980363.shtml.

Fuchs, Christian. "Labor in Informational Capitalism and on the Internet." *The Information Society* 26, no. 3 (2010): 179–96.

Fullana, Judit, Maria Pallisera, and Montserrat Vilà. "Advancing towards Inclusive Social Research: Visual Methods as Opportunities for People with Severe Mental Illness to Participate in Research." *International Journal of Social Research Methodology* 17, no. 6 (2014): 723–38.

Fung, Anthony Y. H., and John Nguyet Erni. "Cultural Clusters and Cultural Industries in China." *Inter-Asia Cultural Studies* 14, no. 4 (2013): 644–56.

Furlong, Andy, Dan Woodman, and Johanna Wyn. "Changing Times, Changing Perspectives: Reconciling 'Transition' and 'Cultural' Perspectives on Youth and Young Adulthood." *Journal of Sociology* 47, no. 4 (2011): 355–70.

Gaetano, Arianne. "Single Women in Urban China and the 'Unmarried Crisis': Gender Resilience and Gender Transformation." In *Working Papers in Contemporary Asian Studies; No. 31*. Lund: Centre for East and South East Asian Studies, Lund University, 2010.

Garnaut, Ross, and Ligang Song, eds. *China: Twenty Years of Economic Reform*. Canberra: Asia Pacific Press, 1999.

Garnham, Nicholas. "From Cultural to Creative Industries." *International Journal of Cultural Policy* 11, no. 1 (2006): 15–29.

Gattegno, Caleb. *Towards a Visual Culture*. New York: Dutton, 1969.

Gauntlett, David. *Creative Explorations: New Approaches to Identities and Audiences*. London: Routledge, 2007.

Genz, Stéphanie, and Benjamin A. Brabon. *Postfeminism: Cultural Texts and Theories*. Edinburgh: Edinburgh University Press, 2009.

Gerbaudo, Paolo. "Protest Avatars as Memetic Signifiers: Political Profile Pictures and the Construction of Collective Identity on Social Media in the 2011 Protest Wave." *Information, Communication & Society* 18, no. 8 (2015): 916–29.

Gibson, Chris, and Lily Kong. "Cultural Economy: A Critical Review." *Progress in Human Geography* 29, no. 5 (2005): 541–61.

Giddens, Anthony. *The Transformation of Intimacy: Sexuality, Love, and Eroticism in Modern Societies*. 1st edition. Stanford: Stanford University Press, 1992.

Gill, Rosalind. "Empowerment/Sexism: Figuring Female Sexual Agency in Contemporary Advertising." *Feminism & Psychology* 18, no. 1 (2008): 35–60.

Gill, Rosalind. "Unspeakable Inequalities: Post Feminism, Entrepreneurial Subjectivity, and the Repudiation of Sexism among Cultural Workers." *Social Politics* 21, no. 4 (2014): 509–28.

Gill, Rosalind, and Andy Pratt. "In the Social Factory?: Immaterial Labour, Precariousness and Cultural Work." *Theory, Culture & Society* 25, no. 7–8 (2008): 1–30.

Glaeser, Edward L. "Are Cities Dying?" *The Journal of Economic Perspectives* 12, no. 2 (1998): 139–60.

Glaeser, Edward L. "Cities, Information, and Economic Growth." *Cityscape* 1, no. 1 (1994): 9–47.

Gong, Xiaobing (恭小兵). "总结:关于80后 [Summarizing: About the Post-80s]." 天涯论坛 *[Tianya Luntan]*, July 11, 2003. http://bbs.tianya.cn/post-210-2-1.shtml.

Goode, Erich, and Nachman Ben-Yehuda. "Moral Panics: Culture, Politics, and Social Construction." *Annual Review of Sociology* 20 (1994): 149–71.

Gordon, Tuula. *Single Women: On the Margins?* Women in Society (Houndmills, Basingstoke, England). Basingstoke: Macmillan, 1994.

Gornick, Vivian. *The Odd Woman and the City: A Memoir*. New York: Farrar, Straus and Giroux, 2015.

Granovetter, Mark S. "The Strength of Weak Ties." *American Journal of Sociology* 78, no. 6 (1973): 1360–80.

Gregg, Melissa. *Work's Intimacy*. London: Polity Press, 2011.

Grossberg, Lawrence. "Is There a Fan in the House? The Affective Sensibility of Fandom." In *The Adoring Audience: Fan Culture and Popular Media*, edited by Lisa A. Lewis, 50–65. London: Routledge, 1992.

Gu, Duhuang (顾笃璜). "苏州昆曲曲家与道和曲社 [Suzhou Kunqu Qujia Yu Daohe Qushe]." 文匯報 *[Wenhui Bao]*, May 18, 2015.

Guo, Shaohua. "When Dating Shows Encounter State Censors: A Case Study of If You Are the One." *Media, Culture & Society* 39, no. 4 (2017): 487–503.

Guo, Yingde (郭英德). 明清传奇史 *[Mingqing Chuanqi Shi]*. Nanjing: Jiangsu guji chubanshe, 1999.

Gurova, Olga, and Daria Morozova. "Creative Precarity? Young Fashion Designers as Entrepreneurs in Russia." *Cultural Studies* 32, no. 5 (2018a): 704–26.

Gurova, Olga, and Daria Morozova. "Creative Precarity? Young Fashion Designers as Entrepreneurs in Russia." *Cultural Studies* 32, no. 5 (2018b): 704–26.

Hall, Stuart. "Encoding/Decoding." In *Culture, Media, Language: Working Papers in Cultural Studies*, edited by Centre for Contemporary Cultural Studies. London: Hutchinson, 1980.

Han, Yujuan (韩玉娟). "新世纪家庭伦理剧女性形象变迁 [Changes of Female Representation in Family Drama of the New Century]." 艺术科技 [*Yishu Keji*], no. 3 (2015): 52–53.

Hansen, Høgni Kalsø, and Thomas Niedomysl. "Migration of the Creative Class: Evidence from Sweden." *Journal of Economic Geography* 9, no. 2 (2009): 191–206.

Harré, Rom. *Social Being: A Theory for Social Psychology.* Basil Blackwell, 1979.

Hartley, John. "Creative Industries." In *Creative Industries*, edited by John Hartley, 1–40. Oxford: Blackwell, 2005.

Harvey, David. *Rebel Cities: From the Right to the City to the Urban Revolution.* London; New York: Verso Books, 2012.

Harvey, David. "The Right to the City." *New Left Review*, II, no. 53 (2008): 23–40.

Hasler, Béatrice S., and Doron A. Friedman. "Sociocultural Conventions in Avatar-Mediated Nonverbal Communication: A Cross-Cultural Analysis of Virtual Proxemics." *Journal of Intercultural Communication Research* 41, no. 3 (2012): 238–59.

Hatton, Celia. "Boyfriends for Hire to Beat China's Wedding Pressure." *BBC News*, February 7, 2013, sec. China. http://www.bbc.com/news/world-asia-china-21192131.

Hay, James, and Nick Couldry. "Rethinking Convergence/Culture." *Cultural Studies* 25, no. 4–5 (2011): 473–86.

He, Wei, and Hui Zheng. "Under the One Child Policy Regime in China: Did Having Younger Sibling(s) Increase the Risk of Overweight and Underweight Status?" *Asian Population Studies* 13, no. 3 (2017): 267–91.

Heelas, Paul. "Work Ethics, Soft Capitalism and the 'Turn to Life.'" In *Cultural Economy: Cultural Analysis and Commercial Life*, edited by Paul du Gay and Michael Pryke, 78–96. London: SAGE, 2002.

Hermes, Joke, ed. "Special Issue: Labour and Passion." *European Journal of Cultural Studies* 18, no. 2 (2015).

Hershatter, Gail. *Women in China's Long Twentieth Century.* Berkeley: University of California Press, 2007.

Hesmondhalgh, David, and Sarah Baker. *Creative Labour: Media Work in Three Cultural Industries.* London: Routledge, 2011.

Hillenbrand, Margaret. "Communitarianism, or, How to Build East Asian Theory." *Postcolonial Studies* 13, no. 4 (2010): 317–34.

Hills, Matt. *Fan Cultures.* Hove: Psychology Press, 2002.

Hinerman, Stephen. "Beatlemania: Girls Just Want To Have Fun." In *The Adoring Audience: Fan Culture and Popular Media*, edited by Lisa A. Lewis, 107–34. London: Routledge, 2002.

Hochschild, Arlie Russell. *The Outsourced Self: Intimate Life in Market Times.* 1 edition. New York: Metropolitan Books, 2012.

Hodgson, Damian, and Louise Briand. "Controlling the Uncontrollable: 'Agile' Teams and Illusions of Autonomy in Creative Work." *Work, Employment and Society* 27, no. 2 (2013): 308–25.

Holloway, Lewis, and Phil Hubbard. *People and Place: The Extraordinary Geographies of Everyday Life*. Harlow: Pearson Education, 2001.

Hong Fincher, Leta. *Leftover Women: The Resurgence of Gender Inequality in China*. London, New York: Zed Books, 2014.

Hong Fincher, Leta. *Betraying Big Brother: China's Feminist Resistance*. London: Verso, 2018.

Hooper, Beverley. "Flower Vase and Housewife: Women and Consumerism in Post-Mao China." In *Gender and Power in Affluent Asia*, edited by Krishna Sen and Maila Stivens, 167–93. London: Routledge, 1998.

Hu, Xiaowen, and Ying Wang. "LGB Identity Among Young Chinese: The Influence of Traditional Culture." *Journal of Homosexuality* 60, no. 5 (2013): 667–84.

Hu, Xin (胡辛), and He Jing (何静). "难以超越的性别视角-1949年后中国男导演的女性电影叙事管窥 [Unsurpassable Gender Perspective: Female Narration by Chinese Male Directors since 1949]." 江西社會科學 *[Jianxi Social Science]*, no. 8 (2008).

Hu, Youwang (胡友旺), Sun Yanbao (孙艳宝), and Sun Xiaoyan (孙小燕). "儒家思想对大学生创业精神的消极影响及其对策 [The Negative Influence of Confucianism on the Entrepreneurship of College Students and Its Remedy]." 湖南师范大学教育科学学报 *[Hunan Shifan Daxuae Jiaoyu Kexue Xuebao]* 11, no. 5 (2012): 122–25.

Huang, Ya Chien. "Pink Dramas: Reconciling Consumer Modernity and Confucian Womanhood." In *TV Drama in China*, edited by Ying Zhu, Michael Keane, and Ruoyun Bai, 103–14. Hong Kong: Hong Kong University Press, 2008.

Huang, Ying (黄颖). "镜像内外的困囿与突围—论新世纪以来中国电影中的女性形象 [The Restraint and Breakout Inside/Outside of the Mirror: On Female Representation of Contemporary Chinese Cinema]." 当代电影 *[Contemporary Cinema]*, no. 12 (2016): 142–45.

Hui, Desmond. "From Cultural to Creative Industries: Strategies for Chaoyang District, Beijing." *International Journal of Cultural Studies* 9, no. 3 (2006): 317–31.

Hung, Kineta, and Stella Yiyan Li. "Images of the Contemporary Woman in Advertising in China." *Journal of International Consumer Marketing* 19, no. 2 (2006): 7–28.

Ibrahim, Yasmin. "Self-Representation and the Disaster Event: Self-Imaging, Morality and Immortality." *Journal of Media Practice* 16, no. 3 (2015): 211–27.

Illouz, Eva. *Cold Intimacies: The Making of Emotional Capitalism*. Cambridge: Polity, 2007.

Inverardi-Ferri, Carlo. "Commons and the Right to the City in Contemporary China." *Chinoiresie* (blog), September 28, 2017. http://www.chinoiresie.info/commons-and-the-right-to-the-city-in-contemporary-china/.

Ip, Penn Tsz Ting. "Desiring Singlehood? Rural Migrant Women and Affective Labour in the Shanghai Beauty Parlour Industry." *Inter-Asia Cultural Studies* 18, no. 4 (2017): 558–80.

Iveson, Kurt. "Social or Spatial Justice? Marcuse and Soja on the Right to the City." *City* 15, no. 2 (2011): 250–59.

Jamieson, Lynn, and Roona Simpson. *Living Alone: Globalization, Identity and Belonging*. London: Palgrave Macmillan, 2013.

Jarrett, Kylie. "The Relevance of 'Women's Work': Social Reproduction and Immaterial Labor in Digital Media." *Television & New Media* 15, no. 1 (2014): 14–29.

Jenkins, Henry. *Convergence Culture: Where Old and New Media Collide*. New York: NYU Press, 2006.

Jiang, Bing (江冰). "论'80后'文字文学 [On 'Post-80s' Writing Literature]." 中国作家网 *[Zhongguo Zuojiawang]*, April 23, 2008. http://www.chinawriter.com.cn/2008/2008-04-23/34533.html.

Jiang, Jin (姜进). 诗与政治: 20世纪上海公共文化中的女子越剧 *[Poetry and Politics: Female Yue Opera in 20th Century Shanghai Public Culture]*. Beijing: 社会科学文献出版社 [Social Sciences Academic Press], 2015.

Jiang, Xiaobin (蒋肖斌). "从《电视红娘》到《非诚勿扰》—电视相亲节目的历史考察 [From 'Television Matchmaker' to 'If You Are the One': A Historical Investigation of Television Dating Shows]." 现代视听 *[Xiandai Shiting]*, no. 9 (2011): 43–46.

Jing, Ji (荆棘). "《欢乐颂》:碗现实主义的毒鸡汤 ['Ode to Joy': A Bowl of Realist Poison Chicken Soup]." 齐鲁周刊 *[Wilu Zhoukan]*, no. 19 (2016): 64–65.

Johansson, Perry. "Chinese Women and Consumer Culture: Discourses on Beauty and Identity in Advertising and Women's Magazines 1985–1995." Doctoral thesis, Stockholms universitet, 1998.

Jones, Gavin W., Zhang Yanxia, and Pamela Chia Pei Zhi. "Understanding High Levels of Singlehood in Singapore." *Journal of Comparative Family Studies* 43, no. 5 (2012): 731–50.

Jullien, Francois. *The Silent Transformations*. London; New York: Seagull Books, 2011.

Kam, Lucetta Yip Lo. *Shanghai Lalas: Female Tongzhi Communities and Politics in Urban China*. Hong Kong: Hong Kong University Press, 2012.

Kanai, Akane. "On Not Taking the Self Seriously: Resilience, Relatability and Humour in Young Women's Tumblr Blogs." *European Journal of Cultural Studies*, 2017, 1–18.

Keane, Michael. *Created in China: The Great New Leap Forward*. London; New York: Routledge, 2007.

Keane, Michael. *Creative Industries in China: Art, Design and Media*. Malden: Polity, 2013.

Keane, Michael. "Television Drama in China: Remaking the Market." *Media International Australia* 115, no. 1 (2005): 82–93.

Kennedy, Helen, and Rosemary Lucy Hill. "The Feeling of Numbers: Emotions in Everyday Engagements with Data and Their Visualisation." *Sociology*, 2017, 1–19.

Kertzer, D. I. "Generation as a Sociological Problem." *Annual Review of Sociology* 9, no. 1 (1983): 125–49.

Kirby, David A., and Ying Fan. "Chinese Cultural Values and Entrepreneurship: A Preliminary Consideration." *Journal of Enterprising Culture* 03, no. 03 (1995): 245–60.

Kitson, Peter J. *Forging Romantic China: Sino-British Cultural Exchange 1760–1840*. Cambridge: Cambridge University Press, 2013.

Klinenberg, Eric. *Going Solo: The Extraordinary Rise and Surprising Appeal of Living Alone*. 1 edition. London: Duckworth Overlook, 2012.

de Kloet, Jeroen. *China with a Cut: Globalisation, Urban Youth and Popular Music*. Amsterdam: Amsterdam University Press, 2010.

de Kloet, Jeroen, and Anthony Y. H. Fung. *Youth Cultures in China*. Cambridge: Polity, 2017.

Knowles, Caroline, and Paul Sweetman. "Introduction." In *Picturing the Social Landscape: Visual Methods and the Sociological Imagination*, edited by Caroline Knowles and Paul Sweetman, 1–17. Routledge, 2004.

Ko, Dorothy. *Cinderella's Sisters: A Revisionist History of Footbinding*. Berkeley: University of California Press, 2005.

Kong, Lily. "From Cultural Industries to Creative Industries and Back? Towards Clarifying Theory and Rethinking Policy." *Inter-Asia Cultural Studies* 15, no. 4 (2014a): 593–607.

Kong, Lily. "The Sociality of Cultural Industries." *International Journal of Cultural Policy* 11, no. 1 (2005): 61–76.

Kong, Lily. "Transnational Mobilities and the Making of Creative Cities." *Theory, Culture & Society* 31, no. 7–8 (2014b): 273–89.

Kops, Manfred, and Stefan Ollig. *Internationalization of the Chinese TV Sector*. Berlin: LIT Verlag Münster, 2007.

Krackhardt, D. "The Strength of Strong Ties: The Importance of Philos in Organizations." In *Networks and Organizations: Structure, Form, and Action*, 216–39. Boston, MA: Harvard Business School Press, 1992.

Kücklich, Julian. "Precarious Playbour: Modders and the Digital Games Industry." *Fibreculture Journal*, no. 5 (2005).

Kuehn, Kathleen, and Thomas F. Corrigan. "Hope Labor: The Role of Employment Prospects in Online Social Production." *The Political Economy of Communication* 1, no. 1 (2013).

Lahad, Kinneret. *A Table for One: A Critical Reading of Singlehood, Gender and Time*. Manchester: Manchester University Press, 2017.

Lahad, Kinneret. "'Am I Asking for Too Much?' The Selective Single Woman as a New Social Problem." *Women's Studies International Forum* 40, no. Supplement C (2013): 23–32.

Lahad, Kinneret, and Haim Hazan. "The Terror of the Single Old Maid: On the Insolubility of a Cultural Category." *Women's Studies International Forum* 47, no. Part A (2014): 127–36.

Lahad, Kinneret, and Avi Shoshana. "Singlehood in Treatment: Interrogating the Discursive Alliance between Postfeminism and Therapeutic Culture." *European Journal of Women's Studies* 22, no. 3 (2015): 334–49.

Lakämper, Judith. "Affective Dissonance, Neoliberal Postfeminism and the Foreclosure of Solidarity." *Feminist Theory* 18, no. 2 (2017): 119–35.

Lam, Joseph Sui Ching. "Escorting Lady Jing Home: A Journey of Chinese Gender, Opera, and Politics." *Yearbook for Traditional Music* 46 (2014): 114–39.

Lao, Bei (老北). "70后、80后与90后 [The Post-70s, the Post-80s and the Post-90s]." 文化中国 [*Wenhua Zhongguo*] (blog), September 19, 2010. http://culture.china.com.cn/book/zxyd/2010-09/07/content_20882161.htm.

Lawrence, David Herbert. *Lady Chatterley's Lover*. New edition. Ware, Herfordshire: Wordsworth Editions, 1928.

Lee, Ching Kwan. "Precarization or Empowerment? Reflections on Recent Labor Unrest in China." *The Journal of Asian Studies* 75, no. 2 (2016): 317–33.

Lee, Ching Kwan, and Yonghong Zhang. "The Power of Instability: Unraveling the Microfoundations of Bargained Authoritarianism in China." *American Journal of Sociology* 118, no. 6 (2013): 1475–1508.

Lee, Haiyan. *Revolution of the Heart: A Genealogy of Love in China, 1900–1950*. Stanford: Stanford University Press, 2006.

Lee, Minha. "Fostering Connectivity: A Social Network Analysis of Entrepreneurs in Creative Industries." *International Journal of Cultural Policy* 21, no. 2 (2015): 139–52.

Lefebvre, Henri. *Writings on Cities*. Edited by Eleonore Kofman and Elizabeth Lebas. Cambridge, Massachusetts: Wiley-Blackwell, 1996.

Lesthaeghe, Ron. "The Unfolding Story of the Second Demographic Transition." *Population and Development Review* 36, no. 2 (2010): 211–51.

Lewis, Tania, Fran Martin, and Wanning Sun. *Telemodernities: Television and Transforming Lives in Asia*. Durham: Duke University Press, 2016.

Li, Chunling (李春玲). "静悄悄的革命是否临近?—从80后和90后的价值观转变看年轻一代的先行性 [Is the Quiet Revolution Imminent?—The Advances of the Younger Generation from the Transformative Values of the Post-80s and Post-90s]." 河北学刊 [*Hebei Xue Kan*], no. 3 (2015): 100–104.

Li, Huan (李欢). "浅析电视剧《欢乐颂》中女性形象的文化认知 [An Analysis of the Cultural Recognition of Female Images in TV Series 'Ode to Joy']." 大众文艺 [Dazhong Wenyi], no. 21 (2016): 205.

Li, Hui (李慧). "对'70后'命名的思考 [Reflection on the Term of 'Post-70s']." 安徽文学:下半月 [Anhui Wenxue: Xia Banyue], no. 8 (2009): 319–20.

Li, Jie. Shanghai Homes: Palimpsests of Private Life. New York: Columbia University Press, 2014.

Li, Li. "The 'Me Generation.'" Beijing Review, February 3, 2008. http://www.bjreview.com.cn/special/2008-02/03/content_101174.htm.

Li, Luzhou. "If You Are the One: Dating Shows and Feminist Politics in Contemporary China." International Journal of Cultural Studies 18, no. 5 (2015): 519–35.

Li, Maizi. "I Went to Jail for Handing out Feminist Stickers in China." The Guardian, March 8, 2017, sec. Opinion. http://www.theguardian.com/commentisfree/2017/mar/08/feminist-stickers-china-backash-women-activists.

Li, Wuwei (厉无畏). "发展创意产业 让世界刮起中国风 [Developing a Creative Industry That Blows China Wind across the World]." 人民网 [People.Cn], March 11, 2011. http://finance.people.com.cn/GB/71364/14119345.html.

Li, Yan (李艳), and Li Hefeng (李禾丰). "创业文化是传统客家文化的精髓 [Entrepreneurial Culture Is the Essence of Traditional Hakka Culture]." 江西农业大学学报:社会科学版 [Jiangxi Nongye Daxue Xuebao: Shehuikexue Ban] 8, no. 1 (2009): 147–50.

Li, Yang (李阳). "曲女性的欢歌—电视剧《欢乐颂》评析 [An Ode to Women—An Analysis of TV Series 'Ode to Joy']." 美与时代 [Beauty & Times], no. 7 (2016): 120–21.

Li, Yinhe (李银河). "中国已经阴盛阳衰了吗? [Has China Already Become High in Femininity and Low in Masculinity?]." 李银河的博客 [Li Yinhe's Blog] (blog), June 4, 2018. http://liyinhe.blog.caixin.com/archives/181848.

Li, Yu (李煜), and Xu Anqi (徐安琪). 婚姻市场中的青年择偶 [Youth Spousal Choices in the Marriage Market]. Shanghai: Shanghai Academy of Social Sciences Press, 2004.

Lian, Hongping. "The Post-1980s Generation in China: Exploring Its Theoretical Underpinning." Journal of Youth Studies 17, no. 7 (2014a): 965–81.

Lian, Hongping. "The Resistance of Land-Lost Farmers in China." Asia Pacific Journal of Public Administration 36, no. 3 (2014b): 185–200.

Liebenberg, Linda. "The Visual Image as Discussion Point: Increasing Validity in Boundary Crossing Research." Qualitative Research 9, no. 4 (2009): 441–67.

Liebler, Carol M., Wei Jiang, and Li Chen. "Beauty, Binaries, and the Big Screen in China: Character Gender in Feature Films." Asian Journal of Communication 25, no. 6 (2015): 584–99.

Lindstrom, Martin. BrandChild: Remarkable Insights into the Minds of Today's Global Kids and Their Relationship with Brands. London: Kogan Page, 2004.

Ling, Qi. "A New Dynamic of Gender Discourses? A Textual Analysis of the Representation of Shengnü in Television Dramas and Women's Magazines' Websites." MPhil diss., The Chinse University of Hong Kong, 2013.

Liu, Haiming. "The Chinese Diaspora: Space, Place, Mobility, and Identity (Review)." *Journal of Chinese Overseas* 20, no. 1 (2006): 150–53.

Liu, Liqun (刘利群), and Zhang Jingjie (张敬婕). "'剩女'与盛宴—性别视角下的'剩女'传播现象与媒介传播策略研究 ['Leftover Women' and Grand Banquet: Study of the Media Portrait of 'Leftover Women' and Strategies behind Media Coverage from a Gender Perspective]." *妇女研究论丛 [Collection of Women's Studies]*, no. 5 (2013): 76–82.

Liu, Min. "Two Gay Men Seeking Two Lesbians: An Analysis of Xinghun (Formality Marriage) Ads on China's Tianya.Cn." *Sexuality & Culture* 17, no. 3 (2013): 494–511.

Liu, Tian (刘天). "传统道德教育与大学生创业 [Traditional Moral Education and College Students' Entrepreneurship]." *中国青年研究 [Zhongguo Qingnian Yanjiu]*, no. 11 (2008): 95–98.

Liu, Tzu-kai. "Minority Youth, Mobile Phones and Language Use: Wa Migrant Workers' Engagements with Networked Sociality and Mobile Communication in Urban China." *Asian Ethnicity* 16, no. 3 (2015a): 334–52.

Liu, Wenjia. "The Dawn of 'Free Love': The Negotiation of Women's Roles in Heterosexual Relationships in Tanci Feng Shuang Fei." *Frontiers of Literary Studies in China* 9, no. 1 (2015b): 75–103.

Liu, Yuan (刘沅). "是'胜女',不是'剩女'—电视剧《欢乐颂》中樊胜美形象解读 [Is 'Winning Woman,' Not 'Leftover Woman'—Representational Analysis of Fan Shengmei in TV Series 'Ode to Joy']." *湖南大众传媒职业技术学院学报 [Journal of Hunan Mass Media Vocational Technical College]* 16, no. 5 (2016): 36–39.

Lloyd, Richard. *Neo-Bohemia: Art and Commerce in the Postindustrial City.* New York: Routledge, 2006.

Lorey, Isabell. *State of Insecurity: Government of the Precarious.* London: Verso, 2015.

Lu, Xun. "Shanghai Girls." In *Lu Xun: Selected Works*, translated by Xianyi Yang and Gladys Yang, 3:332–33. Beijing: Foreign Languages Press, 1980.

Lu, Ye, and Yajie Chu. "Media Use, Social Cohesion, and Cultural Citizenship: An Analysis of a Chinese Metropolis." *Chinese Journal of Communication* 5, no. 4 (2012): 365–82.

Lu, Yuying (吕玉莹), and Zhao Qiang (赵强). "'伪女性主义'宣言书—浅析《欢乐颂》 ['Pseudo-Feminism' Manifesto—An Analysis of 'Ode to Joy']." *戏剧之家 [Home Drama]*, no. 19 (2016): 139–41.

Lucas, Robert E. "On the Mechanics of Economic Development." *Journal of Monetary Economics* 22, no. 1 (1988): 3–42.

Lull, James. *China Turned On: Television, Reform and Resistance.* London: Routledge, 2013.

Luo, Aiping (罗爱萍), Wang Feng (王蜂), and Jiang Yu (江宇). 中国剩女调查 [China's Shengnü Survey]. Guangzhou: 广东人民出版社 [Guangdong renmin chuban she], 2014.

Luo, Wei. "Packaged Glamour: Constructing the Modern Bride in China's Bridal Media." Asian Women 28, no. 4 (2012): 83–115.

Luo, Wei, and Zhen Sun. "Are You the One? China's TV Dating Shows and the Sheng Nü's Predicament." Feminist Media Studies 15, no. 2 (2015): 239–56.

Luo, Yunjuan (罗韵娟), and Hao Xiaoming (郝晓鸣). "媒体女性形象塑造与社会变革—中国妇女》杂志封面人物形象的实证研究 [Shaping Women's Image in Media and The Social Revolution—An Empirical Study of the Cover Figure's Image from Women of China]." 中国传媒报告 [China Media Report] 1 (2015): 87–99.

Ma, Er (马耳). "陈卫与'70后' [Chen Wei and the 'Post-70s']." 豆瓣小组 [Douban Xiaozu] (blog), September 21, 2011. https://www.douban.com/group/topic/22459586/.

Ma, Yan (马艳). "女性励志剧中的人物功能分析 [Analysis of the Characters in Female Empowering Drama]." 中国电视 [China Television], no. 2 (2009): 36–40.

Mannay, Dawn. "Making the Familiar Strange: Can Visual Research Methods Render the Familiar Setting More Perceptible?" Qualitative Research 10, no. 1 (2010): 91–111.

Mannheim, Karl. "The Problem of Generations." In Essays on the Sociology of Knowledge, 276–322. London: Routledge, 1928.

Markusen, Ann. "Urban Development and the Politics of a Creative Class: Evidence from a Study of Artists." Environment and Planning A 38, no. 10 (2006): 1921–40.

Martin, Fran. Backward Glances: Contemporary Chinese Cultures and the Female Homoerotic Imaginary. Durham; London: Duke University Press, 2010.

Martin, Fran. "Intersections: The Gender of Mobility: Chinese Women Students' Self-Making through Transnational Education." Intersections: Gender and Sexuality in Asia and the Pacific, no. 35 (2014). http://intersections.anu.edu.au/issue35/martin.htm.

Martin, Fran, and Larissa Heinrich. Embodied Modernities: Corporeality, Representation, And Chinese Cultures. Honolulu: University of Hawaii Press, 2006.

Massey, Doreen. "Landscape as a Provocation: Reflections on Moving Mountains." Journal of Material Culture 11, no. 1–2 (2006): 33–48.

Mat, Joke. "Jong, Slim En Boordevol Twijfel." NRC Handelsblad, April 8, 2017.

Mauss, Marcel. The Gift: Forms and Functions of Exchange in Archaic Societies. Translated by Ian Cunnison. New York: W. W. Norton, 1967.

McCormack, Donna, and Suvi Salmenniemi. "The Biopolitics of Precarity and the Self." European Journal of Cultural Studies 19, no. 1 (2016): 3–15.

Mcgranahan, Carole. "Refusal and the Gift of Citizenship." *Cultural Anthropology* 31, no. 3 (2016): 334–41.

McLaughlin, Heather, Christopher Uggen, and Amy Blackstone. "The Economic and Career Effects of Sexual Harassment on Working Women." *Gender & Society* 31, no. 3 (2017): 333–58.

McNeal, James U. *The Kids Market: Myths and Realities.* New York: Paramount, 1999.

McRobbie, Angela. *Be Creative: Making a Living in the New Culture Industries.* 1 edition. Cambridge, UK; Malden, MA: Polity, 2016.

McRobbie, Angela. "Jackie: An Ideology of Adolescent Femininity." In *Popular Culture: Past and Present*, edited by Bernard Waites, Tony Bennett, and Graham Martin, 263–83. London: Croom Helm, 1982.

McRobbie, Angela. "Post-feminism and Popular Culture." *Feminist Media Studies* 4, no. 3 (2004): 255–64.

McRobbie, Angela. "Reflections on Feminism, Immaterial Labour and the Post-Fordist Regime." *New Formations*, no. 70 (2011): 60–76.

Mead, Margaret. *Culture and Commitment: A Study of the Generation Gap.* New York: Doubleday, 1970.

Meager, Nigel. "Children Make Observational Films—Exploring a Participatory Visual Method for Art Education." *International Journal of Education Through Art* 13, no. 1 (2017): 7–22.

Meng, Bingchun, and Yanning Huang. "Patriarchal Capitalism with Chinese Characteristics: Gendered Discourse of 'Double Eleven' Shopping Festival." *Cultural Studies* 31, no. 5 (2017): 659–84.

Merriman, Peter. "Rethinking Mobile Methods." *Mobilities* 9, no. 2 (2014): 167–87.

Miller, Toby. "From Creative to Cultural Industries." *Cultural Studies* 23, no. 1 (2009): 88–99.

Mitchell, Claudia. *Doing Visual Research.* London: Sage, 2011.

Mohanty, Chandra Talpade. "Under Western Eyes: Feminist Scholarship and Colonial Discourses." *Feminist Review*, no. 30 (1988): 61–88.

Morgan, George, and Pariece Nelligan. "Labile Labour—Gender, Flexibility and Creative Work." *The Sociological Review* 63, no. 1_suppl (2015): 66–83.

Mu, Guangzong (穆光宗). "'单身社会'来临未必是好事 [The Advent of 'Single Society' May Not Be a Good Thing]." *中国网 [China.Org.Cn]* (blog), August 27, 2017. http://big5.china.com.cn/gate/big5/opinion.china.com.cn/opinion_20_170420.html.

Mulvey, Laura. *Visual and Other Pleasures.* London: Macmillan, 1975.

Munck, Ronaldo. "The Precariat: A View from the South." *Third World Quarterly* 34, no. 5 (2013): 747–62.

Murdoch, Jon. *Post-Structuralist Geography: A Guide to Relational Space.* London: Sage, 2005.

Murphy, Enda, and Declan Redmond. "The Role of 'Hard' and 'Soft' Factors for Accommodating Creative Knowledge: Insights from Dublin's 'Creative Class.'" *Irish Geography* 42, no. 1 (2009): 69–84.

Murray, Derek Conrad. "Notes to Self: The Visual Culture of Selfies in the Age of Social Media." *Consumption Markets & Culture* 18, no. 6 (2015): 490–516.

Nakano, Lynne. "Single Women in Marriage and Employment Markets in Japan." In *Capturing Contemporary Japan: Differentiation and Uncertainty*, edited by Satsuki Kawano, Glenda Susan Roberts, and Susan Orpett Long, 163–182. Honolulu: University of Hawaii Press, 2014.

Nancy, Jean-Luc. *The Inoperative Community*. Minnesota: U of Minnesota Press, 1991.

Natalia Gerodetti, and Martha McNaught-Davis. "Feminisation of Success or Successful Femininities? Disentangling 'New Femininities' under Neoliberal Conditions." *European Journal of Women's Studies* 24, no. 4 (2017): 351–65.

Nealon, Jeffrey. *Foucault Beyond Foucault: Power and Its Intensifications since 1984*. Stanford: Stanford University Press, 2007.

Neff, Gina. *Venture Labor: Work and the Burden of Risk in Innovative Industries*. Cambridge, MA: MIT Press, 2012.

Negra, Diane, and Yvonne Tasker. *Gendering the Recession: Media and Culture in an Age of Austerity*. Durham, NC: Duke University Press, 2014.

Ng, Evelyn G. H., and Catherine W. Ng. "Single Working Women and Motherhood: The Personal and the Political." *Asian Journal of Women's Studies* 19, no. 1 (2013): 9–38.

Ng, Jhony Choon Yeong, Christina Maria Helminger, and Qianyun Wu. "A Generational Cohort Model for Consumers in China: The Rise and Fall of the Great Gatsby?" *A Generational Cohort Model for Consumers in China: The Rise and Fall of the Great Gatsby?* 7, no. 1 (2016): 53–66.

Ngai, Pun. "Gender and Class: Women's Working Lives in a Dormitory Labor Regime in China." *International Labor and Working-Class History* 81 (2012): 178–81.

Ngai, Pun. *Made in China: Women Factory Workers in a Global Workplace*. Durham: Duke University Press, 2005.

Ngai, Pun. *Migrant Labor in China*. Cambridge: Polity Press, 2016.

Niu, Weilin (牛维麟), and Peng Yi (彭翊). 北京文化创意产业集聚区发展研究报告 *[Beijing Cultural Creative Industry Clusters Development Study Report]*. Beijing: 中国人民大学出版社 [People's University Press], 2009.

Nowicka, Magdalena. "Mobile Locations: Construction of Home in a Group of Mobile Transnational Professionals." *Global Networks* 7, no. 1 (2007): 69–86.

Nyíri, Pál. *Mobility and Cultural Authority in Contemporary China*. Seattle and London: University of Washington Press, 2011.

Oberst, Ursula, Andrés Chamarro, and Vanessa Renau. "Gender Stereotypes 2.0: Self-Representations of Adolescents on Facebook." *Estereotipos de Género 2.0: Auto-Representaciones de Adolescentes En Facebook*. 24, no. 48 (2016): 81–89.

O'Brien, Anne. "'Men Own Television': Why Women Leave Media Work." *Media, Culture & Society* 36, no. 8 (2014): 1207–18.

O'Connor, Justin, and Xin Gu. "Creative Industry Clusters in Shanghai: A Success Story?" *International Journal of Cultural Policy* 20, no. 1 (2014): 1–20.

O'Connor, Justin, and Xin Gu. "Shanghai: Images of Modernity." In *Cultures and Globalization: Cities, Cultural Policy and Governance*, edited by Helmut K. Anheier and Yudhishthir Raj Isar, 288–99. London: Sage, 2012.

Ooi, Can-Seng, and Birgit Stöber. "Creativity Unbound—Policies, Government and the Creative Industries." *Culture Unbound: Journal of Current Cultural Research* 3 (2011): 113–17.

Ortega Y. Gasset, José. *The Modern Theme.* New York: W. W. Norton Company, 1933.

Ouyang, Youquan (欧阳友权), ed. 文化品牌蓝皮书:中国文化品牌发展报告 *[Blue Book of Cultural Brands: Annual Report on the Development of Cultural Brands in China]*. Changsha: 中南大学中国文化产业品牌研究中心 [Zhongnan University China's Cultural Industries Brands Research Centre], 2006.

Palmer, Victoria J., Christopher Dowrick, and Jane M. Gunn. "Mandalas as a Visual Research Method for Understanding Primary Care for Depression." *International Journal of Social Research Methodology* 17, no. 5 (2014): 527–41.

Pang, Laikwan. *Creativity and Its Discontents: China's Creative Industries and Intellectual Property Rights Offenses.* Durham: Duke University Press, 2012.

Park, Robert. "The City: Suggestions for the Investigation of Human Behavior in the Urban Environment." In *Classic Essays on the Culture of Cities*, edited by Richard Sennett. Englewood Cliffs: Prentice-Hall, 1916.

Pauwels, Luc. *Reframing Visual Social Science: Towards a More Visual Sociology and Anthropology.* Cambridge: Cambridge University Press, 2015.

Pauwels, Luc. "Visual Sociology Reframed: An Analytical Synthesis and Discussion of Visual Methods in Social and Cultural Research." *Sociological Methods & Research* 38, no. 4 (2010): 545–81.

Peng, Tianxiao (彭天笑). "浅析中国同性恋者选择形式婚姻的原因及影响 [On the Causes and Effects of 'Xinghun' Marriage by Chinese Homosexuals]." 中国性科学 *[Zhongguo Xing Kexue]*, no. 8 (2014): 97–99.

Peugny, Camille, and Cécile Van de Velde. "Rethinking Inter-Generational Inequality." Translated by Peter Hamilton. *Revue Française de Sociologie* 54, no. 4 (2013): 641–62.

Pi, Chenying. "Fieldwork Report: Love Club." *HERA SINGLE* (blog), December 2, 2014. http://www.hera-single.de/love-club/.

Pink, Sarah. *Doing Visual Ethnography.* 3rd Edition. London: SAGE, 2013.

Postigo, Hector. "America Online Volunteers: Lessons from an Early Co-Production Community." *International Journal of Cultural Studies* 12, no. 5 (2009): 451–69.

Poutanen, Seppo, and Anne Kovalainen. *Gender and Innovation in the New Economy: Women, Identity, and Creative Work.* New York: Springer, 2017.

Pyšňáková, Michaela, and Steven Miles. "The Post-Revolutionary Consumer Generation: 'Mainstream' Youth and the Paradox of Choice in the Czech Republic." *Journal of Youth Studies* 13, no. 5 (2010): 533–47.

Qian, Nanyang (钱南扬). "南词引正校注 (Nanci Yinzheng Jiaozhu)." 戏剧报 *[Xiju Bao]*, no. 2 (1961): 60–61.

Qin, Xiaohong (秦晓红). "女性生存状态的中国镜像—论中国电影中的女性形象建构 [Chinese Mirror of Female Existence—On the Construction of Female Images in Chinese Films]." 湖南社会科学 *[Hunan Shehui Kexue]* 3, no. 44 (2006): 138–41.

Qiu, Jack Linchuan. *Goodbye iSlave: A Manifesto for Digital Abolition*. Champaign: University of Illinois Press, 2017.

Qiu, Jack Linchuan. "Locating Worker-Generated Content (WGC) in the World's Factory." In *The Routledge Companion to Labor and Media*, edited by Richard Maxwell, 303–14. New York: Routledge, 2015.

Qiu, Jack Linchuan. "'Power to the People!': Mobiles, Migrants, and Social Movements in Asia." *International Journal of Communication* 8 (2014): 376–91.

Qiu, Jack Linchuan. *Working-Class Network Society: Communication Technology and the Information Have-Less in Urban China*. Cambridge, Massachusetts: MIT Press, 2009.

Radway, Janice A. *Reading the Romance: Women, Patriarchy, and Popular Literature*. London: Verso, 1987.

Rasmussen, Kim, and Søren Smidt. "Children in the Neighbourhood: The Neighbourhood in the Children." In *Children in the City: Home Neighbourhood and Community*, edited by Pia Christensen and Margaret O'Brien, 82–100. London: Routledge, 2003.

Raunig, Gerald. *Factories of Knowledge, Industries of Creativity*. Los Angeles, CA: Semiotext(e), 2013.

Rene, Helena K. *China's Sent-Down Generation: Public Administration and the Legacies of Mao's Rustication Program*. Washington, D.C.: Georgetown University Press, 2013.

Reynolds, Jill. *The Single Woman: A Discursive Investigation*. London: Routledge, 2008.

Rich, Adrienne. *Compulsory Heterosexuality and Lesbian Existence*. London: Onlywomen Press, 1980.

Rofel, Lisa. *Desiring China: Experiments in Neoliberalism, Sexuality, and Public Culture*. Durham: Duke University Press, 2007.

Rose, Gillian. "On the Relation between 'Visual Research Methods' and Contemporary Visual Culture." *The Sociological Review* 62, no. 1 (2014): 24–46.

Rose, Gillian. *Visual Methodologies: An Introduction to Researching with Visual Materials*. London: Sage, 2012.

Rosen, Stanley. "Contemporary Chinese Youth and the State." *The Journal of Asian Studies* 68, no. 2 (2009): 359–69.

Ross, Andrew. *Nice Work If You Can Get It: Life and Labor in Precarious Times.* New York: NYU Press, 2009.

Ross, Andrew. *No-Collar: The Humane Workplace and Its Hidden Costs.* Philadelphia: Temple University Press, 2004.

van Saarloos, Simone. "Op Straat, Tussen de Mensen, Kom Je Jezelf Pas Echt Tegen." *NRC*, February 3, 2017. https://www.nrc.nl/nieuws/2017/02/03/op-straat-tussen-de-mensen-kom-je-jezelf-pas-echt-tegen-6534397-a1544348.

Sarkisian, Natalia, and Naomi Gerstel. "Does Singlehood Isolate or Integrate? Examining the Link between Marital Status and Ties to Kin, Friends, and Neighbors." *Journal of Social and Personal Relationships* 33, no. 3 (2016): 361–84.

Savage, Mike, and Roger Burrows. "The Coming Crisis of Empirical Sociology." *Sociology* 41, no. 5 (2007): 885–99.

Saxonberg, Steven, and Tomáš Sirovátka. "Failing Family Policy in Post-Communist Central Europe." *Journal of Comparative Policy Analysis: Research and Practice* 8, no. 2 (2006): 185–202.

Scheel, Karen R., and John S. Westefeld. "Heavy Metal Music and Adolescent Suicidality: An Empirical Investigation." *Adolescence* 34, no. 134 (1999): 253.

Scholz, Trebor, ed. *Digital Labor: The Internet as Playground and Factory.* New York: Routledge, 2013.

Scotton, James F., and William A. Hachten. *New Media for a New China.* Chichester: Wiley-Blackwell, 2010.

Sennett, Richard. *Together: The Rituals, Pleasures and Politics of Cooperation.* New Haven: Yale University Press, 2012.

Shade, Leslie Regan, and Jenna Jacobson. "Hungry for the Job: Gender, Unpaid Internships, and the Creative Industries." *The Sociological Review* 63, no. 1_ suppl (2015): 188–205.

Sharp, Elizabeth A., and Lawrence Ganong. "'I'm a Loser, I'm Not Married, Let's Just All Look at Me': Ever-Single Women's Perceptions of Their Social Environment." *Journal of Family Issues* 32, no. 7 (2011): 956–80.

Sheller, Mimi, and John Urry. "Places to Play, Places in Play." In *Tourism Mobilities: Places to Play, Places in Play*, edited by Mimi Sheller and John Urry, 1–10. London: Routledge, 2004.

Siebert, Sabina, and Fiona Wilson. "All Work and No Pay: Consequences of Unpaid Work in the Creative Industries." *Work, Employment and Society* 27, no. 4 (2013): 711–21.

SK-II. *SK-II: Marriage Market Takeover*, 2016. https://www.youtube.com/watch?v=irfd74z52Cw.

Song, Jesook. *Living on Your Own: Single Women, Rental Housing, and Post-Revolutionary Affect in Contemporary South Korea.* Albany: SUNY Press, 2014.

Standing, Guy. *The Precariat: The New Dangerous Class.* London; New York: Bloomsbury Academic, 2011.

Stein, Peter J. "Singlehood: An Alternative to Marriage." *The Family Coordinator* 24, no. 4 (1975): 489–503.

Stenberg, Josh. "Three Relations between History and Stage in the Kunju Scene Slaying the Tiger General." *Asian Theatre Journal* 32, no. 1 (2015): 107–35.

Stenberg, Josh, and Jason J. P. Cai. "Mostly Young Women with Quite Traditional Tastes: Empirical Evidence for National Contemporary Audiences of Xiqu." *Theatre Journal* 69, no. 1 (2017): 43–59.

Storey, John. "The Social Life of Opera." *European Journal of Cultural Studies* 6, no. 1 (2003): 5–35.

Su, Xing (苏醒), and Tian Renbo (田仁波). "'城市剩女'群体生存焦虑问题研究 [Research on Living Anxiety of Shengnü in Cities]." *Journal of Qujing Normal University* 31, no. 2 (2012): 116–20.

Sun, Lu (孙璐). "论当代传媒中女性刻板印象的嬗变 [On Changing Female Stereotypes in Contemporary Media]." 传播学硕士论文 [MA thesis of Communication Studies], 苏州大学 [Soochow University], 2004.

Sun, Shengwei, and Feinian Chen. "Reprivatized Womanhood: Changes in Mainstream Media's Framing of Urban Women's Issues in China, 1995–2012." *Journal of Marriage and Family* 77, no. 5 (2015): 1091–1107.

Sun, Wanning. *Subaltern China: Rural Migrants, Media, and Cultural Practices.* Rowman & Littlefield, 2014.

Sun, Wanning, and Jenny Chio. *Mapping Media in China: Region, Province, Locality.* London; New York: Routledge, 2012.

Tan, Jia. "Digital Masquerading: Feminist Media Activism in China." *Crime, Media, Culture* 13, no. 2 (2017): 171–86.

Tan, See Kam, Peter X. Feng, and Gina Marchetti. "Introduction." In *Chinese Connections: Critical Perspectives on Film, Identity, and Diaspora*, edited by See Kam Tan, Peter X. Feng, and Gina Marchetti, 1–5. Philadelphia, PA: Temple University Press, 2009.

Tao, Shun (陶舜). "单身社会来了 [The Single Society Has Come]." 腾讯网 *[Tengxun Wang]* (blog), August 24, 2017. http://view.news.qq.com/original/intouchtoday/n3993.html.

Taylor, Anthea. "Blogging Solo: New Media, 'Old' Politics." *Feminist Review* 99, no. 1 (2011): 79–97.

Themen, Kate, and Jenny van Hooff. "Kicking against Tradition: Women's Football, Negotiating Friendships and Social Spaces." *Leisure Studies* 36, no. 4 (2017): 542–52.

Thomas, Lyn. *Fans, Feminisms and "quality" Media.* Hove: Psychology Press, 2002.

Tian, Xiaoli, and Yunxue Deng. "Organizational Hierarchy, Deprived Masculinity, and Confrontational Practices: Men Doing Women's Jobs in a Global Factory." *Journal of Contemporary Ethnography* 46, no. 4 (2017): 464–89.

To, Sandy. *China's Leftover Women: Late Marriage Among Professional Women and Its Consequences.* London, New York: Routledge, 2015.

Tokumitsu, Miya. "In the Name of Love." *Jacobin Magazine*, January 12, 2014. http://jacobinmag.com/2014/01/in-the-name-of-love/.

Tönnies, Ferdinand. *Gemeinschaft Und Gesellschaft.* Leipzig: Fues's Verlag, 1887.

Torras, Marta Mensa, and Jean M. Grow. "Creative Women in Peru: Outliers in a Machismo World." *Communication & Society*, 2015, 1–18.

Trier-Bieniek, Adrienne. *Feminist Theory and Pop Culture.* Rotterdam: Sense Publishers, 2015.

Tsui, Clarence. "Celine Dion to Perform on China Central Television's New Year's Gala Show." *The Hollywood Reporter*, February 6, 2013. http://www.hollywoodreporter.com/news/celine-dion-perform-cctvs-new-419121.

Tu, Jia-Wei, and Tien-Tsung Lee. "The Effects of Media Usage and Interpersonal Contacts on the Stereotyping of Lesbians and Gay Men in China." *Journal of Homosexuality* 61, no. 7 (2014): 980–1002.

Verdich, Madeleine. "Creative Migration? The Attraction and Retention of the 'Creative Class' in Launceston, Tasmania." *Australian Geographer* 41, no. 1 (2010): 129–40.

Vergunst, Jo. "Technology and Technique in a Useful Ethnography of Movement." *Mobilities* 6, no. 2 (2011): 203–19.

Vlase, Ionela, and Rebekka Sieber. "Narrating Well-Being in the Context of Precarious Prosperity: An Account of Agency Framed by Culturally Embedded Happiness and Gender Beliefs." *European Journal of Women's Studies* 23, no. 2 (2016): 185–99.

de Vries, Dian A., and Jochen Peter. "Women on Display: The Effect of Portraying the Self Online on Women's Self-Objectification." *Computers in Human Behavior* 29, no. 4 (2013): 1483–89.

Wang, Changfeng (王昌逢). "社会性别视角下的 [剩女] 现象分析 [An Analysis of the 'Leftover Women' Phenomenon from the Perspective of Gender]." *中共山西省直机关党校学报 [ZhongGong Shanxisheng Zhi Jiguan Dangxiao Xuebao]*, no. 6 (2010): 46–47.

Wang, Haiping, and Douglas A. Abbott. "Waiting for Mr. Right: The Meaning of Being a Single Educated Chinese Female Over 30 in Beijing and Guangzhou." *Women's Studies International Forum* 40, no. Supplement C (2013): 222–29.

Wang, Hui. *The End of the Revolution: China and the Limits of Modernity.* London; New York: Verso Books, 2011.

Wang, Jing. "The Global Reach of a New Discourse: How Far Can 'Creative Industries' Travel?" *International Journal of Cultural Studies* 7, no. 1 (2004): 9–19.

Wang, Pan. "Inventing Traditions: Television Dating Shows in the People's Republic of China." *Media, Culture & Society* 39, no. 4 (2017): 504–19.

Wang, Tianyue (王天玥). "电视剧《欢乐颂》的意识形态色彩研究 [A Study on the Ideological Colors of TV Drama 'Ode to Joy']." *西部广播电视 [Xibu Guangbo Dianshi]*, no. 9 (2016): 100.

Wang, Yan (王焱). "现代主义与传统文化的璧合—白先勇小说创作概论 [The Combination of Modernism and Traditional Culture—An Introduction to Bai Xianyong's Novel Creation]." 天中学刊 [Tianzhong Xuekan], no. 1X (1995): 66–69.

Wang, Yanjun. "Spouse Selection Amongst China's Post-1980 Generation." Master's Thesis, Central European University, 2012.

Wang, Zhenzhen (王臻真). "消费文化中的性别图景—近年中国电影中的女性形象 [Gender Images in Consumer Culture—Female Representation in Recent Chinese Films]." 当代文坛 [Dangdai Wentan], no. 1 (2015): 103–9.

Wangyi nüren pingdao (网易女人频道). 我知女人心:70后、80后、90后女性情感大调查 [I Know a Woman's Heart: 70/80/90 Female Emotional Survey]. Zhejiang: 浙江大学出版社 [Zhejiang daxue chubanshe], 2011.

Watanabe, Yasushi, and David L. McConnell, eds. Soft Power Superpowers. Armonk, NY: M.E. Sharpe, 2008.

Weber, Max. "The Distribution of Power Within the Gemeinschaft: Classes, Stände, Parties." In Weber's Rationalism and Modern Society: New Translations on Politics, Bureaucracy, and Social Stratification, edited by Tony Waters and Dagmar Waters, 37–58. New York: Palgrave Macmillan, 2015.

Wei, Qiong (危琼). "报纸对'剩女'的媒介形象塑造 [The Media Representation of 'Shengnü' Image by News]." 新闻世界 [News World], no. 9 (2010): 112–14.

Wen, Lifang (温丽芳). "电视相亲节目的前世今生 [The Past and Present of Television Dating Shows]." 山西晚报 [Shanxi Wanbao], February 27, 2010.

Wherton, Joseph, Paul Sugarhood, Rob Procter, Mark Rouncefield, Guy Dewsbury, Sue Hinder, and Trisha Greenhalgh. "Designing Assisted Living Technologies 'in the Wild': Preliminary Experiences with Cultural Probe Methodology." BMC Medical Research Methodology 12 (2012): 188.

White, Allen, Naomi Bushin, Fina Carpena-Méndez, and Caitríona Ní Laoire. "Using Visual Methodologies to Explore Contemporary Irish Childhoods." Qualitative Research 10, no. 2 (2010): 143–58.

Wilkinson, Eleanor. "Single People's Geographies of Home: Intimacy and Friendship beyond 'the Family.'" Environment and Planning A 46, no. 10 (2014): 2452–68.

Wilson, Julie Ann, and Emily Chivers Yochim. "Mothering Through Precarity." Cultural Studies 29, no. 5–6 (2015): 669–86.

Winship, Janice. Inside Women's Magazines. London: Pandora Press, 1987.

Wojcik, Pamela Robertson. The Apartment Plot: Urban Living in American Film and Popular Culture, 1945 to 1975. Durham, NC: Duke University Press, 2010.

Wong, Lok Yee. "The Poetics and Politics of Hong Kong Wenyi Qingnian." MPhil thesis, Hong Kong Baptist University, 2017.

Wong, Winnie. Van Gogh on Demand: China and the Readymade. Chicago; London: University Of Chicago Press, 2014.

Woodman, Dan. "Researching 'Ordinary' Young People in a Changing World: The Sociology of Generations and the 'Missing Middle' in Youth Research." *Sociological Research Online* 18, no. 1 (2013).

Woolf, Virginia. *The Years*. London: Hogarth Press, 1937.

Wu, Changchang (吴畅畅). "欢乐颂:一阕现实主义的'颂'歌? [Ode to Joy: Ode to Realism?]." 上海艺术家 *[Shanghai Yishujia]* 0, no. 4 (2016): 94–96.

Wu, Daozi (吴稻子). "《欢乐颂》热映背后的中国都市残酷物语 [The Cruel Story of Chinese Cities behind the Popularity of 'Ode to Joy']." 端傳媒 *[Initium Media]*, May 23, 2016. https://theinitium.com/article/20160523-mainland-huanlesong/.

Wu, Doreen D., and Agatha Man-kwan Chung. "Hybridized Images: Representations of the 'Modern Woman' across Mainland China and Hong Kong TV Commercials." *Journal of Asian Pacific Communication* 21, no. 2 (2011): 177–95.

Wu, Jing. "Post-Socialist Articulation of Gender Positions: Contested Public Sphere of Reality Dating Shows." In *Women and the Media in Asia*, 220–36. London: Palgrave Macmillan, 2012a.

Wu, Shuping. *Single in the City: A Survey of China's Single Women*. Beijing: Long River Press, 2012b.

Wyn, Johanna, and Dan Woodman. "Generation, Youth and Social Change in Australia." *Journal of Youth Studies* 9, no. 5 (2006): 495–514.

Xiao, Hui Faye. "'Love Is a Capacity': The Narrative of Gendered Self-Development in Chinese-Style Divorce." *Journal of Contemporary China* 19, no. 66 (2010): 735–53.

Xie, Wenqing (谢文庆). "儒家思想对大学生创业精神的积极影响—兼与胡友旺等先生商榷 [The Positive Influence of Confucianism on the Entrepreneurship of College Students—A Discussion with Mr. Hu Youwang et al.]." 湖南师范大学教育科学学报 *[Hunan Shifan Daxuae Jiaoyu Kexue Xuebao]* 12, no. 1 (2013): 116–19.

Xin, Hua (新华). "'70后、80后、90后',时代催生的'话题三重门' ['The Post-70s, Post-80s, Post-90s', the 'Topic Triple Door' Spawned by Eras]." Edited by Li Yanmin (李彦敏). 乡音 *[Xiangyin]*, no. 8 (2008): 42.

Xiong, Yan (熊艳). "《非诚勿扰》何以领跑收视冠军 [How Does 'If You Are the One' Remain a Rating Champion]." 视听 *[Shiting]* 0, no. 6 (2013): 26–27.

Xu, Gary, and Susan Feiner. "Meinü Jingji/China's Beauty Economy: Buying Looks, Shifting Value, and Changing Place." *Feminist Economics* 13, no. 3–4 (2007): 307–23.

Yan, Alice. "How a Ban Is Forcing China's Single Women to Put Their Fertility on Ice Overseas." *South China Morning Post*, August 20, 2017. http://www.scmp.com/news/china/society/article/2107287/how-ban-forcing-chinas-leftover-women-abroad-freeze-their-eggs.

Yan, Wei (闫伟). "《欢乐颂》为都市剧的创新探路 ["Ode to Joy" Discovering Innovative Pathways for Urban Drama]." 人民日报海外版 *[People's Daily*

(Overseas Edition)]. May 9, 2016, Overseas edition edition, sec. 12. http://paper.people.com.cn/rmrbhwb/html/2016-05/09/content_1677453.htm.

Yan, Yan (闫妍), and Qin Hua (秦华). "充分发挥妇女在家庭文明建设中的独特作用 [Full Potential of the Unique Role of Women in the Construction of Family Civilization]." *中国妇联新闻 [Zhongguo Fulian Xinwen]*, May 18, 2015. http://acwf.people.com.cn/n/2015/0518/c99058-27015970.html.

Yang Jianli (杨剑利). *女性与近代中国社会 [The Female and Modern China Society]*. Beijing: 中国社会出版社 [China Society Press], 2007.

Yang, Xianmei (杨先梅). "中国传统文化在大学生创业精神培育中的价值研究 [A Study on the Value of Chinese Traditional Culture in Cultivating College Students' Entrepreneurship]." *国网技术学院学报 [Guowang Jishu Xueyuan Xuebao]* 18, no. 3 (2015): 73–76.

Yang, Yan (羊艳). "解读女性宫廷剧的大众文化意义 [Deconstructing the Popular Culture Significance of Female Historical Court Drama]." *电影文学 [Movie Literature]*, no. 21 (2011): 111–12.

Yang, Yang (杨洋). "《欢乐颂》编剧袁子弹:人生没有弯道超车 ['Ode to Joy' Scriptwriter Yuan Zidan: No Chicane Overtaking in Life]." *壹讀 [READ01. COM]* (blog), May 19, 2016. https://read01.com/gNzjn5.html.

Ye, Pan (叶攀). "'平语'近人—习近平谈妇女如何全面发展 ['Ping Yu' Intimacy—Xi Jinping Talks about Personal Development of Women]." *中国新闻网 [Chinanews.Com]*, October 12, 2015. http://www.chinanews.com/gn/2015/10-12/7565191.shtml.

Ye, Xin (叶辛), and Kuai Dashen (蒯大申). *上海文化发展报告 (2011) [Shanghai Cultural Development Report (2011)]*. Beijing: 社会科学文献出版社 [Social Sciences Academic Press], 2011.

Ye, Zi (叶子). "《欢乐颂2》难复第一季辉煌?主创聊季播探索之路 ['Ode to Joy 2' Unable to Attain the Height of Season One? Show Creator Discusses the Initial Exploration of the Show]." *新浪娱乐 [Sina Entertainment]* (blog), June 7, 2017. http://ent.sina.com.cn/v/m/2017-06-07/doc-ifyfuzmy2393679.shtml.

Yeung, Wei-Jun Jean, and Shu Hu. "Coming of Age in Times of Change: The Transition to Adulthood in China." *The ANNALS of the American Academy of Political and Social Science* 646, no. 1 (2013): 149–71.

Yi, Xiang, Barbara Ribbens, Linna Fu, and Weibo Cheng. "Variation in Career and Workplace Attitudes by Generation, Gender, and Culture Differences in Career Perceptions in the United States and China." *Employee Relations* 37, no. 1 (2015): 66–82.

Yi, Xiang, Barbara Ribbens, and Caryn N. Morgan. "Generational Differences in China: Career Implications." *Career Development International* 15, no. 6 (2010): 601–20.

Yin, Ming (尹铭). "'60后'眼中的'70后、80后、90后' ['The Post-70s, Post-80s, Post-90s' in the Eyes of 'the Post-60s']." Edited by Li Yanmin (李彦敏). *乡音 [Xiangyin]*, no. 8 (2008): 42–43.

Yodovich, Neta, and Kinneret Lahad. "'I Don't Think This Woman Had Anyone in Her Life': Loneliness and Singlehood in Six Feet Under." *European Journal of Women's Studies*, 2017, 1–15.

Yoo, Jin-Seok. "Young Consumers Drive China's New Economic Model." *SERI Quarterly* 6, no. 4 (2013): 113–18.

Young, Iris Marion. "Unruly Categories: A Critique of Nancy Fraser's Dual Systems Theory." *New Left Review*, no. 222 (1997): 147–160.

Yu, Weimin (俞为民). "昆曲的现代性发展之可能性研究 [Study on the Possibility of the Modern Development of Kunqu]." 文化艺术研究 *[Wenhua Yishu Yanjiu]*, no. 1 (2011): 133–55.

Yuan, Yue (袁岳), and Zhang Jun (张军). 我们90后 *[We the Post-90s]*. Hangzhou: 浙江大学出版社 [Zhejiang daxue chubanshe], 2011.

Zeng, Yuli. "'Save Our Boys': China's Made-up Masculinity Crisis." *Sixth Tone* (blog), July 31, 2017. http://www.sixthtone.com/news/1000562/save-our-boys-chinas-made-up-masculinity-crisis.

Zhang, Jeanne Hong. "Gender in Post-Mao China." *European Review* 11, no. 2 (2003): 209–24.

Zhang, Jun, and Peidong Sun. "'When Are You Going to Get Married?' Parental Matchmaking and Middle-Class Women in Contemporary Urban China." In *Wives, Husbands and Lovers: Marriage and Sexuality in Hong Kong, Taiwan, and Urban China*, edited by Deborah S. Davis and Sara L. Friedman, 118–44. Stanford: Stanford University Press, 2014.

Zhang, Kai (张开). "女性观众喜爱电视剧成因分析 [A Study on the Reasons Why Television Drama Series Are Popular among Female Audiences]." 现代传播:中国传媒大学学报 *[Xiandai Chuanbo: Zhongguo Chuanmeidaxue Xuebao]*, no. 6 (2009): 65–68.

Zhang, Lin. "The Contradictions of 'Women's Work' in Digital Capitalism: A 'Non-Western'/Chinese Perspective." *Feminist Media Studies* 18, no. 1 (2018): 147–51.

Zhang, Lin, and Anthony Fung. "The Myth of 'Shanzhai' Culture and the Paradox of Digital Democracy in China." *Inter-Asia Cultural Studies* 14, no. 3 (2013): 401–16.

Zhang, Lin, Pataradech "Tony" Srisupandit, and Debra Cartwright. "A Comparison of Gender Role Portrayals in Magazine Advertising: The United States, China and Thailand." *Management Research News* 32, no. 7 (2009): 683–700.

Zhang, Meng. "A Chinese Beauty Story: How College Women in China Negotiate Beauty, Body Image, and Mass Media." *Chinese Journal of Communication* 5, no. 4 (2012): 437–54.

Zhang, Weiyu, and Chengting Mao. "Fan Activism Sustained and Challenged: Participatory Culture in Chinese Online Translation Communities." *Chinese Journal of Communication* 6, no. 1 (2013): 45–61.

Zhang, Xiaoming (张晓明), Hu Huilin (胡惠林), and Zhang Jiangang (章建刚), eds. 文化蓝皮书:中国文化产业发展报告 *[Blue Book of China's Culture: Annual Report on the Development of China's Cultural Industries].* Beijing: 社会科学文献出版社 [Social Sciences Academic Press], 2002.

Zhang, Xiaoming (张晓明), Wang Jiaxin (王家新), and Zhang Jiangang (章建刚), eds. 文化蓝皮书:中国文化产业发展报告 *[Blue Book of China's Culture: Annual Report on the Development of China's Cultural Industries].* Beijing: 社会科学文献出版社 [Social Sciences Academic Press], 2012.

Zhang, Yuanyuan (张媛媛). "浅析几部国产电影中的女性角色 [On the Female Roles in Several Chinese Domestic Films]." 云南农业大学学报 *[Yunnan Nongye Daxue Xuebao]* 4, no. 6 (2010): 88–90.

Zhang, Yuliang (张裕亮). "铁姑娘、贤内助、时尚女—中国女性杂志建构的女性形象 [Iron Lady, Better Half and Fashion Girl: Women's Image in Women's Magazines in China]." *China Media Report Overseas* 6, no. 1 (2010): 79–94.

Zhao, Feng. "The Evolution from Generation to Post-XX." Translated by Ted Wang. *Chinese Education & Society* 44, no. 2–3 (2011): 76–79.

Zhao, Shanlin (赵山林). "试论昆曲观众的历史变迁与现状 [On the Historical Vicissitude and Current Situation of Kunqu]." 东南大学学报(哲学社会科学版) *[Journal of Southeast University(Philosophy and Social Science)]* 16, no. 1 (2014): 96–165.

Zheng, Chuanjian (郑传鉴). "昆剧传习所纪事 [Kunqu Chuanxisuo Jishi]." 中国戏曲网 *[Zhongguo Xiqu Wang]* (blog), November 6, 2006. http://www.chinaopera.net/html/2006-11/606p3.html.

Zhong, Zhi-Jin, and Mike Zhengyu Yao. "Gaming Motivations, Avatar-Self Identification and Symptoms of Online Game Addiction." *Asian Journal of Communication* 23, no. 5 (2013): 555–73.

Zhou, Ting (周婷). "宫廷剧中女性形象对都市白领女性形象的解构—基于34位都市白领女性对《后宫甄嬛传》看法研究 [The Deconstruction of Metropolitan White Collar Female Image in Historical Court Drama—A Study Based on the Analysis of 34 White Collar Female on 'Empresses in the Palace']." 声屏世界 *[Voice and Screen World]*, no. 7 (2014): 35–37.

Zhou, Viola. "China's Marriage Rate Slumps as More Singles Say 'I Don't.'" *South China Morning Post*, September 6, 2017. http://www.scmp.com/news/china/society/article/2109868/marriage-rate-down-divorce-rate-more-chinese-couples-say-i-dont.

Zhou, Xuelin. "'From behind the Wall' The Representation of Gender and Sexuality in Modern Chinese Film." *Asian Journal of Communication* 11, no. 2 (2009): 1–17.

Zhou, Yiping (周一平), and Zhou Lei (周雷). "2008年改革开放史研究述评 [Overview of Researches on the History of Chinese Economic Reform 2008]." 当代中国史研究 *[Dangdai Zhongguo Shi Yanjiu]*, no. 1 (2008): 102–9.

Zhu, Qi (朱其). "'70后':这个名称意味着什么? [The Post-70s: What Does This Name Mean?]." 美苑 *[Meiyuan]*, no. 5 (2005): 5–6.

Zhu, Ying. *Television in Post-Reform China: Serial Dramas, Confucian Leadership and the Global Television Market*. London; New York: Routledge, 2008.

Zhu, Ying, and Chris Berry. *TV China*. Bloomington, IN: Indiana University Press, 2009.

Zhu, Ying, Michael Keane, and Ruoyun Bai, eds. *TV Drama in China*. Hong Kong: Hong Kong University Press, 2008.

Zito, Angela. "Bound to Be Represented: Theorizing/Fetishizing Footbinding." In *Embodied Modernities: Corporeality, Representation, And Chinese Cultures*, edited by Fran Martin and Larissa Heinrich, 21–41. Honolulu: University of Hawaii Press, 2006.

Zournazi, Mary. *Hope: New Philosophies for Change*. New York: Routledge, 2002.

"中国广告媒体新世代(一): 新媒体刺激市场需求 [New Generation of Advertising Media in China (I): New Media Stimulate Market Demand]." 商贸全接触 *[Hong Kong Means Business]* (blog), April 21, 2016. http://hkmb.hktdc.com/tc/1X0A5VYH.

中国戏曲志全国编辑委员会 [Zhongguo xiquzhi quanguobianji weiyuanhui]. 中国戏曲志上海卷 *[Chinese Xiqu Records Shanghai Volume]*. Beijing: Zhongguo, 1999.

"十九大開幕 習近平發表工作報告 [Opening of 19th National Congress— Working Report by Xi Jinping]." 香港經濟日報 *[Hong Kong Economic Times]*, October 18, 2017. http://china.hket.com/article/1927215.

"延展思考的时空尺度 文化起飞 [Extending Thinking on Time and Space: A Cultural Takeoffc]." 工商时报 *[Gongshang Shibao]*, March 17, 2014. http://www.chinatimes.com/cn/newspapers/20140317000072-260202.

阿里足跡團隊 (Ali news team). "2017天貓雙11全日成交額1682億元人民幣 再刷新紀錄 [2017 Tmall November 11th Full-Day Turnover of RMB 168.2 Billion Breaks New Record]." 阿里足跡 *[Alibabanews.Com]*, November 12, 2017. http://alibabanews.com/article/2017tianmaoshuang11quanrichengjiaoe1682yiyuanrenminbi-zaishuaxinjilu.

INDEX[1]

---

[1] Note: Page numbers followed by 'n' refer to notes.

© The Author(s) 2019
Chow Y. F., *Caring in Times of Precarity*, Palgrave Studies in
Globalization, Culture and Society,
https://doi.org/10.1007/978-3-319-76898-4

Printed by Printforce, the Netherlands